THE COMPLETE AND MAGNIFICENT
HISTORY OF THE PLANTAGENETS
IN FOUR THRILLING VOLUMES

A HISTORY OF THE PLANTAGENETS

The
Magnificent
Century

By THOMAS B. COSTAIN

POPULAR LIBRARY · NEW YORK

THE MAGNIFICENT CENTURY

Published by Popular Library, a unit of CBS Publications, the
Consumer Publishing Division of CBS Inc., by arrangement
with Doubleday & Company, Inc.

Copyright © 1959 by Thomas B. Costain

ISBN: 0-445-08512-6

26   25   24   23   22   21   20   19   18   17

CONTENTS

CHAPTER ONE

A Boy Is Crowned King

OCTOBER 19, 1216. King John was dead. The storm which roared about the towers of the Bishop of Lincoln's castle at Newark and tore at the windows of the room where the royal body lay was sweeping over most of England like a messenger of doom. The people of England, who had been despoiled and torn by civil war as long as John lived, were in an even more sorry plight now that he was dead.

To make clear the difficulties of the situation into which the country had been plunged by the passing of the bad King it will be necessary to cast back and tell briefly what had been happening in the island kingdom. When the united barons forced John to sign Magna Charta at Runnymede on June 15 of the previous year that stubborn monarch had seemed reconciled to his surrender of dictatorial powers. Outwardly compliant, he had been filled, nevertheless, with rage and hate and a determination to undo everything at the first opportunity. For some time thereafter he remained in seclusion, spinning his plans and waiting for the messengers he had sent to the Continent to gain him the assistance he needed. Some of them had carried a highly colored version of Runnymede to Pope Innocent III. Others had been instructed to find mercenaries to fight in the King's behalf and were recruiting professional soldiers at Rouen, Ghent, Cologne, Naples. The Pope, easy to convince because John had made England a fief of Rome and had been ruling, supposedly, as the representative of the Vatican, decided that Magna Charta was wrong and declared it null and void. Stephen Langton, the great Archbishop of Canterbury who had been chiefly instrumental in organizing the baronage against kingly aggression and had been the real leader of the movement, went to Rome to argue for the popular cause. Sitting in the Vatican like a wrathful god, his hands filled with thunderbolts, Innocent refused to listen to Stephen Langton and even forbade his return to England. Without the sagacious prelate to hold them together, the barons failed to present a concerted front when John came raging out of the West with his well-trained mercenaries and proceeded to spread death and desolation.

The barons then took a step which showed the depth of their desperation: they sent a deputation to Paris and offered the crown of England to Prince Louis, the heir to the throne of France, who had married Blanche of Castile, a granddaughter of Henry II. Philip Augustus, the King of France, was a shrewd and ambitious man who had already taken Normandy and Brittany and the Angevin possessions from John, thereby doubling the territory over which he ruled. He was a powerful king, the ruler who paved the streets of Paris and started its great markets and was responsible for its medieval grandeur. Some further explanation of this man should, however, be made. He was the bitterly resentful prince who had circumvented the old lion, Henry II, and had goaded him at Colombières when he was dying in grief and defeat; the same King of France, moreover, who had deserted Richard at the Crusades and had conspired to keep the lionhearted monarch in his German prison; a man of harsh moods and contemptuous tongue, portly and florid now, and still filled with hatred for England and her Angevin kings. Nothing would have suited Philip Augustus better than to scoop the island into the Capetian bag (the inevitable result of the proposal made by the desperate barons), but he was bound by the terms of the treaty of Chinon and did not find himself at this juncture in a good position to oppose that man of equally iron will, Innocent III. The result was that Philip Augustus openly opposed the idea while secretly conniving with his son to organize an army for the invasion.

The ports of northern France were soon filled with transports. The services of Eustace the Monk were secured to direct the naval operations, and this was considered almost a guarantee of success. Eustace, born near Boulogne of a family of the lesser nobility, had entered a monastic order at Saumur but had left the abbey to demand satisfaction from the Count of Boulogne against the murderer of his father. Failing in this, he had broken his vows permanently and had turned to piracy with a small band made up at first of his brothers and friends. They were so successful that disaffected men from all parts of the Continent began to join them, and they soon became the terror of the Channel. Merchant captains sighed with relief when they reached their destination without having sighted the sails of the dreaded Eustace on the sky line. The pirate leader grew to such stature, in fact, that kings bid against each other for his services, and he waxed fat in body and purse. At one time he served John and was rewarded well enough to set up an establishment of his own at Winchelsea. He was a rambunctious fellow, barrel-like in build, as ready to spill blood as to down a flagon of malvoisie. The news that he had thrown in his lot with the French sent a shiver along many a spine in the train of the vengeful John.

The French army landed without any serious opposition and advanced to London. The citizens of that most independent of cities, hating John and all his works, gave nevertheless no more than a guarded and watchful support to Louis. The Cinque Ports did not resist, however, and so the French gained a firm grip on the coast except for the castle at Dover, where Hubert de Burgh held out boldly. Hubert was destined to prove a continuous thorn in the side of Gallic operations.

John, when hard enough pressed, had the Angevin capacity for generalship and he proceeded to take wise measures. He scattered his forces along a line from the coast through Oxford and into the midlands to confine the invaders in the southeast corner of the country. His ablest mercenary captains were placed in command of the forts which made up this line; Engelard de Cigogni at Windsor, Falkes de Bréauté over the shires stretching northward, Peter de Maulay at Corfe Castle in Dorset. Confident that Louis would not be able to break through, John then set about the task of cutting communications between the French and the barons of the North, who were John's most determined foes.

In this plan to check the French the King was greatly aided by a comparatively unknown knight who proceeded to make things hot for the invaders on his own account. He was called

William of Kensham and sometimes William of Cassingham. History is full of such men, unsung heroes who play conspicuous parts in great events but are overshadowed by the leading characters on the stage. William of Kensham organized a band of guerrilla fighters and took the Weald as his base of operations. The Weald was a dense strip of forest, high above the chalk escarpment, which ran dark and forbidding from the western portion of Kent across the whole of Sussex, a barrier of trees, mostly oak, whose roots were sunk deep in soil made up of Wealden clay, Hastings sand, gault, greensand, and chalk. A few industrious husbandmen were scattered through it, striving to turn its occasional open strips of sandy soil known as denes into farming land and pitting it with holes sunk to get at the marl they needed to fertilize the land; subsisting, without a doubt, on the very edge of starvation. A few winding roads cut through it and a number of rather turbulent rivers, but it was difficult of access. The Weald served, in fact, as an almost impenetrable curtain, cutting London off from the southwestern ports.

Little is known about this bold leader except that he was bailiff over the courts of the Seven Hundreds of the Weald, which he held at the usual farm fee of one hundred shillings a year, and so belonged to the ranks of the minor nobility. It is not known where he learned the art of guerrilla fighting, but he soon proved himself a master hand at that kind of warfare. He would issue suddenly from the Weald and demolish a party of French knights, retiring then into the dark depths of the forest, to attack the next day a castle, leaving wherever he went the bodies of Frenchmen dangling from trees. In time he came to command a force of one thousand men, mostly archers. He was a passing cloud of dust, a quick glint of metal among the trees, death riding on the wind. The dread he caused was so great that the French troops refused to venture out on the roads to the south and west, preferring to stay safe behind the walls of London. Louis could do nothing about this fast-riding, hard-hitting guerrilla captain and left him in full possession of the forest barrier.

The people of England, always looking for a hero to take to their hearts and preferring one of relatively humble birth, fixed their attention on William with all the enthusiasm they would show later for Robin Hood and Adam Gurdon and John Ball. He became Willikin to them, Willikin of the Weald.

It was while engaged in his northern operations that John

died at Newark. It seemed at first that his death would make no difference. Louis declared that he had no intention of letting it interfere with his claims on the English throne. The barons supporting him swore openly that they would not accept any of the brood of the hated King as ruler of the land. Actually, however, the passing of the tyrant made an immediate change in the situation. There was now no need for foreign intervention in the civil war. The men who had ridden to Runnymede and put civilization in their debt by forcing from John that great guarantee of the rights of man, Magna Charta, were in a serious dilemma. Bound to the French prince by their oaths, they were realizing that they had sold themselves to a master as autocratic and unyielding as the dead John. The austere and humorless Louis was letting them see already that he despised them as traitors to a royal suzerain and that they would have gained nothing if their efforts placed him in John's place. He did not hesitate to dispose of their lands and castles to the French knights he had brought over with him.

The barons knew also, as did all England, that the invitation to Louis had been based on a false premise. If John had forfeited the throne by his conduct as King and his children were to be barred from the succession, the right did not pass to Blanche, the wife of Louis. There was a candidate who had a better claim than Blanche of Castile, better moreover than John's right had been.

In the southern part of Dorset, in what was known as the Isle of Purbeck, stood a tall chalk range, and in the middle of it there was a gap, looking as though a tooth had been yanked from the jaw of some prehistoric giant. This was called Corfe Gate, and back of it, like a sentry guarding the open space, stood a hill two hundred feet high. Perched on the summit of the hill was the formidable Corfe Castle, a natural stream forming a moat about its base, its strength so great that no man seriously considered the possibility of storming it. Corfe Castle was so strong, in fact, that John had used it always for the custody of his most important prisoners.

At the time of his death the castle in the gap held the most important prisoner ever entrusted to it, a young woman of great beauty, dark of eye and hair, haughty of temperament, but the possessor of so much charm that she was a favorite with the garrison and with the other prisoners at Corfe. She was not held in the close confinement of a single cell but was allowed such liberty as lay within the high walls. She lived in the Gloriet Tower, which had been added in John's time, taking her meals in the Long Hall and being allowed to walk along the walls. She never failed to take advantage of the privilege thus extended to her, pacing the ramparts around the three baileys, back and forth, back and forth, from the Butavant Tower to the Plakement, from the Plakement to the Gloriet, her somber eyes fixed on the southern horizon beyond which, she knew, lay Brittany.

If the law of primogeniture had been faithfully adhered to, this young woman would have been sitting on the throne of England instead of pacing endlessly the ramparts of Corfe and sighing for her freedom. She was the Princess Eleanor, sometimes called the Fair Maid, more often the Pearl of Brittany.

Eleanor of Brittany was a tragic figure. She was the daughter of Geoffrey, the fourth son of Henry II, who had married Constance, the hereditary Duchess of Brittany. Geoffrey was the handsomest of the Plantagenets, the possessor of a figure of elegant symmetry, and a man of the most winning manners. His early death in a tournament in France had been deeply mourned. Eleanor resembled him closely, inheriting from both parents a high temper and a royal share of determination. During the early years, when it seemed certain that her younger brother, Prince Arthur, would succeed the childless Richard as King of England, she was one of the most sought after princesses in Europe. When Richard was in Palestine he offered her in marriage to Saphadin, brother of Saladin, if the Moslem leader would make the pair King and Queen of Jerusalem. Saladin's brother, however, showed no inclination to embrace Christianity, which was a part of the bargain, and so this scheme fell to the ground. Later, when negotiating his release from a German prison, Richard promised as part of the ransom treaty to give the little princess of Brittany in marriage to the son of Leopold of Austria, his archenemy. She accompanied Richard's mother to Germany when that indomitable lady of seventy-two made the journey from England to be sure that nothing would be allowed to stand in the way of the unshackling of her son. There is some doubt as to whether the marriage took place and was broken immediately thereafter or whether the plan was abandoned before the nuptials were solemnized. Certainly, however, the young Eleanor accompanied her grandmother back and was restored to her family in Brittany. A few years later she was offered by Richard to his rival, Philip Augustus, as a wife for the latter's son Louis (the same prince who now sat in London and planned the conquest of England), and the idea was favorably received. It was assumed at the time, however, that Arthur of Brittany would succeed to the throne of England. When Richard decided instead that John should follow him, the French King broke off the negotiations on the ground that the alliance would not now be sufficiently important and brilliant for the heir of France.

The poor little Pearl of Brittany had seen two royal husbands slip through her hands, not to mention the dusky Saphadin, but the greatest misfortune was still to be encountered. When her brother Arthur, contending with John for the crown of England, was captured by the latter at Mirabeau and carried off into the captivity which ended with his murder, Eleanor was sent to England with the Breton knights who had been taken prisoners in the fighting around Mirabeau. With them she was imprisoned in the castle of Corfe. She must have known of the sad fate of her companions in misfortune, all but one of whom starved to death; and their fate served, no doubt, as a final proof of the malignant nature of the man who had shut her off from the world. She was still there when John died at Newark, a woman of perhaps thirty years, still beautiful, still rebellious of spirit. The news of the King's death may have revived her hopes of release, but more likely she had long since come to realize the nature of the trap in which she was caught. The very validity of her claim to the throne made it certain that she would never be allowed her freedom. No matter who might be King of England, it would be deemed necessary, if peace were to be maintained, to keep her buried away. The secret of her whereabouts was so closely held, in fact, that the people of Brittany did not know she was at Corfe. For many years all legal enactments in Brittany were made subject to change in the event of the missing heiress being found.

She had plenty of company at Corfe. Two Scottish princesses, who were being held as hostages for the good behavior of their brother, King Alexander, were there also, and there is evidence that the trio were much together. They were treated with decent respect and were allowed to ride out on occasions, under the strictest guard, of course. It is clear from a succession of items in the royal accounts that they were provided with clothes in keeping with their rank. There is mention of bolts of fine silk and lengths of samite and yards of velvet. Eleanor was allowed robes of dark green with capes of cambric and hats trimmed with miniver. It is on record that she was given "one saddle with gilded reins and scarlet ornaments." There is an item also of a hundred pounds of figs being ordered for the three royal captives. But fine silks and satins and all the figs in the world could not compensate the beautiful Pearl of Brittany for the freedom denied her. No youth came courting her, it being necessary above everything else that the line of Geoffrey should die out and no longer complicate the question of succession. The taste of power, so dear to all Plantagenet palates, was never on her tongue. She ate her heart out on the battlements of Corfe, from which she could see nothing but the green of Dorset meadows and distant hills on the horizon, hoping and praying for freedom, for revenge, for the chance to live a normal life.

Before John had set out on his last campaign he had sent all his children, saving Henry, the heir, to Corfe for safekeeping. Richard, the second son, who was seven years old, was there, a lad of such shrewdness that he was destined to grow into the richest prince in Europe and to buy for himself an imperial title. The two youngest daughters were there also: Isabella, who would marry the Emperor of Germany, and the baby of the family, little Princess Eleanor. Although still in her first year, Eleanor was showing signs already of having inherited some at least of the enchanting beauty of her mother, Queen Isabella. She was an engaging and willful child and a family favorite. Keep her in mind, this little Princess Eleanor: she will play an active part in the drama of the next fifty years.

But not for the Pearl of Brittany any further part in the affairs of England. She was removed soon thereafter to Bristol, and there she died in 1241. What little is known of her character leads to the conviction that she was brave and defiant of her fate to the end.

That she was alive when John died should have rendered the claim of Blanche of Castile to the throne invalid, but the point does not seem to have been raised seriously. It was generally accepted that the issue lay between Blanche's husband as the candidate of the barons and Henry, the youthful son of John.

To complicate matters further, John had made England a fief of Rome during his struggle with the barons. The new Pope, Honorius III, considered the country as under his jurisdiction. The papal legate in England, Gualo Bianchieri, would be the power behind the throne no matter what form of government was set up. He had already excommunicated Prince Louis and all who supported him. This mass banning added to the doubts of the sorely tried English barons.

2

When word came that the heir to the throne, John's nine-year-old son Henry, was being brought by his mother from the doubly stockaded castle of Devizes where the King had left him, William the Marshal rode out to meet them. The latter was drawing close to the end of his days and knew it quite well, and it was in his mind that this would be his last official act. He wanted to spend the few years left him in the company of his children and his young wife, who had been the heiress of Pembroke and had made him a faithful and loving companion in spite of the disparity in their years. He was filled with a fiercely intense longing for the peace of Pembroke Castle, which looked across the waters at Milford Haven, and the easy life of his extensive Irish estates, where a gentle sun came out between showers and everything was lovely and green. The incomparable old knight had fallen into the habit of claiming eighty years. Actually he was seventy-two; a long time to spend in fighting; in the Crusades, in the continuous wars, in the five hundred tournaments which he had won without a single upset.

The desire for comfort which comes with the years had caused him to discard his armor, and he wore instead a padded and gaily colored tabard, which was especially designed for use ahorse, being split on both sides from the armpits down. It was habit perhaps which had induced him to keep under his hat of soft cloth a *coif de fer*, the skullcap of steel which knights wore beneath their helmets. His bearing was still martial and, when the plains were reached from which a glimpse could be had against the sky line of the bell tower of the Abbey of Malmesbury, his eyes were keen enough to catch the first sight of the royal party in the distance.

As soon as she heard of her husband's death Queen Isabella had ridden from Exeter to Devizes to get the youthful heir. She had not been allowed any active part in public affairs while John was alive, but she was to display in every phase of her life from this point on both ambition and energy and, certainly, a taste for mischief. She was riding beside Henry when the two parties met on the plains outside Malmesbury and, despite the interest felt in the new King, it was on the lovely Isabella that each eye rested first. It was customary for ladies of high rank in France to don white for mourning, but those of royal blood were allowed a license in the matter of color and were prone to use black trimmed with yellow or ermine. It is probable, therefore, that Isabella was in black when she met the old marshal; it is certain that she was beautiful to behold, being in her early thirties and at the height of her dazzling charm. She was slender and, as she had stripped off her gloves and tucked them in her belt in the style of the moment, it could be seen that her hands were small and white.

The young prince was riding on the front of the saddle of an old retainer, Ralf of Saint-Samson. The marshal dismounted and went down on one knee.

"Welcome, sir," piped Henry in a high, boyish voice. "I commit myself to God and to you. May God give you grace to guard us well."

It was well spoken. Perhaps he had been rehearsed in what he was to say by his mother or his tutor, Philip d'Aubigny. More likely, however, the salutation was his own thought, for even as a boy Henry had persuasiveness and tact. He had as well the golden hair of the Plantagenets and his mother's high coloring and he was altogether a handsome lad with one physical flaw only, a tendency in one eyelid to droop. William the Marshal was delighted with his good looks and the gentility of his manner, happy to find him so polite and so very unlike the raucous, cruel, tricky, whisker-twitching youth his father had been; a sweet prince indeed to offer the people of England.

"Sire," said the marshal with tears streaming down his seamed and sunken cheeks, "on my soul I will do everything to serve you in good faith as long as I have the strength."

Everyone wept at this, the young prince loudly, the old warrior with the sadness which the sight of youth can induce in the aged, the beautiful Queen with well-bred restraint, the knights in both trains, and the servants who brought up the rear.

Realizing the need for haste, they then fell into line and set out at a sharp pace for Gloucester. Most of the advisers of the late King were there when the royal party arrived. It was decided that, in spite of the difficulties which stood in the way of a proper coronation, the boy should be crowned without any delay. The difficulties were technical and yet of the kind to cause serious trouble later. Westminster Abbey was in the hands of the enemy. Stephen Langton, who alone had the right to officiate, was still in Rome, a virtual prisoner of the Vatican. The crown had been swept out to sea with all the royal regalia when the waters of the Wash had engulfed the wagons in John's train. It was decided under the circumstances to give the crowning a preliminary character, with an eye to a more regular and properly imposing ceremony later.

First, however, the prince had to be knighted, and it was agreed that the old marshal, who had performed the service for King John, should officiate. The coronation which followed was the least pretentious of all, being held in the presence of a small group of bishops and earls instead of an assembly of all the great men of the kingdom in their finest robes and glittering jewels. Perhaps the meager nature of it had some effect on the mind of the boy King and led to the extravagances in which he indulged himself ever after. It may well have been that the memory of the anxious-faced group which shared the plain coronation banquet incited him to the great feasts of his later years; for which hundreds of cattle would be slaughtered and fast-driven carts would come from the seaports with the lampreys for which he developed an insatiable appetite and the plaice and turbot which would be properly calvered for the guests; and which moreover always drained the royal purse. Certainly Henry seemed obsessed with a desire to conduct himself on all public occasions in a most lavish manner.

The crowning was on October 28, one of the most exciting days in the history of the ancient Roman city of Gloucester. Now that John was dead, the people had turned fiercely royalist and wanted to see the French interlopers swept into the sea. They crowded into the old church which good Abbot Serlo had built, and those who could not find places inside the nave with its tall fire-blackened pillars filled the streets for a glimpse of the pretty little Plantagenet. They dissolved into joyous tears when the boy's voice was heard repeating the words of the oath.

The ceremony was carried out, in fact, with every evidence of rejoicing. The prince, who conducted himself with rare dignity, was anointed and crowned by Peter des Roches, Bishop of Winchester, about whom much will be told later. A plain gold circlet, supplied by the Queen Mother, was placed on the head of the third Henry in place of the proper crown, which would never be recovered from the shifting mud of the Wash. In recognition of the irregularity of the proceedings, the ceremony did not include unction or the imposition of hands. An edict was issued immediately, however, that for a month no adult should appear in public without a chaplet on the head in honor of the new King; a command which the people obeyed with enthusiasm.

3

A meeting of the men named in John's will as his executors was held in the royal courts of Lancaster the day after the coronation. The company consisted of the papal legate, the marshal, a few bishops, some noblemen of high degree and position, Aymar Saint-More, the head of the Knights Templars, and Falkes de Bréauté, the ablest and most mercenary of the mercenary captains.

They were a colorful group. The costume of the day, while not spectacular, was both impressive and richly dignified: the flowing draperies, the rare imported materials (for of course men of this stamp did not attire themselves in honest English cloth but had silks and satins and velvets from abroad, sometimes interwoven with gold thread), the lavish use of precious stones. With the rediscovery of the dyeing process, which had lapsed and been forgotten during the Dark Ages, color was being restored in exciting glory. In France and Flanders men were experimenting with the yellow-flowered madder and producing cloth of great beauty, while, more important still, in Italy dyes were being imported from the East. Already a Florentine had discovered a method of extracting orchil out of lichens from Asia Minor. Because of this, the high churchmen in the party were clothed in princely purple.

The nobles were wearing tabards. Mention has already been made of this garment, which was the one fashionable development of the early part of the thirteenth century. It was a major change because it had sleeves, tight-fitting sleeves which covered the shoulders snugly. It had become a jacket to slip over loose draperies and was especially useful for riding because of the slits on each side. Tailors would continue experimenting with it both in fit and material, and it would become padded and tufted and a very foppish garment indeed, and in time would lead to the cote-hardie, that great and useful garment of the latter half of the century.

The shoes of the men who had gathered to discuss the future of England were particularly elegant. Ever since the days of William Rufus, who was sometimes known as King Cornard because of this, the long points of shoes had been filled with tow and then "turned up like a ram's horn." Now fretwork had been introduced and the surface of the leather was raised in squares, each section being stamped with the figures of lions, unicorns, or leopards in gold leaf.

There were two absentees of note and, because of this, the meeting was a brief one. The first was Ranulf de Blundeville, the Earl of Chester, who was on his way from the North and was expected to arrive at any moment. He had been one of the best of Henry II's bright young men, trained in his ways and in his conception of law administration. When Henry's son Geoffrey was killed in a tournament, the King had decided that Constance of Brittany, the widow, must not be allowed to select a second husband for herself. His choice was the young Earl of Chester. Spare, graceless, black-a-vised, the earl did not find favor with the haughty Constance, even though she finally gave in to her dominant father-in-law. She went through the marriage ceremony but, according to a story generally believed, never allowed her new spouse to set eyes on her again. Chester, caring little perhaps, went about the business of governing Brittany in the workmanlike way which Henry desired. After Constance secured a divorce he returned to England, married again, and became recognized as the leading peer of England and the last survivor of the aristocracy of the Conquest. He had become enormously wealthy and carried a great deal of weight in the kingdom.

The second absentee was Hubert de Burgh, the brave knight who had refused to let John's assassins burn out the eyes of Prince Arthur when the latter was a prisoner at Falaise Castle. Hubert, who was now justiciar of the country, could not come because with a garrison of no more than 140 men he was holding out against the French in the stone fortress at Dover which served as the gateway of England. It was just about this time, in fact, that Louis decided he must clear this obstacle from his path as the first step in taking advantage of John's death. He sent two English barons to discuss terms of surrender with the determined castellan. One of them was Thomas de Burgh, Hubert's brother; and, as he came unwillingly, he was loaded with chains.

The herald who accompanied the two emissaries sounded his horn, and brave Hubert de Burgh came to the inner of the

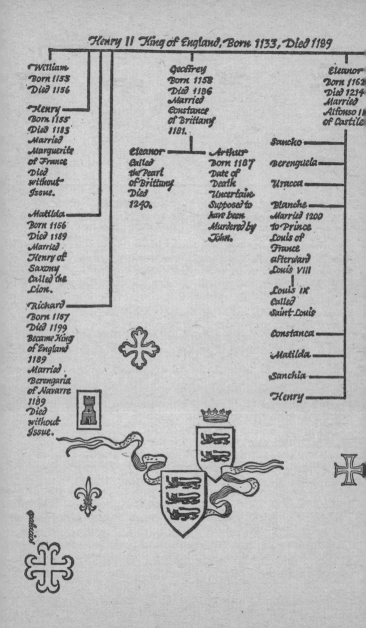

Henry II King of England, Born 1133, Died 1189

William
Born 1153
Died 1156

Henry
Born 1155
Died 1183
Married
Marguerite
of France
Died
without
Issue.

Matilda
Born 1156
Died 1189
Married
Henry of
Saxony
Called the
Lion.

Richard
Born 1157
Died 1199
Became King
of England
1189
Married
Berengaria
of Navarre
1189
Died
without
Issue.

Geoffrey
Born 1158
Died 1186
Married
Constance
of Brittany
1181.

Eleanor
Called
the Pearl
of Brittany
Died
1240.

Arthur
Born 1187
Date of
Death
Uncertain
Supposed to
have been
Murdered by
John.

Eleanor
Born 1162
Died 1214
Married
Alfonso II
of Castile

Sancho

Berenguela

Uracca

Blanche
Married 1200
to Prince
Louis of
France
afterward
Louis VIII
|
Louis IX
Called
Saint Louis

Constanca

Matilda

Sanchia

Henry

Eleanor of Aquitaine, Queen of England, Born 1122, Died 1204

Joanna
Born 1165
Died 1199
Married
William II
of Sicily
No Issue.
Second
Husband
Raimund
of Toulouse.

John
Born 1167
Died 1216
Became
King of
England
1199
Married
Isabella of
Angoulême
1200

Henry
Born 1207
Died 1272
Became
King of
England
under title
of Henry III
1216
Married
Eleanor of
Provence
1236.

Richard
Called
Richard of
Cornwall
Born 1209
Died 1272
Elected
King of
the Romans
1258.

Joanna
Born 1210
Died 1238
Married
Alexander II
of Scotland.

Isabella
Born 1214
Died 1241
Married
Emperor
Frederick II
of Germany.

Eleanor
Born 1215
Died 1274
Married (1)
William
Marshal,
Earl of
Pembroke
1224 (2)
Simon de
Montfort,
Earl of
Leicester
1239.

Edward
Born 1239
Died 1307
Became
King of
England
as
Edward I
1272.

Margaret
Born 1240
Died 1275
Married
Alexander III
of
Scotland.

Beatrice
Born 1242
Died 1275
Married
John,
Count of
Bretagne.

Edmund
Born 1245
Died 1296
Selected
King of
Sicily,
1254, but
never
Succeeded
to Throne.

Katherine
Born 1253
Died in
Childhood.

Four Sons:
Richard,
John,
William,
Henry.
Died in
Infancy.

two parapets between which the drawbridge swung, followed by five archers with drawn bows.

His brother told him of John's death and added that Louis would brook no more opposition. If it became necessary to take Dover Castle by storm he had sworn to hang every man in the garrison, including the leader, who would dangle from the top of the Keep. The Keep was eighty-three feet high, so that Hubert would have plenty of space in which to do his dangling. As a further inducement the brother added, "By your stubbornness you ruin yourself and all your family."

The other courier then spoke up and said that Louis promised Hubert the counties of Suffolk and Norfolk if he would lower his flag at once.

None of this had any effect on the resolute justiciar. "Traitors!" he cried. "If John be dead, then he leaves sons. One more word and I'll command my archers to shoot you down!"

This indomitable soldier was not, therefore, in a position to attend the meeting, but the spirit he displayed in his defense of Dover was putting courage in men's hearts to resist the invaders and it was reflected in the attitude of those present.

The legate presided, but the proceedings were dominated by two men, the first of whom was the marshal. The greatest fighting man of his, or perhaps of any, age, he had a record without a stain and men looked up to him in this crisis and were ready to adopt any course he might propose. The second was Peter des Roches, the bishop who had crowned the young King. Peter des Roches was a Poitevin, a handsome and polished courtier as well as a learned churchman, who had come to England reluctantly at John's behest and remained only for the material advantages he could obtain for himself and the members of his family. His own desire was to serve the Church in Rome and he spent a great deal of his time there. He would have carved out a great career if he had been permanently located in the Eternal City, being an adroit diplomat and full of the new ideas which were sweeping over Europe, the desire for learning, the urge to create beauty which would soon lead to the Renaissance. There was a fascination about this suave churchman with his handsome eye and his exciting talk, but his manner to Englishmen was aloof and superior and the people both feared and hated him.

The purpose of the meeting was to establish a temporary government and to make plans for the ejection of the French. The legate opened the discussion by addressing the marshal.

"You have made our young lord a knight," he said. "We all pray you now to take him into your keeping."

It was clear that the old man was both startled and dismayed by this suggestion. He frowned and then shook his head emphatically. "I cannot," he said. "I have reached my fourscore year. I am very tired."

The rest of the company joined with the legate then in urging him to accept the leadership in the struggle which lay ahead. They crowded about the kindly-eyed old man, telling him he was the Ulysses to whom all turned and in whom they had complete faith. The mind of the marshal was still firmly fixed on the green meadows and peaceful lakes of his Irish estates and his longing for a few years of comfort. He persisted in his refusal and, when they still besieged him with arguments, he fell back on the excuse that nothing should be done in the absence of the Earl of Chester. "His voice must be heard first," he urged.

Chester arrived the following day, and a second meeting was held in the King's Hall. The discussion was opened by one Alan Basset, who declared that he saw no one fitted to lead them save the marshal or the Earl of Chester. The veteran was still unwilling to undertake the task, and when Alan Basset had finished he turned to Chester and exclaimed in a tone of entreaty: "I am feeble and broken in health. Take it upon yourself, Sir Earl of Chester, for God's sake!"

Chester, usually sparing of words, broke into a eulogy of the marshal. "You are so prudent, so feared, so loved, and so wise," he said. "You are one of the greatest knights in the world. I am ready to serve under you and do your behests."

The prospect of a few years of peace still beckoned the old man and he repeated his plea to be allowed the relinquishment of all responsibility. Gualo, who was a shrewd diplomat, then took him into a smaller room with Chester and Peter des Roches. It had grown chilly, and William the Marshal was glad to draw his chair close to the small fire which burned on the hearth. The light thus provided made his eyes seem sunken and tired, and it was clear to all that he had not been using his age as an excuse, that time was running out for him.

Gualo proceeded to use his final argument. The saving of the kingdom was a sacred duty. If the marshal would take the leadership, his reward would be the remission of his sins. This was not a consideration to be lightly dismissed. William the Marshal had not been dishonest, cruel, or covetous, but he had lived a life of violence and bloodshed. There was much in the past, without a doubt, which weighed on his conscience; and, as all men knew, the end of the world was close at hand, when the banked fires would blaze up for evildoers, so that it behooved them to look to the state of their souls. The old man fell into a long and careful study, and finally sighed and said he would act. One stipulation went with his acceptance, however: the care of the young King's person, which had been assigned to the marshal in John's will, must be assumed by someone else until things were settled and the fighting and tumult ceased. It was decided that this responsibility would be laid on Peter des Roches, a step which undoubtedly changed the course of history. The wily Poitevin gained an ascendancy over the youthful monarch which would be used later for selfish ends.

After nightfall the marshal, now the head of the state, summoned three of his closest adherents to his own room. It was, as might have been expected, a small apartment: a hearth large enough only for a small charcoal blaze, a narrow bed, a chair, a crucifix on the wall. It would have been a bare and ascetic lodging to almost anyone else, but it was not lacking in comfort for a man who had spent most of the nights of his life in tents or under the stars. To this room came, therefore, the devoted trio: John, his nephew; John Earley, his squire; and Ralph Mustard, the castellan of Gloucester.

The marshal began at once on a discourse. "Advise me," he said, "for by the faith I owe you I see myself entering into an ocean which has neither bottom nor shore." His eyes filled with tears. "May God help me! They have turned over to me a helpless government, a king without a piece of gold. And as for me, I am very old."

John Earley, who is generally believed to have written later the metrical biography *L'Histoire de Guillaume le Maréchal*, which is the sole source for the story of the marshal's selection, took it on himself to answer. He pointed out that what his master had undertaken could result only in great honor. Even if all the fickle nobility deserted him and surrendered their castles to Louis, he could still take the young King to Ireland and continue the struggle from there. If, on the other hand, things went well, no man would ever have attained such honor on earth.

The marshal recovered his good spirits at this, and there

was a suggestion of mounting enthusiasm in his eyes. He sprang up and began to pace about the room.

"By God's glove!" he exclaimed. "The advice is good and true. If all should abandon us, I would carry the King on my shoulders, one leg here and one in Ireland. I would carry him from island to island and land to land, and I would not fail him ever!"

4

The new head of the state gathered the others about him and it was decided that, inasmuch as the war was a holy one, the royalist forces would wear the white cross of the Crusades. The legate, drawing on the wide powers allowed him by the Pope, supplemented this by putting Wales under an interdict and confirming the ban he had placed on Louis and all his adherents. The meeting was characterized by a growing sense of confidence because the small group of zealous men at Gloucester knew that soon all England would be stirring and that public opinion would be with them. If they could hold out long enough with the weakened resources they had inherited from the dead tyrant, they were certain to win. Time was on their side.

It was decided to hold a national council at Bristol on November 11 and to leave all questions of policy until then. All loyal men were summoned to appear and they came in great numbers, churchman and noble alike, to take the oath of fealty to the boy King. An unexpected arrival was Hubert de Burgh. The French wanted to transfer their activities to the midlands and had concluded a truce with him, thus making it possible for him to leave Dover. Nothing could have been more fortunate. Hubert de Burgh was still chief justiciar and one of the powers of the state. His advice and counsel were needed.

Two important steps were taken at Bristol. The first was the confirmation of Magna Charta, with some changes, the most noteworthy being omission of the clause which bound the King to lay no tax on the backs of his subjects without their consent. This had been one of the great victories of Runnymede and it might seem that the Charter lost validity without it. In all probability the omission was due to the attitude of the Vatican. Innocent III had declared the Charter null and void, but his successor, Honorius III, gave his unqualified approval to the new version, from which the conclusion might be drawn that the removal of the constitutional check had brought about a change of heart at Rome. It must be remembered also that the men at Bristol had been adherents of John, not blindly accepting everything he did but not belonging to the party of the barons. Their willingness to accept the Charter at all was evidence of the change which one year of time had wrought. The confirmation might be considered a shrewd move to make it easier for the barons ranged behind Louis to renounce his cause, but the reason went much deeper than that. In the few months of bitterness and civil war which had elapsed since Runnymede the Charter had come to be accepted by all men as necessary and, in most respects, just. They might dispute over certain clauses, but in point of principle they were agreed. Runnymede was already a victory for the ages.

Other omissions were dictated by the fact that the country was at war. The King's party was sadly in need of funds and supplies to carry on the struggle, and so arbitrary measures, to which men submit when the fate of the nation is at stake, would have to be taken.

It must be allowed, therefore, that common sense and discretion dictated the Bristol attitude to Magna Charta. It was a time for conciliation and not for sharp measures. In the light of subsequent events it is easy to see behind the decisions the wise moderation of William the Marshal and the shrewdness of Gualo.

The second step taken was a decision on the strategy to be followed. It was generally agreed that it would not be wise to risk everything on a pitched battle with the invaders, who still had a great preponderance of strength. It was decided instead to use Fabian tactics while recruiting more adherents and accumulating strength.

Hubert de Burgh, confirmed in his post of justiciar, went back to Dover to continue his defense of that most important fort. William the Marshal, given the power of a regent with the title *Rector noster et Regni nostri,* set about consolidating the royalist position in the West and summoning back the recalcitrant barons. This he attempted to do by writing letters to all of them, pointing out that the death of John had changed the situation and that, with a new king committed to observe the Charter, their duty was to swear fealty and to fight under the three leopards.

While Louis spent the winter months in attacks on castles here and there, dissipating his strength in sieges, the old marshal was skillfully undermining his support and detaching man after man from the French cause.

CHAPTER TWO

The War against the Invaders

PRINCE Louis was a small man, pale of face and austere of expression. He had little in him seemingly of his brilliant and turbulent father, Philip Augustus. A certain saintliness was claimed for him which undoubtedly he inherited from his grandfather, the ineffectual Louis VII, and which would assert itself so magnificently in his son, that great king who is called St. Louis. An anecdote persists that a good friend, one Archambaud de Bourbon, believing that the prince's health suffered from his rigid continence, hired a beautiful young woman to climb into his bed while he was asleep. On waking and finding himself with a bedfellow, the prince ordered her, courteously but firmly, to leave. He was reported to have added, "I cannot commit a mortal sin."

The chaste and reserved prince might be pious, but he was a lion when stirred to fighting pitch. Philip Augustus was easy to rouse to anger and easy to calm down; Louis, hard to rouse, hard to appease. Despite his frail stature he was a champion of mettle, and an old chronicle says, "He put on his cuirass like Judas Maccabaeus." He does not seem to have had much skill in generalship, however, accepting too completely the conceptions of warfare which chivalry had imposed on the Christian world and which would be shattered in a very few years, first by Sabutai leading the armies of Genghis Khan

28

into the heart of the Holy Roman Empire and cutting armies of steel-clad knights to pieces, and later by a plebeian weapon called the longbow in the hands of English churls. His plan for conquering England was to take one castle after another and to enlarge gradually the arc of his control. The weakness of this method was that each castle taken necessitated leaving a garrison behind, thus leading to a stage when all his troops would be roosting in captured Keeps and strutting on alien battlements. This method kept wars going interminably; it led to continuous truces and in the end to a paucity of results. Louis, it seems, moreover, was a poor judge of men. The lieutenants to whom he entrusted the command of his little armies in preference to more experienced English barons were young French knights who were ready to lay their lives down bravely but who had no capacity for leadership.

In February, Philip Augustus summoned his son home to discuss the situation. It was believed that the French King was anxious to avoid papal confirmation of the ban of excommunication laid by Gualo on all Frenchmen under arms on English soil, but this was not the real reason. Philip Augustus had a hide impervious to such darts, having been banned himself on more than one occasion. He had been blowing hot and cold, however, on the English adventure and was beginning to doubt the issue. It was as clear to the French monarch as it was to William the Marshal that time was not fighting on the side of the French.

It was easy to summon Louis home, but it was not easy for the prince to obey. The adherence of the Cinque Ports to his cause had become so doubtful that it was not possible to sail from any of them while between London and the harbors westward lay the Weald in which lurked the ever-watchful Willikin. Louis ventured out from London with a considerable escort but with some trepidation, a state of mind which was justified by subsequent events. They took a circuitous course through Kent and then swung in between the Weald and the coast, hoping to reach Winchelsea, where Eustace the Monk could take them off in his ships. As they passed Lewes arrows began to fall on the rear guard and fast-riding horsemen shouting, "The Rood! The Rood!" closed in on them. Willikin had detected the maneuver and he struck at them so ferociously that the French party was thrown into confusion and started a hasty flight for Winchelsea. The guerrilla band followed on their heels and took many prisoners, including two nephews of the Count of Nevers. They cut off all stragglers and kept up such an incessant attack that the Frenchmen reached Winchelsea in a breathless state.

.They found the town empty and gutted of supplies. The inhabitants had left and the men had joined forces with those of the nearby town of Rye. They returned in full force to hem Louis in on the east while Willikin poised a continual threat of assault on the west. Louis was in a serious plight. Finally, however, a rescue party, riding by way of Canterbury to avoid suspicion, came down through Romney and arrived at Winchelsea just in time to save the prince and his men from dying of starvation. Eustace arrived with some ships off the coast at the same time and took the harried prince and his men aboard.

There was a stormy interview between the French King and Louis when the latter arrived at his father's court. Philip Augustus was not pleased with the way things were going. He declared himself to have been against the venture in the first place (this, of course, was not true) and he found fault, on much sounder ground, with his son's handling of the invasion. It was now a lost cause and he had no intention of spending further money on armies and supplies. Louis protested without making any impression on the imperious monarch. He went then to his wife and begged her assistance.

It is high time to tell something of this remarkable woman known to history as Blanche of Castile. When it had been decided some fifteen years before that a Spanish bride should be sought for Louis, King Alfonso had two candidates to offer, his daughters Blanche and Uracca. The King of France decided that the name Blanche would have a more familiar sound in the ears of his subjects and accordingly she was selected. Seventy-eight-year-old Queen Eleanor, widow of Henry II of England and grandmother of the two Spanish princesses, rode all the way to Castile to make the final arrangements and to escort the bride in proper state to her royal husband. When that wise and indomitable woman reached the Spanish court she must have wondered about the wisdom of the choice. Uracca was a dazzling beauty, so lovely, in fact, that Blanche looked plain beside her. Comparison with this beautiful sister was not fair, however, to the prospective bride. Blanche was comely enough, some reports having it that she bore a slight resemblance to her grandmother; and this was high praise because Eleanor had been the reigning beauty of Europe in her day. The plainer of the two princesses had certain advantages over the more vivacious Uracca which, no doubt, were apparent to the wise eyes of the old Queen. She was serious of disposition and very pious and she possessed, moreover, a gift for management. Eleanor, who had become expert at pulling strings to animate the puppets on the stage of history, must have recognized in this quiet and somewhat repressed granddaughter a kindred spirit.

Louis was well pleased with his bride. The lovely Uracca might have been too giddy and pleasure-loving for the earnest-minded prince, but Blanche was the perfect wife for him. She was as ambitious as he was, as unremitting in her addiction to duty. They became deeply attached, bringing twelve children into the world, six of whom lived. They were model parents, and their life together seems to have been passed without a ripple of disagreement. Taller than her spouse and of a natural sternness of temperament, Blanche dominated Louis as she afterward did her son, the saintly King.

When Blanche found that her formidable father-in-law had turned against any continuation of the effort to annex the crown of England, she took matters into her own hands. Storming into his presence, she demanded that he change his mind. French biographers have compared her to Semiramis, the fabled Queen of the Four Quarters of the World who was fed as an infant by doves and later took the form of a bird. There was nothing dove-like in the outraged advocate of action who cornered the monarch and passionately demanded that he continue to support his son. She left his presence finally with threats that, if he remained obdurate, she would raise the money by pawning her children. It is assumed in the records of the day that the King was disturbed by the picture this conjured up in his mind of his beloved grandchildren held as hostages by Lombardy usurers and, if not actually displayed in shops with tickets on them, at least compelled to exist in a mean form of captivity. It is easier to believe that he had intended always to go on supporting the army of invasion but had sensed that opposition might strengthen the backbone of the prince to more determined efforts. It might have been, again, a ruse on his part to deceive the Pope as to his real attitude. It is still more possible, of course, that he could not stand out against his resolute daughter-in-law. Whatever the reason, he gave in finally and promised Blanche the financial support she was demanding.

Blanche seems to have been fated to play the role of the activating force behind her less aggressive and far from practical men. It was devolving on her now to put drive and initiative behind her brave but decidedly not inspired husband. In later years she would rule France during the minority of Louis IX and through the long years he spent at the Crusades, drawing on the resources of the kingdom to supply him with men and money and supplies, thus making it possible for him to achieve historical greatness.

In the present instance she went to work with a grim resolve to win for her husband the throne of England. She went out and raised more money wherever she could, pawning her personal possessions if not her children. With the funds thus made available she established her headquarters at Calais and proceeded to buy equipment for the mercenary troops she was recruiting and to secure ships for the transport of the army. She harried Eustace the Monk and played so violently on the patriotism of the knights of France that three hundred of them enlisted for service in England.

2

While Louis was in France the marshal was at work. He went on a tour of the southeast corner of the kingdom, winning adherents everywhere. The men of the Cinque Ports, who had been wavering, were ready now to come over in a body. His own son, William, was among the most notable of the converts, and the Earl of Salisbury, a natural son of Henry II by the Fair Rosamonde and more familiarly known as William Long-Espée. Other barons joined the train of the newly appointed head of the state and were with him at a council of war held with Willikin of the Weald. A vigorous plan of action was marked out, and the boy King's supporters began then to hammer so effectively at the outer edges of the French holdings that castle after castle fell to them, Winchester, Farnham, Marlborough, Knap. Willikin swooped down on Dover and burned the camp of the besiegers, hanging Frenchmen as fast as he could get his hands on them. The result of all this furious activity was that Louis, returning around the end of April, had to make a landing at night and dash in great haste for the security of London.

The campaign which followed reflected the weakness of purpose of Louis and his halfhearted English allies. The prince was persuaded to send the largest part of his troops on a thrust into the midlands, where the castle of Mountsorel was being invested by royalists. Resuming command himself of the operations around Dover, Louis placed the Count of Perche in charge of the northern excursion. The count was one of the bravest and rashest of his many brave and rash young men and probably the least suited for such a mission. Finding that the siege of Mountsorel had been raised, Perche felt he must achieve something to justify this elaborate foray and shoved on up the Belvoir road to attack the city of Lincoln. The widow of the castellan of Lincoln, a brave woman named Nicolette de Camville, retired into the castle and defended it so bravely that all the efforts of the French forces were in vain.

William the Marshal now decided that the time had come for a test of strength. The French army was divided, and he knew enough about the character of the young Count of Perche to feel he could be counted upon to make mistakes. Accordingly the veteran got together all the men who could be rallied to the banner of the boy King and approached Lincoln by a northwesterly route, marching from the Stow road to the Old Roman Way. The marshal knew that he was outnumbered, but this did not cause him too much concern. Early that morning a knight named Geoffrey de Serland had ridden out from Lincoln with a message from the resolute Nicolette. A small postern near the western sally port in the walls was open and unguarded. The marshal planned, therefore, to monopolize the attention of the French while the archers under Falkes de Bréauté slipped into the old walled city.

Early in the morning of May 20 the marshal's army appeared on a high ridge to the north. Forgetting his years and his slackening powers, the grand old man rode in the van, his white cross proudly displayed on his breast. He had either forgotten to put on his helmet or had purposely elected to appear without it. At any rate, he led the attack bareheaded, his lank white locks tossing in the breeze. His eyes gleamed with all the old ardor and eagerness for the fray. "God has given them into my hands!" he declared.

Robert Fitz-Walter and Saire de Quincey, the leaders of the English who still fought with the French, rode out to reconnoiter. They were not alarmed by what they saw. The force advancing to the attack was small and lacking in cavalry. They returned and advised the Count of Perche to meet the English in the open country, where the French cavalry would have freedom to attack. The young count had no respect, however, for the military sagacity of his English allies. He decided to see for himself.

The old marshal had resorted to a stratagem. Behind the not too numerous body of his armed men he had assembled all the wagons of his train and a large and motley company of camp followers, servants, and peasantry. They had been given standards to carry, and to the inexperienced eye of the young French leader it seemed that a large army was moving against him. Brushing aside the advice of the English leaders, he decided he could not face such a formidable force in the open and ordered, instead, a concentration of his men in the upper level of the old Roman city, a warren of narrow streets between the castle, where the fair Nicolette still held out, and the cathedral. Here cavalry could not be used and the superior numbers of the French would mean nothing.

In the meantime the archers under Falkes de Bréauté made their way into the city through the unguarded postern. His selection to command the bowmen had been a wise one. Of all the professional soldiers imported into England by John, he was the best, a skilled and cool-headed leader who struck, moreover, with such passionate fury when he got into action that he was sometimes called the Rod of the Lord's Fury. He seems to have had no difficulty in reaching the postern and gaining access from there to the castle. The Frenchmen, packed in the streets below, were thrown into great confusion when they heard suddenly the English cry of "King's men! King's men!" from the battlements and looked up to see the walls crowded with archers. Immediately, it seemed, the air was filled with arrows. The space between the castle and the cathedral was a jumble of alleys and closes and so small that a strong-armed bowman could send a bolt from one end to the other. The French soldiery, having no shelter from the lethal hail and being unable to advance or retreat, began to drop like ripe chestnuts after the first frost. The horses screamed and threshed about savagely when wounded, crushing their riders under them.

The main attacking force, led by the marshal, who had now donned his helmet, forced an entrance into the upper level at the same time that the Earl of Chester attacked the lower part. Chester had no difficulty in scattering the few French detachments which had been posted below and driving them up the sloping streets into the crowded upper town. The

French were now more than ever handicapped by their numbers. Unable to make a sortie, they died under the rain of arrows from the castle walls and gave way before the sharp attack of the marshal in the north and west and the Earl of Chester in the south until they were hopelessly jammed into the maze of lanes about the cathedral.

The fighting was singularly one-sided. Although the English under the marshal lost very few men, the French suffered wholesale slaughter. The Count of Perche, as valiant as he was stubborn and inept, refused to surrender and was cut down in the street fighting after an exchange of blows with the aged marshal. All the English allies with the French were captured. It is probable that, disgusted with the stupidity which was costing them so dear, they had little stomach for the struggle. Most of the French gave in at the same time, three hundred knights in all laying down their arms.

The victory was so complete, and had been won with such small loss, that it was called thereafter the Fair of Lincoln. The exultant marshal, feeling no fatigue after a day of riding and fighting in the saddle, galloped that night to Nottingham, where the legate and the boy King were stationed, to give them the glad news that the largest part of the French army of invasion had been destroyed.

The fact that many of the English barons, including Robert Fitz-Walter, Saire de Quincey, Robert de Ros, and William Mowbray, were captured in the narrow and blood-drenched streets adds a note of ironic regret to this otherwise splendid victory. They had been among the leaders of the popular party at Runnymede, and their names should never be forgotten as long as man has memory for the great deeds of the past; but at Lincoln they were fighting for the invader, they stood under the lilies of France and strove against the English. They had been driven to this course in the first place by the tyranny of John, who threatened not only their possessions but their lives, and they were held by their oaths to the support of the alien they had invited over to help them. If they had prevailed at Lincoln new chains would have been forged for their wrists and Magna Charta would have been disregarded and forgotten.

The victors were men who, for the most part, had stood aside in the earlier struggle for freedom, and some of them had ridden in the small train which accompanied John to Runnymede. It is doubly ironic that at Lincoln they fought for the Charter against the men who had conceived it.

Louis realized the extent of the disaster and expressed a willingness to enter into negotiations for peace. He gave up his interminable and futile siege of Dover and in a mood of the deepest discouragement returned to London. A meeting to discuss terms was held near Brentford and, as the marshal was persuaded to moderation by the desperate need of England for peace, they came close to an agreement. The legate, however, was unwilling to stretch the amnesty to cover four ecclesiastics without instructions from the Pope, and nothing could be signed. Louis in the meantime was hearing encouraging reports from the energetic Blanche of the strength she was gathering for him, and his will was stirred to further efforts.

Hoping that the tide of fortune would still turn for him, Louis settled down in London to wait for the reinforcements that Eustace the Monk would convoy across the Channel.

CHAPTER THREE

The Start of Sea Power

JOHN, that bad man and most execrated of monarchs, must be given credit as the founder of the British navy. While Normandy was under the rule of the English kings and the Channel was a national strait which did not require guarding, there had been no royal navy and no need of one. The necessity for transportation to and from the Continent had been solved by the creation of the Cinque Ports, a federation of the sea towns of Kent and Sussex. In return for certain privileges these towns undertook to supply the kings with ships and men. They were allowed to govern themselves by portmotes and to take flotsam and jetsam (which turned them into more or less open nests of piracy), and a cluster of lesser rights which need not be enumerated, although it is interesting to mention some of them for the color of the words—den and strond, tol and team, blodwit and fledwit, infang and outfang, soc and sac, and mundbryce. This was a convenient arrangement but hardly adequate after John lost all the northern possessions in France. With hostile ports so close at hand, he was compelled to get together the first semblance of a national fleet.

His navy was quite small. In addition to a limited number of fighting ships, none of which exceeded eighty tons, he had available many smaller vessels for the carrying of supplies and troops. They were called sornakes, passerettes, schuyts, and nascellas. Being a methodical man and a first-rate organizer, John devised a plan for the management of the royal ships which led in due course to the formation of the Admiralty. He appointed one William de Wrotham as the head. It is not recorded that William de Wrotham had displayed any great proficiency at polishing up the handles of front doors, but it is almost certain that he had never gone to sea. He was a churchman, as were all state officials, holding the archdeaconry of Taunton. He confined himself to the details of management, and it was his responsibility to supply the silk and canvas for the sails, to purchase or seize the stores of food, and to impress the men needed for the crews. He seems to have been a capable official and to have given his capricious master full satisfaction, but it is recorded that at one time he paid twenty-three hundred marks for the King's favor, *benevolentiam regis*. Probably the post gave ample opportunities for the feathering of personal nests.

John was the first also to perceive the need for adequate dockyard facilities. Although the law of eastern drift had not yet seriously filled with silt the harbors of the chalk cliffs, he seems to have been aware that it would be wise to go farther west for permanent ports. At any rate, he issued orders to William de Wrotham to take over the docks at Portsmouth and to build around them a strong wall with penthouses for stores and tackle. The work was not carried very far because John, as usual, could not bring himself to supply the funds for the purpose.

This curiously contradictory ruler, who, it must be said, was always popular with sailors because of his wry humor and the rough and sardonic edge of his tongue, was the first, moreover, to score a conclusive triumph at sea. The destruction of the French fleet at Damme (in which he had no personal part) toward the end of his reign was the first in that long succession of naval battles which over the centuries built up the tradition of invincibility at sea.

2

All that was left of John now lay in the Norman choir at Worcester between two splendid Saxon saints, Wulfstan and Oswald, as he had requested with his last breath. If the Evil One had taken possession of his soul in spite of the protection thus afforded him, it would neither have surprised nor distressed the men who faced the consequences of his bitter wrongheadedness. Not only did the French standard float over Calais, but above the towers and walls of London as well. Most of the castles of the southeast were in the hands of Louis. Transports filled the ports of Normandy to bring across the reinforcements which Blanche of Castile had collected for her husband. The small group on whom the responsibility of undoing what that worst of English kings had done contained, fortunately, such courageous and shrewd men as William the Marshal, Hubert de Burgh and Philip d'Aubigny, who had been warden of the Channel Islands and was now in charge of the defense of the southeastern coast. On them the lesson of the victory at Damme had not been lost. They were convinced it would be folly to wait and use their ships only to contest a landing. Better to venture out and challenge the power of France in the open waters of the Channel. Accordingly, when Eustace the Monk led his armada from Calais on St. Bartholomew's Day, August 24, 1217, the relatively small English fleet was ready to go into action.

The chronicles agree that it was a bright and sunny day, one of those clear days, in fact, when keen eyes from the chalk cliffs could catch a glimpse of foreign soil across the Channel. The anxious watchers, who had taken possession of rooftops and trees and spires, had a good view of the French ships as they gained mid-Channel, and of what then transpired.

Eustace the Monk was in the first and largest ship in the line, and it would have been obvious to anyone who saw the condition of his vessel that the dreaded sea captain was suffering from overconfidence. He had, at any rate, loaded it so heavily that the water washed over the gunwales with each movement. In addition to thirty-two knights with the bluest of blood in their veins and enough steel on their proud backs to weigh down any ship, there was a trebucket on board (a cumbersome siege engine) and a string of horses intended for the use of Prince Louis. Eustace had collected and equipped the ships, but the commander was Robert de Courtenai. The latter had distributed the 120 knights who made up his personal following in the four vessels which came next in line. There were six other vessels, so loaded with knights and men-at-arms that they swerved and luffed erratically into the wind and were at times almost out of control. Following the troopships were seventy smaller craft carrying supplies.

The English fleet consisted of smaller vessels in the main.

They were all under one hundred feet in length, high in bow and stern, flat-bottomed, and stoutly clinker-built, which means that the planks in the hold overlapped each other. They had one mast only, in the exact center, a single square sail of no great size, made of silk with reinforcements of canvas, and were steered by an oar fixed on the starboard. In battle they were maneuvered by sixteen oars on each side. For this crisis they had been "bearded," the bows strengthened by bands of iron for use in ramming. There were sixteen ships of battle and many more smaller craft.

William the Marshal had contributed one of the largest in the fleet, a cog, which was a stoutly constructed type of vessel with rounded bow and stern. Never having avoided a fight in the whole of his life, he intended to go aboard the cog and take charge of the operations. His attendants knew, however, that the splendid old paladin lacked the seaworthiness of leg needed for participation in the hurly-burly of a naval battle. They persuaded him, with great difficulty, to stay ashore. Hubert de Burgh took his place in command.

The tactics of the English had been planned with the audacity which alone wins battles afloat. They waited until the French armada had passed Sandwich and then issued out behind it. Eustace, standing in front of his tent on the raised platform called a bellatorium, boomed out his delight when he saw what was happening. He was certain that the English were hoping to divert him by a feint at Calais. He was too old a fighting cock, he averred, to be caught by any such transparent device as this. Let them attack the port from which he had just sailed! They would find he had left it strongly guarded and would get well singed for their pains; and in the meantime he would proceed with his task of landing the men and supplies so badly needed by the French army of invasion.

His satisfaction, however, was short-lived. The English had no intention of attacking Calais. They had swung about into the wind and were coming fast after the French transports. By this one move they had accomplished the prime objective of all the maneuvering which precedes a brush at sea; they had gained the windward position and were pounding on after him with a brisk breeze at their backs. Eustace, no doubt, swore many loud nautical oaths as he strove to bring his ships about to meet them. The French vessels floundered and pitched and fell out of line and were, as a result, badly disorganized when the battle was joined. With Hubert de Burgh and Richard Fitz-John, a bastard son of the late King, in the van, the small English ships came on to make the most of the situation, their sails bellying in the western wind, the sailors seated at the oars in readiness, the constables with their archers in the waists, even the grummets (the boys who made part of all crews in ships of the Cinque Ports) clambering up the masts and cheering wildly, and above them the most skilled of the bowmen in the gabies.

The wind played a big part in the English plan of attack. As soon as they came within range, the constables gave orders to the archers to begin. The feather-tipped shafts gained increased speed from the sustained breeze into which they were launched, and took murderous toll of the Frenchmen, still frantically engaged in the task of turning. As the islanders came abreast, moreover, they opened pots of finely powdered lime and the wind carried it into the eyes of the French. As a result the steel-trussed knights were unable to put up any effective resistance when the English, their eyes filled with battle fire above the daggers held in their teeth, their pikes slung loosely on their backs, came swarming over the rails. Even Eustace, that veteran of many sea fights, could not organize a front against them, for both the cog and the ship commanded by Richard Fitz-John had elected to attack him, one on each side. The struggle here was short and the slaughter of the French was tremendous. Only the knights were spared (because of the ransoms they could pay), and Robert de Courtenai was among the prisoners taken.

Eustace valued his life and he disappeared when he realized that the fight was a hopeless one. A search was made for him as soon as resistance ceased, and he was found burrowing down under the ballast sand and bilge water in the hold, surely the largest and least willing frog ever fished out of that malodorous scum. Brought on deck with arms lashed behind his barrel-like torso, the doughty pirate pleaded for his life and offered to pay a ransom of ten thousand marks. This was proof that piracy pays, because few noblemen would have been able to buy their freedom at such a price.

It was a tempting offer, but the feeling against this double renegade ran higher than the cupidity of his captors. "Base traitor!" cried Richard Fitz-John, putting into words the sentiment of the other leaders. "Never shall you again seduce anyone by your fair promises."

It was decided he must die, and accordingly he was

strapped down on his grufe along the rail of the ship, still pleading frantically for his life. A man named Stephen Crabbe, who had once served with Eustace, volunteered to act as executioner.

In later years the legend of the monkish pirate grew and it was believed that, after breaking his monastic vows, he had studied black magic in Spain and had the power to make himself and his ships invisible. If Eustace ever possessed such power this surely was the time to display it. Nothing happened, needless to state, to obscure the body over which Stephen Crabbe hovered with his blade suspended in the air. Perhaps an old grudge put skill and dispatch in the sailor's arm. At any rate, he severed the head from the body with one stroke and the gory locks of Eustace floated from the end of a pike when the victorious fleet put in later at Dover. The pirate's head was a prized exhibit for a long time and was carried about England, still on the end of the spear, to be gazed at and exulted over.

This was a fitting end, no doubt, for Eustace the Monk.

The capture of the flagship gave victory to the English. The other troopships turned and set sail for Calais, and all, or nearly all, got safely back. The reason for their escape was that the English, with the day won, found the booty of the supply ships more to their taste than the glory of capturing knights in shining armor. They took most of the smaller craft, killing the crews or spilling them without ceremony into the sea. On their triumphant return, therefore, the English ships were piled so high with loot that they rode as heavily as the French had done earlier in the day. The men of the Cinque Ports were allowed to keep most of the spoils, but a certain percentage went to the Hospital of St. Bartholomew's, which was established at Sandwich in honor of the victory.

The decisive battle of Sandwich had done more than cut Louis off from his base and leave him powerless to continue his efforts: it had set a pattern which would persist down the ages. From that day on it was recognized that the wooden walls of the navy were the first line of defense and, as it developed, the only line needed. If a prophetic sense had visited the furiously aggressive masters and constables under Hubert de Burgh or the exultant watchers on shore, they might have seen in the haze of the future phantom fleets with great carved superstructures and glistening orange sails which stemmed from their efforts of that day, and mighty frigates mountainously rigged and sailing in line, and steel-encased leviathans with guns capable of hurling shells beyond the horizon; and they might have heard a whisper of the names of great sailor men who would fight and win in the same way, Drake and Howard and Rodney and Blake and Nelson.

CHAPTER FOUR

Peace Comes to the Land and Death Comes to the Marshal

PEACE was signed on September 12 on an island in the Thames at Kingston, with a proud queen mother and an exuberant young king to watch the proceedings. Louis was to withdraw from England and to forswear his claims to the crown. He agreed, moreover, to bring persuasion to bear on his father to restore Normandy and the Angevin provinces to the English King. This was a futile gesture: Philip Augustus, that passionately ambitious monarch, would never yield an inch of the territory he had won. Louis entered into a definite undertaking to restore the Channel Islands to England, expelling the brothers of Eustace the Monk therefrom.

On their part, the English agreed to proclaim an amnesty and to restore all lands and possessions of the barons who had fought for the French. They were to pay the beaten prince the sum of ten thousand marks to finance his withdrawal, Louis being now completely without funds.

The terms were easy. Some violent partisans wanted to force the French to surrender without conditions, but it is worth noting that none of them belonged to the relatively small group which began the struggle in support of the boy King and had borne the heat and the responsibility of it. William the Marshal again held out for moderation on the ground that England needed peace. He wanted above everything else to see the French out of the country and a start made at re-pairing the ravages of civil war. The legate was of the same opinion, although he refused to have the amnesty extended to the churchmen who had allied themselves with the invaders; Rome would attend to the disciplining of its own people. The verdict of history has been that they were right in not holding out for more rigorous terms, that the country benefited im-measurably by the quick ending of hostilities.

The vanquished Louis, somber and chill in defeat, sailed from Dover before the month was out, with his most unpleas-ant task still ahead of him, that of facing Philip Augustus and explaining his lack of success.

The long civil war had come to an end. In November of that year Eustace of Fauconberg was appointed treasurer and the Exchequer began again to function normally at Westmin-ster. Early in the following year, 1218, the judges set out on their circuits and again cases were tried and justice was administered as in the good days of Henry II. Stephen Lang-ton, the great archbishop, was at last allowed to return from his exile in Rome. He landed at Dover in May 1218 and was greeted like a conquering hero, great crowds swarming about him, to kiss his hands, to see his benign and resolute face. He was an old man but as conscious as ever of great tasks to be accomplished. Resuming his functions at Canterbury immedi-ately, he was largely responsible for the affirmation of Magna Charta at a council held in London shortly thereafter.

On Whitsunday, 1220, the boy King was crowned again, with proper robes and regalia and with all the ostentation which had been lacking at his first coronation. Stephen Lang-ton officiated, and the noblemen with hereditary roles to play came forward eagerly to perform them, even the owner of Addington presenting his dish of dilligrout in the traditional manner. The records state that "the feasting and joviality was such that the oldest man present could remember nothing like it at any previous coronation."

2

Queen Isabella had left England in July 1217, returning to the peace of the high-walled city of Angoulême which had been her home until John saw her and stole her away from the man to whom she had been pledged, Hugh of Lusignan. Her purpose was to visit her seven-year-old daughter, Joanna.

The little princess, who was a beautiful child and blessed with a perfect disposition which she could not have inherited from either of her parents, was to marry in due course of time this same Hugh of Lusignan, who was now the Count of La Marche. In his disappointment over the fair Isabella, handsome Hugh le Brun (the Brown) had remained without a wife, and it was through sentimental regard for his old sweetheart that he had accepted Joanna as his future bride in return for assistance to John in one of the latter's abortive campaigns in France. The child was being educated in one of his castles.

Count Hugh was away crusading when Isabella arrived. The Lusignans had played an important part in the struggle for the Holy City, and one of them had been King of Jerusalem. Hugh returned before the end of her visit, browner than ever, and he realized at once that his love for her had not lessened with the years. This was not surprising, for the royal widow at thirty-four was still beautiful, as lissome as ever, her manner gay and seductive. A troubadour would have compared her to a ripe peach hanging on a sun-kissed wall in Provence or an earth-bound spirit of beauty. Why should he wait seven or eight years more while the little Joanna grew up? Here was the lady of his first choice, free and obviously willing. He held out his arms and Isabella walked right into them.

They were married without waiting for the consent of the King's Council in England. This was a mistake. The Council had the power to say whom she should marry or whether she should marry at all. As the second matrimonial ventures of queens are supposed to be dictated by political expediency, it was certain they would not have selected Hugh le Brun for her. They promptly confiscated all her dower lands and stopped the payment of her pension.

Isabella and her devoted Hugh were highly indignant over this. Hugh was in love with his wife, but he was also very much attached to her broad acres and the handsome jointure she was supposed to receive each year. He demanded satisfaction and made many threats against the men who composed the Council. The little princess had not been returned to England, and this provided the pair with a weapon. They announced they would not let her go until the Council relented and handed back the castles which had been the Queen's dower right and the fat and fruitful lands which had gone with them. This threw the Council into an equal state of indignation, and a letter was sent to the Pope, signed by the boy King, requesting the Pontiff to excommunicate his mother and her new spouse, to curse them, as the papal bans read, "within and without, sleeping or waking, going and sitting, standing and riding, lying above ground and under water, speaking and crying and drinking, in water, in field, in town." It happened that, on finding the princess had been freed from her troth, the Council had started negotiations to give her as wife to King Alexander, the Red Fox of Scotland, and thereby cement the peace between the two countries. Joanna not being available, the Council wanted to substitute the tiny Princess Eleanor. Alexander would have none but the oldest daughter of the royal line, and so the Council was compelled, most reluctantly, to come to terms. Isabella received in compensation for her dower lands in Normandy the stannaries in Devon and the revenue of Aylesbury for a period of four years. She received the sum of three thousand pounds as payment for arrears in her pension.

To cast ahead, Joanna was married to Alexander at York in the year 1221. The little Queen won the affections of the Scottish people, who called her Joan Makepeace because her coming had brought about a cessation of hostilities between the two countries. She died in her twenty-eighth year and was deeply mourned by her husband and the people.

Isabella was happy for a time in her second marriage, presenting her husband over the years with eight children. She had been a queen, however, and could not reconcile herself to the rank of a mere countess. Her dissatisfaction grew with the years and led, as will be recorded later, to much trouble for her husband and her son, and much unhappiness for the people of England.

3

William the Marshal, Earl of Pembroke, Lord of Striguil, and regent of England, fell ill in the Tower of London early in 1219. He could eat nothing but mushrooms and partially masticated bread, and he became weak and the flesh wasted from the bones of his once powerful frame. Doctors came from all parts, undoubtedly all five of the established physicians in London, as well as healers of the sick from elsewhere with cures of their own, and quacks in noisy droves. They gave him curious mixtures and they put coral in his mouth at night and they kept the room cooled by the evaporation of rose water.

There was a general belief in the efficacy of warmth, and some of them unquestionably would have liked to bury him up to the neck in a dunghill or in the belly of a freshly killed animal, these being acknowledged ways of checking disease. The old man knew that he had not much longer to live, however, and it is unlikely that he permitted the men of medicine to subject him to such useless indignities.

He remained in the Tower until Lent, his devoted wife remaining constantly at his bedside. Then he was taken by boat to Reading and from there to his manor at Caversham, where he desired to spend his last hours. The members of the Council followed immediately for a final conference with the Good Knight. The King, the legate Pandulfo who had returned to England to replace Gualo, the justiciar, the barons, and the bishops arrived in a body and seated themselves about the narrow couch on which the marshal was lying. The dying man spoke first to the young King.

"Good, sweet sire," he said, "I have served you loyally and I would still serve you if it pleased God that I should remain on earth. But that is no longer His pleasure, and it is fitting for your barons to choose a man who should guard you well, you and the realm, to the satisfaction of God."

Peter des Roches took it on himself to answer. Having had the custody of the King's person, he had succeeded in gaining an ascendancy over the boy's mind. During the two and a half years of his tutorship he had been installing his own relatives and creatures in posts of importance. A young Poitevin named Peter des Rivaux, who was generally believed to be his illegitimate son, had been insinuated into a position in the royal household and was picking up other posts as they fell vacant. It was clear to all that the suave and wily bishop was planning to get full control of national affairs into his clever and unscrupulous grasp.

Placing a hand on the King's head, Peter des Roches declared that Henry was in his custody and would remain so.

This was a direct challenge. William the Marshal, understanding fully the ambitious plans of the bishop, summoned his dwindling strength to raise himself slightly on the couch.

"Not so, Sir Bishop," he said. "The Lord Henry was placed in my care. Because the land had to be defended I delegated his custody to you." A sudden twinge of pain caused him to pause. He then turned to Pandulfo and said to him: "Go now and take the King with you. Tomorrow, if you will be good enough to return, I will tell you what I have decided; and may God guide my counsels aright."

The decision at which he arrived was probably the wisest one under the circumstances. He did not make the mistake of giving the post to any of the active contenders for it, knowing the dissension which would have been caused. On the following day, when the same group had assembled about his couch, he raised himself with great difficulty on his side and addressed the legate. "I will commit my lord Henry into the hand of God," he said, "and into the hand of the Pope—and into yours, you being here in the Pope's stead."

This solution had perhaps been expected. At any rate, there was no immediate discussion or opposition. With the greatest difficulty the marshal raised himself still higher and addressed himself to the King.

"Sire," he said, speaking in a whisper, for his strength was beginning to fail him, "I pray the Lord God that He may grant you to be a brave and good man."

"Amen," piped up the boy.

The Bishop of Winchester now approached the King with the obvious intent of dissenting from the decision. The marshal cried sharply, "Let be, my lord bishop!" and motioned to his oldest son, who was present, to escort the boy to Pandulfo. Peter des Roches hesitated, then stepped back. He could afford to wait.

Committing the custody of the boy King to the legate meant that Pandulfo would assume political as well as spiritual control of the country during the remaining years of the minority, and many were inclined to look askance at this. He had been legate in John's time and had conducted the negotiations which led to the translation of England into a fief of Rome. As a result, he had been regarded as a guileful and even diabolical character. This was not wholly deserved. He was a man of great ability and a careful administrator. The aging marshal had found him co-operative in every way in restoring the country to a peacetime basis.

Having settled this matter to his own satisfaction if not to that of all the ambitious and high-tempered men who made up the Council, the Good Knight composed himself to die. He called in each of his children and explained what he had done to provide for them. He set aside sums for the Church and for charity and for masses to be said for his soul. Then, his mind cleared of worldly responsibilities, he asked that his wife come to his couch.

The beautiful and gentle countess had been the wealthiest heiress in England and had brought him the lands and honors of Pembroke and Striguil as well as the enormous estates in Ireland which had been passed on in the Pembroke family from Strongbow. She had been a loving wife, content to stand by his side and to accept his will in all things; and her grief now was so great that she found it hard to retain any composure.

"My love, kiss me," said the dying man. Then, his voice becoming less distinct, he added, "It will be for the last time."

Later he roused and asked his faithful squire, John Earley, if he had seen the two strangers who had entered the room. He did not know, murmured the old man, who they were; but they were very tall and of a wonderful beauty, although somewhat shadowy. The company in the room, which was made up of the family and all the faithful men who had ridden with him in his campaigns and had shared his life in camp and court and castle, wept loudly at this, knowing that the two strangers, visible only to the eyes of the dying man, had been sent to escort him over the threshold into immortality.

Thus died William the Marshal, conscious to the end and making the sign of the cross, on the fourteenth of May, 1219. The news of his passing plunged the people of England into the deepest grief. They remembered how John in his dying moments had roused himself to commit his son into the care of the marshal, saying, "In his loyalty, above that of any other man, I put my trust." Aymar, the Grand Master of the Templars, who was lying on his deathbed, said to his attendants, "Bury me beside William the Marshal, the Good Knight." Even Philip Augustus, most self-centered of monarchs, fell into a saddened mood when the news reached him. The French King wandered about and asked all whom he encountered, "Have ye heard that the marshal is dead?" It was not necessary, even at an alien court, to explain which marshal was meant. Later Philip Augustus said, "He was the most loyal man I ever knew."

The old man had promised his body to the Templars, and so he was taken to London for burial. As the funeral train passed, people fell into line behind it, barons and bishops, plain soldiers and plain priests, great men and common, and followed on to London. The Templars, who had been growing powerful and rich as the years went on (they owned in Western Europe no fewer than nine thousand manors with wide lands attached), had recently moved their headquarters to a place on the banks of the Thames between the city walls and the King's palace at Westminster. Here they had built their Round Church (which still stands today, looking very small and strange), surrounding it with a cluster of houses for the head of the order and his officers and the cells of the knights, a jumble of stone buildings raising their gables above a gray wall. There was a cloistered chapel of noble proportions along the waterfront, and somewhere in the maze of buildings there was a countinghouse where the banking of the country was carried on. In addition the Templars were spreading out on all sides, using fifteen acres known as Fikettscroft for martial exercises and installing two forges on a road which in course of time would be called Fleet Street.

It was to the Round Church that the body of William the Marshal was carried. Stephen Langton officiated, and it was clear to the knights who filled the small space wearing the plain white robe of their order that the usually composed and sternly realistic archbishop had been badly shaken by the passing of the Good Knight. He paused in his discourse and looked down on the body of the warrior.

Memories flocked through his mind. It is only possible to guess at what he was thinking, but perhaps he recalled some of the things which were most affectionately remembered of the dead man: How he had been so quiet as a boy and so devoid of the sly smartness of adolescence that his companions thought little of him, calling him William Waste-meat because of his great size, and now those who laughed at him were dust and forgotten, and all Christendom knew that William the Marshal had saved England; and how he had commanded the rear guard when the Lion of England, Henry II, was retreating from Le Mans and he checked Richard the Lionhearted in his pursuit of his defeated and dying father, killing Richard's horse and saying to that ungrateful son, "I leave *you* to the devil!" Certainly there was in his mind a picture of the marshal riding to the Fair of Lincoln without a helmet, his face lighted up and saying to those about him, "See, the hour has come!" an old man leading youth to victory. Finally there was in the mind of the archbishop a deep sense of regret. He thought of the longing which William had felt for a few years of peace and comfort before he passed over the border and how this wish had been denied him.

Then the archbishop raised his voice and put into words the thought which was in every mind, "Here lies all that remains of the best knight of all the world who has lived in our time."

CHAPTER FIVE

The Minority and the Rise of Hubert de Burgh

AFTER the regent died the people about the King split into two camps. On one side were the Englishmen, Stephen Langton, Hubert de Burgh, the Earl of Chester, Philip d'Aubigny, the family of the marshal, the heroes of Runnymede. The latter, sad to relate, were now beginning to follow the marshal into the shades. Saire de Quincey died in 1219, and others in quick succession thereafter, Robert de Vere, William Mowbray, the earls of Hertford, Hereford, and Norfolk. Robert Fitz-Walter, at peace with the state but not happy, went off to the Crusades.

In the other camp were those who had come into the kingdom at John's invitation, most of them men of great ability and of a fierce ambition. They had no sense of patriotism, these Normans and Poitevins, save to their own purses and their desire for power. At the head of the foreign faction was, of course, Peter des Roches. That determined churchman had chosen to disregard the old marshal's declaration and had kept the custody of the boy King. Behind him were the mercenary captains, Falkes de Bréauté, Peter de Maulay, Engelard de Cigogni, hard-bitten soldiers who had been awarded castles and land and had no intention whatever of giving them up. Falkes de Bréauté, in particular, had feathered his nest so successfully that he had become one of the greatest of landowners. He had married the widow of the Earl of Devon and he held castles all through the midlands, where he acted as sheriff of no fewer than six shires. He was intensely ambitious and intended to keep every castle and every hide of land in his acquisitive Norman fingers. Naturally these men drew together, the land-hungry soldiers and the creatures of Peter des Roches, realizing that their prosperity depended on being strong enough to fight for the favor of the young King.

No one was appointed regent in William the Marshal's place, but the death of the old warrior had left one man supreme in the eyes of the people of England, Hubert de Burgh. The popularity of that brave soldier had started when the story of his refusal to allow the mutilation of Prince Arthur became generally known and believed. It grew by leaps and bounds when he stood so bravely at Dover and defied the French invaders, and it reached its height when he took out the ships which won the great naval victory off Sandwich. Here, then, was a candidate ready-made for the leadership.

In view of the great career he carved for himself, and the spectacular fall to which it led, there has been much speculation about this knight who ruled England through most of the minority. Little is known, actually, of the man himself. It is only too clear that he was intensely acquisitive and ambitious, and it has been assumed, because of the bitter antagonism he created, that he was overbearing and even, perhaps, bumptious. The passionate eagerness with which his enemies sought to unseat him indicates certainly that he was not a bluff, blundering soldier hewing blindly to the line of duty as he has sometimes been pictured.

From the facts which are known about his life an entirely different portrait appears. He is believed to have been descended from Robert de Mortain, a half brother of the Conqueror, which would mean that a small tincture of royal blood ran in his veins. If this were true, time had been unkind to the family of De Burgh, bringing it far down in the scale. Hubert's father was a member of the lower reaches of the nobility in Norfolk, a dependent perhaps of the great William de Warenne. As a young man Hubert and his older brother William went to court, seeking chances to further their fortunes. There they came in contact with Prince John, the youngest son of the royal family. John seems to have taken a liking to the landless pair. When he went to Ireland in 1185 he took

William and settled large estates on him. William remained in Ireland and established the family of Bourke, or Burke, which was destined through the centuries to play a prominent part in Irish history. Hubert went into John's service and rose to the post of seneschal of Poitou. Later John appointed him chief justiciar. This was the most important position in the kingdom after the Archbishop of Canterbury, followed by the constable, the marshal, the steward, the chamberlain, and the chancellor.

The matrimonial record of the poor young man from East Anglia makes a truly fantastic story. He was married four times, his first three wives being rich widows, his fourth a princess of Scotland, and each marriage not only left him richer than before but marked a step upward. The first wife was Joan, daughter of William, Earl of Devon, and widow of William de Brewiere the younger. The second was Beatrice, daughter of William de Warenne, the great lord of the east, to whom no doubt the family of De Burgh submitted as their feudal head. Beatrice was the widow of Lord Bardulf. Her first husband had probably been chosen for her; her second she chose for herself, and she brought to young Hubert a very fine estate indeed. Her preference for a knight of comparatively low degree, whose sword was his fortune, is proof enough that he was a man of good address. When she died in 1214 he took as his third wife a former queen of England.

When John, the youngest of the Plantagenets, had been called Lackland because all his father's possessions had been promised to his older brothers, it was arranged to improve his lot by a rich marriage. Avisa, the heiress of the Earl of Gloucester and granddaughter of the great Robert of Gloucester who had been Stephen's chief opponent in the years of the anarchy, was the greatest catch in England. She was a handsome young woman with huge estates in the West, extending into Glamorgan. John had no financial worries after his marriage to Avisa, but when suddenly and unexpectedly he became King of England and saw by an unhappy mischance the radiantly lovely Isabella of Angoulême, he put pressure on the high churchmen of the kingdom and secured a divorce on the grounds of consanguinity, Robert of Gloucester having been an illegitimate son of Henry I. It is perhaps needless to state that King John kept a large part of the Gloucester estates for himself. With what was left, however, Avisa made her second husband, Geoffrey de Mandeville, the richest peer in England; a match which John arranged himself and for which he collected from the bridegroom a fee of eighteen thousand marks. Avisa was a widow again when Hubert de Burgh's wife Beatrice died, and she was no longer young. Certainly she had reached the stage where continual child-bearing had played havoc with the figure and the usual trouble with teeth had begun. All medieval ladies seemed to suffer from bad teeth and were much concerned with ways of holding handkerchiefs in front of the face to conceal the fact, being much addicted also to mulled wine as a means of improving the breath. By the most favorable reckoning Avisa was in her middle forties and older than Hubert de Burgh. It is said that she was still attractive; and certainly she was the possessor of broad acres and fine manors and large herds of cattle.

Hubert's willingness to wed the aging Avisa was a further proof to the critical baronage of his ambitious nature. When he brought his matrimonial record to a climactic high point by wedding the Princess Margaret, sister of the King of Scotland, in 1221, four years after the one-time queen's death, the indignation of the nobility reached a high peak of bitterness. But Princess Margaret, fourth of the great ladies to love and wed this remarkable soldier of fortune, remained devoted to him for the rest of his life. No rough, uncouth soldier, this: a man, rather, of ingratiating manner, an adept courtier, handsome perhaps, but of pleasing mien certainly, of shrewd political sense, deft, adroit, quick-witted. His rise under the ill-tempered and hard-to-please John and his matrimonial success would not have been possible to a man lacking in these qualities.

That the great baronial families never regarded him as anything but an upstart in spite of the exalted connections he made by marriage is a further indication of the character of the man. He must have been too aggressively dedicated to success, too prone to brush aside any obstacles in his path, too demanding of concessions on the part of others while making none himself. Some of the other qualities of the climber remained in him even after his great success came. He was inclined to take the defensive and seems to have been a little ill at ease in his dealings with the men of the great families. In this connection an anecdote survives which is worth telling. When it was believed that William Long-Espée, the Earl of Salisbury, had died on his way back from Gascony, Hubert decided that his nephew Raimund should marry the widow, the Countess Ela. But that high-spirited lady, who had been the central figure of a great mystery and romance in her youth, was very much in love with her husband and she sent the candidate for her hand packing, a much discomfited man. Shortly afterward William Long-Espée turned up safe and sound. He had made a desperate crossing of the Bay of Biscay and had been driven ashore. He complained to the King of Hubert's plans and the improper haste with which he had acted. Hubert hurried to make his apologies to the indignant husband and seems to have been almost abject in his attitude.

Hubert was, however, a man of great ability and decision and, with the exception of Stephen Langton, there was no one else with the strength and the prestige to assume the control of affairs. The archbishop was now a very old man, and although he would continue to raise a decisive voice in all deliberations, he lacked the physical strength to assume actual leadership. Without any assumption of title or formal declaration of accession, therefore, Hubert de Burgh gathered the reins into his own hands.

He was aided in this assumption of power by the young King, who had been growing up and developing an impatience with the restrictions which hedged him about. Peter des Roches had come to represent this restraint, and Henry was eager to slip from the clerical leading strings. He was happy to turn to the masterful soldier and escape from the influence of the churchman.

In his early teens Henry was becoming tall, straight, graceful of carriage, and rather handsome in a fair-haired, high-complexioned way. The droop in the one eyelid was now a little more pronounced, and the men who saw most of him were beginning to wonder about it. Was it the outer manifestation of a certain slyness of character? For Henry, although he strove to appear ingenuous and anxious to please, was showing qualities which were more nearly an index of his real character, the qualities which would be so pronounced in the man. Although outwardly agreeable, he was actually very critical of what was done for him. Once he railed bitterly at the sons of William the Marshal because he now thought the terms exacted from the Fench invaders had been too easy; a fledgling hedge bird delivering judgment on an eagle. His manners were winning, but he could not always conceal the fact that he was contemptuous of those about him. The passionate rages of John had dwindled in Henry to a sarcastic turn of speech, but he was as determined as his father had been to brook no restraints on his right to rule as he saw fit. It was becoming only too clear that he had no stability in either his likes or dislikes and that the boyish traits which had so pleased his supporters in the dark days of the struggle had been, in part at least, assumed.

After his second coronation he approached Grosseteste, the Bishop of Lincoln, who was to play a remarkable part in his long reign, and asked for information as to the nature of the grace wrought in a king by the unction. The bishop replied that it conferred on kings the sevenfold gifts of the Spirit as in confirmation. The boy thanked him earnestly, and the story was passed along as an evidence of the serious turn of his mind and of his desire to acquire a true understanding. It seems more likely to have been a gesture, a deliberate effort to create that exact impression. He was already showing an inclination to win by persuasion the things his father had rudely grasped as his right. If the anointing at Westminster had conferred the sevenfold gifts on Henry, the effects, alas, soon wore off: for no king was more prone to disregard the obligations of his office, to break promises, to play fast and loose with the people whose welfare should have been his first consideration.

Already it was clear enough that the boy's charm was superficial and that he was going to prove, although in a far different way, as hard to hold in check as his father. There was none of the savagery of John in the new King; he would not be cruel or wantonly destructive, but he would be selfish and willful, and his hand on the rudder of state would be uncertain, unskilled, unpredictable.

On the other side of the shield he was devout (all men were devout in this splendid century), he was generous, and with a real tendency to learning. He became well versed in poetry and he had a fine discrimination in matters of art, most especially in architecture, becoming known later as Henry the Builder. These qualities, admirable in themselves, were not of the kind most needed in a man called to kingship.

It was natural for a boy of this disposition to weary of the restraints of tutelage and to develop impatience with those who exercised authority over him. Peter des Roches, suave, diplomatic, and ever watchful as he was, was unable to hold the King on leash. He fell out of favor suddenly. This was an excellent thing, for otherwise the Poitevin would have taken into his venal hands the administration of the kingdom. Henry at fourteen wanted to escape from his tutor, and it was at this stage that Hubert de Burgh took up where William the Marshal had left off.

The question as to when Henry would come of age was causing much discussion. In France a king's majority began legally when he was fourteen, that having been the age of Philip Augustus when his father gave him a share in the authority of kingship. In England the rule seems to have been to leave the decision to circumstances. For six years Hubert de Burgh was the real head of the state, and he governed with a firm hand in spite of the tides of opposition which surged about him. Peter des Roches had departed the kingdom and gone on a pilgrimage to Compostela as soon as he lost favor (he would come back when things were more propitious), but the foreign influence was still being exerted in insidious ways in the dark little offices at Westminster where the business of government was being carried out. In addition, the powerful barons of England were now openly resentful of the new head of the state and bitterly critical of the wealth he was acquiring for himself.

The next years, in spite of this opposition, saw many forward steps taken. The administration of the realm was firm and consistent in the best traditions of Henry II.

2

The years of the minority were made difficult by a chronic lack of funds. It had been found hard, after the expulsion of the French, to get into operation the various processes of law by which money came to the offices of the Crown. Debts had been accumulating in the meantime, the greatest being the sums owed to the Vatican.

The papacy had always taken an annual toll from England as a matter of course. Starting with the Rome penny, as it was called in Anglo-Saxon days, the yearly tribute took the form of Peter's pence after the Conquest. One of the duties of the Archbishop of Canterbury was to supervise the collection of Peter's pence, which he did with the assistance of the bishops. It did not amount to a very large sum in the days of the Norman kings, particularly as a habit had developed of sending to Rome only a relatively small part of what was collected. A letter from one pope of the period complained that it "was collected faithfully but paid faithlessly." Another papal letter complained bitterly that only three hundred marks had reached Rome while the bishops had retained more than one thousand marks of the amount collected. The actual work of collection devolved on the parochial priest. His duty it was to gather in the tithes, holding suspended over any grumblers or defaulters in his flock the threat of excommunication.

Peter's pence, of course, was collected in all Christian countries subject to Rome and served as one of the main sources of the papacy's still inadequate revenue. England was on a different footing, however, since John had declared the kingdom a fief of Rome. He had agreed to pay an annual tribute of one thousand marks, seven hundred for England, three hundred for Ireland. During the first years of the minority it was impossible to pay this tribute. In addition to war debts, it was necessary to give ten thousand marks to Louis of France and half of that sum to make up arrears in the pension of Richard's widow, Berengaria, who had been allowed by John to exist in poverty. Fortunately the Pope who succeeded that man of wide vision and iron will, Innocent III, was sympathetic to the difficulties of the nation and permitted the tribute to go unpaid. Cencius Savelli had been chamberlain at the Vatican under Innocent, a gentle old man, well loved by everyone. When he was selected to succeed under the title of Honorius III, he brought to the papacy one fixed idea, that the work of Innocent must be carried on, particularly his plans for continuation of the Crusades.

That Honorius was willing to let the payments lapse did not mean, however, that the return to normal conditions in England would find the Crown with a clean slate. He was a careful administrator, a believer in close attention to detail, and a shrewd financier. During his term as chamberlain he had written *The Book of the Revenues of the Church*, and it surprised no one when he demanded payment from England of all arrears.

The necessity of making up the unpaid tribute hung over the early years of Henry's reign like a dark cloud. The King himself had no desire to avoid the debt, but the writs he issued for the money due Rome were often returned because there was no money in the treasury to pay them. It followed that the arrears were paid off in installments extending over a long period of years.

Honorius, and the popes who followed after his death on

March 18, 1227, at the Lateran, found it necessary on occasions to send special representatives to England to supervise the collection of funds for the purpose, and this led to a very great evil, the stimulation of usury. The money for Rome was paid through Italian banking houses, and when Master Otto or Master Martin sat at Westminster to inquire into sums due their master, they generally had a keen-witted Florentine financier sitting beside them. When men were unable to meet their obligations the banker was often willing to make a loan for the purpose. The bankers did not always return to Italy, and this led to a firm establishment of the Lombardy moneylender in the country. He became a much more feared exponent of usury than the Jew because he had papal sanction and was, presumably, under the protection of the Church.

At a later stage of Henry's reign the Vatican discovered one flaw in this arrangement. Two great Italian banking houses failed, the firms of Buonsignori and Ricciardi. The collapse swept away the sum of eighty thousand florins which had been gathered in England for transfer to the papacy.

In addition to the regular forms of tribute there were many other payments which kept draining the island of money, special subsidies for this and that, obventions and legacies for the Crusades, mandatory income taxes, benefices, penitentiary fees, compositions, fines, procurations, pecuniary penances, indulgences. Even more expensive still, and infinitely harder to swallow, was the practice of giving church appointments in England to Italians. This began as soon as John made the grievous error of declaring the country a fief of Rome. Hundreds of posts fell vacant during the years of the interdict, and no effort was made to fill them. As soon as the ban was lifted the legate began to fill them with Italians. They came swarming into the country, eager to enjoy the fat livings and causing nationwide indignation by the ostentation with which they conducted themselves. This practice continued after John's death, although as years went on it took the form of absentee holding. The Italian appointees fell out of the habit of going to England, preferring to remain in Rome and have the revenues paid them there. This was just as well, perhaps, because the men thus favored with canonries and prebends never fitted themselves to fill their offices by learning English and they did less harm by staying out of the country. Much of this was nepotism, the posts being awarded to the relatives of popes and cardinals, but a part of it was the result of a practice which had grown up to relieve the poverty of the papacy. A huge staff was maintained at the Vatican, and the funds were not sufficient to maintain an adequate pay roll. Each nation was expected to assist by appointing a number of these clerks and officials to livings while they continued to work in Rome.

England was suffering a much heavier drain on her financial resources, however, than any other country. A survey of the situation in 1231 led to the conclusion that many hundred livings in England were in the possession of Italians while substitutes, paid starvation wages, carried on the work. The annual payments made to foreign holders of benefices amounted to seventy thousand marks, which was more than the revenue of the government. Years later one of the popes agreed to establish a limit by which no more than eight thousand marks could be paid to foreign benefice holders, and this was estimated as five per cent of the income of the Church in England. On that basis of reckoning the amount taken from the Church had been running as high as forty per cent.

The strain was felt more during the minority than at any other time. In 1221 Stephen Langton made such a strong presentation to the Pope of the spiritual stagnation in many of the parishes affected that Honorius made a sweeping concession. As the sinecures fell vacant through death, the right to appoint successors would revert to England. Had this guarantee been carried out, the evil of absenteeism would gradually have been eliminated; and so the archbishop was well content with what he had accomplished. Unfortunately the clamor in Rome for subsistence continued as great as ever. When one comfortably endowed Italian died there would be a scramble to step into his shoes. In too many cases letters were received in England making Italian appointments with the words *Non obstante* marked on the margin, which meant that no restriction on foreign appointments must be allowed to stand in the way. *Non obstante!* The phrase became odious to English eyes and one to which, unfortunately, they became well accustomed as the years and the decades rolled on.

Naturally there was plenty of nepotism and simony in England as well. Henry did not differ from other kings in having candidates of his own when desirable posts fell vacant. As he grew older he became more and more addicted to favoritism. There was a dark little room behind the Exchequer at Westminster, and here he was known to sit when questions of appointments were being threshed out. Frequently his candidates were foreigners—Poitevins, Gascons, relatives from Angoumois or Provence; and seldom were they fitted to perform the functions of the office.

It has been recorded that John Mansel was invested with livings running from three hundred to seven hundred in number during the years that he served the King in various capacities. This is undoubtedly an exaggeration, but it may safely be assumed that the total of his appointments was large to the point of absurdity. These livings were not conferred on a humble official for his own individual profit. The revenue thus secured was either for the royal purse or for the benefit of friends and relatives of the King. In fairness to Rome, also, it should be pointed out that Westminster followed the same principle of giving livings to state officials while they continued to fill their governmental duties because the Crown was too poor to pay them.

3

The importance of Hubert de Burgh continued to increase during the last years of the minority. He was the first of a long succession of commoners who rose to posts of almost supreme power and lived in some, at least, of the magnificence of royalty. Lacking their stature, he was still the forerunner of such great and fascinating figures as Jacques Coeur, Cardinal Wolsey, Cardinal Richelieu, Fouquet. He had been created Earl of Kent and was firmly establishing himself in Wales, being castellan of the three fortresses of Montgomery, Carmarthen, and Cardigan. The Tower of London had come back into his hands, and he resided there a large part of the time although he had set up a palatial residence of his own on a piece of land which later became Whitehall. The royal castles of Dover, Canterbury, Rochester, and Norwich were in his hands, to mention the most important only.

He was the sheriff of seven counties. The sheriff is today a relatively unimportant local officer; in these early days he was the King's representative and the embodiment of the law in his county, the lineal descendant of the Norman viscount. He lived in a royal castle in the county seat and, although he had to call the knights of the shire to pass judgment on cases tried in the shire courts which met for a day every four weeks, he presided at the shire moots with powers which could be made arbitrary, and the hundred-moots were called at his will. He was the manipulator of *scotale* and the controller of *scot and lot;* he conducted inquests, collected taxes, and managed the machinery of law enforcement.

Needless to state, Hubert de Burgh did not fulfill the duties of his seven shrievalties himself. He engaged deputies for that. But a large part of the revenue of each came to him and stayed in his heaping purse.

His marriage with the Scottish princess had been highly successful. They seem to have been a devoted couple, and certainly Margaret remained loyal to him through thick and thin. One daughter had been born to them who was named for her mother but was always called affectionately Meggotta. Henry had not yet acquired the interest in architecture which earned him later the name of Henry the Builder, and so the Tower lacked at this time the additions which are linked to him, the Water Gate, the Cradle Tower, the Lantern, in the latter of which the King would one day have his bedroom because of the view it allowed of the river. The resplendent justiciar, filled with a sense of his importance and so drunk with power that he paid little heed to the growing resentment of the nobility, resided with his princess wife and his dearly beloved Meggotta in the White Tower. He took his meals, undoubtedly, in the Banqueting Hall, the only apartment in this gloomy pile of masonry (where even the gray partitions were ten feet thick) which had a fireplace. The flames jumped and roared on the huge hearth, lighting up the long table where Hubert and his company sat down to meat well basted with sauces fragrant with spices from the East and washed down with wines from Gascony. At the far end the musicians played the pure and rather haunting airs of the day, blowing softly on the tibia (the grandfather of the flute) and twanging the harp, while the flames lighted up the pictures of the history of Antiochus which covered the walls.

Kings could travel about the lands they ruled in simplicity and without fear. The boy who would soon become the King of France and be known as St. Louis developed the habit of sitting under a tree by the side of the road and talking to all who passed or attending services in churches so humble that they lacked seats. Much later Louis XI of France would fall into the habit of disguising himself in menial attire and issuing out to discover for himself what people were thinking and saying. But when men of common birth ruled, they found it necessary to travel in state. Hubert de Burgh, borrowing from

Thomas à Becket when the latter was chancellor and William de Longchamp, the hobgoblin who governed England when Richard went to the Crusades, rode out, accompanied by a long train: knights, men-at-arms, archers, scriveners, confessors, almoners, body servants, cooks, barbers, jugglers, acrobats. He took pains to cut an imposing figure himself in polished chain mail, a scarf dyed bright with madder knotted about his steel-encased neck, the quillons of his sword sparkling with jewels. No matter where he might ride, it was not necessary for him to seek the hospitality of other men. He owned so many castles and manors that wherever he went he could always repair by nightfall to lodgings of his own. The roll call of Hubert's possessions has a fantastic sound, tall castles of dark stone perched above traveled roads or guarding strategic fords, crenelated houses behind spiked palisades and guarded by stagnant moats. When Meggotta attained her fifth birthday she was given three manors in widely separated parts of the country, Sussex, Leicestershire, Lincolnshire. It has been estimated that the justiciar owned estates in fifteen counties.

The possession of so many tenements or freeholds entailed the employment of great armies of men: stewards and seneschals to handle the accounts, men-at-arms, yeomen of the eweries and of this and that, larderers and pastry cooks and kitchen knaves, grooms and blacksmiths and carpenters, villeins to till the soil, all wearing the iron badge of Burgh around the neck or stamped in color on the sleeve. Conceive of the work of the armorers in covering the backs of the men-at-arms who would ride behind their master to war and in making ailettes for the shoulders and chausses of steel for the thighs and covering kneecaps with water-hardened leather! How the forges must have blazed and roared in making the shields which had changed from kite shape to flatiron, the prick spurs, the two-edged swords!

The administration was honeycombed with men of his own choosing. Ralph Nevil, Bishop of Chichester, owed his rise to the chancellorship to the influence of Hubert and worked hand and glove with him. Ranulf the Breton, treasurer of the royal household, was another appointee of the all-powerful justiciar. Stephen Segrave, who was Hubert's chief colleague in all matters of importance and who later would play Thomas Cromwell to his benefactor's Wolsey, was a man of his exact stamp, able, ambitious, not too scrupulous. It was the same all down through the lower reaches of officialdom, men of ability and an eye to the main chance holding posts to which they had been appointed by Hubert and considering that their prosperity depended on his good will.

The landless youth from Norfolk had come a long way up in the world.

CHAPTER SIX

The Faith of the Century

THERE has been so much discussion of the looting of England by the hierarchy at Rome, the bitter warring of high churchmen whose shoes "shone with boocles of silver" and whose girdles had silver harneys, and of the excessive wealth of the monasteries that an impression may have been created of spiritual bankruptcy. This is so far from the truth that a hasty amendment seems now to be demanded. The hold of the Church on the hearts and imaginations of the people was deep enough and great enough to bring about one crusade after another and to keep the roads of Christendom filled with pilgrims. It inspired them to the building of the great churches, those wonderful testimonials to richness of faith. It led men by the tens of thousands to devote their lives to contemplation in the abbeys which raised their rooftops everywhere, in secluded vale and on stark moor.

Early in the thirteenth century a magnificent manifestation of this faith was provided by the work of two men, working independently and without knowledge of each other, one in Spain and one in Italy. Out of the efforts of St. Dominic and St. Francis of Assisi came the mendicant friars, the humble preachers who went about on foot, staff in hand, tending to the spiritual and bodily needs of the poorest classes, asking no earthly reward, a field hedge their cloister, a begging bowl their sole possession. The first years of the great century saw at its freshest and finest this fervent striving of man to achieve the purposes of God. As time went on the Dominicans and the Franciscans grew into huge orders. With growth came the inevitable companion, organization, and then, finally, permanence and wealth; but nothing could blur the memory of the glorious start. To the first symbol of the age, which must be the church spire reaching higher and ever higher into the sky, could now be added a second, the humble friar in his brown or white robe of coarsest cloth, his feet bare and scarred, the light of service in his eyes.

Dominicans went out to preach, the Franciscans to serve. The founder of the Franciscans had a conception of selflessness directly opposed to monasticism, which took a man out of the world. It was not their own souls with which the brown friars were concerned; it was the souls of the downtrodden, the leper, the thief, and the doxy. They were sworn to poverty so complete that some of them did not own as much as a breviary. "I am your breviary!" cried Francis to one of his followers. They must own no property; they must give no thought to the morrow. It was a perfect conception but one which, because of its perfection, attracted too many converts; and with growth it changed and became in time something quite different.

The Franciscan order became of great importance in England. It flourished there, growing with more rapidity than elsewhere. After the founder himself, the great men of the order came from England—Adam Marsh, Haymo of Faversham, Duns Scotus, William of Ockham. Above all, there was that fascinating and mysterious figure, Roger Bacon, that bright light in the Dark Ages, that great genius who laid a slow train which smoldered for centuries and then exploded finally into scientific discovery and advance.

The first Franciscans landed in England on September 10, 1224, a party of nine men, only four of whom were in holy orders, under the leadership of Friar Angellus of Pisa. In the party were three Englishmen, Friar Richard of Ingeworth, Friar Richard of Devon, and William of Esseby, a novice. They were received with suspicion at Dover, these unpriestly strangers whose pockets were empty. They were locked up for the night and ejected from the gates of the town early the next morning. Taking then the pilgrimage trail to Canterbury, they stayed for two days of rest and prayer before going on to London to begin their work in accordance with the strictest teachings of the founder, the beloved Poverello: to serve and obey, to be humble and charitable, to perform manual labor and to save neither copper coin nor stalk of lentil against the morrow. They had given away all their worldly possessions when they joined the order, and each owned nothing now but a tunic of patchwork stuff, a pair of breeches, and a cord for the waist.

They began at once to tend the sick in the crowded and poor sections of the city. At first they lived in a small house in Cornhill which had been loaned to them. This they cut up into individual cells, filling the walls with dried grass. Some years later a London mercer gave them a house near Newgate, close to the city slaughter ground and thus in the section generally called Stinking Lane. It was a dwelling of bare plank walls, a proper base for the work to which they were dedicated.

Richard of Ingeworth and Richard of Devon went on to Oxford and obtained a house there in the parish of St. Ebbe. It was their good fortune, therefore, to give the order its first great impetus in England. The university city had been ripe for a spiritual awakening. In the hospitia (the houses where groups of students lived under the stern eye of a principilator) which clustered on School Street were men of fine minds and deep fervor who had been restive and unhappy. They had been studying, probing, seeking, unwilling to bury themselves away from the sins of the world in the easy way of monasticism and yet seeing no other outlet for their zeal. They were men of great learning like the gentle and wise Adam de Marisco, or, as he is better known, Adam Marsh. To men like this the coming of the humble Franciscans was a direct answer. Here, at last, was a way to fight the evil and greed of the world. They began to join in large numbers. While the order continued to spread in all directions Oxford remained the core, the spiritual as well as intellectual center. The King, who was sincerely devout, sent beams from Savernake for the chapel which was being built for them in the university city. Robert Grosseteste, one of the great men of the age, as will become apparent soon, was filling a post which one day would be called chancellor and he acted as rector of the Franciscans. Under his watchful eye the Franciscan school achieved an international reputation. Adam Marsh taught there, and his gentle philosophy supplemented perfectly the teachings of the founder. They now had a choir, not, however, like the resplendent edifices rising all over England; a place of bare walls, as plain as a certain manger in Bethlehem. Some years later the King's brother, Richard of Cornwall, would build them a church and bury there his third and beautiful wife, Beatrice of Falkenstein.

The order grew so rapidly throughout England that in thirty years it had 49 houses and 1,242 members. Haymo of Faversham had played a large part in its growth and had been instrumental in developing along practical lines the precepts of the founder. He it was who insisted that it was better to gain a living by work than by begging. St. Francis had insisted that his followers subsist on whatever they were given so that all their time could be used in the care of the poor. Haymo's conception was more practical, a belief that a few hours of labor each day with hoe and mattock, saw and hammer, would suffice to provide the brothers with food and still leave them free in the service of the needy. This was more acceptable to English members. The begging bowl went out of use.

In a still more important respect the order in England grew far away from the original conceptions of the Poverello. Francis had wanted men of small learning, even of an ignorance to match that of the poor people they served. In England the trend was in the other direction. It was men of learning who were attracted to the order, and those who came to the top were the most illustrious scholars of the age. The man chiefly responsible for this was Grosseteste, himself the most vigorous and enlightened of thinkers.

2

Robert Grosseteste was born at Stradbrook in Suffolk about the year 1175. His parents were humble people, and it was due to the aid of friends that he was able to go to Oxford and later to Paris. He became renowned for his learning and, on his return to Oxford, was rapidly promoted to a controlling post at that institution.

If Grosseteste had possessed any inclination to secular activity, he would have become the greatest man of the century. But his nobly proportioned head with its massive brow (from which came his name) was the head of a scholar. His understanding of science was so profound that he started Roger Bacon on the path to his great discoveries. He was a preacher of mighty power and eloquence. Above everything else, he was a man of sublime courage: the unrelenting critic of the King, a thorn in the side of popes, a rod for the backs of venal churchman and indulgent monk.

In the year 1235 he was elected Bishop of Lincoln, which at that time was the largest see in England, comprising Lincoln, Leicester, Buckingham, Bedford, Stow, Huntingdon, Northampton, and Oxford. The clergy had fallen into slack ways, and the new broom wielded with furious energy by the venerable man with the forehead of a dreamer but the zeal of a crusader swept out concubinage (the flaunting of it, at least), drinking, loose ways of living. He put a stop to such profane practices as the holding of games in churchyards, the Feast of Fools (a form of mummery at which many priests had been disposed to wink), the soft indulgences of refectory and chapter house. To accomplish these reforms it was necessary to visit the monasteries in his extensive province and, as a result of what he observed, he lopped off the heads of many abbots and priors. Rumblings of discontent rose on all sides, and even the canons of his own chapter at Lincoln became bitterly antagonistic. They denied his right to make visitations and carried their case to Rome. The feud continued for six years, and even when Pope Innocent IV gave a decision in favor of the bishop the stubborn canons refused to give in with good grace.

Grosseteste was the great opponent of plurality. When the King desired to make John Mansel the prebend of Thane, the bishop came up to London and threatened to excommunicate the acquisitive royal clerk if he did not withdraw at once. Mansel not only resigned his pretensions in a great hurry but persuaded the King to give in as well. Once Grosseteste threatened also to lay the royal chapel at Westminster under an interdict because of some slyness the King was up to, and Henry retreated quickly.

It was the determination of Rome to treat England as a fief and to demand an ever-increasing share of its revenues which roused the fighting bishop to his most courageous stand. He opposed the appointment of Italians to benefices in his territory and made visits to the papal court to protest against such exactions. On one of these visits, when Innocent IV was in temporary exile at Lyons, he preached a sermon denouncing the evils existing within the shadow of the Vatican and roused Innocent to an almost incoherent state of indignation. On returning to England after this bold defiance of the head of the Church, the bishop began an investigation which uncovered the fact that Rome was taking out of England each year the sum of seventy thousand marks, which was three times larger than the income of the King; and with this weapon in his hands he thundered still more boldly against the policy of the Vatican, not concerned that Pope and King were in alliance and equally resentful of his attitude.

Through it all he remained in high standing even with those he attacked most openly and persistently. He was on friendly personal terms with the King, his advice was sought by the Queen on occasions, he carried on a voluminous correspondence with the prominent men of the country, the cardinals protected him from any hostile action as a result of the Pope's resentment.

Shortly before his death in 1253 he received through the papal commissioners an order to appoint to a canonry at Lincoln a nephew of the Pope, Frederick of Lavagna. The demand was couched in the most positive terms and carried the obnoxious clause *Non obstante*. The stouthearted bishop decided to disregard precedent by refusing, and his decision was conveyed in a letter to the papal executor which has been kept and studied down the centuries as a model of reasoning and firmness. He made his chief point that to continue the filling of important posts in the Church with Italians who could not speak the language and would never set foot in the country would make it impossible for the Church to minister properly to the spiritual needs of the people. No faithful subject of the Holy See, he declared, could submit to such mandates, not even if they came from "the most high body of angels." He went on to protest that "as an obedient man, I disobey, I contradict, I rebel!"

Innocent IV literally boiled over when this letter reached his hands. "This raving old man, this deaf and foolish dotard!" he cried. He went on to say that the English bishop had gone too far this time. He would be punished as he deserved. A command would be sent to the King of England for his prompt arrest. The punishment he would receive would make him a horror to the whole world.

One of the cardinals, Giles the Spaniard, had enough independence to advise against any action. Grosseteste, he said, was "a holy man, more religious and of a more correct life than ourselves." Other cardinals joined in with the same opinion. The Pope, refusing to look at them, as was his custom when annoyed, grumblingly gave in. The letter, unanswered, was committed to the files. For once the imperious *Non obstante!* was disregarded and Frederick of Lavagna had to be provided for elsewhere.

Even if Innocent had decided to discipline the outspoken bishop, it would have been of no avail, for while the cardinals discussed his case that stouthearted man was dying at his manor in Buckden. On the night of St. David's Day he breathed his last. He had lived seventy-eight years and in every conscious moment of his long span of existence he had been selfless, resolute, clear-seeing, filled with the kind of faith which knows when to warn and does not hesitate to oppose. The world had lost its soundest teacher, the Church its finest son.

The night he died Faulkes, Bishop of London, heard a sound in the air like the ringing of a great convent bell. He roused himself and said this could mean only one thing, that the noble Robert of Lincoln had died. Some Franciscan monks, passing through the royal forest of Vauberge, heard the same bell tolling.

Innocent IV had a different kind of intimation of the passing of his venerable enemy. He dreamed that Grosseteste came to him and wounded him in the side; and for the rest of the time that he had left of his own life he insisted he could feel the effects of the blow.

3

It is unfortunate that so little is known of Adam Marsh. He was the confidant of king and prince and, in the later years, adviser of the men who led popular opposition to the weak and vacillating Henry. Completely lacking in ambition, he had a clarity of vision and a fineness of judgment which would have elevated him to a prominent place. Roger Bacon, the most critical and outspoken man of the age, referred to him as "perfect in all wisdom." His piety led him to prefer the seclusion of the Franciscan school at Oxford and the wider scholastic arena of the university. He played a large part in the growth of Oxford and at the same time he saw, perhaps to his dismay, his reputation as an intellectual grow throughout Christendom. The stature he attained was so great that in the concluding years of his life a determined effort was made to elect him Bishop of Ely. He did not want a high place in the Church, being certain in his own mind that he was unfitted for administrative duties. It was undoubtedly with a sense of relief that he closed his eyes for all time before his appointment could receive the sanction of Rome.

This gentle scholar and man of God was to do his greatest work, as will be seen later, in the influence he exercised over Simon de Montfort. Adam did not live to see the brave Simon leading the armies of the baronage against the King and calling the first Parliament in which common men were allowed to sit. That privilege was withheld from him, but there can be no doubt that he molded the thinking of the leader of the popular cause.

Duns Scotus came later in the century, and the period of his greatest influence was in the opening years of the fourteenth. This learned man, who is claimed by the Irish but is generally conceded to have been born somewhere in the border country between England and Scotland, earned a place in the front rank of teachers and established a school of thought directly opposed to that of Thomas Aquinas. As Thomas was a Dominican and Duns a Franciscan, the antagonism between the two orders fanned the controversy over the beliefs and philosophies of the two men into a blaze of hatred. The sharpest clash was over the doctrine of the Immaculate Conception, which Duns supported with great earnestness and ingenuity, but the important differences were more general. Thomas Aquinas was a constructive thinker; Duns Scotus took the stand that no actual conception of the omnipotent God was possible to the human mind and that all men could accept was what revelation had supplied. The Thomists called their opponents Dunces, and the word made a place for itself in the language which would have distressed the eminent doctor had he lived to realize it. The controversy reached its peak, however, long after the two principals were moldering in their graves. It was perhaps not surprising that, as time rolled on and men began to delve more and more into the nature and meaning of things, the teachings of Duns Scotus fell into disrepute, culminating in such a low place in scholarly esteem that in 1535 one Richard Layton wrote to Thomas Cromwell, chancellor to Henry VIII, "We have set Dunce in Bocardo and banished him Oxford forever, and is now made a common servant to every man, fast nailed up upon posts in all houses of common easement."

There was not a hint of this eclipse in the days when the

brilliant Duns was teaching at Oxford and writing his mighty effort, *Opus Oxoniense,* or in his later years in Paris. Scholars from all over the known world sat at his feet, delighting in the ingenuity of his dialectics and the forcefulness of his presentation. The influence of his ideas can be traced in the writings of most of his contemporaries. He never took staff in hand and walked the countryside barefoot, but his work, and the reputation he gained therefrom, helped more than any other single factor to maintain the prestige of the Franciscans through this period.

Although the sharpest phases of the great controversy came after his death, Duns must have experienced some enmities in his lifetime. There was a rumor after his death at Cologne, where he had been sent to aid in establishing a university, that he had been made a prisoner and buried alive. The fact that such a wild story could gain circulation and some measure of belief is evidence that the great scholar had enemies who might be expected to go to any lengths.

William of Ockham, an Englishman born in the Surrey village of that name, was a student under Duns Scotus and became leader of the whole Franciscan order. He proved a stormy pilot, preaching the doctrine of Franciscan poverty in the teeth of papal disapproval and being driven into exile. This, however, is a story of the succeeding century.

Roger Bacon, that remarkable man whose enrollment in the ranks of the brown friars was sufficient in itself to lend the order distinction for all time, merits a later chapter to himself, where the magnitude of his work and the impenetrable nature of the mystery which surrounds him may be told.

4

The Crusades had been in a sense a direct development of the idea of pilgrimage which had seized on Christian people as early as the second century and had been growing continuously ever since. Beginning as an intense desire to manifest faith, pilgrimage had been fed by a number of more concrete motives: to bring back relics, to secure indulgences, to obtain absolution of sin. The great pilgrimage was, of course, to the Holy Land. Second in importance, and the one most commonly adopted, was to Rome, where the sites of early Christian martyrdom served as magnets as strong as the Vatican itself. All countries had shrines which drew visitors, the most famous being the tomb of St. Thomas the Martyr at Canterbury and the shrine of St. James at Compostela in Spain.

In the thirteenth century the difficulties and the dangers of a pilgrimage to Palestine had been heightened by the fact that the Holy City was again in the hands of the infidels. To make it possible for courageous souls to perform this supreme act of faith there were, however, the two knightly orders of the Templars and the Hospitalers. The former had been formed to protect pilgrims on the road to Palestine, the latter to provide care for the sick and needy. They had grown into great and wealthy organizations; but, although other considerations now seemed to come first with them, they were still functioning along the routes the pilgrims took and as far as possible in the Holy Land. The Templars were making their headquarters at Acre, where they had built Castle Pilgrim. This mighty fortress stood on a high promontory extending out into the waters of the Mediterranean and contained within its walls woods and pastures and orchards. It was deemed strong enough to stand siege forever. The Hospitalers had institutions in Cyprus, Acre, Rhodes, and Malta and did a great deal to ease the sufferings of the pilgrims and reduce the mortality.

The march to Palestine continued throughout the century, and for a very long time thereafter, on a truly amazing scale. Statistics are not available save the records kept at the ports of Marseilles and Venice. The ships of the two knightly orders took six thousand pilgrims each year from Marseilles and even more from Venice, from which port two annual round trips were conducted. When it is considered that ocean voyaging was confined to small ships which seldom ventured out of sight of land and that lack of the right winds could keep a vessel in port for weeks, that moreover the whole conception of travel was one of adventuring into strange and mythical lands, the magnitude of what was happening can be better comprehended. Ships were built for the pilgrimage trade alone, and the maritime powers found it necessary to frame laws and regulations for the protection of travelers from the rapacity of sea captains and innkeepers. Books were written and sold in great quantities containing information for pilgrims.

The pilgrims came from all countries, earnest-eyed zealots and feverish penitents with sins to expiate, tramping the overland route to Constantinople and from there by way of Heraclea, Edessa, and Antioch to Jerusalem, or taking ship at Marseilles, Venice, or Genoa and landing at the port of Jaffa. There were hospices in the passes of the Alps and in all ports for the help and accommodation of the seekers after grace. Generally the traveling was done in groups in which at least one would have some knowledge of other languages and so be able to act as interpreter.

There was a recognized costume for pilgrims consisting of a gray cowl, scrip and scarf, and a red cross on shoulder, a broad belt to which were attached rosary and water bottle and sometimes a bell (to make the walking easier), the hat broad-brimmed and turned up in front. Over their shoulders they carried a sack and gourd. This costume became familiar everywhere, but it is probable that the pilgrim would have been recognized without it. His eye, fixed on the horizon, had a fanatical light; his feet moved at a sclaffing gait; fingering his beads as he walked, he sang the words of *Jerusalem Mirabilis* or, if he came from the Teutonic countries, the crusading songs of Walther von der Vogelweide.

The cost has been exaggerated, some estimates being as high as one hundred silver marks per person. This was perhaps the figure which a knight would have to meet when he traveled with squires, grooms, and the necessary number of horses. The passage from Venice to Jaffa was one mark, but this was the fare only and did not take into consideration the food which became exorbitantly high. The poor pilgrim depended on begging and a free roof when he was ashore.

Shipmasters competed for the trade of the pilgrims. While waiting in port they set up tables on the bows of their ships and invited the gray-cowled men to come aboard and partake free. They made all manner of promises, particularly in the matter of malvoisie, a wine from Crete which was supposed to be the only cure for seasickness. This was a great inducement because the poor pilgrims dreaded *mal de mer* more than anything, more than the blinding sun, the plague, or the loud screeching of Moslems on the raid.

Once aboard, of course, this soft indulgence ceased. The pilgrim would discover that the efforts of the masters had more than filled the ship. He slept on the lower deck, being allotted six feet of space by two but seldom being able to claim that much. It was customary to sleep with the head to the side of the ship, the feet pointing inward; but it was only a very broad man, or a very pugnacious one, who could insist on his full two feet of space. The stench was unbearable to sensitive nostrils, for the hold directly underneath was filled with sand and bilge water. The sand was seldom changed and, as it was used for sanitary purposes and for the burial of those who died en route (in cases where it was necessary to bring the body back), the atmosphere became extremely foul. To complicate matters further, sheep and cattle were carried on board and stabled on the lower deck with the pilgrims. Most passengers brought hens with them in the hope of having fresh eggs, and they cackled endlessly in the daytime and roosted wherever they could at night.

The food supplied was meager and of wretched quality. After the first few days there was no bread, and the sea biscuit which took its place was hard and far from nutritious. The salt pork and fish turned rancid, especially the fish, which was thrown into the vats without gutting. The wine was thin and sour. There were two meals a day, and the only respect in which early promises were lived up to was that a pan of malvoisie was provided in the morning.

The only moment of the day when the devotional aspect of pilgrimage obliterated the sordid details of mere existence was at the evening services. Everyone attended, the pilgrims bareheaded, the sailors with their hoods thrown back on their shoulders, the ship's confessor beginning with a *Salve Regina.* The sailors would remain and say an exclusive *Ave* for St. Julien, while the seekers after grace sought their allotment of deck space below and prepared for slumber by the light of lanterns suspended from the low beams. There was a continual feud between the pilgrims and the crew over this use of lanterns. They were a constant danger, and many ships were burned at sea as a result of lanterns breaking or the curtains catching fire in the cabins fore and aft where travelers of noble rank slept.

What a picture the ships presented at night! Conjure it up in your mind: the horn lanterns swinging with the movement of the ship, sometimes leaving the whole lower deck in darkness, then steadying to show the long rows of sleeping men, the callused soles of feet turned upward, the passage between the uneasy pilgrims piled high with supplies; the animals penned at each end stamping and struggling, the hens roosting everywhere, sometimes on the breasts and shoulders of the sleepers; a sailor at each end in long pants of sailcloth and with bare feet; a priest pacing anxious-eyed as though aware that the wing of death would brush the shoulders of three quarters of these brave men, and wondering what more could be done about their souls.

The overland journey from the seaport to Jerusalem was comparatively easy after the hardships of the sea voyage. There were droves of wily oriental traders to meet the ships with offers of donkeys (most pilgrims desired to ride into Jerusalem as Christ had done) and with supplies of food and every conceivable kind of relic for sale. The business of fleecing the humble men who had come so far for the good of their souls had been very cleverly organized. Guides were always available for trips throughout Palestine, to see the manger in Bethlehem, to visit the spot along Galilee where the miracle of the loaves and fishes took place; to see, in fact, every place mentioned in the Bible. All that was necessary was for a pilgrim to mention something he wanted to see and there would be a native who knew exactly where to go. The pilgrims traveled in large bodies, knowing that to venture out alone was certain to result in mysterious disappearance. Although under treaty protection and watched over by the Templars and the Hospitalers, they were not only in continual peril but were humiliated at every turn, called "dogs of unbelievers" and pelted with offal by Arab boys as they plodded by or rode their stubborn little donkeys.

In Jerusalem the movements of the pilgrims were carefully supervised. They went about in processions planned and watched over by the Franciscans or the Templars, visiting the Dome of the Rock and the Mount of Olives and even venturing down into the narrow and airless alleys to see the house near the southern wall where the Last Supper was held. Their stay in the Holy City was generally limited to a week because more and more of them kept arriving and the tempers of the oriental masters of the city were too short to allow overcrowding.

The casualties were extremely heavy. In 1066 the Archbishop of Metz led a company of seven thousand pilgrims to Jerusalem. Two thousand only came back. This percentage may be accepted as an indication of the degree of risk the men in gray took. They dropped of exhaustion along the dusty trails and they died like flies in the malodorous holds of wallowing ships. Some died of Eastern fevers and other strange diseases; many were cut off from their companions and sold into slavery. Some could not face the rigors of the return voyage and settled down to finish their lives in crowded ports or olive groves.

The rewards, however, were great. Those who came back from Jerusalem were venerated by everyone and were permitted ever after to wear a cross of palm leaves on their hats; from which custom rose the term "palmer." The penitent pilgrims had to announce that they were seeking the absolution of a sin in either one of two ways. They wore a chain of iron around the waist (which would spring apart or disappear when the sin had been forgiven) or carried a fagot in their hands. In the latter case they were permitted to burn the fagot publicly when they reached Jerusalem as a sign that they were no longer in danger themselves of burning.

It was customary to bring back a "pilgrim sign" as proof that their destination had been reached. This took the form of something which could be worn on the cap after the order of the palm leaf. Returning from Compostela, after praying before the shrine where the bones of St. James, son of Zebedee, were kept, it was customary to wear a cockleshell; from Amiens, a badge of the head of John the Baptist; from the shrine of St. Thomas, the Canterbury bell.

5

England had seen armies on the march—Harold in breathless haste from victory at Stamfordbridge to death at Hastings, William leading his steel-clad Normans eastward to London, the handsomely caparisoned knights of Prince Louis going confidently to the Fair of Lincoln—but never anything to equal the curious phenomenon of mass movement which happened around July 7 and December 29 of each year, the march of the Canterbury pilgrims. The pilgrims walked to the cathedral city by three routes, from Dover, from London, and from Winchester. The latter was the one most commonly used because it led direct from the West and South of England and it drew most of the European visitors who sailed from Norman ports to Southampton. It was called the Pilgrims' Way or sometimes the Old Road.

This road converged on Winchester, the ancient capital, and there the pilgrims were allowed hospitality free for one day and one night in any of the church establishments or at Strangers' Hall. The road from there ran due east, a rutted and stubborn track over hills and down valleys and across unexpected fords. It followed at first the course of an ancient

British road, the antiquity of which has been proven by the ingots of tin occasionally dug up from the sides where they had been hidden by tin merchants when thieves attacked them.

Sometimes an invalid would be carried in a sling between horses. Still less often the creaking of a hammock-wagon would be heard, the only form of traveling vehicle of the time, bearing some great lady or person of advanced years to the scene of the martyrdom. The hammock-wagon consisted of a seat, shaped like the rockers of a hobbyhorse, perched on springless axles, and it was such an uncomfortable way of achieving distance that the need for absolution must have been great in the case of all who adopted it. Pilgrims were expected to walk, and walk they did, in gray cowl and round hat and with staff in hand, the penny which must be left at the shrine carried on a string around the neck or clutched in one hand as an identifying mark. Thus they marched, nobleman and lady of high degree, socman and franklin and buxom dame, rich man, poor man, beggarman, thief. They marched in ever-increasing numbers as the years went on. The Jubilee of the Translation in 1420, just after the great victory at Agincourt which had left men jubilant and filled with a thirst for adventure and, moreover, possessed of French spoils to pay the cost, brought one hundred thousand people to Canterbury, most of them by the Pilgrims' Way. Conceive of the confusion which resulted when the unorganized masses drew near their destination and the weary files converged on the gates of Canterbury.

The hardest bit was over the high escarpment of the Weald. Here the roads were chalk and so the constant pressure of feet cut ever deeper into the spongy surface until the clay banks on each side, topped by high beech and yew, seemed like drifts of snow. The dense forests of the Weald were filled, according to popular report, with wild beasts and wild men. The deep chalk pits, falling off abruptly from the edges of the road, were a constant peril. All in all it was a welcome sight when the plodding pilgrims glimpsed the green of peaceful Kentish lanes.

It was a pleasant amble downhill to Canterbury, past hamlets where every house offered accommodation, at a price, past Chilham Castle and the village of Old Wives Lees and Knockholt Green, past the grave of the giant Julaber (the natives were always ready to show the way to this sight although Julaber was as mythical as Blunderbore), and so on through Westgate into the sacred city. Canterbury, once a sleepy town which the martyrdom of Thomas à Becket had turned into a busy city with twenty-one watch towers and a cluster of churches, was still gray and austere around the curving course of the Stour. There were always pilgrims walking to Canterbury, seeking grace with penny in hand, but for the two great occasions, the anniversaries of the murder of St. Thomas and the Translation, the old city girded itself to meet the invasions and to profit thereby; and did both exceedingly well. The doors of St. Thomas Hospital, the large spittlehouse built by the Martyr himself on stone arches across the Stour, were always wide open for the needy but capable of looking after a mere fraction of the impecunious who arrived. Every householder was under orders to take the travelers in and was always glad to do so at a good, round price. For the nobility there was the priory of Christ Church, where gracious rooms overlooked the avenue of elms, Les Ormeaux, which became corrupted in time to The Omers. For common men with money in their pockets there were many inns, most particularly the Chequers of the Hope, which boasted of its Dormitory of the Hundred Beds. During the teeming anniversary days, when more than twice the population of London camped in little Canterbury, the most earnest efforts of the church authorities could not cope with the situation, and most of the pilgrims slept under hedges or in the shelter of rick-stavels; finding the company of the stars more congenial, perhaps, than the snoring occupants of a hundred beds.

The carcasses of oxen and sheep were roasted whole and offered for sale on all open pieces of land, together with pots in which soup simmered, and those who could afford such a luxury were permitted to dip a spoon. The inns had capons turning on spits and maw-mennies and other stews on the fire, and mountains of loaves which the White and Brown Bakers had labored for days to produce. It was impossible, however, to feed such multitudes, and the wise pilgrims, forewarned, always had a pouch in which they carried food of some kind.

Mass was celebrated in all the churches and in the open on streets black with people as far as the eye could see. It took days for all the visitors to file through the cathedral, past the Martyrdom and the shrine, after dropping their pennies in receptacles at the entrance. The pilgrimage could not have failed to become the most lucrative business in all England.

Finally the pilgrims would visit the open booths in the neighborhood of High Street and Mercery Lane, where the greatest profits were reaped. Here tokens and pilgrim signs were on sale. Every pilgrim bought something. Those who could not afford the costly ampullas, lead bottles containing a drop of the Martyr's blood (which flowed continuously from a well and then turned from water to blood), had to content themselves with the *caput Thomae,* brooches with a carved representation of the mitered head of the saint. This ended the pilgrimage and, equipped with proof that they had completed their journey, the weary walkers turned homeward, rich man, poor man, beggarman, and thief.

The road over the chalk escarpment and through Chantries Wood and up St. Catherine's Hill seemed much longer on the homeward journey and more beset with danger. But what of that? They were full of the wonders they had seen. A life sanctified with new grace stretched ahead.

CHAPTER SEVEN

The Decline and Fall
of Hubert de Burgh

ONE day in January 1227 a special meeting of the Council was called with Henry presiding. He was now fully grown. A truly kingly sword was strapped to his belt, and he looked kingly himself; straight and tall and handsome in a rather more restrained mold than the familiar Plantagenet brand of blazing good looks. His manner was determined and assured.

He announced that he was now of age, having reached his nineteenth year, and that he would assume at once the full powers and responsibilities of kingship.

It was clear enough that Hubert de Burgh had been aware in advance of what Henry planned to do and that he had acquiesced. He retained the royal favor to the full and proceeded to implement a policy which was designed to fill the pitifully bare coffers of the crown. Steps were taken to tighten the forest laws and bring full ownership back to the Crown. Owners of land by royal patent were ordered to bring their proofs to Westminster and to secure confirmation anew. They found that confirmation entailed the payment of a fee, the size of which was arbitrarily decided by the highest powers. It is estimated that as much as one hundred thousand pounds was raised in this way. Landowners, needless to state, were very unhappy about it, particularly the great barons who had not been exempt. They laid the blame on Hubert de Burgh, and the feeling against the overbearing upstart (to mention the least hostile of the things said against him) continued to mount. If he knew how much he was disliked, which is doubtful because he seems to have been somewhat insensitive on that score, he did not alter his course or make any effort to placate the baronage.

The late twenties were taken up largely with trouble in Wales. The southern portion of Wales had been overrun by the Normans, but in the North a valiant prince named Llewelyn ab Iorwerth was holding out. He had married Joanna, an illegitimate daughter of John, but this connection with the English royal family did not prevent the Welsh leader from contesting every foot of mountainous soil and striving to break the circle of Marcher castles which hedged him in.

Llewelyn, who came to be called the Great in history, had begun his fighting career when he was ten years old. Wales had been split with dissension then, but he had drawn the country together under his personal rule. The bards now called him Prince of Aberffraw and Lord of Snowdon and they sang his praises with all the fervor and exaggeration of which they were capable; which was a great deal indeed. "There fell by his hands," sang the minstrels after one battle, "seven times the number of the stars!" He was the Devastator of England, and the sound of his coming was "like the roar of the wave as it rushes to the shore." His helmet of battle was "crested with a fierce wolf."

Llewelyn looked down from the peaks of Snowdon and saw Hubert de Burgh, who had already made Montgomery a threat to Welsh independence, starting to build another great castle in Arwystli. Instead of sending Henry his usual yearly gift of goshawks, sparrow hawks, and falcons, the Welsh prince came down from his high fastnesses with fire and sword. The campaign which followed was a series of humiliations for the English, and in the end they had to promise to raze the new castle to the ground. The justiciar had once jokingly referred to it as Hubert's Folly, and his enemies now pointed out that he had indeed been a prophet.

Henry was burning with martial zeal, but not for the kind of guerrilla fighting which brought him nothing but defeat and loss in Wales. It irritated the young King to be tied down to such small-scale operations. What he wanted was to lead a great army into France and wrest back the imperial possessions his father had lost. It was a constant mortification to Henry that all Englishmen laid the blame for the loss of the French provinces on John Softsword, and he was never going to be happy until he had balanced the scales. It galled him that no one in England wanted war and that Hubert opposed every move he made to draw the sword. It was particularly galling that he found his hands tied at a time when discontent was reaching a high point in France.

In 1228 the Count of Brittany, Peter of Dreux, took up arms against the French King. Rumors flew through England when a deputation arrived in the country at Christmas, made up of Norman and Poitevin knights, headed by the Archbishop of Bordeaux. On the surface it was no more than a visit for the exchange of seasonable civilities, but in the King's green-draped chamber at Westminster conferences were held in great secrecy at which he was promised an active uprising in both North and West if he would lead an army into France.

Henry took fire. He saw an opportunity to regain all the lands which had belonged to his grandfather, Henry II, Normandy and the Angevin provinces and the vast and fair expanse of Aquitaine. He agreed to take an army of invasion into France the following year. Hubert de Burgh was still opposed to the plan, as were most of the King's advisers (except those who had estates to regain in Normandy), but this made no difference. They were commanded to organize the full resources of the kingdom for the blow which was to be struck.

An army was recruited in due course and ships were gathered at Portsmouth to transport the troops and supplies to Brittany, where forces would be joined with Peter of Dreux. The date of sailing had been set, October 13, and Peter of Dreux came over to England to swear fealty to Henry for his duchy. It was discovered then that the army which gathered at Portsmouth was much smaller than had been anticipated. The country still lacked stomach for a resumption of the costly French wars. But meager though the army was, it was found that the vessels gathered to transport it were not numerous enough for the task. It was, in fact, a sorry fiasco. Henry was certain the miscalculation had been deliberate, particularly when it was reported to him that some of the casks which were supposed to contain funds for the campaign were filled instead with stones and sand.

"Old traitor!" cried the King, turning on his justiciar. He

drew his sword and rushed at Hubert, swearing that he would have his blood.

The Earl of Chester, who was one of the few leaders with something to gain if Normandy came back to the English Crown and who therefore favored intervention, was wise enough in spite of that to interfere. He placed himself between the two men and persuaded the King that Hubert was not to blame. Henry cooled down but only after an agreement had been reached, to which all his ministers, including the justiciar, subscribed, that a more powerful thrust would be organized in the spring. Hubert's consent was wrung from him because he now saw the danger of opposing the wishes of the King. He was convinced in his own mind, however, that a thrust at France could be nothing but a costly failure. England lacked everything for a successful war against the more powerful nation across the Channel, men, money, arms, ships, the will to fight.

The invasion took place with great pomp and circumstance. A large army had been gathered and there were adequate supplies. In May 1230 the King set sail with a fleet of 230 vessels, a truly magnificent armada. The treasury had been depleted, but there was no thought of this in the mind of the proud young monarch when he landed at St. Malo and was given a wildly enthusiastic welcome. It was a glittering and magnificent start. All the great nobles of England were with him, their banners making a brave show when elevated over the walls of St. Malo. Henry himself had come ashore like a conqueror, decked out in shining armor and looking very handsome in a mantle of white silk.

But the results fell dismally short of expectations. The rising in support of the English King did not take place except in Brittany, where Peter of Dreux was irrevocably committed to the cause. The appearance of a foreign army on French soil had cooled the resolution of the French nobility. Some of them broke their promises by rushing to arms under the banners of Louis.

Henry rode at the head of his troops through Poitou. He captured one small castle in the Gironde and made a triumphal entry into Bordeaux. The French paid him the sorry compliment of ignoring him. A thrust into French territory would have been met sharply and decisively, but as long as the dilettante soldier was content to parade through the safe reaches of the territory which still remained under English control, Blanche of Castile was content to leave him to his own devices.

Henry became ill with dysentery and decided that he had done as much as could be expected of him. Leaving the eldest son of the Good Knight, who had become marshal in his father's stead, to command the forces which were being left behind, he sailed back to England in October. The most inglorious of campaigns had come to an absurd end.

If Henry's pride smarted from his lack of success, he had a ready excuse to offer himself. He had received no more than half-hearted support. His knights had spent their time drinking and wenching and had shown no sign of honest martial ardor. An evil influence had been at work to account for this pusillanimous attitude. The King knew the answer to that because there were plenty to whisper it in his ear: Hubert de Burgh.

2

Peter des Roches returned to England late in 1231, and the King went to Winchester as his guest at Christmas. The dismissal of Hubert de Burgh was decided on during the visit.

Henry was as variable as a weathercock in his likes and dislikes, and the suave bishop had no difficulty in winning him back. The latter was full of the stimulating talk for which the young King hungered, news of the capitals of the world, what was being said in Paris and Rome and the East, the state of affairs in Poitou and Gascony, which the bishop had visited, the great movements beginning in all the arts. Henry succumbed again to the charm of the polished churchman, and it became very easy to convince him that all the difficulties under which he had been laboring, most particularly his poverty, was the fault of Hubert de Burgh. The wars in Wales, which had cost the Crown so much and had been so ineffective, had been controlled by lukewarm hands. The French campaign had been a failure for the same reason. Get rid of the incubus, urged the bishop. Make a clean sweep of the leeches and fortune hunters brought in by Hubert and now serving him as master. Henry listened eagerly and agreed.

Not sufficient has been said about Peter des Roches to give an adequate picture of this man who was plotting to rule England. He was in every respect remarkable. It was not because he had felt called to a spiritual life that he had taken holy orders, but because he was realistic enough to see that the path to preferment led through churchly portals. A fiercely combative man, he was a soldier rather than a priest, and at various stages of his career he had shown himself not only an able leader of troops but a most capable military engineer; this, in addition to his more useful gifts as a diplomat and administrator. With all his brilliant parts, however, he failed of greatness, and this was due to his lack of integrity. Back of his suavity and charm, he was venal, grasping, devious, and unscrupulous. There was not a shred of generosity or inner grace in him.

History supplies no picture of him and no hint of his outward guise. So much is known of the manner of man he was, however, that the imagination may be allowed some latitude in picturing him, this first-class villain who held the center of the stage through the first scenes of Henry's reign. Having lived the life of a soldier and traveler and not the sedentary existence of a churchman, he would be lean and hard rather than paunchy and soft. Discipline and hardship make the soldier clean of body and habit, so it may be assumed that Peter of Winchester had acquired this addiction to a well-scrubbed austerity of body, a claim which could not be made for some high-ranking figures in the Church, even the saintly Edmund of Abingdon being somewhat careless in his ablutions if not actually averse to water. It is certain that Peter had not fallen into the ways of lavishness in dress, being both too intelligent for such display and too well versed in the ways of the world. Still, his vestments would be of the cleanest and finest of linen; the orphreys he wore (bands of velvet down the front of the priestly cope) would be of modest black and in the best condition; the ring on his thumb (common men called this a thumbstall, after the sheath of the tailors, or even a poucer) would be set with a handsome and costly stone.

The plot against Hubert de Burgh was carefully prepared before any outward moves were made. Peter des Rivaux was appointed treasurer of the royal household and was confirmed in that position for life. He was given custody of the King's personal seal and his authority was quietly broadened. Hubert's own right-hand man, Stephen Segrave, was drawn into the plot and was found quite willing to betray the master who had made him. Segrave began to work secretly for the enemies of the justiciar, bringing to them proofs of maladministration and the diversion of funds. They were all ready to proceed when something happened to put into their hands the kind of weapon which they could use best.

In December 1231 a band of masked men made an attack on a group of foreign churchmen as they emerged from an ecclesiastical council at St. Albans. It was completely unexpected, and there was much shouting and protestation and a hurried scramble back within the church portals. One foreign churchman, an Italian named Censius, failed to reach shelter, however, and was carried off a prisoner. He was not released until he had paid a ransom to his captors.

The reason for the raid was soon made clear. A band of men, mostly from the North and calling themselves the Brotherhood, had been organized to drive the Italian holders of benefices out of the country. They proceeded to ride about at night, masked and disguised, and won the immediate approval and support of people everywhere. The willingness of the populace to applaud was easily understood; the hatred of the interlopers who waxed fat on English livings had been growing more intense all the time and, as an additional reason, the raiders carried letters which indicated they had the sanction of the Crown.

The attacks on foreigners began to take on a nationwide character. It developed later that the original Brotherhood had consisted of no more than eighty members, most of them audacious young men under the leadership of one Robert Tweng, a bachelor knight from Yorkshire who had assumed for the purpose the name William Wither. It was soon apparent that raids were being carried out by men who did not belong to Tweng's band, most of them men of ill will who took advantage of the situation to ride out masked and who cloaked their activities under the pretense of belonging to William Wither and his group. Italians with prebends or other profitable benefices who had been rash enough to take up residence in the country which paid them their fat yearly fees were visited at night and robbed. The grain was taken from their barns and distributed to the poor, or kept for the personal use of the raiders as the case might be. Some Italians went into hiding and some fled overseas. Papal messengers were waylaid and relieved of all papers to prevent bans of excommunication from being brought in and issued. It became certain that all the incidents reported could not have been the work of the original band.

The bishops held a council in February 1232 and excommunicated everyone connected with the depredations. This does not seem to have had any effect. At any rate, the raids went on.

Word reached Rome in June. Gentle Honorius was dead and had been succeeded by Ugolino of the counts of Segni, a relation of Innocent III, under the name of Gregory IX. The new Pontiff was a man of great firmness of character and of very great learning, although he failed to attain in the pontificate the full stature of his illustrious relative. Being embroiled with Frederick II of Germany at the time, and finding that versatile and violent monarch as much as he could handle, Gregory does not seem to have taken the situation in England with any particular seriousness. The note he sent to Henry was, at any rate, surprisingly mild. He rebuked the King for allowing such things to happen and he chided the Church in England. Naturally, of course, he commanded the excommunication of all whose part in the raids had been proven, but adding that they should be sent to Rome for his absolution. The impression is left that Gregory entertained a secret suspicion that the Brotherhood had some right to voice their dissent with conditions in this illegal but forthright way.

By this time the truth was out in England. It had been discovered how small the original Brotherhood had been and the identity of the leader had been revealed. Robert Tweng was excommunicated and then packed off to Rome. The Pope, discovering that the young knight's actions were due to his pique over the giving of a church, to which he held the right of presentation, to an alien without his consent, treated the culprit most kindly. Tweng was not only absolved but was allowed to continue holding the right of presentation.

In England the activities of the Brotherhood had ceased and masked men no longer rode the highways by night. The investigation had been dropped, however, and the whole nation knew the reason. Preliminary inquiries had uncovered the fact that many prominent men both in Church and State had either been involved personally or had given the ring-leaders the sanction of support; so many, in fact, that the crown officers shied away at once and reported the case closed.

Neither the actual participants nor the men of prominent rank who had lent support to the movement paid any form of penalty. Punishment was reserved for the one man mentioned who unquestionably was innocent. It had been known from the start that the documents of royal sanction were forged, and the whisper had gone out that Hubert de Burgh had either supplied these false credentials or had winked at their use. The whisper originated without a doubt in the fertile brain of Peter des Roches, who could not fail to see at once the splendid possibilities in what was happening. It was inconceivable that Hubert de Burgh could have been guilty of such an absurd mistake. He had earned the name of a stern and relentless upholder of the law and, if he had seemed lax in following up its prosecution of the Brotherhood, it undoubtedly was because he also knew the prominence of the men involved. He had everything to lose and nothing to gain through the activities of Tweng and the Brotherhood.

When the investigation was dropped, however, it was given out that the involvement of the justiciar in the plot had been established.

3

On August 8, while the King was at Shrewsbury, the blow fell. Hubert was commanded to surrender all the royal castles in his possession to Stephen Segrave, and the latter was appointed chief justiciar in his place. Henry, who tended to swing fiercely from one extreme to another, was no longer content to dismiss his minister and let matters rest; he was determined to ruin Hubert as well. On August 13 a second order was issued which took away all the personal possessions of the latter. The royal offices at Westminster were swept clean of Burgh men. Stephen Segrave and one Geoffrey of Crowcomb, the steward of the royal household, went to work on the papers which had been seized.

Hubert de Burgh was not surprised. He had been realizing for some time that forces were working to bring about his dismissal from office. He was dismayed, however, at the unexpected ferocity of the attack. At first he did nothing, sitting disconsolate in the Tower. This inertia changed to active consternation when he found that London had turned bitterly and turbulently against him. From the narrow windows of the White Tower he looked down on streets packed with angry, jeering people, on bonfires blazing in open spaces, on torches carried exultantly to celebrate his fall.

Hubert had made the grievous mistake of offending London. Some years before there had been an occasion when a group of apprentices had set up a quintain outside the walls of the city. A quintain was a wooden target at which knights practiced tilting in preparation for the time when they would face live opponents in the lists. The apprentices were trying their skill with homemade lances when some youths of the court happened to see them. Taking umbrage at this open aping of their betters, the scions of gentility returned in a body to teach the sons of common men a lesson. In the melee which followed the young courtiers got the worst of it and were driven off with broken heads and torn clothing. The incident grew into a riot when the court elected to punish the youth of London. It was asserted that one bold citizen named Constantine Fitz-Arnulf incited the townspeople to destruction of property by raising the French battle cry of "Mont joy and St. Denis!" an indication that London sympathies had been with Louis of France and not Henry. Fitz-Arnulf was arrested and brought before Hubert de Burgh.

Hubert had always been a stern administrator of the law, quick to punish, quick to call on the services of the executioner. He ordered that Fitz-Arnulf be hanged without giving him the privilege of trial, and the sentence was carried out immediately. Not content with this, he punished a number of other ringleaders by having their feet cut off.

London had never forgotten. From that time forward the head of the state had encountered in the great city on the Thames a steady and undeviating opposition, an unceasing dislike. Hubert de Burgh was a brave man, but he was unnerved now when he saw below the tossing of angry torches and realized, for the first time fully, that any man who incurred the enmity of London would come to rue it someday. The trained bands of the citadel of wool had forgotten his heroic war record and remembered only the body of Constantine Fitz-Arnulf dangling on a gibbet. They thought no longer of the sea battle off Sandwich but recalled the arbitrary way in which he had punished Londoners for a disturbance forced upon them by the young gentry of the court.

The deposed minister decided that it would be wise to get away from London and he departed stealthily at night. He made his way to Merton Priory, a famous institution behind a high triangular wall where Thomas à Becket and many other great men had gone to school, and settled down to the urgent task of preparing his defense. There was little time for this, a hearing having been set for September 14 and the demand made on him that he be prepared to account for all funds which had passed through his hands during his long term in office.

All England was now in a ferment. The nobility shared the jubilation of the Londoners and clamored for the punishment of the upstart. The common men of the kingdom, whose opinions in this crisis were of no weight, however, were disturbed and unhappy. They had been dazzled and alienated somewhat by the magnificence of the man during his days of power, but this had not obliterated their memories of his heroic stands at Chinon and Dover and the sweep of his sails over the Channel in pursuit of the ships of Eustace the Monk. They were stunned and apprehensive over the dislodgment from the high wall of authority of this first great Humpty Dumpty of humble origin. Did it mean a return to baronial supremacy and the sharp medicine of feudal justice? The common men waited anxiously, certain that Hubert had been their friend, fearful of the consequences of his sudden fall.

Henry was like an excited boy over his success. Directing the moves from Westminster, he drank in the ugly rumors which were circulating about Hubert and perhaps came to believe them himself, even though he had had a hand in the concocting of them. It was not only being said that the justiciar had looted the treasury and that he had mismanaged the military operations. Darker things were now being openly charged. The fallen minister had removed opponents from his path by the hand of the assassin and the cup of the poisoner. He had administered a lethal dose to stout old William Long-Espée after the return of the latter from abroad. He had encompassed the deaths of William the Marshal, son of the Good Knight, and of Archbishop Richard, who had succeeded Stephen Langton at Canterbury. He had seduced the Princess Margaret and then married her in the hope of succeeding to the throne of Scotland.

The campaign of calumny went even farther and spread tales of black magic which he had used to gain his ends. It was said that his hold over the King had been the result of evil charms. He had stolen a precious stone from the royal treasury which had the power to render anyone who wore it into battle safe from all harm and had given it to Llewelyn of Wales. The last tidbit was circulated avidly, although no attempt was made to explain why no one else had known of the existence of this magic stone or why Hubert had given it to his most active opponent instead of keeping it for his own use.

Behind the high walls of Merton, Hubert heard what was being said and knew that the scales had been weighted, that his trial would be no more than a formality. He refused to leave the priory, claiming the right of sanctuary. Henry stormed into action. He hurried off a letter to the Lord Mayor of London, asking that the citizens organize themselves and bring Hubert de Burgh back dead or alive. It was night when this missive was received, but the Lord Mayor responded at once by ringing all the bells of London. The townspeople, roused from slumber, poured out of their houses in instant response and were delighted when the word was circulated of the service the King had asked of them. The night was spent in preparation, and by dawn the march was begun. It was estimated that as many as twenty thousand men had armed themselves, and the roads into Surrey were black with unorganized but eager citizens.

It was fortunate that among the men around the King at this juncture there was one with a cool head. The old Earl of Chester, who had no love for Hubert de Burgh and no desire to shield him from punishment, was apprehensive of the results of this appeal to mob rule. He pointed out to the King that the situation was certain to get out of control. The strength of London, once allowed to assert itself, might be turned later to less agreeable objectives. Henry was brought finally to a realization of the danger. Fortunately, also, the Lord Mayor was a man of great common sense, Henry Fitz-Alwyn, a son of the renowned Roger FitzAlwyn who had been the first to hold the office. The FitzAlwyns were drapers and believed in the motto which the members of that powerful guild carried under the two lions, "Unto God only be honor and glory." The Lord Mayor had enough of conscience to see the danger in the situation and he was quick to issue an order to the trained bands to break up and return home.

Reluctantly the long marching lines halted, turned, and retraced their steps to London. At the head of the line they displayed the chains which had been forged for the limbs of the now thoroughly hated ex-minister.

The excitement died down, but Hubert was not reassured thereby. It was quite clear to him that his opponents, with the young King urging them on, would be satisfied with nothing but his ruin and death. The deposed justiciar, who had laughed when the French prince threatened to hang him from the battlements of Dover, succumbed now to an emotion quite new to him, a feeling of panic. He fled from Merton Priory, intending to join his faithful princess wife at Bury St. Edmunds.

The events which followed in rapid succession were like a mirror held up for one brief moment to the beliefs, the moods, the deep faiths, the contradictions, of the Middle Ages. Hubert progressed no farther than a crossroad settlement in the forests of Surrey where Brentwood now stands and where he sought lodging at a manor owned by one of his nephews, the Bishop of Norwich. He had retired for the night when there was a sudden clamor of horses' hoofs on the road outside and loud voices demanding entrance. Not waiting to dress, the deposed minister escaped from the house and made his way in the dark to the chapel of Boisars, which was nearby, and there his pursuers found him, kneeling before the altar with a cross in his extended hands. Dragged out by command of Geoffrey of Crowcomb, who had charge of the pursuit, he was taken to the crossroad smithy, and the blacksmith, routed out in turn, was ordered to forge fetters for his wrists and ankles. Rubbing the sleep from his eyes, and recognizing the prisoner, the stout smith refused.

"It is my lord Hubert de Burgh," he said. Remembering Dover and Sandwich and forgetting everything else, he threw down his hammer. "I'll never make chains for my lord Hubert de Burgh!"

No manner of threats could make the brave smith change his mind, so Geoffrey of Crowcomb and his men placed the prisoner on horseback, bound his feet under the animal's belly, and took him to London and the Tower. Here he was lodged far down under the spacious apartments where formerly he had dined in state, in the lowest of the remote cells of the White Tower.

The high churchmen of the land had been as anxious as the nobility to get rid of the arrogant climber who had raised himself above them. Violation of sanctuary, however, was an offense they could not condone. The Bishop of London felt called upon to inform the King that, unless the prisoner was taken back to the chapel, he would excommunicate everyone connected with this act of violence, beginning with Henry himself and going all the way down to the groom who held the bridle of Geoffrey of Crowcomb's horse. Reluctantly the King gave in and the deposed minister was restored to the sanctuary from which he had been torn. A large force was placed on guard and a patrol thrown about the little chapel; and then the whole nation waited and watched to see what would happen.

Henry was burning with impatience to have the obnoxious Hubert safely out of the way so that he could start on the long-anticipated gratifications and excitements of personal rule. The men about him were urging him on to arbitrary extremes. The watch about the chapel of Boisars was conducted, nevertheless, with a scrupulous regard for the traditions and ethics of sanctuary. None of the followers of the fugitive was permitted to communicate with him, but his servants carried food to the chapel each day. Hubert, never moving more than a few feet from the altar, answered the proposals which were sent in to him with resolute negatives. Would he agree to go into exile? No. Would he give himself up on the royal promise to spare his life and make his punishment life imprisonment? No.

The Earl of Chester, one of the most determined of his opponents but also the fairest of them, died while the siege was in progress. Hubert, informed of this and realizing, perhaps, that one of his few props had been taken away, read a service for the soul of the departed, crying earnestly, "May the Lord be merciful to him!" Nothing could express more vividly the curious addictions to form, the inhibitions, the deep devotions of the age, than this picture of a fugitive, faced with debasement and perhaps death but scrupulously supplied with food to maintain his solitary vigil (a little reminiscent of the custom of offering wine to a condemned man after his stomach has been cut away in the gory business of drawing and quartering), bowing reverently before the altar in the darkness of the encircled chapel and saying prayers for the soul of one of the stiff-necked men who had brought him to this pass.

Finally it occurred to the tradition-bound group about the King that a little logic might be applied to the solution of this strange situation. Why go on supplying the stubborn man with food? The daily rations were discontinued. Hubert de Burgh held out as long as he could. Then, a pale and weakened version of himself, he came to the door of the chapel and gave himself up.

Another ride to the Tower followed, the legs of the prisoner tied again under the belly of the horse and all London turning out to watch the ignominious finale of Hubert de Burgh's defiance of the law.

Placed on trial early in November, the prisoner refused to plead or submit to the judgment of the court of earls sitting to hear his case. Instead he threw himself on the King's will. This was probably the wisest course for him to pursue, but it carried with it his willingness to surrender all his possessions.

It has been explained earlier that the Knights Templars had established themselves in elaborate quarters on the banks of the river outside the city and that they had become the nation's bankers. They were ideally situated to act in that capacity, being subject to no laws other than their own and having military strength to defend themselves and their stores against any form of aggression. It is likely that, for security, they had located the countinghouse somewhere in the center of the group of buildings which made up the New Temple, approached no doubt through winding passages and many strong doors. The vaults were located as a matter of necessity immediately beneath the countinghouse, for the men of that day were not yet accustomed to banking practices and had the habit of dropping in at odd moments to demand that their particular possessions be produced for visual inspection.

When the officers of the King visited the New Temple with the demand that everything held there for Hubert de Burgh be surrendered, they were told that nothing could be yielded up, even to the King, except with the consent of the depositor. This negative answer, delivered by the white-cloaked knight who presided over the banking operations, was respectful but quite firm, and it was clear that it would be backed by force if necessary. The corridors were filled with knights wearing the red cross of the Templars on the shoulder, silent men who observed the rule of the order, "I have set a watch on my mouth," and whose first duty was vigilance, which they followed even to the extent of sleeping in secure and peaceful London in shirt and breeches and with a lamp burning by the bedside. They were prepared, it was apparent, to fight and die, if need be, rather than permit any violation of the rules of the order.

The messengers of the King carried back the answer, and Hubert was brought out from his dark cell and ordered to agree to the seizure of all his wealth. Realizing the futility of refusal, he made a gesture of despair and did what was demanded of him. The paper was returned to the New Temple, and the silent custodians of the nation's wealth repaired to the vaults below where the treasure of the once great justiciar was kept.

It proved to be a tremendous haul. Hubert de Burgh had been feathering his nest in real earnest. The eyes of the King must have gleamed with excitement when he saw what the chests yielded up—gold, plate, rings sparkling with precious stones, imposingly high standing-cups (there were 158 cups of gold or silver, all elaborately decorated), uncut gems. There was so much, in fact, that the servants of the King advised against taking it all at once. A large part was left in the Temple in boxes with the royal seal.

Feeling ran higher than ever against the prisoner when this proof of his rapacity was uncovered. The new men about the King, covetous of a chance to accumulate wealth for themselves, insisted that his guilt had been proven and that he should be put to death. It soon became apparent, however, that the evidence available would not justify the verdict for which they clamored. It was not difficult to prove venality, but the charges of murder and of dabbling in black magic were found to be based wholly on idle rumor. The verdict finally arrived at, after much searching of all possibilities of suiting the royal will, was mild enough on the surface. He was deprived of all offices and honors save his earldom. The savings turned over by the Templars were confiscated to the Crown, but he was permitted to keep his private landholdings. He was to be held in close captivity in Devizes Castle until such time as he took the vows of the Knights Templars and left England for service in the Crusades.

His captivity was close indeed. He was held in solitary confinement in the main tower of Devizes, shackled to the wall. When he heard that Peter des Roches was demanding the custody of his person, which meant only one thing to the prisoner, an intent to do away with him, he contrived with inside help to make his escape and got as far as Devizes Church, where he sought sanctuary. Now the familiar pattern was reenacted, but with a few differences in method and result. He was dragged from the church and taken to the lowest vault in the castle, where he was chained to the dungeon wall with three pairs of iron rings instead of the usual one. The bishops of Salisbury and London repaired at once to the kingly presence and demanded that the prisoner be re-

stored to sanctuary. Hubert was, accordingly, taken back to
the church and a patrol was established around it. One diver-
gence was made from the previous formula, however; no food
was allowed the harried fugitive sitting on the frithstool beside
the altar.

The ending was different and more to the taste of the
people of England, who were beginning to think the persecu-
tion had been carried far enough. Two of Hubert's friends,
Richard Siward and Gilbert Basset, who had already fallen
out with Peter des Roches and were ready for any act of
defiance, rode to the church, scattered the patrol, and carried
him off with them. They reached the Wye and found a boat to
take them across the river to Chepstow. Hubert de Burgh had
reached a sanctuary at last which could not be violated. He
was in territory where the King's writ did not run.

There he remained for two years.

CHAPTER EIGHT

The Passing of a Great Man

IT had been part of the misfortune of Hubert de Burgh that his companion in the shaping of a sound and moderate national policy had died before the surge of opposition came to flood tide. Stephen Langton, one of the truly great figures of English history, passed away on July 9, 1228.

He was an old man when permitted to return to England in 1218, and the years which followed were hard for him. He stood like a guardian angel with drawn sword before the Charter and allowed no hostile hand to be laid on it. When he saw to what a sorry pass the country had been brought by absenteeism and papal exactions, he returned to Rome in 1220 to lay the facts before Honorius; riding slowly and painfully for nearly three months over rough and rocky roads. The Pope, who was eminently reasonable in all things, lent an attentive ear to the arguments of the great archbishop. The result was that Pandulfo was recalled and a promise made that it would no longer be deemed necessary for a legate to reside permanently in England. As a result the primate returned the following year, in great peace of mind and great discomfort of body.

In 1222 he held a synod at Oseney and dictated the drafting and adoption of a new series of constitutions which were so sound in form and yet so advanced in conception that traces of them are still included in ecclesiastical law.

In 1225 he girded himself to the task of riding all the way to Salisbury, where something very interesting was happening. It becomes necessary at this point to pause and tell of a truly great experiment which was being tried in the design and building of English churches.

2

In 1174 a fire destroyed the Norman choir at Canterbury and the task of rebuilding it was delegated to a great architect named William of Sens, who was brought over from Normandy for the purpose. William of Sens proceeded to make the restoration a reflection of the very best in French construction. In the course of the work, however, he fell from a scaffold and was so badly injured that the completion of the building passed into the hands of a native assistant who is known as William the Englishman. This truly great man, an unsung genius who flashes out of obscurity for this one brief moment, realized that the opportunity had been placed in his hands to cut English architecture free from French leading strings and to create a type of structure which would be forever England. He succeeded in directing into original lines what his predecessor had started, and in doing so began a movement which was reflected immediately in all construction work and came to be called Early English. It was an escape from the massiveness of Norman building into something more delicate and lofty and at the same time an avoidance of the excesses to which the French turned. The pointed arch took the place of the semicircular and led to great developments in high vaulting. The flying buttress came into existence. The sturdy pillar of earlier days changed to more slender and refined piers. The personal contribution of William the Englishman can be found in Canterbury's Trinity Chapel and especially in the unbroken vista stretching eastward from the choir.

The new movement was well under way when the conviction became fixed in the mind of good Bishop Richard le Poor of Salisbury that the old cathedral erected there by St. Osmund on a hill so high that no word of the services could be heard when the wind was blowing was no longer adequate. He felt that the time had come to see what English brains and hands could accomplish, and on the pleasant meadowland which stretched down to the winding Avon he began the erection of a new cathedral which would be from foundation to the topmost pinnacle of the spire, in conception and execution, in every stone carved for pillar or flying buttress, in every length of timber planed and dressed for altar or rail, as English as the penny and the longbow. It was in his mind also that a greater cohesion of style would be possible if the work could be done in one generation and not allowed to drag over centuries.

The start was made in the year 1220, the direction being put in the hands of an architect and builder named Elias de Derham. This selection proved a most fortunate one. Elias de Derham, appointed a canon of Salisbury and given full control, proceeded to put into effect with skill and dispatch the ideas of the bishop. He gathered about him the best masons in England and he set up a system of prompt delivery of the fine gray stone from the Chilmark quarries sixteen miles away and the black Purbeck marble from the south of Dorset. He obtained some of the "strange devices" which William of Sens had used to unload Caen marble from the ships plying the Channel, and these he used to hoist the carved stone into position on the high walls when the usual system of ramps proved too slow. The work progressed so smoothly, in fact, that by 1225, when Stephen Langton came to Salisbury, a portion of the cathedral was already completed. The Lady Chapel was finished and roofed and slated, and enough of the nave was standing to allow the consecration of three altars. In thirty-three more years the work would be completed (save for the tower and spire, which were built the following century), a record for speed which astonished the world of the thirteenth century in which it was wrought.

It is a matter for deepest regret that no pen has set down in detail what the aging archbishop saw when he reached Salisbury. The pleasant meadows around the rising gray walls had been turned into a town of shops and cutting houses where the chisels of the masons turned the Chilmark stone into graceful forms and the finer tools of the stone carvers evolved the magnificent figures which made the west elevation a portrait gallery of amazing variety and imagination. He must have talked to the artists who were doing all this, the men who spent their whole lives at the work to which they were dedicated. They were different from other men, these absorbed workers in wool tunics of red or green or blue, in shoes of leather bound with thongs, in hoods of soft moleskin, whose eyes turned so often to the sky from which their inspiration came, their faces calm and unvexed by the frets of life in town. He would have been interested in the schools which they had set up in the workshops, where a new generation of young men were learning to carry on.

It is quite possible that Stephen Langton encountered the King during his visit. Henry's favorite summer home was at Clarendon, a few miles away, and he had fallen into the habit of wandering over to inspect the proceedings. The King knew many of the workmen by name and he talked to them at great length.

Stephen Langton preached the dedicatory sermon in the Lady Chapel, a small but beautifully symmetrical structure with tall slender columns of the Purbeck marble and an arched ceiling of subdued coloring in which burnished red and the voluptuously rich blue of the Middle Ages predominated. The crowds which came to hear the aging primate would be too large for the limited space of the chapel and must have spread out to fill the covered part of the nave. The text from which he spoke is not recorded. This is unfortunate. The man who had led the struggle for Magna Charta must have sensed a continuation of the same spirit, the same urge to better the lot of mankind, in what was transpiring at Salisbury. It would be stimulating to know what he had to say on that score. He realized, no doubt, that the chisel of the mason would be as potent in the end as any words he might utter that day. Perhaps he had enough vision to foresee the truth: that not one sentence he spoke would be preserved, while the beautiful walls of Salisbury would stand for centuries and create reverence in countless hearts.

3

In his last days the archbishop felt, as William the Marshal had done, the need for a closing period of peace and contemplation. He was more fortunate than the old warrior, moving to the archiepiscopal manor of Slindon, on the edge of the Downs, where he was free at last of the cares of office and the bitterness of political strife. His brother Simon joined him there. Simon had been exiled because he had acted as chancellor to Louis during the brief period when the French prince ruled in London, but he was allowed to return late in 1227. For a few months the brothers, between whom there was a deep bond of affection, were together at Slindon. They sat and looked across the water toward the Isle of Wight and talked, no doubt, of the stirring days through which they had lived.

Stephen Langton was buried in St. Michael's Chapel at Canterbury in an unadorned stone coffin, and there he remained for more than a century in the peace he had so greatly deserved. On the death of Lady Margaret Holland in 1439 an illuminated alabaster tomb of sufficient size to contain the body of the deceased lady and her two warrior husbands of high lineage was placed in the center of St. Michael's. To make room for the newcomers, the simple tomb of the great archbishop had to be moved. Space, apparently, was at a premium; at any rate, it was deemed necessary to make a hole in the wall and place him there. The dust of Stephen Langton has remained in this anomalous position ever since, partly in and partly out of the cathedral. To those who reverence his memory it is disturbing to think that he has been thus exposed to wind and rain and the drifting snow while the great cathedral has been filled with the bones and the elaborate tombs of nonentities. It may be, however, that in the end his will be the advantage: that on the last day he will be the quicker to issue forth and go to meet his Judge.

Stephen Langton was fortunate that death came to him in the early part of the thirteenth century. He had been one of the first to sense the awakening which was sweeping men on to great things, and it was easy to die in the belief that, out of this burgeoning of intelligence and spirit, a shining new world would emerge. It was with this belief, no doubt, that he closed his eyes.

CHAPTER NINE

The Poitevins Rule England

WITH the fall of Hubert de Burgh, Peter des Roches found himself in a position to exercise full control of the realm. With his usual perspicacity, however, he saw that he himself was regarded with suspicion and dislike and that it would be wiser to keep himself in the background. Accordingly he delegated a representative to assume the post of first minister to the King. The representative, of course, was his son, Peter des Rivaux, who has already been mentioned. Peter des Rivaux was not a man of much personality or showy abilities, but he had a tremendous capacity for solid work and on all counts he was the perfect sword arm for the wily bishop to employ. He assumed at once the office of treasurer and from this foothold proceeded to put into effect the ambitious plan of the bishop for the consolidation of all power in the realm. The custody of escheats and wardships (where crown officials could most easily wax prosperous) was given over to him. He was made chief justice of the forests. All the King's houses passed into his active stewardship. A clean sweep was made of the shrievalties, and the appointment of new sheriffs was left in the hands of the fast-climbing Poitevin. He was careful to retain three of the most strategic in his own hands, Sussex, Staffordshire, and Shropshire, although some records say he had twenty-one. Finally he was made castellan of many of the great castles which had been in Hubert de Burgh's hands, Dover and the strong fortresses in the Marcher country.

All this was on the surface and did not depart too much from the activities of Hubert at his peak; underneath, however, a revolution was being effected. Authority was being centralized as it had never been before, and the new first minister was undertaking the active supervision of all administrative branches. The business of government was being overhauled and fitted together into one piece, a change which had merit when compared with the chaos of earlier centuries but which had one supreme weakness, that in the wrong hands it amounted to despotism and tyranny.

There was little doubt in most minds that power had now fallen into the wrong hands. Without understanding fully what was going on, and perhaps not aware of the new concept of organized control, men sensed that things had reached a highly dangerous stage. Mercenary bands were being imported from the Continent as in the dark days of John's reign. It was a disturbing picture: tight-lipped officials sitting in the Westminster offices and managing all affairs of state down to the most minute details of a scutage dispute; foreign soldiers keeping watch on the battlements of Dover and swaggering in the streets of London; a callow king excited and exuberant over this taste of what he believed to be absolute power.

Peter des Roches, always arrogant, had become insufferable in his pride. He looked on the English people with scorn. On one occasion, when the King was urged to listen to those who should be regarded as his natural advisers, the peers of England, the bishop laughed and said in loud and truculent tones, "There are no peers in England!" a remark which flew from one end of the kingdom to the other and caused the barons to hate him more than ever.

In spite of the growing tide of discontent, however, the wily churchman was skillful enough to prevent any immediate consolidation of his opponents. The whispering campaign he maintained kept the barons at odds with each other. The King's brother, Richard of Cornwall, had shown a tendency at first to side with the barons. He was a calculating young man, however, and Peter des Roches managed to win him back by flattery and promises. He accomplished the same results with the powerful earls of Chester and Lincoln. Realizing that the opposition to his party would always center around the sons of the Good Knight, the five young Marshals who constituted the strongest and wealthiest family in England, the bishop sought by every means to build up a counterbalance among the other nobles of substance and power, and for a time succeeded in this.

The barons were realizing for their part, but much too late, that it had been a mistake to combine with the foreigners against Hubert de Burgh. With all his faults Hubert had been an able administrator and he had ruled as an Englishman who understood the people and their ways. Now he was a fugitive across the Wye, and the Poitevins, with the help of a few unscrupulous Englishmen, were ruling the land.

2

Stephen Langton had been succeeded as Archbishop of Canterbury by Richard Grant, sometimes called Richard of Wethersted. The name Grant seems to have been applied because of his commanding height. He had been chancellor of Lincoln and reached the primacy as a compromise choice.

He was one of the bitterest of Hubert de Burgh's opponents, and the outstanding event of his brief two years as archbishop was a visit to Rome, where he proceeded to give a most uncompromising and uncomplimentary report of the King's minister. Gregory seems to have been convinced, Richard having a convincing tongue as well as a forceful personality. The primate was returning in a triumphant mood to England when he died in the Franciscan monastery at Umbria. He was buried there in his finest robes. Robbers opened and rifled his tomb, but they found it impossible to take the costly archiepiscopal ring from his finger and ran away in great fear. When news of his death reached England, the whispering campaign against Hubert de Burgh acquired a new impetus. The archbishop's death, it was declared, had been due to poison administered by agents of the justiciar.

The incident is worth reciting only because of the light it casts on the estimate in which Hubert (this was just before his fall) was held. His power was believed to be so great that he had agents everywhere and no one who offended him or threatened his control was safe from his vengeance, even if hidden away in the most obscure corner of Christendom.

The election of a successor to Richard of Canterbury proved an unusually difficult matter. The Canterbury chapter, which had the right, nominally at least, of choosing the archbishop, decided to assert itself and rushed through the election of one of its number, a man of advanced years who was so unfitted for the post and so much of a nonentity generally that both Pope and King were indignantly opposed to him. When the doddering appointee reached Rome, eager for confirmation, Gregory got rid of him by putting him through an examination before a board of cardinals. The poor brain of the chapter's choice became fuddled in the face of the probing by gimlet-sharp cardinals, and he failed to answer a single question to the full satisfaction of his inquisitors. He was flatly rejected then and sent back to England. Two other candidates were brought forward and both were rejected. It then occurred to the Pope that there was in England a man of great holiness about whom all Christendom had been hearing.

The twelfth century had seen the multiplication of the great monasteries in England, first the Benedictines, who were called the Black Monks, and then the reforming offshoot, the Cistercians or Gray Monks. One of the largest and best endowed was the Benedictine abbey of Abingdon. Within sight of its walls, in a small town wedged into a neck of land where the Ock emptied into the Thames, a couple named Rich had raised a family of five children. The Rich family typifies the deep and unswerving faith of the times: Reinald, the father; Mabel, the devoted and fanatical mother; Edmund, the spiritual eldest son; two other sons and two daughters, all of whom were intended for the Church, despite the fact that they owed their surname to their fine share of land and other possessions. Reinald retired to the monastery of Eynsham to spend the last years of his life in contemplative peace. Mabel wore a hair shirt next to her skin and clamped it tight with iron stays. She rose without fail at midnight and spent the remaining hours of darkness in prayer and supplication. When Edmund was a small boy she gave him presents to induce him to fast. He needed little in the way of inducements: from his earliest boyhood he refused food on Sundays until he had sung the psalter through. His brothers and sisters were almost equally devout.

It is with Edmund that history is concerned. He grew up a handsome lad and fully in accord with his mother's rigid conceptions of devotion. When he and Robert, his next-of-age brother, went to Paris to become students at the university, their mother convinced them it would be ungodly to travel in ease as became scions of a wealthy family. They begged their way and depended on alms while there. They remained in

Paris for several years, eagerly acquiring knowledge, each receiving a haircloth shirt from their mother on graduating. After her death Edmund went to Oxford, where he became the first great teacher in that rapidly growing institution. It is not recorded where he taught, but no doubt he gathered his students about him in one of the thirty-two houses on School Street which were given over to the uses of the university. Certain it is that he had a great influence over the students who flocked in from all parts of England, filled with the first thirst for learning which the race had manifested. He was a clear and convincing speaker and an earnest expounder.

It was during his Oxford days that Edmund acquired his reputation as the saintliest man in England. He always wore a hair shirt as his mother had done, bound in tightly, perhaps, by the iron stays she had bequeathed him. He never used his bed but slept lightly and briefly in a chair or on the floor, rousing himself at midnight to resume his meditations and prayers, not wishing to waste a moment more than was necessary in forgetful sleep. He made a knot of ropecloth and beat himself unmercifully with it. His knees became callused from the long hours he spent on them in prayer.

Edmund had not yet taken priestly orders, but from his own funds he constructed a chapel in Oxford for the better training and care of his pupils. They paid him a mere pittance (a few shillings a year, no more), but he had so little regard for any kind of reward that he would take the small pieces of money, cover them in a flowerpot on his window sill, and say, "Ashes to ashes, dust to dust." It was understood that the needy could help themselves to the coins buried in the earth, and no doubt many of them did.

It was during his term at Oxford that he had a vision of his mother coming to a blackboard covered with geometric problems which he taught as part of the quadrivium (the advanced course at the university) and substituting for them the three circles of the Trinity. This warning from beyond the grave led him to take holy orders. He soon became the most noted orator in the country. People flocked to hear him preach, attracted by his clarity, his simplicity, and his avoidance of disputation. His eloquence reached its stage of highest manifestation in 1227, when at the express command of the Pope he went out through the country and preached the latest Crusade. It is recorded that on several occasions rain fell all about the crowds who listened to him but that never a drop touched tunic or hood of the attentive audiences. He made many converts in these years of his pulpit eminence, particularly old William Long-Espée, the Earl of Salisbury, who had been a rough-and-tough fighting man all his life and had given small thought to eternity. After the earl's death his widow Ela depended on Edmund for spiritual guidance, and it was on his advice that she built and endowed Lacock Abbey.

He was appointed treasurer of Salisbury Cathedral in 1219 and he continued in that office for fifteen years, his reputation for saintliness growing all the time. It was freely recognized, however, that his gentleness made him a poor financial administrator. He gave away his own stipend with such open-handedness that he would have nothing to live on for at least half of each year and would be compelled to eke out an existence with the help of friends.

He had been appointed prebend of Calne, an ancient town snuggling quietly in the midst of Salisbury Plain, and he was here at his prayers one afternoon when a great shouting arose outside his window. A servant, almost breathless with excitement, rushed into the oratory to tell him the news. Remaining on his knees and seeming to take small interest, Edmund heard that a deputation had arrived to notify him of his appointment as Archbishop of Canterbury. What he said on hearing this astonishing word has not been recorded, but it was clear that he was deeply disturbed. He had no desire for such high preferment and he doubted his fitness for the post. He remained in prayer for several hours. In the meantime the members of the deputation, who had expected to be received with joyful acclaim, had become puzzled and resentful. They partook of a frugal meal, the household being, as usual, poorly stocked, while listening to the low murmur of the prayers rising from the humble man in the oratory.

The mood of the disgruntled deputation changed when at nightfall Edmund emerged to greet them. He was now approaching his sixty-fifth year, his frame was frail from a lifetime of privation, his eyes were deeply sunk in his wasted countenance. With the first word he spoke, however, his magic asserted itself. The group of churchmen who made up the delegation listened in astonishment and awe as the ascetic preacher told them he could not accept the honor. He had neither the strength nor the capacity, he said, to undertake the headship of the Church. He was better fitted to the humble work he was doing and he earnestly entreated that this message be taken back to the chapter and acted upon.

Although impressed with the humility of Edmund's attitude, they crowded about him, urging him to reconsider. They told him of the impasse which had been reached at Rome and of the quick agreement as soon as his name had been advanced. Edmund, filled with a premonition of what this translation to greatness would mean, remained unconvinced. He accompanied them to Salisbury, however, and to the cathedral where from a multitude of tents and sheds the walls of the nave were rising in majestic grandeur. Here the bishop and other high officers of the see joined in urging him to consent. It took a long time to beat down his doubts and his conviction of unworthiness. In the end, however, he gave in and a triumphant *Te Deum* was sung over him in the midst of the bare high walls.

And then something came to pass which can only be compared to the change made in Thomas à Becket by his elevation to the archbishopric. The saintly Edmund of Abingdon, realizing the responsibilities of his office and the great need the Church had for uncompromising leadership, became as bold as a lion. He knew that he must fight the Pope who had selected him in order to save England from the spiritual loss resulting from absenteeism and plurality, that he must oppose the King and his bad councilors, that he must purge the Church of evils. The gentle, soft-spoken, scholarly Edmund, better fitted to the soft debates of the cloisters and to rapt prayer on callused knees than to facing selfish and worldly men, drew his sword with firm resolution and took up the good fight.

3

The first organized opposition to the new form of tyranny under the Poitevins came, therefore, from the bishops. To the great surprise of everyone, and the consternation, no doubt, of Henry and his chief officers, it was the gentle and saintly man they had plucked from the obscurity of a country cathedral who led the attack. Without waiting for his consecration as archbishop, Edmund called together his suffragans at Westminster and won their support to a move against the men who ruled the pliable King. They passed a resolution of censure which did not mince words.

"Lord King," it read in part, "we tell you, in the name of God, that the counsel you receive and act upon—that, namely, of Peter, Bishop of Winchester, and of Peter des Rivaux —is not wise or safe but is dangerous as regards the realm of England and dangerous to yourself. These men hate and despise the English nation and, when the English assert their rights, they call them traitors. They estrange you from your people and alienate the affections of the people from their King. . . . We solemnly warn you that we shall put into effect against you the censures of the Church. . . ."

Two months later, having been consecrated in the meantime, the new archbishop led a deputation of the barons and the bishops to confront the King. Edmund was spokesman and he delivered his warning with all the force and eloquence of which he was capable. Henry gave way easily. Lacking resolution even in his ill-doing, he promised an investigation of conditions. Promises meant nothing to Henry, however, and he continued thereafter to act in concert with the men against whom the criticism had been directed, even taking them with him on a tour of the country in the spring. The sharp attack of the archbishop had shaken him, without a doubt, but it would take a touch of steel to bring him to the distasteful fulfillment of his pledge.

CHAPTER TEN

·The ·Five ·Sons of the Good Knight

WILLIAM the Marshal left five sons, the first, named after his father, succeeding to the earldoms of Pembroke and Striguil and the hereditary post of marshal of England. At no other period of English history has one family possessed as much power and wealth as the Marshals at this juncture. In addition to their enormous estates in England and Wales, they owned all the possessions in Ireland which Strongbow had accumulated, nearly all of Leinster, and, by virtue of a rather extraordinary arrangement made with Philip Augustus when he was King of France, they retained their Norman estates at Longueville, Orbec, and elsewhere.

There was an equal number of daughters, Matilda, Isabella, Sibilla, Eva, and Joanna, handsome and high-spirited girls who had married representatives of other powerful families, Bigod, Warenne, Clare, Derby, Braose, Warin, Valence. Isabella, the second of the five daughters, who was the real beauty of the family, was first married to Gilbert de Clare and brought six children into the world. On her husband's death in 1230 she was still so beautiful that the King's brother, Richard of Cornwall, who had been looking for a wife among the princesses of Europe, gave up the quest and elected instead to take the young widow as his bride. They seem to have been quite happy and had four children before Isabella died at a relatively early age. Matilda, the eldest daughter, had married Hugh Bigod, Earl of Norfolk, and it was through this connection that the post of marshal of England came finally into the Howard family. The alliances thus created added immeasurably to the power of the Marshals as a family.

Henry was King of England, but it is certain that he was a poor man compared to the head of the Marshals, who lived in semi-royal state. While the first son lived they never used their power to oppose the King, but it was recognized that potentially they were strong enough to dictate to the Crown if the need should arise.

Before telling of the part the five sons took in the affairs of England, particularly in forcing Henry to abandon the Poitevins, there is a story about them which should be related because of its bearing on what was to follow.

It goes back to a quarrel in Ireland between the Good Knight himself and the Bishop of Ferns over two manors which each of them claimed. Old William had no doubt in his mind at all that the land belonged to him because he had taken it in the civil wars, and he retained possession without paying any heed to the shrill claims of the churchman who resorted to every legal means without success and finally proclaimed a ban of excommunication on him. No one seems to have been concerned over what had happened, least of all the Good Knight himself. When the marshal died, however, King Henry began to worry about the state of his soul. Would the ban issued at Ferns keep him in purgatory until some means could be found to have it lifted? Some years later, the bishop being still alive, the young King summoned him to London. Together they walked into the Round Church, where the tomb of the great warrior stood against the wall.

The bishop was a choleric man, and his sense of wrong flared up as soon as he stood in the presence of his former enemy, even though the body of the marshal had been moldering into dust for years. Without waiting for royal prompting as to what was expected of him, he stepped forward and shook an admonitory finger at the stone coffin.

"Oh, William," he said, speaking as man to man, perhaps in the hope that some response or sign might be elicited from the tomb. "Oh, William, who are here entombed and bound by the bonds of excommunication, if those possessions of which you have wrongly despoiled my church are restored with adequate compensation—by the King, or by your heirs, or by any of your family—then I absolve you."

A moment of silence followed in the small circular space of the church. Then the indignation of years mounted still higher in the mind of the old bishop. He took a step forward, his face mottled with the intensity of his feelings, his outstretched hand trembling.

"But if not," he cried, "I confirm the sentence that, involved in your sin, you shall remain in hell forever!"

Henry was dismayed beyond measure. He was afraid that, in his desire to do something for the grand old man who had secured for him the crown of England, he had made things worse. With the shrill voice of the bishop ringing in his ears, he hurriedly summoned the eldest son of the family, who was now Earl of Pembroke and marshal of England, and told him what had occurred. Would it not be a sensible thing, he hinted, for the family to give up the two manor houses in question?

William the son was not at all disturbed. He declared that, in the first place, the lands had belonged to his father, that they had been fairly won in time of war, and that his father had died legally seized of them. It is not recorded that he used the most important point, which must have been, however, in all their minds, that the papal legate had offered his father remission of all his sins if he would assume the burden of the kingdom after John died, that the old marshal had done so and had driven the French out of England, thereby assuring to Henry the possession of the throne. This promise had come directly from the Pope at Rome and would override any earlier ban pronounced by a bishop.

At any rate, the young marshal declared that he had no intention of being intimidated into relinquishing the land.

When the bishop heard what had been decided he fell into a state of such sustained anger that he hurried to demand an audience of the King. "What I have said, I have said!" he cried. He went on then to prophesy the end of the family. "In one generation the name shall be destroyed. The sons shall be without share in that benediction of the Lord, 'Increase and multiply.' Some will die a lamentable death and their inheritance will be scattered. All this, my lord King, you will see in your lifetime."

Having thus said his last word on the subject, the old bishop returned to Ferns.

2

William, the oldest of the five brothers, remained head of the family for twelve years, fighting in all the wars with such stoutness that he was considered a worthy successor to his great father. He resembled the Good Knight closely, being tall and magnificently put together and having a handsome head of light brown hair. He became Chief Justiciar of Ireland and crushed all opposition there with thoroughness. He also succeeded in giving Llewelyn a drubbing when that ever-aggressive chief of the Cymry elected to invade the Marshal domain in Wales.

King Henry was very fond of William the second and offered his youngest sister, Princess Eleanor, to him in marriage. Mention has already been made of Eleanor, when as an infant of one year she had been at Corfe Castle with the Pearl of Brittany as well as her own brothers and sisters. She was now about seven years old and a very pretty girl, more attractive even than her oldest sister Joanna, who was Queen of Scotland and noted for her beauty and her wonderful disposition. Eleanor would never be noted for her disposition. She was a young lady with a mind of her own and a foot to stamp when things did not suit her. It was already evident that she would grow up into a woman of individuality and character as well as beauty.

The King's offer created immediate opposition. The members of the Council wanted to find a royal husband for the little princess. As a matter of principle also they were against allowing any more commoners to take wives of royal blood. William himself did not think well of the idea; he would have to wait too long for his wife to grow up. Henry persisted, and so in due course the match was arranged. When Eleanor was ten years of age the ceremony was performed, but it was not until five years later, at which time William was in his middle forties, that the marriage was consummated.

It will be recalled that the first William had married the heiress of Pembroke when he was about the same age and she was in her teens. That had been a most successful marriage, and there was every reason to believe that the union of their son with the princess would have turned out equally well. Eleanor was deeply in love with the tall and handsome marshal. She had fulfilled her early promise and was now a very great beauty indeed. During the brief term of married life which fate allowed them she went everywhere with him, riding by his side when he hunted, sitting with him when he transacted business. She would have gone with him to the wars in France (Henry's farcical effort to regain his lost territory occurring at this time) if that had been allowed.

William died with tragic suddenness at the end of one year of complete happiness with his high-spirited bride. He had returned from France and had seen his sister Isabella married to Richard of Cornwall, his great friend, and had seemed in good health. Three days later he was dead. History records nothing of his death except the abruptness of it, and it can only be assumed, therefore, that some inner disorder was the cause. His bride of sixteen was so overcome with grief that she was sure everything worth while in life had come to an end. She took an oath never to wed again (a dramatic manifestation of the intensity of her grief which would cause much trouble later) and contemplated entering a nunnery for the rest of her life.

Henry was stricken with grief also and seemed to think the death of his stanch lieutenant another proof of the punishment exacted from the Plantagenets for the death of Thomas à Becket. At any rate, on hearing of the fatality, he exclaimed, "Alas! Is not the blood of the blessed Thomas the Martyr yet avenged!"

3

Richard, the second of the five sons, had been abroad for eleven years, administering the family estates in Normandy. In the expectation that his life would be spent there, he had married Gervase, a daughter of Alan le Dinant. On William's death he returned to England and took over the estates and offices of the family.

There had been little of his famous father in Richard as a boy. He lacked the towering height and the great strength of the head of the family, being inclined to the sickly side. By sheer determination, however, he had overcome his frailty and had acquired enough soldierly reputation to have been offered the post of marshal of France. He had in full measure the shrewdness and the stanch spirit of the old marshal and in addition a clarity of vision all his own. This young knight, in fact, about whom history has little to say because he died so soon after taking office, was cut to the measure of greatness.

Had he lived he might have saved England many years of bitter strife.

Peter des Roches realized that the Marshal family, with this resolute second son at the head of it, might become too powerful for him to cope with, and characteristically he decided to take the offensive. Richard had no sooner been confirmed in his offices and estates than the power behind the throne attacked. A court official named William de Rodune, who acted as representative of the Marshals, was dismissed and a Poitevin put in his place. Richard, surprised and infuriated, responded in kind, demanding of the King that he get rid of his foreign advisers. The issue was joined.

Peter des Roches struck again immediately, sending royal troops on some flimsy pretext to seize the lands of two supporters of the Marshals, Gilbert Basset and Richard Siward (the two knights who later effected the escape of Hubert de Burgh), and, for added measure, turning the confiscated estates over to his own son, Peter des Rivaux, into whose insatiable maw everything worth while was being gathered. At the same time messengers that Richard had sent to Normandy were held up and searched, on the supposition that they might be carrying treasonable instructions.

The Good Knight had always acted on a deep sense of loyalty to the King he served. He had ridden to Runnymede with John, even though he knew that the cause of the barons was a just one, and it is doubtful if any circumstances could have brought him to the point of drawing sword against his anointed sovereign. His son Richard, seeing things in clearer focus, had no such scruples. He realized that Henry had become the servant of the Winchester party and that, for the good of the realm, action would have to be taken. Although making no secret of his readiness to intervene by force of arms if necessary, he proposed, nevertheless, that strife be averted by a conference, and he was on his way to meet the King's representatives when a messenger stopped him at Woodstock. His sister Isabella, married to Richard of Cornwall and in a position to know what was going on at court, had sent him warning not to attend. The King, who was completely a tool of Peter des Roches, summoned the young marshal to attend another conference to be held some months later. When Richard did not appear he was proclaimed a traitor, his offices were taken from him, and it was announced that his possessions were forfeit.

Without further delay the head of the Marshal family drew the sword and set up his standard against the King. From his castle at Chepstow the young marshal saw the West blaze into rebellion behind him. Llewelyn the Great lost no time in throwing in his lot with the rebels. His wife Joanna had been detected in an infidelity with an English nobleman, and Llewelyn had caught the paramour and hanged him publicly. He had been champing for a chance to avenge himself on the royal family and he emerged from his fastnesses with a strong force, going into action at once. In the fighting which ensued the King's forces had all the worst of it, being routed at Grosmont and Monmouth.

Henry, lacking the steel to fight on in the face of defeat, came to terms at this stage and agreed to get rid of his foreign advisers. Richard of Pembroke was to be received back into favor, and all his possessions and honors were to be restored.

Believing the King's word, Richard hurried over to Ireland, where his enemies, the Lacys, had taken advantage of his involvement at home to seize some of his castles. The Lacys proposed a truce, but when the young earl rode out to the Curragh of Kildare to discuss terms he was set upon by a large force of armed men. In the fighting which ensued he was badly wounded and died later in the castle of Kilkenny, to which he had been carried. It was said that the surgeon who attended him brought about his death by unskilled cauterization of his wounds.

Thus died the man who would inevitably have commanded the forces of liberty and who might perhaps have held Henry to recognition of the responsibilities of his high office. He left no children.

4

Henry did not like the younger Marshals, but the reason was probably not a personal one. They were an obstacle to his enjoyment of the fattest source of revenue in the kingdom. When a man of large possessions died without a male heir his estates passed to the courts of chancery and the King was in a position to benefit hugely. Twice the holders of the enormous Marshal estates had died without issue, and each time there had been a cadet to step up and claim the inheritance. It is not improbable that Henry thought often of the Bishop of Ferns raising his angry forefinger and shrilling his prediction that all the Marshals would die without heirs. Why did they not get along about the business?

After the sensational murder of the able and resolute Earl Richard, the third son, Gilbert, was confirmed as head of the family. It was done in a grumbling spirit, and the lack of cordiality was so evident that the new marshal considered appealing to the Pope. The ill will of the King reached a head on the following Christmas, which the court spent at Winchester. Henry usually went to Winchester because it was a wealthy see and willing to pay all the holiday expenses. The nobility of the land flocked after him and found accommodation in the many monasteries and castles which clustered about the ancient capital and in the taverns of the town.

Earl Gilbert came there with the rest and presented himself on the holiday morning. The whole court was beginning to hum and shine with Christmas hilarity, for Henry loved Christmas, loved to celebrate it as a day of high jollity with, of course, religious undertones.

The Christmas matins had been sung just before dawn with all the proper ceremonial. The bishop himself, wearing his dalmatic, had chanted St. Matthew's Genealogy, after being escorted by the acolytes to the rood loft, where candlesticks were elevated above him. It had been a solemn occasion. The King had spent it on his knees, thrilling to the deep gloom of the edifice, the drone of the bishop's voice, and then the rich chorus of the monkish voices in the *Te Deum* which followed. He loved ritual. It uplifted him, made him feel more than an earthly king, gave him, perhaps, a sense of participation in heavenly rule.

Now the festivities of the day were starting and everything would be done with the refinement and magnificence which the Normans had introduced into such celebrations. The yule log had been dragged in already while gleemen sang the popular carol of the day, *To English Ale and Gascon Wine*, the refrain of which ran:

> *May joys flow from God above,*
> *To all those whom Christmas love.*

The wassail bowls were ready with the fragrant hot spiced ale and the roasted apples. The meats were making on the spits, pig and boar and goose, and the kitchens were still busy preparing such holiday delicacies as dilligrout and karum pie.

There was no hint of seasonal good cheer, however, about the reception which Earl Gilbert was tendered. Court officials demanded his name (the best-known name in the kingdom) and then refused him admission. Gilbert persisted but was told with curt finality that his presence was not desired. He returned to his own quarters and dispatched a note to the King, complaining bitterly of what had happened.

King Henry received the message in the midst of the festivities. Gleemen were singing in the galleries and everyone was sprawling happily in the warmth of the great fires. "Each must drain his cup of wine, and I the first will toss off mine," someone had sung as the King waited for the French mystery play to begin.

Henry had now reached his thirties and had become a little stout and florid. He had been letting a habit grow on him of loose talking. With or without provocation his high-pitched voice would suddenly be raised in comment which was as twisted and baseless as it was ill-natured. On this cheerful Christmas Day, with the flames warming his well-turned thighs stretched out before the fire, he lapsed into a most indiscreet mood when the message reached his hand.

"How is it," he demanded, "that Earl Gilbert turns his heels threateningly upon me?"

Earl Gilbert had turned his heels only when no other course was open to him, but this royal habit of twisting facts was quite familiar to all about the King. Henry had lost his Christmas joviality. He frowned into his cup of wine and continued to talk of the faults of the Marshal family. Finally he turned his attention to the previous incumbent and declared in a bitter voice that Earl Richard had been a "bloody traitor."

When this was reported to Gilbert he left Winchester in a white fury, and there was never any love lost between the two men thereafter. The King persecuted his marshal, finding fault with him and threatening to dispossess him. He made the occasion of Gilbert's death a reason for attacking his memory and assailing the rest of the family.

For Gilbert died, and without issue, after a very few years of directing the fortunes of the Marshals. He had been sickly as a boy and on that account had been intended for the Church. All through his life he seemed to feel the need of proving that he had become strong and hard and a true son of his great father; and it was this which led to his early death.

Although Henry had forbidden tournaments on the ground that he did not want his subjects killing each other in sport, Gilbert attended one at Ware and in a spirit of bravado appeared in the lists on an Italian horse which no other man had dared mount. The charger threw him and, his foot catching in the stirrup, he was dragged for some distance. He died from the injuries.

5

Henry went into a tantrum when the fourth son, Walter, came forward to claim the inheritance on Gilbert's death. He refused to confirm him in the earldom and the hereditary post of marshal, indulging in a tirade which began with the conduct of the Good Knight himself. This was something new. The King had lashed out at all the sons often but had spared hitherto the memory of the man who had put him on the throne.

"Your father William," he charged, "was tainted with treason. He saved Louis from being taken when in England." This was a reference to the moderate terms which the old marshal had given the defeated French prince in order to bring the civil war to a close. There had been some criticism then, and the thought had been festering in the King's mind. Now, for the first time, it had been put into words, a proof of the brevity of the royal memory and Henry's small capacity for gratitude.

"Your brother Richard," went on the King, "was taken prisoner and slain in arms against me." Gilbert, he went on, had been killed in an act of disobedience. He, Walter, the claimant, had been at the tournament when his brother had died and was therefore equally guilty. This was the only fault which could be found in Walter's record, but the King made the most of it, asserting loudly his decision to withhold all honors from him.

It took a year for the royal displeasure to cool, but finally Walter was allowed to succeed. He went to Gascony with the King the following year but had no opportunity to display his mettle. He married Margery, the widow of John de Lacey, Earl of Lincoln, on his return, but the union remained unblessed by children. Three years later he followed his three older brothers into the grave, dying suddenly at Goodrich Castle on March 24, 1245.

There was still one son left, Anselm. One month after

Walter's demise, before anything had been done about his investiture as head of the family, he also died and was buried beside Walter at Tintern. He had been married to Maud, a daughter of the Earl of Hereford. It is perhaps superfluous to state that they had no children.

That five brothers had thus died in a space of fourteen years and that none of them had left any children could easily have been coincidental, but no one in that age believed it anything but the result of the curse pronounced by the Bishop of Ferns. The choleric old man had been in his own grave for years, but he least of all would have doubted that his prophecy had exacted this bitter toll for the two manor houses and the few hides of land around them which William the Marshal had seized. This much was fact: The possessions of the family were broken up among the daughters, or rather among their husbands; the hereditary post of marshal was vested in the husband of the oldest daughter, and from their children descended in time to the family of Howard; the name Marshal no longer existed among the great families of England.

6

It was neither strange nor unusual for men to die at an age which later would constitute the prime of life. Despite remarkable advances in several important aspects which will be noted later, the practice of medicine in the thirteenth century was still shrouded in medieval mumbo-jumbo. What little was known of disease was a heritage from the early Greek and Arabian teachers, and even these sources had become suspect. The works of Aristotle were forbidden at a synod held in Paris in the year 1210, under the same great pope, Innocent III, who had done so much to encourage the building of good hospitals, and it was not until 1231 that Gregory IX passed a decree permitting them to be used again in the universities of Europe. Even after that the biological works of Aristotle were seldom consulted. There had been one great shining light in the prevailing darkness, the medical school at Salerno, and near the close of the twelfth century a German army under Henry VI sacked it, taking away the teachers as prisoners and selling their wives and daughters at auction. Salerno never recovered from this blow, and though other schools rose to prominence at Montpellier in France, and at Naples and Palermo, they seemed unable to attain the stature or to match the fine spirit of Salerno.

Matthew Paris is authority for the statement that in his day there were only five reputable doctors in London and six in Paris. It may be taken for granted that the handful of men thus distinguished had little learning to put them much above the practitioners of quackery.

The thirteenth century was still, therefore, a time when physicians believed that red curtains draped around a couch would cure smallpox (the first glimmer of belief in the value of dyes); that men could cure heart palpitations by carrying a piece of coral in the mouth; that some medicines were useful only if boiled in the skins of fat puppies; that the effect of medical brews was heightened if they could be imbibed from a church bell; that asses' hoofs attached to the shank checked the effects of gout. Midwives, in difficult cases, would fold their arms and allow the mother to die, then remove the infant by the Caesarean method, hoping to find it still alive. Even Roger Bacon, that great and advanced leader, father of the scientific approach to knowledge, is found recommending prescriptions such as this: powdered pearls, rubies, sapphires, and amethysts, emerald dust and finely ground gold, mixed together in a gold pot, then exposed to the air for eight days (but covered when the moon came out!), and then administered in doses after eating. This was a general specific, but clearly a remedy which could be given the very rich only.

There was little capacity shown in the identification of diseases. Those believed to be infectious in the thirteenth century were the plague, certain fevers, smallpox, itch, erysipelas, and leprosy. The treatment in all such cases was isolation, the patient being left to settle the issue with nature. There was a deeply rooted impression, although the better men strove to eradicate it, that all other ailments came from God and that it was sacrilege to interfere.

It is easy to understand, therefore, why there is such a paucity of information about the nature of the disorders from which men died. It would usually be recorded as the ague, a quartan fever, or such. Almost invariably the dark whisper of poisoning would spread and loose accusations would be made at the expense of anyone who stood to benefit by the death. Hubert de Burgh, who undoubtedly had no knowledge whatever of the nature and use of poisons, was widely accused of a dozen deaths by that medium.

It was an age when many children were born and few survived; and that ten of the children born to the first Marshal and his wife lived to maturity is proof that it was sound stock. Bearing that in mind, it is still not strange that all the sons died at a relatively early age. It is much harder to account for their lack of progeny. Some of them married widows who had already brought children into the world, and it may be taken for granted that certain of them at least had illegitimate children.

The Bishop of Ferns had lived to a ripe old age, but not long enough to see the fulfillment of his prophecy.

CHAPTER ELEVEN

The Royal Weathercock

IT is necessary now to cast back to the murder of Richard the Marshal in Ireland in order to trace the final stages of the struggle between the leaders of the English party and the Poitevins who had remained in full control after the fall and disgrace of Hubert de Burgh. When news of the death of Richard reached England the King acted with suspicious haste to fulfill some of the conditions to which he had agreed. He ordered Peter des Rivaux to account for all the funds which had passed through his hands in the multiple offices he held. This, the familiar first step to charges of malfeasance and even of treason, so intimidated the bishop's jackal that he made an unsuccessful attempt to escape to France and then fled to Winchester for sanctuary. To rid himself of the still more detested Peter des Roches, the King sent him to France as a peace mediator.

The rapidity of Henry's surrender, however, did not have the effect of suppressing the ugly whispers which were circulating in England. It was being said that letters had been sent to Ireland with the King's signature in which the opponents of Richard were urged to encompass the marshal's death and promising a share of his lands as a reward. The friends of the murdered man followed up the story and got their hands finally on the incriminating documents.

Henry was confronted with the evidence at the next session of the Council. It was in the royal castle of Gloucester, to which the court had come in its continuous processional from one town to another (when the supplies of food in one place had been exhausted in feeding the multitudes who traveled in the wake of the King they would move on), and there was a touch of justice in this. It had been in Gloucester Castle that a handful of loyal knights had decided to fight for the young King and had selected William the Marshal as their leader. Now they were to accuse Henry of the murder of the son of the man who had saved him his crown.

The documents were placed in the King's hands, and he read them in a state of unconcealed confusion and fear. Bursting into loud tears, he declared that his signature had been signed to the letters without his knowledge. Pressed for an explanation, he groveled and acknowledged that he had fallen into the habit of allowing his chief officers to sign his name and affix the royal seal to documents he did not read.

The atmosphere in the great hall of the castle had become distinctly hostile. Hands went to sword hilts and murmurs of indignation rose from all parts of the hall. It was an indication of the poor esteem in which Henry was held by his subjects that they dared express their resentment so openly.

The gentle old archbishop had no hesitation at all in declaring his feelings. Fixing his eyes on the face of the very much discomfited ruler, he said, "Examine your conscience, Sir King, for not only those who caused this letter to be sent but all who were aware of the treachery designed are as guilty of the Earl Richard's murder as if with their own hands they had done the deed."

He had put into words the thought in every mind. Henry had acquiesced, at least, in the murder of the son of his great benefactor.

The consequence of this revelation was that Henry, to justify himself, turned on Peter des Roches and his party with a fury equal to that with which he had unseated Hubert de Burgh. He summoned Peter des Rivaux from Winchester (and would, no doubt, have dragged him by force if right of sanctuary had been claimed) and reproached him bitterly for the things he had done and the evil counsel he had given. Peter was sent to the Tower, and it was expected that he would be treated with the rigor which Hubert had experienced. Through the magnanimity of the archbishop, however, he was released soon afterward and allowed to retire into obscurity at Winchester. The less important officers were removed in a great hurry, and for a time it looked as though a clean sweep would be made.

Even Hubert de Burgh was forgiven in the orgy of appeasement which followed. He was pardoned and his personal landholdings were restored to him. The once powerful minister, rheumatic from his confinement in prison and so chastened in spirit that nothing could stir up again the ashes of his once inordinate ambition, settled down to a quiet life with his devoted wife and daughter.

2

Henry was so lacking in steadiness of purpose and so inconstant in his personal likes and dislikes that the principals in this seesaw for power continued to rise and fall in favor during the period which followed. Within two years the King had summoned Peter des Rivaux back from retirement and given him the keepership of the wardrobe. Continuing in this humble role for many years with great patience, the minor Poitevin villain was suddenly elevated to the custody of the royal seal. This might have led to his complete reinstatement, but strong hands intervened and Henry weakened under pressure as usual. He contented himself with making Peter a baron and fitting him into the post of treasurer of the royal household; and there the subservient Poitevin remained until his death, never allowing himself to raise his head again for a glimpse of the heights.

Peter des Roches went abroad and fought for the Pope in a campaign against the Romans. He returned to England two years later in broken health and loaded with debts. He seemed disposed to settle down at last to the administration of his bishopric and the straightening out of his finances. The King, who had been loudly blaming him for all the ills of the state, veered around once more and seemed on the point of falling for a third time under the influence of that most ingratiating of men. The bishop was restored to a post on the Council. The aging man did not stir himself, however, to take advantage of this. His years had caught up with him and he was tired.

The last glimpe history affords of him was in a Council debate over a crisis which had arisen in the East. Genghis Khan, that great scourge from the steppes of Tartary, had brought his conquering armies to the edge of the desert country where the Saracens held sway. The desperate Saracens cried out for help to Christianity on the ground that the Holy Land must be protected from the onrushing Mongol horde. A Saracen emissary came to England, and there was a faction in the Council which favored the idea of extending help, seeing in this situation a new form of crusade. Peter des Roches, still the complete realist, was against interference, which he predicted would be costly and futile. He said in an exasperated rumble, "Let the dogs devour one another and perish." His point of view prevailed.

He died in 1238 and was buried in Winchester Cathedral.

Hubert de Burgh tumbled into disgrace a second time when Meggotta, his daughter, contracted a secret marriage with the young Earl of Gloucester, Richard of Clare. The earl was a minor and had been a ward of Hubert's. The King, who wanted to bestow the young man, the most eligible bachelor in England, on one of his own choosing, promptly charged Hubert with having arranged the match. Hubert entered a weary denial, declaring that the young couple, who were very much in love, had been married clandestinely and without the knowledge of either of Meggotta's parents. There was plenty of evidence to support this, but Henry, who needed money as usual and hankered for what little his ex-minister had left, contended that the marriage was a breach of the conditions under which the broken man's estates had been restored to him. While a suit to deprive Hubert of his land dragged along, the young couple were separated and poor Meggotta died of a broken heart. The sixteen-year-old bridegroom, who seems to have been deeply attached to his young wife, was forced into a second marriage before Meggotta had been three months in her grave. Hubert mourned his daughter deeply and did not seem to mind what might happen to him after that.

It might have been expected that the twilight of the Great Upstart, inasmuch as he had tumbled into such complete obscurity, would be a peaceful one. When it seemed certain, however, that his end was close at hand, the old charges were brought against him. The whole tissue of absurdities which had been woven into the original indictment when he was at the height of his power and it had seemed he could be dragged down only by sheer weight of accusation was revived. The charge of poisoning and assassinating his opponents, of using witchcraft to gain his ends, all the long discarded and forgotten rumors, were dragged out from the files at Westminster and dusted off and brought against him. Even the story of the casks which were supposed to hold money for the King's first campaign in Poitou and which were found to contain nothing but sand and stones was refurbished and brought against the broken old man. It was generally believed that the purpose in thus attacking him was the likelihood that he would pass away before the case could be settled and thus justify the Crown in seizing all his possessions.

Hubert de Burgh, crippled with disease, his memory almost gone, had only one answer to give the King when brought into court. "Had I wished to betray you," he declared, "you would never have obtained the kingdom." He was thinking, no doubt, of how he had thrown the plan of French conquest into confusion by refusing to give up the castle of Dover and stubbornly straddling their lines of communication.

The old man had enough shrewdness left, however, to entrust his defense to an able advocate, a clerk named Laurence who had been his steward and was now at St. Albans. Hubert had reason to know that the mind under the tonsured poll of this obscure clerk was sharp and clear and that he had an almost uncanny knowledge and command of the law. Laurence justified the faith reposed in him and by a splendid display of logic and legal reasoning tore the case against his former master into shreds and tatters. When he was through, the innocence of the accused had been established to the satisfaction of everyone, except perhaps Henry himself. The King had to be placated, however, and so the court closed the case by confiscating to the Crown four of the castles still belonging to the defendant. That the decision had been no more than an attempt to save the King's face was made evident later when the castles were restored.

It is strange that, after the triumph he had scored, the clerk Laurence disappeared completely from sight and, seemingly, spent the rest of his days in obscure activities in the monastery at St. Albans. If Henry had possessed any gift at all for governing he would have drafted the brilliant clerk into his services, as Henry VIII would do later when he discerned the possibilities in a man named Thomas Cromwell concealed in the shadow cast by the great Wolsey. But Henry had already found a man who pleased him, one John Mansel, and for many years thereafter would look to and act upon the advice which this favorite adviser would whisper in his ear. It will be seen later that Mansel was a man of considerable ability but that he possessed the same stubbornness of mind and the same blindness to public opinion from which the King himself suffered.

Hubert de Burgh died on May 12, 1243, and was buried at Blackfriars in London. His wife married again, her second husband being Gilbert, third of the Marshal sons. His own son, John, by one of his first marriages, was not allowed to succeed him, and the earldom of Kent lapsed for the time being. Thus ended the dream of establishing a great family which the once hated upstart had always kept in his mind.

even held that friend-ship a wanted considerable ability in
its possessor that were sudden as it would jumped had the state.
blunders at again, Vienna from which out. Why him.

CHAPTER TWELVE

England's Most Unpopular Queen

HENRY was twenty-nine when he married. This was not due to
any disinclination on his part for the state of matrimony. On
the contrary, he had been anxious to have a wife and had
striven hard to find one.

As a boy he seems to have admired the Scottish princesses
who were held at Corfe Castle as hostages, and his first
thought when old enough to take a mate was that he would
wed Marion, the younger of the two, even though she was a
number of years older than he was. As Princess Margaret, the
elder, had married Hubert de Burgh, the Council refused to
sanction this plan, holding that it would be derogatory to the
royal dignity to have one of his own subjects as a brother-in-
law.

Disappointed in his first choice, Henry sought a bride in
three different European courts in turn. It was considered
wise to cement relations with Germany, and the Bishop of
Carlisle was sent to Vienna to propose a marriage between
Henry and a daughter of Leopold of Austria. A son of Henry
of Germany carried off the lady, however, under the very
nose of the discomfited bishop. Matches were then proposed
for him with a daughter of the Count of Brittany and a Bo-
hemian princess, without results in either case. Henry began

to believe that some malign influence was at work or that a more positive force was working against him. When the charges were revived against Hubert de Burgh for the last time, the King added a new item to the familiar farrago of claims, that it had been Hubert himself who had secretly connived to prevent him from marrying. He even went to the extent of asserting that in one instance Hubert had conveyed to the prospective bride the information that he, Henry, was "squint-eyed, silly, and impotent, that he had a sort of leprosy, and that he was incapable of enjoying the embraces of any noble lady." This absurdity may have been based on something which had happened, an intrigue, perhaps, to prevent one of the matches from being carried through, but it is indicative of the character of the King that he would publicly refer to the matter in this highly undignified form.

It is hard to understand why the many casts made in the matrimonial waters failed to get more than nibbles. Henry was handsome enough, he was of agreeable address, his tastes were cultivated, and he had a reputation as a man of learning. The English throne was ranked in the top bracket of international importance, and the country was attaining once more to some degree of opulence. No reasonable explanation has been found; but the fact remains that Henry, anxious as he was to find a wife to share his throne and sit by his side, finally gave up in despair and for the space of four years made no further efforts in that direction.

Perhaps by way of compensation the young King turned his attention to aesthetic concerns. He became much interested in poetry and minstrelsy and still more deeply in the great developments which were being seen in architecture. The title of Henry the Builder, which was given him later, was well deserved, for he became an intelligent leader in that field and left monuments behind him to attest his vision and taste. He was sincerely devout (so much so that his fellow monarch, Louis of France, had to order churches closed in advance in order to get him by them), which put him in complete sympathy with the movement to create a purely English type of cathedral and church. The preaching of St. Bernard had roused in the Christian world a deep reverence for the Virgin Mary, and from this had grown the tendency to have Lady Chapels in all important edifices. Henry's first venture in building, therefore, was the beautiful Lady Chapel at Westminster. He was dreaming and planning at this early stage also of rebuilding the abbey; a work which he accomplished later.

It was in his mind that he would make Windsor Castle into a great King's residence, worthy of the nation and the throne. The First King's House, which Henry I had erected for his lovely Saxon bride, had been badly damaged in the sieges to which it had been subjected, although the Hall and St. Edward's Chapel still remained, in a somewhat battered condition. Henry's mind was already filled with a picture of what he would do: a three-sided wall to enclose the level ground west of the Norman keep which could allow for three baileys (courtyards devoted mostly to domestic activities), and in the lower of these there would rise a much handsomer house than the one the first Henry had provided. He was planning royal chambers for himself and the Queen (when he succeeded in persuading someone to be his Queen), a large and magnificent chapel to be dedicated to Edward the Confessor, his favorite saint, and a Great Hall which would be the finest thing of its kind in the kingdom. All this he brought to pass in due course.

When Henry reached the age of twenty and nine it was agreed in the Council that the problem of finding a wife for him must be solved at once. The choice fell on Joanna, daughter of the Earl of Ponthieu in Normandy. It is probable that the girl's mother had been angling for Henry because it is on record that she sent him a present of a costly table of Sardinian ivory, whatever that is. A favorable response was received from the parents, and Joanna herself was said to regard the prospect with approval. The marriage contract was drawn up and ambassadors were posted off to Rome to obtain the consent of the Pope.

The ambassadors had reached a point within a few days' journey of their destination when word was received from Henry that they were to return at once to England. He had changed his mind. A princess had been found who more closely touched his fancy and who, moreover, was ready to become Queen of England. It was unfortunate that the ambassadorial party did not ride a little faster or spend fewer nights in Paris so that they might have completed their mission before being recalled. Joanna of Ponthieu might or might not have made Henry a good wife, but the lady on whom his choice had fallen was to prove the most unpopular queen England ever had.

2

Provence at this stage of history was smaller than it had once been and much smaller than it would become later. It was, in fact, a mere slice of land east of the Rhone, too unimportant for egress to the Mediterranean, too restricted to contain any city of size save the old Roman town of Orange. It was still, nevertheless, the symbol of the South, the cradle or literature and minstrelsy, the core of European culture and sophistication. Here the troubadours loved and sang, finding the Courts of Honor a fitting background for the cultivation of the muse, their inspiration waxing in the lovely gardens and the plantations where the white mulberry grew.

The Count of Provence was Raimund Berenger V, who made his headquarters in quite restricted splendor at Courthezon, close to Orange. The classic age of the troubadour was passing and the high-flown sentiments which had made the *sirventes* a tedious form of enjoyment were giving way to a more robust form of *ballada* after the fashion of Barnard of Ventadour, who sang:

> *"You say the moon is all aglow,*
> *The nightingale is singing.*
> *I'd rather watch the red wine flow,*
> *And hear the goblets ringing."*

Raimund was determined to maintain the old standards and had gathered about him so many singers who still waxed ecstatic over a lady's eyebrow and filled their verses with classic allusions that the impression was created of a court of great brilliance. He was a composer himself, and his wife Beatrice, who had been a princess of Savoy, was as famed for her compositions as her beauty. It was in this rarefied atmosphere that the couple raised a family of four daughters who were to become more famous for their loveliness than the court was for its culture. The charm of the Provençal princesses was on an ascending scale, each one to arrive being more highly praised than those before her. Marguerite, the first daughter, was fresh and pretty with dark hair and fine eyes. Eleanor, the second, was thought at first to have transcended all comparison and was known as La Belle, although Sanchia, who followed her, was of such subtle charm and fascination that she was described as "of incomparable beauty." It remained, however, for Beatrice, the fourth daughter, to set men's hearts thumping and the fingers of troubadours to fevered twanging of lyres. Two of the balladists at the Provençal court were temporarily deprived of reason for love of the entrancing Beatrice.

The father of these four fair charmers was so poor that his household, which is described as "noisy with youth," traveled about from one château to another in order to take advantage of all the food which was grown, sometimes staying in one place no more than a single night. Money was so scarce that clothes were handed down, from mother to daughter, from one child to another. The officers of the household had patches on their elbows; the minstrels sometimes did not get the suppers for which they sang. But the atmosphere was always gay, the intoxication of Provençal gardens made up for the lack of the vinous kind, and when supplies were exhausted the court trumpeter, Mort-du-Sommeil (Death of Sleep), would sound his horn and a laughing cavalcade would ride on to the next château, confident that ahead of them the harvests had been good and that there would be fat capons and plenty of stubble geese for the table.

Count Raimund was so poor, in fact, that he never possessed enough money to make up a suitable dowry for any of his beautiful daughters. He had an asset of much greater value than gold, however, an officer named Romeo of Villeneuve, who possessed such a shrewd head on his threadbare shoulders that he could devise ways and means of snaring kings for the lovely brood without paying out as much as a single coin. This Romeo had already managed to marry Marguerite to King Louis of France. It would have been a most successful match if the mother of Louis, Blanche of Castile, had not become so accustomed to running the kingdom and keeping the royal household under her thumb that she could not share her son with another woman. Blanche made so much trouble for the young couple that they were only happy in their castle at Pontoise, where the King's chambers were directly above those of the young Queen and there was a discreet winding stair connecting them. The two married lovers used to meet on the stair in great secrecy, after setting watchers to give them warning if the formidable tread of the Queen Mother were heard on either floor.

About the time that Henry's proposal of marriage was sent to Joanna of Ponthieu, the nimble mind of the machiavellian Romeo was considering means of attracting his attention to

Eleanor La Belle, who was now fourteen and ready for marriage. The scheme he evolved was roundabout but sufficiently ingenious to accomplish its purpose. Eleanor had begun already to dabble in versification and had completed a long and romantic poem about one Blandin of Cornwall who had fallen in love with Princess Briende and underwent all manner of adventures and tests for her sake. Romeo saw to it that a copy was sent to Richard of Cornwall (who might be expected to see a compliment in it to himself), written in Eleanor's own fair hand and with a note from her as well. Richard, who was passing through the South of France on his way back from the Crusades, was as charmed and flattered by this attention as the wily major-domo had conceived he would be. If he had not been married happily to Isabella of Pembroke, he might have sought the hand of the royal poetess himself, having heard glowing reports of her beauty and refinement. He did the next best thing; he sent the poem (it is still in existence and a perfect sample of adolescent fervor) to Henry and hinted that here, perhaps, was the very best consort for him. Henry was as much dazzled by the genius of the fair Eleanor as his brother had been, and his imagination became inflamed with the reports he heard of the court of Provence and the charms of Eleanor La Belle. He decided to jilt the Ponthieu heiress and propose himself instead as a husband for the second of the daughters of Provence. Fortunately his Council agreed that there would be an advantage in having Louis of France as a brother-in-law, and negotiations were started at once. Procurators were hurried off to Provence to act for the King, the bishops of Ely and Lincoln and the abbot of Hurlé.

Henry proposed to give his bride the reversion of his mother's dower, but Raimund Berenger objected to this on the score that his daughter would have to wait for the Queen Mother's death before having any adequate provision. Henry had become so enraptured by this time over the prospect of getting the belle of Provence as his bride that word of the count's objections threw him into a panic, as no doubt the shrewd Romeo (whose hand is seen at every stage of the negotiations) had intended it should. He decided at once to lower his own demands in the matter of the bride's dowry, having set his figure at twenty thousand marks. Without a moment's delay he wrote to his representatives and instructed them to reduce their demands, even specifying the steps by

which they were to come down: first to fifteen thousand
marks, then to ten thousand, to seven thousand, to five thousand, to three thousand. They were not told that if the count
demurred at the lowest figure (he was certain to do that, not
having anything like that amount in his bare cupboard of a
treasury) they were to accept the lady empty-handed, but
such was Henry's intent. After sending off his bargaining
instructions the King fell into a still greater panic, thinking
that he had perhaps compromised his chances, that in Provence they would scorn him as a pinchpenny and niggler. He
then sat down in a very great hurry and wrote to his procurators that "they were to conclude the marriage forthwith."
They were to do so with money or without, so long as they
procured Eleanor for him and conducted her safely to England. When the question of the bride's dowry was thus dismissed, Count Raimund promptly agreed to accept the reversion of the Queen Mother's dower rights for his daughter and
the marriage contracts were signed, the major-domo rubbing
his hands with satisfaction, no doubt, as he watched the
proceedings.

3

The boy who had been crowned with a circlet of plain gold
belonging to his mother and in makeshift clothes, and had
then sat himself down to a chine of beef with a few noblemen instead of the usual elaborate coronation banquet, decided that his wedding would make up for all this, that it
would be the most dazzling ceremony in the memory of man.
He spent the time before his bride's arrival in feverish activities. The royal tailors made wedding clothes for him of gold-
threaded baudekin and a whole wardrobe for Eleanor on the
same scale. It was his intention to have her crowned immediately after the marriage, and a splendid diadem was designed,
studded with precious stones and costing fifteen hundred
pounds, an enormous sum in those days. Chaplets of gold
filigree, rings of beautiful design, and jewel-encrusted girdles
were among the many articles he ordered for her.

Fearing that she would find the royal quarters at Westminster dingy after the glories (*sic!*) of Provence, he decided to
have the palace redecorated. The Queen's chamber was
provided with handsome new furnishings, and the walls were
covered with historical paintings. He gave instructions for the
Great Chamber to be painted a good green color and that a

French inscription was to be lettered in the great gable. He had no money for all this—in fact, he was in debt for the dowry of his sister Isabella who had married the Emperor of Germany—but this did not concern him. He went on spending, freely and lavishly, with both hands.

He was not the only one who was busy in England. All the nobility were getting ready for the event, and the citizens of London were going to unheard-of lengths by way of preparation. They were cleaning up the streets and setting up cressets of oil at corners to provide illumination. They were planning pageants and spectacles on a most elaborate scale. Moreover, they were going to have a conspicuous part in the ceremony of crowning the young Queen, figuring, perhaps, that they were entitled to that much after the way Henry had been gouging them by forced loans over the years and suspecting, furthermore, that the cost of the wedding would fall on their shoulders finally. They were placing orders for riding equipment in such a rush that the saddlers around St. Vedast's were busier than ever before, and horse clawers were at a premium.

The bridal train, with an impressive retinue of relatives, knights, ladies-in-waiting, troubadours, and jugglers, traveled slowly. From Navarre they rode down through the vineyard country of Gascony and on to the fair district of the Loire, where Queen Marguerite met her sister, accompanied by a great train of knights and servants, the knights with red noses and blankets under their armor and gloves instead of gauntlets because the weather was freezingly cold. Marguerite was delighted to see her sister but was perhaps just a shade condescending. Was not Louis considered a much more powerful and important king than Henry?

The party landed at Dover on January 4, 1236, after a pleasant enough crossing. Eleanor was in the best of health and spirits when Henry met her, and they seemed to like each other at once. There could be no doubt of Henry's feelings, certainly. He paid her extravagant compliments and handed out gold and presents to her attendants as though he were another King Midas. They went at once to Canterbury, where the archbishop married them; and when Henry saw his bride in a gown of material which shimmered like the hot sunlight of Provence, tight-fitting to the waist and then flaring out in generous pleats to her feet, the sleeves long and lined with ermine, he became her captive and never did recover his freedom thereafter.

The bridal party then rode to London for the Queen's crowning, and here a procession of citizens greeted them, three hundred and sixty of them on horseback, the men in tunics of cloth of gold, their wives with fur-trimmed cloaks, each carrying a cup of gold or silver to be presented to the royal couple. The new Lord Mayor, Andrew Buckerel, a pepperer (as grocers were called), cavorted in the lead. The ride from the Tower to Westminster was through clean streets hung with silk banners and trumpeters at each corner blowing furious fanfares for the lovely young Queen. There could be no doubt that Eleanor La Belle had made a most favorable impression, and no one who saw her on this cold but sunny day, without a hint of fog or cloud or smoke in the sky, would have believed that on a raw and gloomy day much later the citizens of London would pelt her barge on the Thames with stones to drive her back to the Tower, calling her a harridan and a witch.

The crowning was followed by a banquet which perhaps blotted finally from Henry's mind the painful memory of his humble start as King. Never before in the history of merrie England had there been such feasting. The nobility were out in full force, performing their hereditary parts in the ritual. The Lord Mayor served wine to those who sat at the head table, the finest wine that Gascony could supply. Food was lavishly provided for the spectators who had braved the cold to walk from London and who packed the gardens and road-ways about Westminster. At the finish everything which had figured in the ceremony was given away to those who had served the newly married couple, even the Queen's bed being claimed by the chamberlain.

The start had been more than auspicious, but Henry promptly destroyed the fine effect of it by not sending back the large train of attendants accompanying the Queen. Louis of France had packed them all off as soon as he married Marguerite (Blanche of Castile, that managing woman, saw to it), but Henry liked them so much he could not part with them. Three uncles had come to England with the Queen. One of them, William, the bishop-elect of Valence, gained an immediate hold over Henry, who considered him wise and enlightened and listened to everything he said. Peter of Savoy, another of the trio, a very handsome and superior-mannered man, made such an impression on the gullible Henry that he was created Earl of Richmond and given (or, rather, sold for three feathers) a strip of most valuable land on the Thames for the building of a permanent home which became known as the Savoy. The third uncle, Amadeus, was also given valuable lands, which he promptly sold at a fine price. Even Thomas of Savoy, the father of this brood, was given a grant of a groat on every sack of English wool which passed through his territory.

The King, in the first flush of his enthusiasm for the wonderful thing which had happened to him, filled the pockets of the rest of the train with gold and even granted life pensions to many of them. One Richard, a musician, was made the King's special harper and was allowed forty shillings and a tun of wine a year. Henry of Avranches, a poet, was put on the household list as the King's versificator, which made him the first poet laureate. Master Henry wrote some verses about Cornishmen which made hackles bristle in the duchy, but this did not lose him possession of his hundred shillings a year. All this, however, was of small importance; what counted most seriously was the fatuous King's granting of pensions to all the Queen's relatives running into thousands of marks.

The Provençals were a most superior lot. They voiced the greatest contempt for everything English and looked down their long noses at the native population. They shuddered at the weather and sang mournful songs about their beautiful, sunny Provence so far away; but they were only too glad to stay and in many cases never did go back to beautiful, sunny Provence. The English people conceived a hatred for them which grew with each day.

Henry, it will thus be seen, was one of the most generous of men but with a perverse habit of displaying his generosity in all the wrong quarters. He never had any left over, certainly, for his subjects who paid the bills. The royal wedding and the orgy of spending which preceded and followed it left him in a most serious financial position. All the money granted to him for his sister's dowry, amounting to two marks on each knight's fee of land, and for his own marriage expenses, had vanished. Not a penny had been sent to Germany, and the royal spendthrift, moreover, acknowledged that he had gone deeply into debt as well.

The dissatisfaction of his subjects was so great that less than three weeks after the wedding a great council was held at Merton to discuss the King's situation and the new danger which had arisen from the influx of foreigners. The barons most emphatically affirmed that no change was to be made in the laws or the methods of government.

The attitude of the Council should have been a warning. Henry preferred instead to listen to the advice of his new friends. They said to him in effect, these poverty-stricken but haughty relatives of the young Queen: "Be firm. Don't give in an inch to these English traitors. Let them know you are the King." This was the kind of advice Henry liked to hear. It coincided with his own thinking, the inner convictions which he had never dared state openly and unequivocally, although he had often given intimations of the reactionary ideas he harbored. Now, following the advice of the feudal-minded Provençals, he came out into the open. He let it be known that he intended to take the full task of government into his own hands. To this end he appointed a new council of twelve to act under him and follow out his orders. William of Valence was at its head, and none of the leading men of the kingdom were included.

On the twenty-ninth of April the Common Council of the kingdom gathered to protest these arbitrary measures which were in direct contradiction to the Great Charter which Henry had sworn so often to observe. Their indignation was so vigorously expressed that the King, never of stout enough resolution to face the whirlwind he continuously sowed, took his adored Eleanor to the Tower of London. They remained in the safety of its high stone walls until, in a somewhat cowed mood, he gave the barons his solemn promise to reform.

The promise had been made without any intention of keeping it. The new council of twelve was retained, with William of Valence at its head, and several of the officials who had served during the regime of Peter des Roches were called back to office. Henry, with his land-hungry in-laws whispering in his ear, was being firm in his own fashion.

4

The Queen, having conceived a poor opinion of the people over whom her husband ruled, was never happy unless surrounded by her relatives and favorites from Provence. In addition to those who remained permanently there was a constant stream of visitors. It is recorded that when the four sisters were together the two elder, Marguerite and Eleanor, insisted on the two younger sitting on stools in their presence because they were not queens. This irked Sanchia and Beatrice very much, neither realizing that fate (without any assistance from the archschemer Romeo) would provide both of them with crowns ultimately and that Beatrice particularly would live a most romantic and exciting life.

Henry found himself now under constant pressure to aid not only the immediate family of the Queen but her mother's brothers and sisters as well. There were, unfortunately, a great many of them. Thomas of Savoy had brought a succession of brilliant sons and beautiful daughters into the world while lacking the means to provide for them. They came flocking and honking into England like a sord of hungry mallards. Boniface, the eleventh child, must have been a special favorite with his niece Eleanor, because she manifested a great desire to help him. Boniface, bold and handsome in a dark and masterful way, was full of ambition; but what prospects were there for an eleventh child in a state as lacking in prosperity as the mountainous slopes of Savoy? Intended by nature to be a soldier, he had found it necessary to go into the Church, where sinecures were always available for the younger sons of ruling families. When a very young man he had been made Bishop of Bellay. This, however, did not content him.

The chance to provide for Boniface came soon enough through the death of Edmund Rich. Although he had acted as archbishop with some of the spiritual conviction of Anselm and at times with flashes of political insight and courage, Edmund had been an unhappy man. His duties had involved him in continuous conflict; with the Pope over the exactions of the Vatican, with Henry because of the latter's weakness and his wrongdoing, even with the monks of his own chapter at Canterbury because of the easy and voluptuous ways into which they had fallen. He lacked the stern fiber of that resolute man, Robert Grosseteste, and finally he reached the stage where he could fight no longer. The last straw was a letter from Gregory IX, the most demanding of pontiffs, instructing him to find three hundred livings for Italian incumbents. At this the gentle and unworldly scholar, who had been drafted into the leadership of the Church against his will, threw his hands in the air. This was in the summer of 1240 and the archbishop had reached his seventieth year.

Edmund did not resign. Over his shoulders, wasted by a lifetime of fasting and deprivation, he slipped the robe of the Cistercians. Crossing the Channel, he made his way to the

Cistercian monastery at Pontigny where Thomas à Becket and Stephen Langton had found refuge when kept out of England. He said simply, "I have come to lay down my bones among you." He continued to live there as one of the brothers until the heat of summer became so great that he was advised to go to the priory of Soissy where the weather would be more moderate. On departing he said, "I will return on the feast of St. Edmund." He had spoken truer than he knew. The feast of St. Edmund falls on November 20. On the sixteenth day of that month he died at Soissy, and it was four days later that his body was brought to Pontigny for burial.

With the saintly Edmund gone, it occurred to Eleanor at once that the chance had come to do something for her favorite uncle. She began to urge his appointment as Archbishop of Canterbury.

It would have been difficult to conceive of a less likely candidate for that exalted post. Boniface was a man of the world, hard and covetous and completely lacking in spiritual qualities. He spoke no word of the language and shared with the rest of his family a sense of superiority over the English. He was already unpopular with the people of the country. The year after Eleanor's marriage to Henry he had visited England and had been entertained with such magnificence that the King had been compelled to demand a gift of twenty thousand marks from the Jews, with the threat that they would be expelled from the kingdom if they refused. It had been believed at the time that part of this money had vanished into the empty, capacious pockets of the visitor.

By this time Henry's affection for his young wife had reached the fatuous stage and he could deny her nothing. With reluctance and inward misgivings (it is hoped) he sent the *congé d'élire*, the official permission for an election, to the monks of the Canterbury chapter, accompanied by a demand that they choose Boniface of Bellay.

The monks had often shown themselves obstructive and set in their convictions, but they were not at this time in a position to oppose the King. Before leaving Canterbury, Edmund Rich had placed the chapter under the ban of the Church. Henry's peremptory instructions in favor of Boniface were accompanied by a promise to do what he could to get the ban lifted. The unhappy monks proceeded, therefore, in a long procession, two abreast, into their handsome chapter house and, seating themselves on the bench around the circular wall, cast their votes for the foreigner. The favored uncle of the Queen thus became the second man in the kingdom.

It was a long time before he could get his appointment confirmed at Rome. Gregory died early in 1241, worn out by his struggles with the German Emperor. The latter had defeated the armies of the Pope and had seized ships carrying cardinals to the general council of the Church which Gregory had called just before his death. He continued to hold the cardinals as his prisoners, and as a result there were only ten members of the Sacred College in Rome when the need for an election arose. He agreed to allow his prisoners to attend the conclave, but with one condition, that they would return to his custody if they did not elect his own candidate, Cardinal Ottobuoni.

The imperial candidate stood no chance whatever of election. The fact that Frederick favored him was enough to destroy his chances. There had been at no time, however, any sentiment in his favor. The favored candidate was an Englishman, Robert de Somercote, who had been created cardinal deacon of San Adriano in 1234.

Cardinal Somercote had been a protégé of Stephen Langton and, perhaps through the influence of the latter, had been made chaplain to the King. He was noticed favorably by Gregory while serving in that capacity, and a summons to Rome put him in the way of rapid preferment. He is said to have been much the same type of man as Adrian IV, who had been Nicholas Brakespeare of Abbots Langley in Hertfordshire, the only Englishman to become Pope. Somercote was a strong and reserved man, firm in his judgments and of proven discretion. On one occasion when the imperial armies were marching on Rome he was the only member of the cardinalate with the courage to remain by the side of the old Pontiff. It was believed that Gregory had thought him worthy of the succession. If the votes of the conclave had been cast for the Englishman, he would undoubtedly have pursued the vigorous policy of Gregory, which also had been the course followed by Adrian IV during his brief years of dramatic incumbency a century before. It was found when the ballots were cast, however, that the reluctance of the cardinals to elect an alien had not been overcome. Only nine votes had been registered, and of these six had gone to a compromise candidate, the oldest member of the College, Godfrey Castiglione of Milan.

When the smoke rose from the burning ballots in the Palace of the Sun and the news was conveyed to the outside world, there was another startling piece of information with it. Cardinal Somerçote was dead. The first version of what had happened was that he had died before the election, that he had been poisoned by his opponents who feared his strength and had gone to this extreme to get him out of the way. Later it was said that he was poisoned after the balloting because a new election had been decided upon and the opposition, convinced he would win if this were done, had chosen to remove him from their path. The truth was never ascertained, but it was generally believed that Somercote had not died a natural death. This was probably the closest that England ever came to having another Pope.

Godfrey was confirmed in the post on October 25 and took the name of Celestine IV. Then, adding intensity to a situation already charged, Celestine died on the tenth of November, his death being followed immediately by that of his closest supporter, the cardinal bishop of Ostia. The sixteen-day Pope had been of such advanced years that the strain to which he had been subjected might have exhausted his small store of strength. Such an explanation was not accepted in the inflamed state of Roman opinion. The poisoners were still at work! Panic swept the city. All the remaining members of the Sacred College fled for their lives and went into hiding.

For two years thereafter it was found impossible to appoint a successor. A few of the cardinals, the bolder spirits, returned to Rome, but the majority remained in hiding. Frederick, the German Emperor, railed at them as cowards and sons of Belial. Month after month passed and still nothing was done. The Emperor finally sent troops to seize the estates of all the cardinals who had not returned to their duties.

Finally in June 1243 a small conclave was held at Anagni and Sinibaldo Fiesco was elected, a member of the noble Genoese family of Lavagna, who assumed the name of Innocent IV. He was a man of great ambition and grim resolution, which caused him to oppose the Emperor as bitterly as his predecessors. "Christ established not only a pontifical but a royal sovereignty," he declared, "and committed to blessed Peter and his successors the empire both of earth and heaven." The clash which followed immediately resulted in the new Pontiff fleeing from Rome and establishing himself in French territory at Lyons.

It was to Lyons, therefore, that Boniface had to go for confirmation. He had not thought it necessary in the meantime to remain in the country over which he was to exercise spiritual sway. In his absence Henry sequestrated the revenues of Canterbury and cut severely into the possessions of the see, selling off timber and livestock and diverting the funds into the royal coffers. When the King went campaigning in Poitou (if it could be called that), he left Walter de Gray, the Archbishop of York, in charge of home affairs. The latter managed the vacant sees with such a firm hand that he was able to send Henry at Bordeaux, in addition to large sums of money, ten thousand measures of corn, five thousand of oats, and five thousand sides of bacon. If he had realized this, Boniface might have returned earlier. As it was, he preferred to remain as commander of the papal guard, to which the new Pontiff had appointed him. He was so interested in the politics of the Vatican, in fact, that he did not arrive in England for his enthronement until four years later.

It did not take long for the people of England to realize that Boniface of Savoy was the strangest primate the country had ever seen. After a succession of old men which stretched back into the mists of the past, sometimes men of great ability and inspired qualities of leadership, always of some degree of saintliness, it was disturbing to see the leadership of the Church in the hands of a worldling in his thirties, a soldier, moreover, contemptuous and grasping. The only thing which could be counted even slightly in Boniface's favor was his prepossessing appearance. He soon became known throughout England as the Handsome Archbishop.

Boniface was as able in his way as any primate of the past. Having one objective only, to make a fortune for himself, he proceeded to employ his very considerable abilities to that end. Realizing that he could not accumulate wealth until he had put the affairs of the see on a better basis, he reduced his staff, made economies in all departments, sold off what was left of the timber. As a quick means of personal aggrandizement he persuaded the Pope, with whom he remained a great favorite, to grant him the first fruits on all vacancies in the province of Canterbury. He proceeded to fill the vacancies, allowing the new incumbents one sixth of the income and keeping five sixths for himself. His pockets filled quickly.

It then entered his head that what Robert Grosseteste had done for the spiritual improvement of the Church could be carried on with an eye to personal profit. He began to make visitations, and when he detected proofs of slackness (his sharp eye found them everywhere) he imposed fines on the delinquents, keeping the money for himself. Sometimes he agreed to forgo visitation when a sufficient inducement was offered.

Finally he came to London, expecting figuratively to find gold coins hanging in the clerestory of St. Paul's like hops on a string, and silver in enticing piles in the churches whose modest spires rose everywhere above the tenements of the old town. He took possession, without permission, of the town house of the Bishop of Chichester and then turned his guards loose on London to exercise a concession the King had given him (and which he had no shadow of right to give), that of purveyance. The armed Poitevins visited markets and shops and took whatever they wanted without making payment. London, incredulous that such things could be happening, did nothing at first. Soon, however, rumblings were heard in the Shambles and in Barking. Wherever men gathered there was talk of what must be done. The anger of London, sometimes slow to rouse, was always hard to appease.

Ecclesiastical London had decided to resist visitation. When Boniface came to St. Paul's, his guards in chain mail at his heels (and all of them from Savoy), he was greeted by a strange silence. No organ sounded, no processional of cathedral officers in ceremonial robes, no censers swinging, no chanting of plainsong. St. Paul's, in fact, was as empty as a cavern under the sea. Finally the dean, old Henry of Cornhill, came doddering up to explain that there had been some mistake. Boniface excommunicated old Henry in a towering rage. Then, not being content with such an insignificant reprisal, he sent his men scurrying in all directions for candles and proceeded to dash them out on the paving stones while he cast into outer darkness everyone connected with the see of London.

The Handsome Archbishop now decided to visit St. Bartholomew's and sent a command for everything to be in readiness at the appointed hour. He must have been aware as he made his way through the crowded streets that he walked in an atmosphere charged with menace. If he had understood the mettle of London he would have known that the scowls on the faces he passed were not mere idle resentment, and his ear would have told him that the trained bands were marching before him, behind him, in parallel streets. The great city was getting ready to act.

As soon as he appeared at the entrance of St. Bartholomew's the bells began to ring, the boom of the organ rose from the interior of the church; it was plain that a service had just begun. Boniface saw at once that it had been timed to prevent him from making his inspection. He was white with rage when the aged sub-prior, who did not seem aware of what was going on, came up to receive him.

"Where are the canons?"

The old man gestured in the direction of the stalls, and the wrathy archbishop saw that the canons, to a man, were already on their knees in prayer and could not be interrupted. He was sure, in spite of the soberness of their faces, that they were laughing at him.

Boniface fell into such an uncontrollable fury that he knocked the venerable sub-prior down and then, as he lay on the stone floor, struck him on the head and face, the blows having all his vigor behind them.

"Thus, thus," cried the furious primate, "will I deal with English traitors!"

He called loudly for a sword so he could finish the helpless old man at his feet. As none was offered him, he reached down and crushed his victim against a spondyl between two of the stalls with such force that several bones were broken. The service was brought to an abrupt end, and the canons crowded between the irate archbishop and his victim. In the struggle which ensued the rochet was torn from the back of Boniface and it was discovered that he was wearing under it, not a penitential hair shirt as might have been expected, but a coat of chain mail!

Even the violent archbishop sensed the impropriety of what had been revealed. He seems to have desisted at once and to have left the church, taking his followers with him.

Word of what had happened had already reached the streets, which were filled with the rising tumult of the angry mobs. Boniface, an experienced soldier, knew that he and his men would be torn to pieces if they did not get away quickly. He succeeded in breaking his way through the people and led his men to the river. Here they secured boats and crossed to Lambeth. The mobs followed to the other side of the water and milled about the palace.

"Where is the bloody aggressor?" they cried. "Come out, infamous assailant of helpless priests! Come out, extorter of money, married priest that you are!"

In the meantime the canons of Bartholomew, acting on instructions from the Bishop of London, went in a body to tell the King what had happened. Henry refused to see them.

Boniface managed to slip away from his palace at Lambeth and took a boat down the river to Westminister. He had no difficulty in gaining admission. The King seems to have taken a serious view of the incident at first, fearing that Boniface had been hasty and ill-advised. Queen Eleanor did not agree with him. She supported her uncle, declaring indignantly that he could not have done otherwise when confronted with such impudent opposition. She even persuaded the weak-kneed King to issue a proclamation warning the people of London not to take part in a controversy which was purely ecclesiastical.

However, the Handsome Archbishop left the country soon afterward and remained away for seven years.

5

There can be no doubt that Eleanor was beautiful. No description of her is available, but it is probable that she inclined to the ivory and brown of the South rather than the dazzling gold-and-pink loveliness of the former Queen. Peter Langtoft speaks of her as "The erle's dauhter, the fairest may of life." Even after people began to entertain a wholesome dislike of her they remained fascinated by the legend of her learning, and the women never did lose their interest in the clothes she continued to import from France. England even then was under Latin influence in all matters of dress. There had been insouciance in the trousseau Eleanor brought to the court of Henry; the parti-colored *cotte*, the gold or silver girdle in which a dagger was carelessly thrust, the wide goring at the hips, the daring effect of red silk damask and decorations of gilt quatrefoil, the mantle of honor over the shoulders, the very high and very new type of wimple into which the head receded until the face seemed like a flower in an enveloping spathe, the saucy pillbox cap.

That she failed to produce an heir until after nearly four years of marriage added to Eleanor's unpopularity. A land tired of succession quarrels had no place in its affections for a barren queen. There was excitement, therefore, and even a resurgence of her early popularity when it became known in the first months of 1239 that she was with child.

On June 18 of that year a healthy male child was born at Westminster. It was quite late at night when the happy event occurred, but all London was awake and waiting. As soon as a loud clangor of bells conveyed the intelligence that the child was a boy, the city was illuminated and the streets filled with excited people. Already the descent of the royal infant had been traced back from Matilda, the Saxon wife of Henry I; to Margaret, her mother, who had been Queen of Scotland; to Edward the Exile, Edmund Ironsides, Ethelred, Edgar, Edward, Alfred. There it was to con, to talk over, the proof of descent from Alfred the Great, Alfred of glorious memory! For the first time in many years Henry had succeeded in making his people happy.

Four days later the child was baptized and given the name of Edward, which again delighted the people because it was so completely English. By this time, however, the first flush of enthusiasm, the first glow of content, was beginning to wear off. Henry was up to his old tricks, demanding gifts for the heir from everyone. He was so demanding as to the nature and value of the gifts, in fact, that one of his Norman officials who stood beside the font remarked dryly to those about him, "God gave us this infant, but our lord the King sells him to us."

Not one of the nobles in their handsome surcoats of silk or samite or their wives in somewhat less costly grandeur had any conception of the importance of the event they were witnessing, that the infant held before the font, this son of vacillating Henry and grandson of the vicious John, would prove to be one of the greatest, if not the very greatest, of all English kings, that after a wild and unpromising youth he would assume office with an intensified sense of responsibility and govern so well that he would be called the English Justinian. They would perhaps have been unhappy and indignant if they had been given a glimpse of a future in which common men sat in the great council of the nation known as Parliament and that the tall man into which this child would grow, after killing in battle the great leader who first called "loyal and honest men" from all counties to sit in deliberation with baron and bishop, would be the one to adopt the idea and give it the sanction of long usage.

There was nothing of this, of course, to be read in the wrinkled face of the rather long infant on whom the holy water was sprinkled this warm day of June. The common people, massed outside and well fortified with the stout English ale always drunk on such occasions, had more prescience than the bowing and chattering people of the court. The boy was descended straight from Alfred, he was to bear the fine name of Edward: it stood to reason that he would grow into a proper man. The common people had high hopes for this prince.

It soon became apparent that the lord Edward was going to be of kingly appearance. He was called Edward with the Flaxen Hair. His eyes were blue, his complexion high, his features fine. He grew quickly and strongly. Some slight dismay was felt when it was found that one eyelid drooped in close imitation of his father's defect, because that famous squint of Henry's was generally believed to be the manifestation of slyness and his other maddening qualities. Would the boy develop the traits of his sire? The heir, however, showed early signs of being different from his father in most respects; a rugged, high-spirited, hot-tempered lad, always willing to exchange a blow for a blow but always fair about it, with a love from the very start for horses and dogs and weapons.

As soon as he had weathered an infantile illness or two (in the course of one Eleanor scandalized the monks of the Cistercian monastery of Beaulieu by insisting on remaining with them to nurse her son back to health) he was taken to Windsor Castle, where Henry's ambitious building plans had been partly carried out, and there he was put in charge of one Hugh Giffard. His tutor soon found out other things about the boy: that he was quick in understanding, an excellent scholar up to a point; that he had an inherent sense of honor. Edward was beginning to grow very tall for his age, and it was certain that he was going to overshadow in height both his father and his grandfather, the thickset John. People began to call him affectionately Longshanks. The name stuck to him, and it is as Edward Longshanks that he is most often referred to in history.

CHAPTER THIRTEEN

Queen's Men, King's Men, and the Villain of the Piece

HENRY was now determined to rule the country without a responsible government. His new council of twelve was subservient to him, and he began to give all administrative posts of importance to men who had been serving him, for the most part, in minor capacities. He had always wanted to do things this way, and his own inclination was, therefore, the main contributing factor in the decision. It was plain to see, nevertheless, that he had been urged to it by the greedy newcomers. They wanted to have to themselves the goose which laid the golden eggs.

But Henry had not been cut to the measure of a dictator. Born with a belief in the absolute power of kings, he lacked the capacity and the personal discipline to make proper use of the power he was now wrongfully assuming. He was too indolent for the role. He must have men to do the work, and it was characteristic of him to lean on his wife's relatives. They suited him perfectly: they were courtly, sophisticated, believers in the kind of government he wanted. He liked to have them around him and, in order to cut a good figure in their eyes, he was prepared to squander the wealth of the realm on them.

As soon as he selected the council of twelve with William of

Valence at the head of it, however, it became only a matter of time until the barons would rise against him. But the murder of Richard the Marshal had removed the one man capable of leading the forces of discontent, and the breaking of the storm must wait the appearance of another leader.

The bitterness of his subjects was made abundantly clear when Henry decided to go to war with France. Of all the wide Angevin possessions, only a small province in the southwest remained to the English King, made up largely of Gascony. Henry dreamed of winning back the empire of his grandfather and he kept an eager eye on developments south of the Channel. It was largely through the influence of his mother that he decided to make the effort at this juncture.

It has already been told that Isabella could not reconcile herself to the loss in rank which resulted from her marriage to the Count of La Marche. She had been Queen of England and of the Angevin possessions beyond the seas, and three times each year she had worn in public a crown on her lustrous hair. Whenever she found herself now in the company of women who outranked her and took advantage of it, she would return in a great rage, her fine eyes blazing, her color high. She was the widow of a king and the mother of a king, she would declare, and she could not live under such rebuffs.

In 1241 Louis decided that his brother Alphonse was to rule over Poitou and took him to Poictiers to receive the submissions of the nobility. Hugh of La Marche obeyed the summons with the greatest reluctance. Isabella accompanied him with even greater unwillingness, and it did not improve her state of mind that she was ignored for three days. Finally she was summoned to the royal presence.

Blanche of Castile was seated beside the King when the former Queen of England made her entrance. It does not need stating that the two women had hated each other from the time when Blanche's husband had tried to take John's throne. The presence of the dowager Queen of France did nothing to soothe the ruffled feelings of Isabella.

There was silence in the room while she walked to the far end where Louis and his mother were seated on raised chairs. Neither rose to greet her, nor did they speak. Isabella compelled herself to voice a brief expression of her loyalty, although each word must have cost her an effort. Louis nodded in response but said nothing. His mother, her eyes fixed triumphantly on this once admired Queen who had been her bitter rival, remained silent also. Isabella accepted their attitude as a dismissal and swept out of the state room in a towering passion.

Louis was a man of rare magnanimity, and it may safely be assumed that this slight to the ex-Queen of England was the work of Blanche of Castile. Blanche had suffered a great deal at the hands of beautiful women. As a girl she had been eclipsed by the attractions of her lovely sister Uracca. The court of Philip Augustus, to which she had come as the wife of Prince Louis, was a brilliant one, the center of beauty and chivalry and fashion. The bride from Spain could not have failed to resent the women of the court, who, she knew quite well, considered her plain and dowdy. She had sought release by interesting herself in affairs of state and she had been almost fiercely in favor of the invasion of England on the invitation of the barons. Her rivalry with Isabella had been long-range, but it had been deep-seated.

The humiliation of the ex-Queen who had tossed her cap over the windmill (and her royal prerogatives with it) had a result which Blanche could not have expected. The Count of La Marche was still in love with his wife and he resented the coolness of her reception as much as she did. She accompanied him when he arrived at the palace sometime later, ostensibly for the purpose of taking the oath of fealty. It was during the Christmas festivities, which may account for the way things fell out. Hugh stomped into the presence of the new ruler of Poitou and in a loud voice disputed Alphonse's right to the control of the Poitevin realm. He then turned and left the palace. Before the ale-drowsy officials could order his detention, he and Isabella had mounted their horses and galloped out through the courtyard.

Having thus committed themselves to rebellion, the daring pair put their heads together and planned the first steps in a conspiracy to unite the provinces of the South and West against the French King. Raimund of Toulouse, who shared their desire to prevent the whole of France from being snared into the Capetian net, fell willingly into line. The barons of Gascony met secretly at Pons and agreed to join the conspiracy, while some of the nobility of Poitou met at the same time in Parthenay and swore to throw off the yoke. All that was needed was the active support of England, and this Henry was eager to give, so eager that he committed himself to the confederacy without consulting any of the great barons of

England. The first intimation they had of what was in the wind was when they were summoned to a general council in January of the following year and asked to provide financial support for the war.

The barons were furious at having been ignored. They realized also that the quarrel with France had been provoked by the King's mother and, falling back on the fact that the truce between the two nations had some time to run, they refused aid to the King as long as it remained unbroken. Henry disregarded them and went ahead with his preparations. He equipped a small army consisting of three hundred knights and some companies of Welsh mercenaries and made a landing at Saintonge. As Eleanor accompanied him, Walter de Gray was made regent with instructions to raise whatever reinforcements and funds would be needed.

The campaign proved a disastrous failure. On his previous invasion the French armies had paid Henry the doubtful compliment of leaving him alone, but this time it was different. Poitou had been overrun before he arrived. When he managed to make contact near Taillebourg with the troops that Hugh of La Marche had raised, he found himself confronted by a superior French army which, clearly, was filled with the determination to exterminate the invaders. With hostile troops ringing his position on three sides it was an uncomfortable time for the King to discover that other men could be as ready as he to break promises and repudiate obligations. Word was brought to him that Hugh, convinced it was a lost cause, was negotiating with the French.

When the two men met and Henry charged his mother's husband with treachery, the count was evasive at first. He studied a hill in the near distance above which French plumes were showing and a cloud of dust raised by the approach of cavalry at a bend of the road. Turning then to the angry and spluttering King of England, he denied that there were treaty obligations between them to prevent him from taking whatever steps he deemed advisable in these circumstances. There had been no promise between them that one would not make peace except with the consent of the other.

Henry declared he would produce documents to prove the promises on the strength of which he had come to Poitou.

The count gave his shoulders a shrug and said he had signed no documents. If any promise had been exchanged, it had been the work of his wife and he had not been a party to it.

There was only one course open to the English, to withdraw before the French could cut off their retreat. This they succeeded in doing, although in his hurry to get away Henry had to leave behind his war chest and all the rich equipment of his chapel royal. The Count of La Marche promptly gave in to the French King on a promise of favorable terms. Henry, spluttering and raging, made a hasty retreat behind the Gironde and from there watched his victorious brother-in-law sweep across the country north of the river.

A conspiracy is never any stronger than its least reliable member, but Isabella's husband cannot be charged with the full blame for the swift and ignominious failure of the confederacy he had been chiefly instrumental in forming. A thing of shreds and patches to begin with, it now fell completely to pieces. He brought a degree of opprobrium on his name in which no one else shared, however, by turning his coat and assuming command of a French army in a drive southward against his former allies. Raimund of Toulouse, never a resolute partner, was brought to his knees. This left Henry with nothing to do but conclude a truce with the victorious Louis which reduced his possessions in France still further. The venture had cost him forty thousand pounds and whatever respect his subjects had entertained for him.

Whether in an effort to cover up his failure or because he did not realize the almost comic role he had played, Henry sent orders ahead of him that he was to be met on his return by all the nobility and that, moreover, he was to be welcomed home in great state. The nobles gathered at Portsmouth, fully accoutered and surrounded by their attendants in livery. They waited a long time while reports trickled in of the adverse winds which were making it impossible for the King to return. Finally the word came that dissension had broken out in Gascony and that Henry had gone there to act as peacemaker. The nobles returned to their homes, their resentment over the poor result of the campaign heightened by the inconveniences to which they had been subjected.

Henry and Eleanor spent a pleasant winter in Bordeaux. There was much entertaining and feasting and staging of brilliant pageants at which the guisers of Provence sang their love lyrics and twanged on their lutes. The royal couple were chiefly concerned in arranging a marriage between Henry's brother Richard of Cornwall, whose wife Isabella had died recently, and Eleanor's sister Sanchia. The latter was affianced to Raimund of Toulouse, but the weak part played by the latter in the recent fighting was a good enough excuse for breaking the bond. A new marriage contract was drawn up and signed, Sanchia occupying a stool, no doubt, during the ceremony of signature, for Richard, although the wealthiest man in England and perhaps in Europe, was still only a prince.

Henry returned to England in the spring and was received at Winchester in a fair imitation of the great state he had demanded. The streets were lined with flags and the banners of the nobility while trumpeters blasted out a royal welcome. Henry, smiling and full of excuses for the lack of results in the war to which (he said blandly) he had been sent by his barons, settled down to the somewhat farcical routine he called governing the country.

The first business to claim his serious attention was getting Richard and Sanchia married. As usual, he burbled with enthusiasm over the arrangements, declaring it must be made an occasion to remember. Beatrice of Provence, mother of the bride, came to England to see her third daughter wedded, but Raimund Berenger was detained by state difficulties which his wife solved by getting a loan from Henry of four thousand marks. The cost of the wedding was chiefly defrayed by a levy imposed on the Jews of the country. It was an arbitrary proceeding, each of them receiving notice of the size of the donation required. Aaron of York, the richest of them, was assessed four hundred gold marks and four thousand silver. An idea of the extravagance of the festivities may be gleaned from the fact that thirty thousand dishes were prepared for the wedding dinner alone.

2

Ex-Queen Isabella seems to have taken things into her own hands after the disastrous failure of the confederacy. No records exist by which her course of action from that point on can be charted, but there is no doubt that from the first she was not reconciled to French domination. She must have realized that nothing more could be expected from her son. Henry had demonstrated that he was neither a military leader nor an organizer of causes. Her own husband was almost as unstable. Hugh's easy submission to Louis must have galled his implacable wife. Inasmuch as his treacherous change of sides was the price he paid for retaining the lands and honors of Lusignan, it may have been that Isabella, who was completely realistic where property was concerned, did not blame him for that move.

If that were true, she soon ceased to allow such considerations to control her actions. She had had five sons by her second marriage, and it must have been clear to her that anything which widened the breach between the French Crown and the family of Lusignan would make it still more difficult to provide for all of them. She had always been vain, capricious, and troublesome, and at this state she seems to have permitted the worst sides of her nature to take possession of her mind to the exclusion of everything else.

Two years later the court of Louis was thrown into great excitement by a story that two of the royal cooks had attempted to poison their master. Whether or not they were guilty, it was certain they would confess when put to the torture, which had become almost an art in France. They babbled abjectly, declaring among other things that they had been in the pay of the ex-Queen of England. Louis had been long-suffering in respect to the troublesome Lusignans, overlooking their arrogance and defiance of him, even forgiving them the recent hostilities. This final offense, in which he seems to have believed, had to be dealt with, however, in the manner prescribed for such crimes. An attempt to take Isabella into custody failed because she had been warned in time and had fled. Her husband was arrested, however, and thrown into prison with his eldest son, charged with complicity in the poisoning plot.

There was no evidence against the mother of England's King save the confession of the two cooks. It may have been no more than a sense of panic which caused her to fly to the monastery at Fontevraud, the burying place of many Norman and Plantagenet kings and queens. Here she was received by the abbess and promised sanctuary. Because of the nature of the charge against her, she was placed in the secret room.

The abbey of Fontevraud was a most unusual institution, consisting of a nunnery with three hundred members and a monastery with two hundred monks, rigidly segregated and under the rule of the abbess. It had been established to help the lowly and downtrodden and contained a hospital for lepers and a home for fallen women.

Isabella said a prayer at the row of stately tombs where Eleanor of Aquitaine lay between her husband, Henry II, and her son, Richard the Lionheart, and was then escorted to the dark apartment where she would be free from molestation. No description is available of the secret room at Fontevraud, but it undoubtedly was a small hole in the thick masonry surrounding the hearth in the refectory of the nuns, approached by narrow steps from an exit somewhere in the vaults, this being the method commonly followed in castles and religious institutions. This much may be taken for granted: it was an airless hole without any natural light, lacking in all comforts and just large enough for a narrow couch and a few domestic utensils.

Here the one-time lady of England existed in safety but great discomfort and unhappiness while her husband and son were charged with a share in the plot to kill the French King. Whether or not Isabella was guilty, it is certain that neither of the men had been involved. There does not seem to have been a shred of evidence against them, and the two cooks had already been executed and could not be tortured into more confessions. The proceedings took the form, therefore, of a challenge to trial by battle. None of the champions of France, however, were ready to meet on the field of honor anyone as tainted with treason as Hugh of Lusignan, and so nothing came of that. Finally the prisoners were allowed their freedom, although they emerged discredited and dishonored.

No further effort seems to have been made to secure the person of Isabella. To try a former queen of England on a charge of attempted murder with no evidence but confessions under torture would create a difficult situation and lead to more war. It is certain that she could have been found and brought to book if there had been any desire to place her on trial. She continued to exist in the secret room, and there she died in the following year. When her body was carried out from the dark enclosure in the stout walls there was nothing to remind those who tended her of the great beauty which had once caused her to be known as the Helen of Europe. Her face was wasted with privation, and her once beautifully proportioned body was reduced to skin and bones.

She was buried in the common cemetery of the abbey, but some years later, on the insistence of Henry, she was given a final resting place in a stone coffin with the other kings and queens.

The ex-queen's coffin looks very small in contrast with those occupied by Henry II, Queen Eleanor and their son

Richard of the Lion Heart; a proof that the rigors of her confinement had been such that she had been reduced to the proportions almost of a child.

3

The disgrace of the family of Lusignan had the effect which Isabella should have foreseen earlier. Her husband lost most of his possessions. There would be enough for Hugh, the first son, but what of the four younger sons and three daughters? There was only one way to provide for them, and that was to send them to England and let Henry assume the burden.

In 1247, a year after their mother's death, four of them arrived at Dover—William, Guy, Aymer, and Alice—the rest being too young to venture from home. They were in charge of the cardinal bishop of Sabina, who was going to England as papal legate; a healthy group of young people whose natural good looks were somewhat marred by the way they wrinkled their noses in disgust at the English climate, the people, and everything they could see of England itself.

Instead of being annoyed by the responsibility thus heaped upon him, Henry was delighted with his young relatives and made it his concern (but not at his own expense) to provide for them handsomely. He married Alice to John de Warenne, Earl of Surrey. William was given one of the great heiresses of England, Joan de Munchensi, a granddaughter of William the Marshal. This was a most important match, because on the death of Joan's father she came into a fifth interest in the huge Marshal holdings. The division gave the penniless William and his bride the family castle of Pembroke and the liberty of Wexford in Ireland. As though enough had not been done, Henry bestowed a yearly pension of five hundred pounds on William and at various times other rich plums, including the castle of Goderich.

Because he owned Pembroke Castle, the acquisitive William concluded that he should have the earldom as well. It was an absurd claim, because his wife's mother had been the fifth daughter of the Good Knight and the other daughters had brought sons into the world. With characteristic disregard of the rights of others, however, William assumed the title and swaggered through life in the belief that he was now the representative of the great marshal. He seems to have combined in himself all the worst qualities, being effeminate, proud, cruel, boastful, and covetous. In order to justify his pretensions, he organized tournaments (nearly all of which Henry stopped, having no faith in the prowess of the young man) and went to enormous expense in importing the best blooded horses and the finest armor.

Guy does not seem to have stayed long, but Henry filled his saddlebags on his departure with so much gold that more horses had to be secured. It would have been a wonderfully fine thing for England if Aymer had returned at the same time, because the youngest of the trio of brothers was to prove himself more troublesome and obnoxious even than William. He had been intended for the Church and could have ranked even with Boniface in point of unsuitability, being violent, overbearing, grasping, and brash. Henry, with his usual lack of judgment about people, seems to have taken a particular fancy to Aymer. He went to infinite pains, and aroused a corresponding amount of indignation among his subjects, in finding benefices for him. Aymer received the rich church of St. Helen in Abingdon, the rectory of Wearmouth, and many other profitable livings. His appointments were so numerous, in fact, that the young man had to appoint a steward to collect his income. This was no more than a beginning. The chapter of Durham stoutly refused to elect him as their bishop on the ground that he was too young and ignorant, and not all the threats Henry made could lead them to a change of mind. Then in 1250 the Bishop of Winchester died and Henry insisted that Aymer be selected to succeed him. The Winchester chapter refused, using the same arguments employed at Durham and adding for good measure that the King's candidate was not yet in holy orders, being no more than an acolyte.

What his representatives, John Mansel and Peter Chacepork, had failed to do, Henry now decided to take on himself. He went to Winchester and, assuming the seat in the chapter house reserved for the bishop, proceeded to exhort the monks in the most extraordinary way. "I was born in this city," he declared, "and baptized in this church: wherefore you are bound to me by the ties of great affection and ought not to oppose my will in any way. . . . My brother Aymer, if elected, will for a long time enlighten this church, like the sun, with the rays of his noble and royal extraction, and of his most willing kindness and youth in which he is pleasing both to God and man." At the end of a long discourse he came to the one point which mattered, that if the monks opposed him he would find means to punish them most severely.

The poor monks, realizing that an appeal to Rome would do them no good, gave in most reluctantly and chose the youth of noble and royal extraction as their spiritual leader. A year later the appointment was confirmed by the Pope at Lyons, and the new bishop, now one of the most richly endowed men in England, began to live in high and mighty state. The monks of Winchester soon had good reason to repent of their weakness in electing Aymer. He oppressed them and on one occasion kept them shut up in their chapter house for three days without food. Some of them ran away and took sanctuary in the monasteries.

A curious situation developed out of the arrival of Henry's relatives. Eleanor remained loyal to her own uncles and cousins, the Provençals and Savoyards, and wanted all the plums for them. Henry's preference had been transferred to his half brothers, and he was determined to make them wealthy and influential. The two parties, as was to be expected, began to clash, openly and bitterly. The public, wryly amused at the struggle between the rival bands of harpies, called them the Queen's Men and the King's Men. They had no reason to find any satisfaction, however, in the situation. Between them the warring relatives were gobbling up all the offices in the kingdom and filling their pockets with the national wealth.

The two parties clashed with particular bitterness on one occasion. Aymer, taking advantage of the absence of Boniface, placed an appointee of his own as prior of the hospital of St. Thomas the Martyr at Southwark, which was within the province of Canterbury. Eustace of Lyons, a high official at Canterbury, ordered the man to vacate and, when this had no effect, seized him and put him in one of the episcopal prisons. Aymer got together an armed force and set the archbishop's manor at Maidstone on fire. He then attacked the palace at Lambeth, tearing the doors off their hinges and getting possession of the person of Eustace of Lyons, who had just been ready to sit down to his dinner, and put *him* in prison. The clash was so sudden and violent that the nation gasped with surprise. Bans of excommunication (which were hurled about these days as freely as maledictions) flew back and forth, and it looked as though something in the nature of civil war in the world of copes and miters would be the result. Boniface came back and did some excommunicating of his own, including everyone who might have been concerned in the episode with the sole exception of the royal family. Henry, taking on himself the role of peacemaker, summoned both Boniface and Aymer to attend him when he went to Winchester for the Christmas festivities. After a bountiful breakfast, supplied most generously by the townspeople (Henry did not forgo his intention, however, of demanding two hundred marks from them as a gift), he called the two prelates together and forced them to exchange the kiss of peace, after Aymer had declared that he had not directed the violent measures of his people. This brought the incident to a close.

The need to provide for all the Queen's Men as well as the King's Men kept Henry in a poorer state than ever. Acting on the advice of his Council, he was prepared to sell his plate but did not believe anyone could be found to purchase it. His councilors, after saying to him, "As all rivers flow back to the sea, so everything you now sell will return to you in remunerative gifts," expressed the opinion that the citizens of London were in a position to act as purchasers. The King became almost apoplectic with rage at this information.

"These clowns!" he cried. "If the treasures of Octavian were for sale, the city of London would purchase and suck it all up. If they are rich enough to buy my possessions, they can afford to give me the money I need."

On many occasions after that he compelled them to make pay tallages or even forced loans. The Queen's Men and King's Men, as a result, were able to continue eating off gold plate.

4

Enter the villain!

Parliament had been meeting regularly, generally around Hilarytide, and had been countering Henry's petulant demands for money, money, and more money with specific counterdemands. He must adhere to the provisions of the Charter, he must stop going into debt for foreign relatives, he must appoint responsible men to the posts of justiciar, treasurer, and chancellor. The King's answer to this was to help himself to money illegally and to put more and more power into the hands of one man, a man who suited him perfectly but did not suit the rest of the nation at all.

John Mansel had been for many years a minor official in

the King's household. In some records he is first noticed as the King's chaplain, in others as his secretary. He was of obscure parentage, the accepted belief being that he was the son of a country priest and, therefore, illegitimate. Some say he was raised as a servant or as a member of the song school at Westminster. His rise in the service of the King was rapid, and in the period following the disastrous second campaign in Poitou (in which he fought bravely) he was appointed to reside at the Exchequer and to handle the rolls of receipt, although it is uncertain if he was allowed at any time the title of Chancellor of the Exchequer. Becoming one of the King's advisers, he displayed such an uncanny sureness in sensing the kind of advice the King wanted to hear that, lo and behold, he was soon chief adviser.

In addition to his duties at the Exchequer, he was deep in the affairs of the embattled royal household; and here he seems to have moved with amazingly sure feet, avoiding the daggers of Poitou on one hand and the poniards of Savoy on the other. He became the departmental jack-of-all-trades, and the King seems to have depended on him whenever a knotty problem required unsnarling either at home or abroad. No more tactful man ever lived. When Henry's daughter Margaret, who had been married in magnificent state to the youthful King of Scotland, was reported held in solitary confinement by the regents in charge of the kingdom, it was Mansel who was sent to straighten things out; and what happened is a story which will be told in its proper place. He was sent on European missions having to do with peace treaties and the marriage of the royal children. He even interposed once in a London civic dispute, deposing several aldermen without bringing down on his head the wrath of the great city.

He was, in fact, the perfect servant for a ruler who wanted to keep all power in his own hands but was incapable of exercising it. Mansel, remaining a priest of not too exalted rank and having no definite title in state organization, did most of the work and was rewarded with a full share of the enmity of the public.

He became the most hated man in the kingdom, after the uncles and sisters and cousins and aunts. The nobles could not reconcile themselves to a priest of minor standing (he was even charged with being secretly married) wielding so much power. He had made himself, as it happened, most peculiarly vulnerable by his greediness in the matter of benefices. Honest, it may be assumed, in his handling of royal revenues, he depended on church appointments for his personal gain. No ecclesiastical post was safe from him. He was the pluralist of pluralists. It is probable that he held at one time as many as three hundred livings, and in some records the number is given as seven hundred. The estimates of his yearly income vary from four thousand to eighteen thousand marks. That he died in poverty may be accepted as an indication that he was acting as depositary for this steady flow of income and that much of it was finding a final resting place in a more exalted pocket than that of plain John Mansel. Certainly he would not have been allowed so to corrupt the machinery of appointments for his own sole gain. He was retaining, this handy man of the King, a considerable share of the revenue, nevertheless. During the first visit that the King and Queen of Scotland made to the English court after the trouble which Mansel had helped in straightening out, he gave a stately dinner for them at his home in Tothill Fields. Seven hundred dishes were prepared for the first course alone. He was reported to have said, on acquiring a benefice which paid only twenty pounds a year, "This will provide for my dogs." He was called bitterly "the richest clerk in the world."

There can be no doubt that Mansel, although a skilled administrator, was a bad influence in the Council of the King. The advice he whispered in the King's ear confirmed the latter in his stubborn shortsightedness. "Don't agree under compulsion," or "Remember that you are the King," was always the gist of it. Lacking completely in perspective, this ubiquitous clerk continued, as the situation became more strained and the wrath of the baronage mounted, to preach non-compliance. Indifferent to the temper of the people, he never changed his mind and was in part, at least, responsible for the King's refusal to make concessions. It is not surprising that the barons, aware of how matters stood, included in their terms a demand that John Mansel be dismissed.

The years rolled on. More children were born to Henry and Eleanor. The King became involved in absurd international adventures and fell more into debt all the time. He rebuilt Westminster Abbey and added more walls and more towers to the Tower of London. He continued to disregard the Charter and to rule as he saw fit, a slack kind of rule, raising revenue by illegal tallages and the bludgeoning of Jews into forced loans. The tide of national discontent rose higher each year until it threatened to swamp the weakening walls of royal privilege, behind which Queen's Men and King's Men still battened on the indulgent zany and most of the work of administration had fallen into the hands of a stubborn-minded and acquisitive clerk.

CHAPTER FOURTEEN

The Home Life of the Royal Family—
Richard of Cornwall

HENRY has appeared often enough in these pages in his official capacity for his measure as a king to be understood. Eleanor as Queen is as easily understandable: haughty, passionately conscious of her high destiny, contemptuous of the lower orders, unwilling to yield an inch from her conception of what was due royalty. It is only fair now to depict them as private individuals, as husband and wife, as father and mother of a growing family. It is a much pleasanter picture which emerges.

They were a devoted family. Henry was deeply attached to Eleanor and remained so to the end of his days except for a few furious but brief rifts. He is one of the few kings who seems never to have taken a mistress, a strange degree of constancy to find in a son of John. Eleanor was a faithful and, as far as can be seen, an affectionate wife. They loved their children as wholeheartedly as any butcher and his mate in the Shambles or any pair of villeins in wattled cottage and toft. The children returned this love in full measure. Edward, the first child, was militant in his devotion to his parents. He never forgave London the enmity which developed between its citizens and the Queen, even though he never trod on their privileges as she had and so must have realized how wrong she had been. As he grew older and began to have the clarity of vision and the level sense of values which were to make him such a splendid king, he must have seen that Henry was a fumbling and weak figure as head of the state; but if he did, he never allowed it to show. He might have seen the shortcomings of Henry himself, but he would brook no criticism in any other quarter of this Skimpole of a king who expected everything to come his way and tossed his money about with an urbane smile and a shrug for the morrow.

The other children were equally loyal to their parents and to one another. Margaret, the oldest daughter, who married Alexander III of Scotland, was passionately devoted to her husband but at every stage of her brief married life longed for her childhood home; for the beautiful mother, the smiling, talkative father, the handsome brothers and sisters, for the woods about Windsor, the park at Woodstock around which many of her fondest memories clustered. She made repeated visits to England, taking Alexander with her, and by doing so lost for her husband much of the loyalty of his Scottish subjects.

It remained for Edward to sum up the feeling which animated the royal family when he was in the Far East on a crusade and received word there of the deaths of an infant son and of his father. Edward bore the loss of his fine boy with fortitude but broke into loud lamentations when he learned of Henry's demise, not caring, seemingly, that he had become King of England. His uncle, Charles of Anjou, was puzzled enough at his attitude to ask for an explanation. Edward answered, "The loss of children may be repaired by the same God who gave them; but when a man has lost a good father, it is not in the course of nature for God to send him another."

2

Henry and Eleanor were almost as continuously on the wing as Raimund Berenger and his family had been in Provence when Eleanor was a young girl. They kept moving from Westminster to Windsor, to Wallingford, to Clarendon, to Winchester or Gloucester. It was necessary, therefore, to establish a family base for the children. Windsor was selected, partly because of the security it offered, partly because the Queen had always been fond of that great Norman castle.

The new buildings had been completed by the time the children began to arrive. A curtain of masonry had been erected along the chalk ridge, ending in a tower called the Belfry. Another wall was carried back to connect with the keep, thus providing a line of granite defense. Within the enclosed space thus provided Henry had made for himself a series of handsome buildings, a King's chamber sixty feet long, a chamber for the Queen, a chapel called St. Edward's, which was seventy feet long, and a Great Hall which was much larger still, a quite magnificent apartment in full keeping with the King's grandiose ideas. These chambers were all paneled and beamed and hung with tapestries which gave them a warmer feeling than most of the royal residences.

When Edward began to grow up into an active and high-spirited boy, it was deemed advisable to provide special quarters for him, and new lodgings were built against the keep. From that time on he always had his own household, tutors, squires, grooms, valets, and cooks, his own chaplain and confessor. It was a noisy household, filled with talk of hunting and fighting, the clash of quarterstaves, the roar of laughter which followed the success of practical jokes. The other children seem to have been lodged in the family quarters already described, where each of them had servants of his own. They arrived with great regularity. Of those who survived infancy, Margaret was born on September 29, 1240, and named after the French Queen. Beatrice was born on June 25, 1242, and named for her maternal grandmother. Edmund, the second son, arrived on January 16, 1245. Katherine, the last child, was born on November 25, 1253. There were four other sons who died in infancy, Richard, John, William, and Henry.

The King was devoted to all his children, although he seems to have displayed some preference for Edmund, who became known as Crouchback. Whether this was due to a deformity, which might explain Henry's special solicitude for him, or was merely a nickname bestowed on him when he was at the Crusades has never been satisfactorily settled. Edmund, at any rate, was handsome, sunny of disposition, and likable. When at Windsor, Henry always had his children around him. The birth of Margaret had left the Queen in a weakened condition, and this depressed his spirits so much that he paid small attention to the child. When he was told, however, that she gave great promise of beauty, he became quite exuberant and rushed to her cradle to give her the one kind of present he seems to have considered worth while, twelve ounces of gold.

Although indolent and averse to the concentrated work which personal rule involves, Henry was fond of detail in a way all his own. He liked to inject himself into such matters as the costumes his servants and officers were to wear. This man, he would direct, was to have a tunic made of cloth at fourteen pence a yard and with fur lining. Another one was to have the same kind of tunic but without the fur lining. He personally directed certain charities, setting aside days for the royal palaces to be thrown open so that the poor could enter and be fed. On one occasion he took a leaf from the book of the mother of Thomas à Becket and had his children weighed. When the combined weight of the royal brood had been ascertained a corresponding amount of silver was donated to charity.

Henry was a gourmet and gave great attention to the matter of supplies for the royal table. It was one of the duties of sheriffs and bailiffs to keep the King well fed, and Henry saw to it that they did, requisitioning four hundred hens once from Buckingham, eels from Bristol on another occasion, and herring pies from Yarmouth. He was inordinately fond of salmon pasties and saw to it that there was always an assortment on hand. Once he became very wrathy on learning that his children were being given the iron-flavored wine of Wiltshire, which was comparatively cheap, and he peremptorily instructed the officers to give them nothing but the best imported wines. He failed, however, to detect an economy which was put into effect at the expense of the royal children. The archbishop of York, who was left in charge at Windsor when the King and Queen were elsewhere and who seems to have had a parsimonious streak in him, gave an order that all good fat deer caught in the forests about Windsor were to be sent away for the use of the King, the lean ones to be kept for the children.

The royal children were spared one experience which might have been humiliating for them. Conscience-stricken over the state of royal finances, Henry and his consort decided to economize. As might be expected, they made a sort of public ritual of their resolution and arranged things so their subjects bore the brunt of the economy program. They reduced the wages paid to their servants and always dined out as the guests of wealthy people. The nobles, the bishops, the most prosperous of the citizens of London were all honored in turn. It was, of course, a great privilege for those selected to provide meals for the royal family and the members of their court, but a very expensive one, particularly as it was always the King's expectation that he would be given a suitable present by his host on taking his departure.

Giving presents to people in the train of visiting celebrities was a favorite pastime of this monarch of muddle and misrule. Even so small a matter as the proper reward for Clair and Lancelot, the fiddlers of Guy of Lusignan (one of the dependent half brothers), was deemed worth his attention, with the result that the sum of thirty-three shillings and fourpence was set aside for each. In 1227 he directed that fifty pounds of almonds, fifty of raisins, and a frail of figs (a frail was a basket capable of holding up to fifty pounds, a great deal of figs, surely!) should be sent to the unfortunate Pearl of Brittany, who was then being kept in Bristol Castle.

It may have been that the affection existing between the King and his children was due in some measure to the fact that he himself never quite grew up and could enter wholeheartedly into their pleasures. One of the great interests in his life was the creation of a menagerie. There had not been one in England, and Henry was determined to correct this deficiency. He started off with three leopards which the Emperor of Germany sent him, a delicate compliment to a king whose flag was emblazoned with the leopards of England. They were placed in cages in the Tower of London, a fitting place of captivity when it is considered how many great Englishmen during the centuries which followed would be kept there in cages of forbidding stone. Lesser animals were added, and then to the great delight of the King an elephant was obtained from the East. Henry had all the affection of a boy for the pachyderm and wept as bitterly as any of his children when the news reached them that their huge pet, finding the atmosphere of the Tower oppressive, perhaps, had died. His indignation was great when he learned that the constable of the Tower, a caitiff of blunted susceptibilities, had buried the body in the Tower ditch, and he sent off a peremptory order for the bones to be dug up at once and shipped to Westminster for a more fitting interment. Richard of Cornwall sent the King a herd of buffalo which proved a vexatious problem because they could not be kept with the rest of the menagerie. Finally the great favorite of all was added to the collection, a white bear. All members of the royal family loved the bear, but it became in a sense a symbol of the King's tyranny over London. He was always demanding that something be provided for Bruin; a muzzle, a chain of iron, a daily fee of fourpence to provide the animal with suitable food.

It was no secret to those about him that Henry had never quite shaken off his adolescence, as shown by his exaggerated notions, his sudden passions and abrupt shifts of mood. There was a strange creature about the court who had been a priest but was now kept as a jester. When the King's half brother Aymer came to England from Poitou he and Henry would indulge in rough games with the not-overly-bright clown, pelting him with clods in summer and snowballs in winter, laughing uproariously the while.

Sometimes a saying of curious wisdom would issue from the mouth of this uncouth court fool. One evening at court he suddenly piped up in his shrill voice: "Hear ye, hear ye, my masters! Our King is like unto the Lord Jesus Christ."

The King turned his head expectantly. It was quite clear that he was pleased, anticipating some complimentary allusion.

"Why so, sir fool?" he asked.

"Because the Lord was as wise at the moment of his birth as when he was thirty years old. So likewise our King is wise at this moment"—the jester paused and winked slyly at the company—"as when he was a little child!"

Henry's high neighing laugh did not join in that of his courtiers. The King was not amused.

The troubles of the royal couple, their discontents, their fears, their jealousies, were freely displayed before the princes and princesses. The children grew up, therefore, in full knowledge of the situation which existed, and their sympathies were strongly aroused in their parents' behalf. They probably shared in the exultation of their mother when she learned that the original copy of Magna Charta had been destroyed in a fire at the papal palace in Rome. She believed this meant that the Charter had ceased to exist and they would never again have to bother about its vexatious clauses and restrictions! They undoubtedly joined in their father's perturbation when the royal cupboard became so bare that orders had to be issued to John Mansel to raise money by pledging a valuable image of the Virgin Mary. Henry was sincerely devoted to the ritual of the Church, and it would take a serious crisis to bring him to such a pass.

The whole family shared in a most distressing misfortune, the loss of their home. The Second King's House, as the new buildings at Windsor were called, began to fall to pieces. They were of stout enough construction, but there had been a miscalculation as to what the chalk ledge would hold. Seams opened up in the walls and a tendency to sag was noticed. Then the Almoner's Tower gave way. The crenelated ramparts buckled and heaved; the walls crumbled and finally down they came with a resounding crash and a cloud of dust which mounted higher than the top of the keep. The children were hastily removed to the First King's House, and it was well that they were, because next the curtain toppled over the edge of the escarpment and even the King's chamber, which they had hoped would stand, began to show signs of disintegration. After making some renovations the third Henry, a much crestfallen and indignant man, moved with his family to what was left of Henry I's quarters.

Although a builder of taste and perception, Henry had very bad luck with his undertakings. His efforts to raise a stone wharf on the Thames side of the Tower of London resulted in two costly cave-ins and a rumor in London that the spirit of Thomas à Becket was interfering with the work. He persevered, nevertheless, and finally succeeded in erecting a stone crib which stood resolutely and permanently against the currents and tides of Thames water.

3

Princess Margaret's early days were spent at Windsor. Soon after her birth Edward was given the royal castle of Eltham as his residence, and her companions at first were Edmund and a daughter of the Earl of Lincoln who lived as a ward with the royal family. Later there were more brothers and sisters and more wards, and so Margaret's childhood was a pleasant one.

She more than fulfilled the promise of beauty which had sent Henry so eagerly to her cradle with his hands full of gold; a dark and lively child, full of the joy of life, a little impulsive, a little hasty of temper. When she was still a small girl the King of Scotland died, leaving a son named Alexander as his heir. The boy was a year younger than the English princess, but in order to assure a continuance of peace between the two countries a marriage was arranged between them. There was much sadness at Windsor when it was known that little Margaret was to be taken away. The princess herself seemed well disposed to the idea of being a queen and having a crown of her own, but she dreaded the separation it involved. The Scottish prince was crowned Alexander III when he was eight years old, and the marriage was solemnized at York two years later. It was an imposing ceremony and, of course, involved the bride's father in unnecessary mountains of debt as well as practically ruining the Archbishop of York, who had to entertain hundreds of visitors. The departure of the darkly lovely bride for her new home was not as keenly felt when it was seen that the youthful couple had conceived a romantic liking for each other.

But the reports which came back from Scotland soon thereafter were most disturbing. The stern regents of Scotland, John Baliol and Robert de Ros, had decided that their King and his bride must be kept in rigid separation until they were old enough for matrimony. Margaret was placed in Edinburgh Castle under conditions which amounted almost to imprisonment. Finally a letter from the little Queen herself was smuggled out of the castle and reached her parents. It painted an even more alarming picture. She was a prisoner, she was suffering from ill-health, her appeals to the stern Scottish lords had no effect. She begged her father to lead an army into Scotland and set her free.

The consternation of the royal parents was so great that they would gladly have done as she wished. First, however, a physician of high standing, Master Reginald of Bath, was sent to Scotland to see about the health of the young Queen. He found Margaret pale and far from well and in a state of intense unhappiness. Master Reginald, unfortunately for himself, complained publicly about the treatment of the English princess. He took ill and died with suspicious suddenness, and it was believed in England that he had been poisoned to prevent an unfavorable report from being made.

The matter had now reached a stage where official action was necessary. Two crown commissioners were sent to Scotland, the Earl of Gloucester and John Mansel, with a large train. They were received coldly by the regents, and their right to visit the young Queen was denied. John Mansel was too resourceful to fail in his mission because of such a rebuff. The two commissioners dressed themselves as knights in the livery of Robert de Ros and as such they were rather grudgingly admitted at the gate. Once inside, they drove the custodians away from the portal and the signal was given to the rest of their company, who had lurked out of sight at the foot of the steep incline. The party rode at top speed up the black whinstone road and were inside the courtyard before any resistance could be offered.

They found that great pile of masonry which frowns down on the Scottish capital and which is sometimes called the Castle of Damsels to be as Margaret had said in her letters, "a sad and solitary place." She existed in a few cheerless rooms with a small group of stern and disapproving servants. She took her meals on the vaulted ground floor and, as she was served the same food as her attendants, it may be taken for granted that the fare never varied: strong mutton, oatmeal cakes, and pease bannock. All she could see from her chamber window in the tower was a patch of sky above the castle walls and, across the enclosure, the little chapel called St. Margaret's after that fine queen who had been the mother of Good Queen Mold, Henry I's Saxon bride. The only hint of liveliness about the place was an occasional skirl of bagpipes.

The commissioners found the unhappy little Queen very pale and thin and, obviously, in poor health. Her spirit had not been touched, however, and she talked to them eagerly and vehemently. She begged them to return to England as fast as their horses would carry them and to convince her father that he must use force if necessary to get her out of the clutches of these grim guardians.

It had been an easy enough matter to force an entrance into the castle, but it now became apparent that getting away would be much more difficult. Armed forces had been collected in the city, and the road down from the fortress was strongly blockaded. It looked as though the Earl of Gloucester and that scheming fox, Master Mansel, and all their company were doomed to share the captivity of the lady in whose behalf they had come. The regents knew, however, that such a course would provoke war, and they were not prepared to go that far. There was much parleying back and forth, and finally the commissioners and their attendants were permitted to make their exit from the Castle of Damsels and to return to England as fast as the little Queen had requested.

The result of the report they took Henry was that he moved north with a large enough force to leave no doubts as to the belligerency of his intent. The regents, startled at this development, came to a conference to discuss more suitable living conditions for the young Queen. It was agreed to allow her fuller freedom of movement, some opportunities to enjoy the company of her youthful husband, and to put in charge of her household two noblemen who were friendly to the young couple: Patrick, Earl of Dunbar, and Malice, Earl of Stratherne.

An anecdote must be related in this connection. Roger Bigod, Earl of Norfolk, who was marshal of England because he was the son of Matilda, oldest daughter of William Marshal, interceded for Robert de Ros, who lay heavily under the King's displeasure. There was a good reason for Bigod's championship, his wife being a Scottish princess, but Henry took it amiss. He glared at his marshal and declared that anyone who could beg easy treatment for such a man must be a traitor himself.

"You lie!" said the earl. "I have never been a traitor and I never shall be. And it's not in your power to harm me."

Henry fell into a towering rage. "Ha! I can seize your corn and thresh it and sell it!" he retorted.

"And I," declared Bigod, "can send back your threshers without their heads."

The quarrel simmered down after others intervened. Robert de Ros suffered no other punishment than dismissal from office. But from that time on Roger Bigod was on the popular side in the great struggle between the barons and the King. Henry's sharp tongue was always doing him disservice.

Things went much more smoothly after this, and in the course of time Alexander and Margaret were judged old enough to live together. It proved a happy marriage. There was only one drawback, the suspicion and disfavor with which the Scottish nobility regarded Margaret's desire to go on visits to her royal father and mother. The first visit was to her parents at Woodstock Castle. Margaret was sixteen then and had become a beautiful woman, with lustrous dark hair and proud brown eyes. When Henry learned that the party was drawing near he got to horse and rode out to meet his daughter. As soon as the visitors hove in sight he set his horse to the gallop in his great impatience. Margaret, certain that the solitary horseman approaching was her father, put spurs to her own horse and left her escort far behind. Henry leaned over from his saddle to embrace her, and Margaret laughed happily and said she had been longing for this moment for years.

Her first child, a daughter, arrived at Windsor on her next visit, and there was furious resentment in Scotland over the birth of their princess on foreign soil. Nothing could keep Margaret from returning to England, however. She was never popular with her subjects as a result, and her husband suffered from their belief that he was being influenced to favor the English connection. He wept bitterly when she died at Cupar Castle after a long visit in England, but the flinty eyes of his nobility were dry. They were glad to be rid of the Sassenach woman.

4

There was a poignant mingling of joy and unhappiness for the royal parents in the brief life of their last child, Katherine, who was born on November 25, 1253. It was apparent from the first that the infant gave great promise of beauty, but as she lay silently in the costly nest provided for her and showed no signs of reaction to sounds when old enough for some manifestations of an awakening interest in life, the Queen and her attendants realized that the little princess was deaf and dumb. Henry was abroad when she was born, and on his return a year later he was as delighted at the extreme beauty of his small daughter as he was distressed over her disabilities. She was lovelier than the impulsive Margaret or the equally pretty second princess, Beatrice, and her disposition was sweet and even. Her patient smiles led Henry into an orgy of spending for her. He ordered gold cloth for dresses for his little Katherine and he distributed among her servants and nurses a sum the equivalent of several hundred pounds in modern currency.

The royal parents watched over their latest child with a solicitude they had never displayed before. All the doctors of London, all five of them, must have been consulted in the parental determination to see her cured, and there was much corresponding with authorities before the bitter truth was accepted that Katherine would never be able to hear or speak. She continued of an angelic disposition, but she did not grow as she should, adding greatly to the grief of the parents. Finally she was sent to Swallowfield, where the air was believed to possess special qualities, and placed in the care of one Emma St. John. As the child displayed a great interest in animals, many pets were found for her, even a young kid which was caught in the woods. This small playmate did something to sweeten the last months in the life of the unfortunate princess, although nothing served to lengthen it.

The grief of the King and Queen when she died was so intense that both fell seriously ill. Henry's first act on recovering sufficiently to leave his couch was characteristic: he ordered one Master Simon de Welles to make a brass figure for the tomb of the dead child in Westminster at a cost of fifty-one pounds, twelve shillings, and fourpence. On second thoughts he was convinced that this tribute fell far short of expressing the intensity of his grief. Mere brass would never do. An order was given accordingly to the King's goldsmith, William of Gloucester, to carve the figure in solid silver. Henry seems to have been satisfied with the work the goldsmith produced, for he paid seven hundred pounds from the royal coffers, which, it is needless to state, perhaps, were in a sorry condition at the time.

This was one of the few extravagances with which his subjects found no fault. There was general grief over the death of the child, and a poet of the day spoke of her as falling fast asleep after one glimpse at a world she did not like.

5

At all stages of this long reign and in every mention of the home life of the royal family the figure of the King's brother, Richard of Cornwall, looms up prominently, and so it may be in order to deal with him and his career specifically.

The first mention in history of Richard is when he was taken at the age of six to Corfe Castle with a priest, two trumpeters, and a washerwoman. He was kept at Corfe for several years under the tutelage of Sir Roger d'Acestre, who must have found his royal pupil bright and receptive. It is very evident that Richard demonstrated from his earliest years a degree of shrewdness and a capacity for order in direct contrast to the scrambled confusion of Henry's thinking and living. He was a most likable boy, of an easy temper but always firmly certain of what he wanted to do.

At first the second son was awarded honors and properties with great caution. He was given nothing outright, in fact, all gifts being "during pleasure." To be granted seizin of the honor of Eye, for instance, was of little consolation when a legal string was attached by which it could be yanked back at adequately endowed, the young Richard began to wax prosperous at an early age. He disagreed continuously with Henry over decisions of state (and always seems to have been right), and the reconciliations which followed invariably resulted in some advantage for the younger brother, an honor or two, some manor houses, an additional slice of revenue. It was not until his second marriage, however, that he and Henry came to definite terms. On wedding Sanchia, Richard renounced his rights to lands in Ireland and Gascony in return for an irrevocable endowment of his estates in Cornwall and the honors of Wallingford and Eye.

From that point onward the acqusitive Richard began to display the Midas touch in everything he did. He soon had enough ready wealth to finance campaigns and to supply deficiencies in the royal coffers. On one occasion he loaned Henry two thousand pounds to pay the expenses of an expedition into Wales. He loaned money to bishops and barons, and always on the most solid security. It is not on record that the farsighted younger brother ever experienced loss as a result of putting money out on loan.

It has been generally believed that he owed his great wealth (for he became known in due course as the richest man in Europe) to the tin mines of Cornwall, the stannaries, and the labor of slaves who toiled and moiled in getting out the metal. The truth is that his possession of the mines proved profitable to him, but they did not play any very great part in the building of his considerable fortune.

In the first place, the worker in the stannaries, although he had no better legal status than a villein, was not bound to remain at his labor over buddle and smelty. He could at any time shoulder his poll pick and go out "bounding," which meant prospecting for new stores of tin or hunting along the streams for "shode," as rough boulders of the metal were called. The mines were not very deep at this time; in fact, most digging was done along "shammels," a crude stage of boards just below the surface. Adits, or drainage tunnels, kept the diggings dry and reasonably well ventilated. Here, with much back-breaking labor over windlass and horse-whimsey, but not in complete darkness or great discomfort, the miners hewed out the splendid tin for which all Europe competed and from which alone the best grades of pewter could be made. So much store was set on keeping up the quality of output from the stannaries that the King's inspectors kept their stamping hammers sealed when not in use. This would seem to indicate that the profits from English tin were enormous, but it is a matter of record that during the years when he "farmed" the tin Richard of Cornwall's income from this source never ran above three thousand marks a year.

He was in a position in 1247 to achieve the greatest coup in a career as brightly studded with successful deals as a midsummer sky with stars. There had been no issue of money since the days of Henry II, and it was decided that the minting of a new coinage could no longer be postponed. The King's brother seems to have been the only man in a position to assume such a formidable undertaking, and so an agreement was made by which he would "farm" the Mint for fourteen years. Richard set to work in a thoroughly businesslike way and succeeded in putting the manufacture of money on a better basis than ever before. It must be explained that the only coins in actual existence were silver pennies and halfpennies. There was continual talk of pounds, marks, and shillings, but no such pieces of money had ever existed. They were what is called coins of account and were used for purposes of calculation only. The problem before Richard, therefore, was to call in the old pennies—clipped, shaved, sawed, and depreciated as they were—and to make enough new money to replace the old and to supply the need for new.

The agreement reached was that Richard would finance the operation and divide the profits equally with the King. The first step taken was to establish local mints, each of them with four moneyers, four keepers of the dies, two goldsmiths, and a clerk. Capital was needed for the establishment of the branch mints, and Richard followed a method which has been employed successfully ever since. He loaned each branch the sum of one thousand pounds and kept a share of the profits by way of repayment. Under an ordinance of March 1248 tenpence in every pound was allowed the Mint as its profit, while sixpence (half of which would go to Richard, half to the King) was set aside as the royal share. Richard was thus in a position to make a great deal more on his financing of the local mints than out of his share of the net profits.

For many centuries the Trial of the Pyx had been a method of approving new money before it was put into circulation. A group would be called together in the Tower of London, consisting of the King, his chief officers, twelve citizens of

London, and the controller of the Mint. A selection of the new coins would then be tested and weighed by goldsmiths. When the time came to put Richard's issue to the official test it was found that the new pennies were well and truly made. The necessary approval was given.

The first division of the profits was made in 1253, when the King and his brother each received £5,513. The total profit that Richard of Cornwall collected was in the neighborhood of £11,000, but this did not take into account the money he made on his loans, which has been estimated at £20,000 in all. This was an enormous fortune and made it possible for the farseeing Richard to undertake the greatest deal of his career, which will be described in due course.

During the fourteen years that he conducted the minting operations about one million pounds' worth of pennies were made and put into circulation. The task had been carried out with complete success.

When he left for Germany to engage in an adventure which would put a crown on his brow, his brother, the King, decided that he could now indulge himself in an experiment on which Richard had frowned. Henry had always wanted to have the finest money in the world, gold to wit, and as soon as Richard turned his back he began to lay his plans for the minting of gold pennies. One gold penny was to be worth twenty silver ones and they would be, decided Henry, the most beautiful coins ever issued from the stamps. The King lingered long and lovingly over the sketches, changing, adjusting, throwing them out, and starting over again. The design he finally evolved was much the finest that had ever been stamped on an English coin, and Henry had good reason to be proud of it.

He soon discovered, however, that he should not have rushed into his grand scheme without giving due heed to his financial and commercial advisers, all of whom had been against it. The beautiful gold pennies proved a drug on the market. Few people could afford to have them in their possession, and the matter of changing them was a continual source of trouble and annoyance. It reached a state where men refused to accept gold pennies. The handsome new coins, so lovingly designed and so accurately stamped, remained piled up in the shops of the moneyers. A most difficult situation developed because of the amount of capital thus tied up unproductively. The merchants of the country complained bitterly, and finally London sent a deputation to the Exchequer to tell Henry to his face that the issue was a failure and that in addition it was depreciating the value of gold. They demanded that the new pennies be withdrawn so that financial equilibrium could be restored.

"Never!" cried the King, his face red with anger.

It happened soon after that nature took a hand in complicating the situation still further. An unseasonable frost came, and the crops suffered, and the leaves of fruit trees drooped and turned brown and sere. The moon, usually benign but now prompted by some diabolical agency (or so men supposed), had a mischievous effect on the tides, and the catch of fish suffered. The run of jack barrel was small, and no longer did plaice and sole come riding in with each wave from the North Sea as though willing to be caught, salted, packed in casks, and sent around to fill the stomachs of hungry Englishmen. Money became as scarce as food, but still the stubborn King would not give in. The gold pennies continued to collect dust and to tarnish in the safe boxes of the mints. It was not until the year 1270, in fact, that Henry would acknowledge his mistake by permitting the coins to be melted. It had been a costly fiasco.

While on the subject of Richard of Cornwall, it should be mentioned that he had the habit of marrying beautiful women. His first wife was Isabella, the handsomest of the rosy-complexioned, chestnut-haired Marshal daughters. Sanchia of Provence, the second, was acknowledged to have a softer and more winsome type of good looks than either Queen Marguerite of France or Queen Eleanor of England, although the fourth sister, Beatrice, was growing up now and threatening to excel them all. It is possible that the Earl of Cornwall would have cast his eyes in the direction of the radiant Beatrice if Sanchia had died somewhat sooner. Beatrice had married Charles of Anjou, however, before the gentle Sanchia fell into one of the declines which carried away so many of the women of this day and age. To cast ahead of the story, Richard won as his third bride the greatest beauty in all Europe, a snow-white German princess named Beatrice of Falkenstein. He loved all three wives, but it is reasonable to assume that he approached matrimony with a calculating eye and made sure that he was getting the best the market had to offer.

It will be clear by this time that Richard of Cornwall had all the qualities the King should have possessed. He would have made a good king, much the kind that Henry VII proved to be nearly three hundred years later. Without a doubt he would have kept the country at peace and put the administration of the laws on a sound basis. He had none of the qualities which make bad kings, cruelty, pride, stubbornness, lust for power, power, and more power. Paradoxically it was a good thing for England that Henry was the one to arrive first in the world and not Richard. It needed a ruler of the stamp of Henry, treacherous, vacillating, wrong-headed, to drive the baronage into a rebellious mood and so reap the democratic gains which came later.

CHAPTER FIFTEEN

Simon de Montfort

SIMON de Montfort was a Norman. The family name was derived from a small castle called Montfort l'Amauri in the lower corner of the duchy, but the importance of his ancestors was far greater than this might suggest. They traced descent back to Charles the Bald, and one of the warrior counts (all the Montforts were great fighting men) had married an heiress of Evreux with wide possessions as well as illustrious connections.

The Montforts were one of the families which were squeezed when the French took Normandy away from England in John's reign. They had fought at Hastings, and one of them, called Simon III in family annals, had become Earl of Leicester through marriage with Amicia de Beaumont. When Philip Augustus of France completed his seizure of Normandy it became necessary for men who held possessions on both sides of the Channel to choose which they intended to be, subjects of England or France. The fourth Simon in the Montfort line elected to serve the kings of France. John promptly declared a confiscation of all his lands and honors in England, although five years later he agreed to put the estates and earldom of Leicester in the hands of Ranulf of Chester "to be held for the said Simon." In the meantime De Montfort had been entrusted with the terrible task of crushing the Albigenses, a powerful sect of Catharistic dissenters from the Church of Rome who were located in great strength around Toulouse. He was a remarkable man, tall and handsome in person, thorough and able as a soldier, and animated with a fanatical zeal which enabled him to consider his mission a crusade. He had succeeded in crushing the schism with great cruelty by the time he fell in battle before the city of Toulouse in 1218. His eldest son, Amauri, continued the work with indifferent success but was made constable of France and showered with honors which his father had earned.

The only other surviving son of the Scourge of the Albigenses was named Simon, the fifth of the line. It is not known where he was born, and although 1208 is accepted as the likely date of his birth, this is a conjecture. He grew up to resemble his father in person—a tall and powerfully built youth with the dark good looks of the South. It was difficult in times such as these to form early judgments of the sons of great families. They were almost certain, because of the privileges of their class, to be pleasure-loving, arrogant, even cruel. How far the young Simon shared in these characteristics is not known, but it was apparent from the first that he took after his famous father in other respects than the nobility of his countenance and the magnetic darkness of his eyes. He had early the strong will and soldierly ability which were so marked in the sire. Other qualities which he inherited would develop later, as well as some magnificent characteristics, and some faults, which were all his own.

That he came to England at all was due to the selfishness of his older brother. In 1220 the Council ruling England during the minority had formally confirmed Chester in the possessions and earldom of Leicester. Amauri protested loudly and bitterly but, getting no satisfaction, proceeded to make a deal with young Simon. If the latter would yield all claims to share in the continental possessions of the family, he should have in exchange whatever he could salvage in England. The cadet accepted this one-sided arrangement, having in all probability no alternative.

Young Simon arrived in England, therefore, in 1229, as handsome and promising a soldier of fortune as ever set foot on English soil. He seems to have had some education but, naturally enough, he spoke no word of the native language. The Chester claims to Leicester had by this time the sanction of years, and the quest of the young claimant seemed hopeless. He had sold his birthright in France to his older brother for something less than a mess of pottage.

Henry, a few years his elder, took an immediate fancy to him, however, and would have been happy to make a settlement in his favor. There could be no interference with the rights of such a powerful noble as Ranulf of Chester, and this the King realized, although he dropped a hint in the ear of the young stranger that the matter might be arranged to suit him at some later date. In the meantime a pension of four hundred marks a year would be given him if he cared to enter the royal service. The claimant was very much disappointed but had enough common sense to accept the King's terms.

The following year Henry, in his shining armor, made his descent on the coast of Brittany which has already been described. Ranulf of Chester was one of the army leaders, and among the lesser members of the royal train was Simon de Montfort, ready and eager to display devotion to his new master. Because the expedition proved the most spectacularly unsuccessful of all Henry's military fiascoes, the chance did not come, but the presence of the young knight led to a very happy development in his family claim. He met the old earl and made a plea for the return of the possessions of his immediate ancestors. Ranulf of Chester had on several earlier occasions displayed a rare degree of magnanimity, but his capacity for generosity now attained its highest peak. Perhaps he had been mellowing with the years or perhaps his possessions were so wide that he put small store in the honors of Leicester. Whatever the reason, he consented to step aside and allow the young stranger to secure his inheritance.

Simon de Montfort described this incident as follows: "He consented, and next autumn took me with him to England, and besought the King to receive my homage for my patrimony, to which, as he said, I had more right than he; and he quit-claimed to the King all that the King had given him therein; and the King received my homage and gave me back my lands." Ranulf seems to have been very thorough in his generosity, initiating each legal step necessary to confirm the transfer. It is certain that he had taken a liking to the Norman cadet, an easy thing to do because the newcomer had ingratiating manners and a way of making friends; most of whom, as it developed, remained loyal to him through all his shifts of fortune and his political ups and downs.

As a result of the Earl of Chester's compliance, Henry

issued instructions on August 13, 1231, that Simon de Montfort was to have seizin on all the lands his fathers had held and which belonged to him by hereditary right. The gamble the younger son had taken had paid him well after all. He was now a peer of England, in high favor at court, and presumably on his way to fortune.

Young Simon soon discovered, however, that there was a worm at the core of his apple of content. The Leicester estates, spreading over a dozen counties, had been divided several generations back between Amicia and a young sister. To make matters worse, the men who had been in charge during the years when his land had been in royal hands had not only done well for the Crown but had feathered their own nests. They had driven off the stock and cut the wood and depleted the game. The once proud demesne was now in a condition of impoverishment. Although not yet ranked a full earl, the new owner had to maintain a household of some size and dignity, and the revenue did not equal the cost. After two years spent in the most awkward poverty he considered making a second deal with his sharp older brother by which he would sell back the title and honors he had recovered. Most fortunately he took no more than a tentative step in that direction. Perhaps he was discouraged by the fear that he would be overreached again by that Norman of Normans, Amauri de Montfort.

The one sure avenue of escape from this embarrassment was to marry an heiress. That Henry did not arrange one for him is proof that there was none of sufficient wealth available in England at the moment. Simon, in a condition of mind which bordered on desperation, was on the point of wedding a middle-aged widow, Mahaut, the Countess of Boulogne, when fate in the guise of Louis of France intervened. Mahaut had broad lands and many castles and would gladly have married the handsome young nobleman, but the French peers thought it would be a mistake to hand over such large estates to a man who had entered the service of England. Mahaut was forbidden to marry him.

Simon then paid court to another widow, Joan, the Countess of Flanders. Joan was even more blessed with worldly goods than the dowager of Boulogne, having great stretches of land and royal parks stocked with deer, and doppings and nyes and springs and sieges of game birds, and here and there great castles topping Flanders' ridges and baileys filled with blooded stock. There was a suspicion that Simon had already contracted marriage with this mature catch when the first wind of it reached the French court. Countess Joan swore that, although willing to marry Simon, she had not done so. The prospective groom was ordered to depart forthwith.

Forced thus into the same position in which Henry had once found himself, Simon de Montfort gave up the idea of marriage for the time being. His fortunes would have to be repaired in some other way. There was relief for him, no doubt, in the decision. He was too much of a romanticist to relish marriage with a wife so much older than himself; and he had, moreover, fallen in love.

2

Behind Henry's chamber at Westminster there was a small chapel where he performed his daily devotions. It was beautifully decorated, for everything about the King had now a touch of sophisticated taste. The walls had hangings of his favorite color, green, and there were many articles of great rarity in this secluded corner where the master of England swore daily homage to a greater King.

One cold winter evening, immediately after the royal family had ridden back in great discomfort from the Christmas festivities at Winchester, when noble and bishop and great lady muffled themselves to the nose in fur-trimmed cloaks and lesser men remained indoors in huddled misery over smoking fires, on the evening of January 7, 1238, to be exact, it was apparent that there was some unusual activity afoot in the King's chapel. All the candles were lighted and a large brazier had been carried in filled with blazing charcoal to heat the tiny room, and Walter, the chaplain of St. Stephen's, was on hand in full canonicals. An air of secrecy was being maintained. All members of the royal retinue were elsewhere, even the Queen, from whom the uxorious King did not like to be parted, and the whole train of scornfully witty uncles and cousins, and the comfortably pensioned minstrels and the fat-paunched makers of rhyme. There were servants about, in fact, to bar the way if any curious souls attempted to see what it was all about. Only three people were admitted, and one of these was King Henry himself.

He was in a state of nervous excitement, as may reasonably be deduced from the known circumstances, chattering and quipping and smiling with pleasure, as was his wont at such moments. He was carrying out a little conspiracy at the expense of his Council and all his bishops and the nobility of England, and this pleased him mightily. He was pleased even though it was clear to him that there would be trouble about it. His realization of the certain consequences is evidenced by the fact that he had not dared take the Queen into his confidence.

The other two were Simon de Montfort and Henry's youngest sister, Eleanor, his favorite sister, in fact. The young widow who, as it will be recalled, had been so heartbroken over the death of her first husband, William of Pembroke, that she had sworn an oath of perpetual widowhood had developed into a woman of great beauty and charm, a slender and vital young creature with dark hair and the bluest of Plantagenet eyes. She had regretted almost from the first the impulsive manifestation of her youthful grief which had bound her, in a sense at least, to the Church. Certainly she had regretted it from the moment her eyes had rested on the dark and expressive face of the tall young Norman. The mutual attraction between them had deepened rapidly into a love which would continue throughout their lives, unchanged by swift alterations of fortune, never wavering when political considerations aligned them against the royal family.

How the consent of the King had been obtained to their union is a matter of conjecture, of course, but the reasons for secrecy in the matter are quite plain. No member of the royal family was supposed to wed without the consent of the Council, and Henry had known only too well the storm which would have been evoked if he had told his barons he intended to give his lovely sister to a man so newly attached to his service, a commoner, moreover, who had not yet given any proof of special merit or unquestioned loyalty. There was also, of course, the matter of that vow. Henry had a well-grounded suspicion that the church leaders were going to raise a whirlwind of protest about his ears.

It was typical of the King to decide under these circumstances that the marriage of his well-loved sister and his new friend should be solemnized anyway and to hold the services privately. Let the news get out later! Trouble in the future held no terrors for Henry: it could be met when it came, and in the meantime let the vows be exchanged, then eat, drink, and be merry at the wedding supper. He entered into the proceedings with a light heart. "Himself he placed his sister's hand in the earl's," and he knelt with the newly wed couple when Walter said mass over them.

The marriage of a royal princess under such romantic circumstances, with the King himself playing the part of a stealthy cupid, could not be kept secret long, and so the storm was quick in breaking. It raged about the King, the bitterest protests coming, as had been expected, from churchmen. Eleanor had not taken the veil and since the death of her husband she had lived much at court, where she was a general favorite. The rest of the time had been spent at her own castle of Odiham, where she kept a miniature court of her own and maintained a normal and gay life. Still, she had taken the vow of chastity, and it was the opinion of all churchmen that the placing of the ring on her finger had bound her indissolubly to Christ. The archbishop declared at once that the marriage was not valid. The barons joined in, adding as it were the rumble of secular anger to the treble of priestly disapproval. The objections of the laity were on two grounds: they had not been consulted and they were against the giving of such a supreme favor to a man of foreign birth. Richard of Cornwall was bitterly incensed and acted as spokesman for the nobility. Was this the result, he demanded to know, of all his brother's promises that he removed his own countrymen from the Council, to replace them by aliens, that he deigned not to ask the assistance of his constitutional advisers before bestowing his wards in marriage on whomsoever he would?

The news spread throughout the country, and there was an almost universal chorus of angry dissent. The barons were on the point of an armed uprising. London was filled with talk of intervention. Henry had known the wedding would stir up criticism, but he had not reckoned on anything like this. He was bewildered and frightened and at the same time angry that he had been involved—innocently, he thought—in so much trouble. In his mind already he was blaming his sister and the man of her choice. In an almost abject mood he promised to have some form of arbitration of the matter, although what results might be expected from such a course was not very clear.

The bridegroom was more realistic in the steps he took to counter the storm. He sought out Richard of Cornwall, with whom he had always been on friendly terms, and won him over by letting him see how much Eleanor's happiness had depended on the marriage. The princess was a radiant bride and ready to fight Church and State, Westminster and London and Canterbury and the whole nation if necessary, for the content she was finding in the union. The King's brother withdrew his objections. Since they lacked his support, the wrath of the barons fizzled out in a flurry of words.

Simon then demonstrated his sound political sense. He collected as much gold as he could from tenants and friends and set off hurriedly for Rome to get a confirmation of the marriage from the Pope. Henry did what he could by writing to the Pontiff that his dear brother and faithful servant, Simon de Montfort, was desirous of discussing matters touching his honor. Whether it was the groom's great gift for negotiation or the support he stirred up in the Curia by the judicious use of his gold, the result was that the Pope promised to pronounce sentence in his favor through his legate in England. The promise was carried out.

Simon de Montfort returned to England in a jubilant frame of mind over the success of his mission. He went at once to his castle of Kenilworth. In this immense stronghold, which covered eleven acres with its mighty walls, he had left his young wife. He was in time for the arrival of his first child, a son, who was given the name of Henry. The winds had veered to a favorable direction and the royal weathercock had swung with them. The King not only acquiesced in the use of his name but acted as godfather of the child.

There was not at this time a cloud as large as a man's hand in the sky, not a sign of rift in the relationship between the happy husband and father and his indulgent brother-in-law.

3

In his first appearances on the stage of English history Simon de Montfort does not show to advantage. He was ambitious and calculating. He had been prepared to marry either one of two women, both of whom were years older than himself, in order to mend his fortunes. From the very first he had been arrogant in manner and highly provocative in his opinions. This picture is more severe, however, than the facts warrant. It must be pointed out in his defense that he was in these respects a true son of his age, that he had acted in a manner common to all men of high station who faced life as penniless younger sons.

The adventurer who had raised his eyes so high and had been rewarded by the hand of a lovely princess must have displayed from the start some trace at least of the magnificent qualities which later would dictate the part he was to play in history. He won the friendship at once of men who were recognized as possessing the finest minds in the country. The first of these was Robert Grosseteste, who was archdeacon of Leicester when the young Norman came to assume his title and lands. There seems to have been an immediate liking between them, the great churchman sensing the splendid qualities dormant in the newcomer: his passionate religious convictions, his great capacity for loyalty to a cause, his sound judgment. Grosseteste did not lose touch with Simon when he left Leicester to become the Bishop of Lincoln but continued to correspond with him. Until the end of his life the great-hearted old bishop gave the Earl of Leicester his best advice and his deepest affection. It was through Grosseteste that Simon came to know Adam Marsh and Walter Cantilupe, who was later the Bishop of Worcester. Adam Marsh, a gentle Ulysses, whose letters to Simon are justly acclaimed the finest of their kind, continued to be his friend and mentor. Walter Cantilupe stood at Simon's right hand and was his chief prop and stay at all stages of the civil war. There can be no doubt that these wise and courageous men saw great possibilities in the ambitious young Norman at the very beginning. None found any reason later to change his mind.

In the letters which passed back and forth among the members of this illustrious circle the admiration of the churchmen for the young peer is manifest. Adam Marsh wrote to Walter Cantilupe at a time when Henry and his new brother-in-law were embroiled over affairs in Gascony, "Thanks to the eternal mercy of God, a new light of heavenly justice seems to rise in the King's mind for the affairs of the Earl of Leicester." He wrote letters to the Archbishop of Rouen most earnestly commending Simon to him. To Simon himself he addressed many letters for the purpose of blowing the coals of the earl's religious convictions to a still warmer blaze. "Work I beg of you, to gain the salutary comfort of the divine words," ran one letter. "Meditate often upon the Holy Scriptures." That Simon was receptive to such advice is evident from another letter. "What noble rewards, illustrious earl, will you receive in the kingdom of God for the happy solicitude with which you plan to purify, enlighten and sanc-

tify the children of God by a government which well befits it."
This extract is from one of the later letters,[1] addressed to
Simon when the latter had achieved political stature and was
pressing for improvements in the government of the kingdom.
That Adam Marsh was heart and soul with the popular cause
is made clear in the course of the correspondence. "I shall
take no rest," he declared once, "until I have learned of the
success of your cause." It may be assumed from this that the
national needs were close to the hearts of this remarkable
coterie. Grosseteste died before matters came to a head, but it
is inconceivable that he would have failed to station himself in
the forefront of reform.

The wisest men in the land might perceive the promise of
greatness in the newcomer, but others were less observant. To
the members of the nobility he was just another foreigner,
elevated over their heads by the perverse preference of the
King. The same view, no doubt, was held by the common
people. Most women were attracted to him, partly by reason
of the curiosity always felt in a royal romance. The Queen
shared this predilection even though the Queen's Men regarded him with active antagonism. To the uncles and aunts
he was another head tussling successfully for a place at the
trough of royal favor.

The King's Men, when they descended on the bounty of
Henry a few years later, made Simon the object of bitter opposition. Never being one to accept a slight or rebuff in silence, he made more enemies than friends during the first
years of his residence in England. It is certain, however, that
in the never-ending friction between the King and his subjects
his sympathies were with Henry. He was, after all, a stranger, unfamiliar with the temperament of the people, unaware
as yet of the deep differences in English and French conceptions of the relationship of king to subject. Henry was his
benefactor, his friend, the brother of his beloved Eleanor. It
would have been strange indeed if he had failed to range
himself on the side of the topsy-turvy tyrant, even though in
court circles he encountered black looks and undercurrents of
hostility.

4

The marriage of Simon and Eleanor, in spite of temperamental disagreements, may be termed one of the great ro-

[1] These extracts are from *Simon de Montfort* by C. Bémont.

mances of the century. There can be no doubt that the princess was deeply in love with her commoner husband. She clung to him through thick and thin, through poverty and exile, a passionately devoted wife. Simon could not have failed of a corresponding devotion. Eleanor was hard to resist, a beauty even in this day of great pulchritude among the daughters of ruling families, coquettish, willful, capricious, in all her moods charming. She came to her second marriage with the faults still of a childhood during which she had been a general favorite. Love of fine clothes was a passion with her, and she spent much of her time in the adornment of her person and the dressing of her fine hair. She seems to have been subject to gusts of anger which were soon over. Adam Marsh, who wrote to her as freely as he did to her husband, took her to task sometimes for this tendency to fly into tempers as well as for the extravagant taste she showed in matters of dress. In one note he urged her to "display all your industry and tact in putting an end to these irritating disputes." The troubles which had evoked this piece of advice were not entirely of Eleanor's making, for their mentor proceeded to explain that by her sweetness and good advice she should be able to bring Simon to more prudent conduct. The quarrels of the lovers whose marriage had set all England by the ears were never serious and may be considered to have been no more than the salt of a happily wedded life.

Simon and his princess bride had, nevertheless, plenty to disturb them. Eleanor brought an intricately involved mass of assets and debts instead of a proper dower, largely because the Marshal family had not yet been sufficiently pressed to return the estates with which she had been endowed at the time of her first marriage. She had an annual income of four hundred pounds for which she had bartered her share of the Irish holdings of the acquisitive Marshals; a most one-sided arrangement which Henry should never have approved. Simon's position remained one of intense pecuniary difficulty. Naturally the extravagant habits of Eleanor made things worse.

It was a regal life they lived at Kenilworth. The castle was an immense clutter of buildings around Caesar's Tower, which was counted impregnable with its double ramparts and moat. The manors and hunting lands extended over twenty miles of wooded land. Here they lived and ruled in feudal state. They had a mill for the grinding of the tenants' grain and a market each Tuesday for the exchange of commodities. They had their own courts of justice, where prices were regulated, disputes settled and crimes tried; they had their own prisons and gallows. The earl and his bride began to collect a library, to act as patrons of literature, to entertain the most intelligent men in the kingdom. Their household was enormous and, although little was given the retainers in the way of pay, the drain on their combined purse was little short of ruinous.

Eleanor continued to be extravagant, but at the same time she became a good chatelaine and managed her end of this gigantic establishment with some shrewdness. This is attested by a curious document which has, by the greatest good luck, survived down the centuries. It is called *The Household Roll of Eleanor, Countess of Leicester.* The countess took it with her to France when she had to flee England near the end of her life. As she spent the rest of her days at the nunnery of Montargis, it is probable that the manuscript was kept in the archives there. Five hundred years later it was discovered and taken back to England, to provide an authentic picture of the life of a great castle in the thirteenth century.

It does more than that, however: it offers to the imagination an enticing picture of the daughter of the royal house playing the part of wife and domestic manager. Back of the precise items about food and drink and the prices thereof one sees the figure of Eleanor proceeding about her tasks, her assistants following at her heels with much jingling of keys and swishing of baskets, and no doubt much suppressed chatter and an occasional giggle. A preoccupied frown is on her face, her voice is often raised in sudden exasperation but dissolves quickly into laughter, her sense of justice is brought to any disputes with (or so we trust) the precepts taught by gentle Adam Marsh. This is not entirely fanciful, for it is recorded that, during the long periods when the warrior head of the family was away at the Crusades or fighting in Gascony, the princess he had married in the secrecy of the King's chapel spent her time quietly in the management of affairs at their chief castles of Kenilworth and Odiham and in raising their brood of children, seven in all, who accumulated rapidly about them.

The Roll deals with the humble details of everyday life and most particularly with costs. Take, for instance, the item of beer. It is possible to get from the prosaic notes entered in a clerkly hand a rather complete picture with reference to beer. Consumption was, of course, enormous, despite the fact that it was flat and insipid stuff. It was made without hops, and those who could afford to do so added spices and other ingredients to give it more taste. The brown-cheeked men in russet or green, bow at shoulder and quiver at belt, who gathered at Kenilworth for the assizes of beer and bread or the court-leet where offenders against the peace were put on trial, drank a great deal of the castle brew and more still at the taverns thereabouts, where they were prone to contribute a farthing for the addition of fennel, the licorice-flavored spice.

It may have been that Eleanor possessed a latent tendency to feminist doctrine, because she used a breweress in Banbury for the making of much of the beer consumed at Kenilworth. Although the idea of feminine equality was never voiced, women assumed a managing role throughout the Middle Ages. Men were so continuously away at war and, it must be confessed, so lacking in practical sense that their wives controlled the households and superintended the planting and harvesting of crops. In the cities they were partners in the shops, and it was as often as not a feminine hand which fell heavily on a careless apprentice, a feminine voice which drove the shrewdest bargains. It is on record in the Roll that on one day in April the countess purchased 188 gallons of beer from the stout breweress at a price which ran a little in excess of a halfpenny a gallon.

Wines were relatively expensive because the homemade varieties were not good, and cultivated palates demanded the finer kinds imported from Guienne and Gascony. The word bastard has always been much on the tongues of Englishmen, perhaps because it has such a good rough roundness to it, and it was applied to many things, to ships and sails and paper and to cloth of inferior quality as well as to the unfortunate and innocent victims of illicit love. It occurs frequently in the Roll, but there it is used to denote a sweet Spanish wine which resembled muscatel and which, apparently, was mixed with native wines to redeem their somewhat metallic flavor.

The information supplied about food has to do largely with meat. The usual varieties were eked out by the flesh of the kid and by venison, the latter being so highly favored that men would risk their lives to bring down a buck in forbidden woods. It was only in the warm seasons, however, that fresh meat was available. During the long winter, which was regarded as the season of the devil, people lived on salted meat and smoked fish. Sometimes, when spring was long in coming, the supply would run short and the contents of the soup pot would be far from satisfying. The consumption of fish at all seasons was tremendous, and in the Roll the names of a wide variety are to be found: sturgeon, conger, ling, mullet, mackerel, stockfish, sea bream, bar, flounder, salmon, plaice, dories, and sole. There was also much consumption of oysters, crabs, and shrimps, as well as fresh-water varieties, the dart, crayfish, eels, and lampreys.

The word *pullagium* occurs frequently to designate all forms of poultry and game, possibly also the strong-fleshed birds which were greatly liked for the medieval table but have since ceased to be considered edible, the peacock, swan, heron, and bittern.

The price of eggs, according to the Roll, was in the neighborhood of fourpence a hundred. They were used in great quantities for the table and, of course, in the preparation of such dishes as bread, puddings, and pastries. Men were immensely fond of pastry and did not mind if the lard which entered into it was strong. There is mention of one Easter Sunday when twelve hundred eggs were used at Kenilworth. They were no doubt stained the yellow of the anemone or pasqueflower and given to the tenants according to the usual custom.

The range of prices for table commodities was extremely wide, owing to the rarity of the much-prized foods from the East. Rice could be purchased for one and a half pence a pound, but the saffron to be used with it (no self-respecting matron would serve rice unless colored with saffron) was ten to twelve shillings a pound. Almonds cost twopence, but ginger was one hundred times as high. Cloves, the most treasured of all spices, cost from twelve shillings a pound up. There were many spices in more or less regular use which are little heard of today, such as galingale.

Except for items of this kind, Kenilworth seems to have been self-supporting. They raised their own cattle and sheep, and the broad fields between the stretches of green forest produced grain in abundance. The soil was fertile and so the crops were plentiful. The nobility and the people of the cities were hampered and irked by Henry's nonsense, but the man on the land does not seem to have suffered much by the misgovernment. The peasants in russet tunics who tilled the fields around Kenilworth always had full bellies and would have agreed that England was a merrie country.

Eleanor was temperamental and no doubt a little giddy, but the existence of the Roll is all the proof needed that she endeavored to meet her responsibilities in a thorough way.

CHAPTER SIXTEEN

The King Quarrels with
Simon de Montfort ·

FOLLOWING the birth of a child it was customary for the
mother, after a specified period of purification, to go publicly
to church and return thanks. On August 9, 1239, Simon de
Montfort and Eleanor, his wife, came to London for the
ceremony of the Queen's churching.

The young countess was in glowing health. Her own son
Henry, who had been born eleven months after the secret
marriage, thereby setting to rest (or so they thought) certain
malicious rumors which had been going about, was now eight
months old and a fine, healthy boy. The King seemed to have
forgotten completely the chidings he had absorbed as a result
of the unorthodox circumstances of their marriage. He could
throw off easily all such unpleasant things. The sun of royal
favor, in fact, had been shining high in the heavens. Simon
had been given possession of the London palace of the Bishop
of Winchester for the time of their stay in the city. It may
have been one of the bastel houses in the heart of the old city
which were always a source of surprise to anyone entering for
the first time. They were gloomy and unimpressive from the
street, over which they loomed darkly, but, once the copper-
studded door had been passed, they startled the eye with the
magnificence of a Great Hall, an arching maze of bog-oak

timbers and high galleries, a never-ceasing drone of priestly chantings from handsome chapels. It may have been, on the other hand, one of the newer seats out along the river toward Westminster, where ample land was available. Here, over stone walls, the houses raised their crenelated battlements and flying buttresses and the stone chimneys which were a continual wonder to common people who lacked chimneys of any kind. Whichever it was, the Earl of Leicester and his vivacious Eleanor were lodged in high state.

They were surprised, therefore, and most unpleasantly shocked to be received with angry looks when they put in an appearance at Westminster during the evening before the churching. The King indulged in a tirade of reproach, his high, thin forehead inflamed with anger, the velvet skirts of his super-tunic rustling and swishing as he strode up and down. Simon, he declared, was excommunicate. What effrontery was this, that he dared to come into the royal presence? Did he regard himself as above the laws of the Church or did he count too much on the unrequited favor of his liege lord?

The explanation of this totally unexpected outburst was given bit by bit as the King spluttered and fumed at them. Simon had owed a debt of 2,080 marks to Peter Mauclerc, the Duke of Brittany. When the creditor decided to go on the Crusades the collection of this debt was left to the courts of Rome. The papal officers had first threatened to lay an interdict on the lands of Leicester, then, finding it impossible to get blood from a stone, had transferred the debt to Thomas of Savoy, the Queen's uncle. This was unpleasant for the Earl of Leicester from two standpoints. In the first place, the King and Queen had been put under immediate pressure to obtain a settlement for the Queen's uncle, and in the second, it happened that Thomas of Savoy had married Joan, Countess of Flanders, after her betrothal to Simon had been broken, and this gave an edge of malice to his demands for payment. The King was furious that this trouble had risen to plague him and he raved at the debtor. Finally he ordered the astonished couple to leave. They were to betake themselves from his sight and never return.

The earl and his wife left Westminster by river boat. They were sick at heart over this sudden turn in their fortunes. Eleanor was finding it impossible to reconcile the royal attitude with the affection and extreme kindness her brother had always shown her. They had as yet no conception of the lengths to which he could go when thoroughly angry, but they had convincing evidence on reaching the water steps of Winchester House. Here they found the lock set against them. Henry had sent messengers galloping ahead to see that they were not allowed to enter.

Simon and Eleanor, as angry now as the King, collected their evicted servants and their possessions and found quarters in a London inn. This translation from the glory of an episcopal palace to the acrid smokiness and the cramped rooms of a tavern was sufficient to rouse their feelings to fighting pitch. As soon as they had seen their people settled the indignant pair rode back to Westminster to demand an explanation.

Henry met them with a still more astonishing blast. In the presence of members of his court he declared that they would not be allowed to attend the churching of the Queen. When a reason was demanded he left his chair and strode over to face the earl at close range.

"You seduced my sister!" he charged. The habit of losing all restraint and permitting himself to say anything that came into his head had been growing with the years. Perhaps not fully aware of the effect his statement would have, but certainly not concerned, he proceeded at once to enlarge on it. "To avoid scandal I gave my consent to the marriage, in my own despite. You went to Rome and corrupted the Curia most wrongfully in my name."

Having thus with a few furious words tarnished beyond any repair the good name of the sister who had always been his favorite, the vitriolic King went on to demonstrate that anger over the matter of the Mauclerc debt was at the bottom of his outburst. Simon, he said, had cited him as security without telling him of it. That he might be held responsible for the debt had caused him to lash out thus with the accusation which would be the most harmful.

The contemporary chronicles say that Simon de Montfort blushed and betook himself from the royal presence, a highly unperceptive reading of the character of this passionately proud man. If Simon de Montfort's face registered the emotion stirred in him by the insult thus publicly offered his wife it would be with the pallor of an anger too great for words. It is recorded that he said nothing and withdrew at once from the court, and this may be accepted as the truth.

The King, his anger mounting to still greater heights, hurried off orders to the commune of London to have the pair lodged in the Tower. As usual, however, Richard of Cornwall was there to prevent his brother from letting his temper carry him too far. Richard saw to it that the order was rescinded and then sent word to his sister that it would be wise for her to leave the city at once. As soon as night fell the Earl of Leicester and his wife, accompanied by a small party of their people, took boat again on the Thames and made off quietly down the river. They went to France and took up residence there.

2

Was there any truth in the charge of incontinence which Henry had made against his sister? It was widely believed at the time, if for no other reason than because the King himself had made it. It has been given little belief since. The date of the birth of Eleanor's first child seems to be the only proof needed that it was a libel. A sorry impression is left of the character of the King when his statement is brushed aside. He had idly and falsely, in a moment of petty passion, laid this shame on a sister who had been a lifetime favorite.

The Earl and Countess of Leicester lived in France for seven months. Henry remained antagonistic and did many things to show his spleen, and then suddenly veered in his feelings and invited them to return. Eleanor could not leave because she was expecting another child, but Simon arrived in England in response. He was welcomed by the King as though no rift had occurred between them. The court, taking its cue from the weathercock King, greeted him with a semblance of friendliness. Soon after his arrival Eleanor gave birth to their second child, a son who was named Simon.

Henry undoubtedly was quite sincere in extending the hand of friendship to the man he had injured so deeply, having forgotten by this time the sense of wrong which had led to his outburst. While accepting his protestations of regard, Simon felt no inner response. The insult had been of a nature no man could forget or forgive, particularly one of such fiery pride as the Earl of Leicester. It had been impossible for him to take the customary steps to protect his honor, and now he was obliged to bow and accept the proffer of renewed friendship. But Simon de Montfort neither forgot nor forgave.

Richard of Cornwall was organizing a party of English knights to go to the Crusades, and Simon was pledged to take the cross with him. His return to England had been partly for the purpose of making the necessary arrangements. It was a very expensive matter to go crusading. A knight required many horses for himself and his followers and a corresponding amount of arms and equipment. He needed also a substantial supply of gold because he paid his way both going and returning. Simon, who found the costs of peacetime living too much for him, encountered a great deal of difficulty in raising funds. He did not leave with Richard of Cornwall but went first to get Eleanor, who was insisting on accompanying him as far as possible. They traveled together to Brindisi, where the German Emperor, perhaps on prompting from his consort, who was Eleanor's older sister, had loaned for her use a huge, echoing stone palace overlooking the sea. Here she stayed with her small staff of servants, her mind filled with the dangers her husband was encountering in the East.

The Crusade proved to be a fruitless effort because a truce had been arranged before they arrived. That Simon found some way of distinguishing himself is evident, however, from the fact that the "barons, knights, and citizens of the kingdom of Jerusalem" wrote to Frederick of Germany requesting that he make Simon their governor pending the time when Conrad, the Emperor's son, would attain his majority and be capable of assuming the reins. Nothing came of it, but the incident makes it clear that the young earl had displayed some of the qualities of leadership which were to be so magnificently proven in later years.

CHAPTER SEVENTEEN

Simon de Montfort as the Seneschal of Gascony

NOTHING remained to Henry of the great Angevin possessions in France save Gascony, the southwest corner. Gascony was a land of hot sunshine, sloping down from the purple Pyrenees to the marshy lands along the Bay of Biscay. In the dunes the Gascons walked on stilts, and everywhere else they strutted with an equal stiff-leggedness through sheer pride, a canny and clever race who obtained a little more distinction than they perhaps deserved when a member of their clan, one M. d'Artagnan, was borrowed, a few centuries later, for the pages of a great adventure story. They were not particularly happy at remaining under English rule. From the year 1057 they had been governed by the dukes of Aquitaine and they had been kicked like a football between England and France after Eleanor, a lovely and self-willed young woman, became their duchess and married first Louis of France and then Henry II of England. They still cherished memories of the beautiful Eleanor, but this was a slender chain to hold their allegiance to the land where her descendants still reigned.

Gascony, in fact, wanted above everything to be independent, having no more love for the French than for the English, but independence was not easily obtainable for a small and poor province surrounded by strong and avaricious neighbors. The proud men of Bordeaux and Béarn and Bigorre felt eyes on their backs all the time, the eyes of the Count of Toulouse and the kings of Navarre and Castile, each of whom aspired to the mastery of Gascony; and, more than all, the orbs of the King of France, the likeliest of the feudal tomcats to swallow the Gascon mouse.

Unfortunately for their aspirations, the Gascons had never been able to establish any unity among themselves. Their counts and viscounts were a bitterly contentious lot, always fighting among themselves and burning towns and ravaging countrysides. The nobles were, for the most part, anti-English. There were a number of strong cities such as Bordeaux, Bayonne, Dax, and Bazas which thrived on the wine trade and were inclined in consequence to be pro-English. If the people of the cities had been able to live at peace among themselves they would have been strong enough to keep the rampaging nobles in order. They in turn, however, were split into two factions, the wine merchants against the less fortunate ones who lacked a share in that profitable business.

The cleavage in Bordeaux was particularly marked. This beautiful city lying on the west bank of the Garonne, with the great vineyards of Médoc behind it, was torn by a rivalry which suggests the struggles in Italy between rich and dynastic families. The Coloms were wine sellers, wealthy, aggressive, and notably pro-English. The Solers, whose interests centered in land, were not quite as rich as their rivals but had been holding the whip hand because of a special aptitude for political activities. The city had the right to select its own mayor and to fill the council or jurade, and because the Solers had a wily leader in one Rustengo de Soler, they had been monopolizing these offices. Rustengo had been in the wine trade at an early stage of his career, as witness an occasion during the reign of John when a cargo of his had been confiscated. Retiring with a considerable degree of wealth, he had become a landowner and was inclined to look down on those who still engaged in his earlier occupation. He lived in the city in a stone house which was large enough to accommodate some of his sons and their families as well as a great many servants and armed adherents. The house of old Rustengo had become the center of all Soler activities, and from it he craftily directed the government of the city with the dignity of a Montague or a Capulet and with more than a hint of the fine trappings of a doge of Venice.

Henry had appointed a succession of seneschals to represent him in Gascony, with conditions growing progressively worse all the time. The province had been brought close to the point of chaos by the bitter clashing of factions and the incapacity of the men the King had sent to govern the country.

2

On May 1, 1248, Henry appointed Simon de Montfort seneschal of Gascony. There was general approval of the move and a feeling that at last the right man had been found to curb the contentious Gascons and establish order in the land. At first Simon held back from accepting, knowing perhaps how much he would be hampered by the vacillation and the interference of the King. He demanded an absolutely free hand for seven years, a grant of two thousand marks a year, and the military support of fifty knights. Henry, unwilling to allow a subject so much authority, gave in with reluctance and agreed grumblingly to all the conditions. He kept none of them, of course, after the first few months.

Simon went about his task with great energy and foresight. Blanche of Castile had resumed the regency of France when Louis set off for the Crusades again, and the new seneschal went to her first. They agreed to a truce for two months. He then traveled on to Gascony, arriving in considerable state with his train of fifty knights and proceeding at once to let the robber barons and the quarreling citizens know that he intended to be master. That he made mistakes at first is only too clear, particularly in the severity of the methods he adopted. From the first moment, however, that the hoofs of his weary steed raised Gascon dust from the hot white roads he demonstrated something which would later make him the great benefactor of the English. His policy was to break the power of the nobility. The reason for this was partly one of sound policy. Only among the commercial classes in the cities and towns was a pro-English sentiment to be found, and it was the part of wisdom to work with them. The reason went much deeper, however. Simon de Montfort, scion of a distinguished line, bred to feudal traditions, had ideas stirring about in his head which would have shocked his equals and outraged the king who employed him, and which perhaps were a puzzle to himself. He had an awareness of something wrong in the world and a slowly awakening willingness to assist in setting things right.

He found that much of the dissension in Gascony stemmed from the activities of one of the most powerful counts, Gaston of Béarn. Gaston was a cantankerous and selfish schemer and an unpleasant fellow personally for whom Simon had a great dislike. Inasmuch, however, as the mother of this rancid individual, Grasenda, had been the first wife of Raimund Berenger, he was a half brother once removed of Queen Eleanor. There was never any way of being sure how far the Queen's sympathies would carry her in anything having to do with a relative of hers, and this made it necessary to deal carefully with Master Gaston. Simon accordingly concluded a truce with him before turning his attention to the other troublemakers. The Viscount of Gramont, one of the most persistent, was taken prisoner and thrown into a dungeon at Le Réole without the formality of a trial. A storm of protest resulted, but there must have been good reasons for dealing with him in such a summary manner. The viscount was left in his cell for seven years, long after Simon de Montfort gave up his post in Gascony. The next victim of Simon's vigorous methods was the Viscount of Soule. Frightened, no doubt, by the fate of his fellow viscount, he refused to appear when summoned to court. Simon reached out promptly and captured him at Mauléon and made him pay a fine of ten thousand molas. The most important step taken was in connection with the King of Navarre, who was persuaded to an arbitration of his differences with the English Crown.

Peace descended suddenly on Gascony. This brand of firmness was new to them. If the methods of the seneschal were unexpected, however, they were easily recognizable. The awed citizens saw in this kind of thoroughness the gift to Simon from his stern and relentless father who had been called the Scourge of the Albigenses. They did not like the taste of this severe medicine, but for the time being there was nothing they could do but mutter their discontent.

After three months in Gascony, Simon hurried to England to report what he had done, leaving a surprising degree of quiet behind him. As he returned to his post immediately and continued to govern with the same firm hand, it may be taken for granted that Henry had approved and had sped him back with the royal blessing.

3

Simon de Montfort's first duty on returning was to settle the strife which was turning Bordeaux into two hostile camps. An election for mayor was approaching, and the Columbines, as the wine merchants were called, were determined to defeat the party of the Solers. Old Rustengo was so far advanced in years now that he had become practically bedridden, but this did not hamper that wise old political leader in his efforts to maintain control. From his huge house in the shadow of the Gothic cathedral of St. André he pulled the strings with all his old cunning, and it was expected that the Soler interests would win.

On the night of June 28, with the voting set for the following day, the Columbines came out in full force, filling the old Roman town with the clamor of their marching and singing. The Solers responded by pouring out in equal numbers, and soon there was fighting in the streets. Simon de Montfort had retired to his chamber, but he emerged at the first sound of conflict, issuing orders to both parties to return to their homes. The Solers, lacking the sagacious presence of old Rustengo, disregarded the order and continued to harry and attack their opponents. The seneschal threw himself into the melee on the side of the Columbines, and the fighting reached such a serious phase that men were killed on each side. Simon succeeded in driving the rioting Solers back to the house of their leader, which he invested and attacked. Rustengo was quick to surrender, ordering his followers to lay down their arms. The ringleaders on both sides were placed under arrest, including the old man, who was hauled from his bed and thrown into prison with the rest. Rustengo, however, was treated with every consideration, being allowed a comfortable chamber and as many servants as he needed for his personal comfort.

After an investigation the seneschal placed the blame on the Solers, who had disregarded his orders to disperse although the Columbines had been willing to obey. He therefore released the leaders of the latter faction but kept Rustengo and several of his most active followers in prison. The voting was held and the party of the wine merchants won.

It was unfortunate that Rustengo died while still in prison. His sons, who had been allowed their freedom, screeched in all the market places of Gascony that Simon de Montfort was responsible for his death. A deputation headed by one of the Soler sons went to England to demand satisfaction. Henry heard them, believed what they said, ordered all the confiscated property of the faction to be restored, and was preparing some action to clip his seneschal's wings when a deputation from the other faction arrived, headed by William Raymond Colom, who had been elected mayor. After listening to them Henry, that somewhat less than resolute arbitrator, changed his mind and had the Solers thrown into prison.

No purpose would be served by recording all the sudden ups and downs which followed and the continual shifts in the position and favor of the King. Certain episodes must be introduced, however, to make clear the parts played by King and seneschal.

Simon was in Paris in March 1250 in an effort to negotiate a five-year truce with Blanche of Castile. Word reached him there that the anti-governmental factions in Gascony were planning a revolution on a wide scale, and he sent an important letter to Henry, important chiefly because it happens to be the only letter of his which remains in existence. He first advised the King that the forces of rebellion would strike after Whitsuntide and then pleaded for an audience to decide on the steps necessary under these circumstances. "Forasmuch as the great folk of the land," he wrote, "look upon me with evil eyes, because I uphold against them your rights and those of the common people, it would be peril and shame to me, and great damage to you, if I went back to the country without having seen you and received your instructions. . . . Nor can they be checked by an army as in a regular war, for they only rob and burn, and take prisoners and ransom them, and ride about at night like thieves in companies."

Before going on with the account of what developed it is advisable to pause and comment on the phrasing of this letter. It is clear that the seneschal is determined not to take any steps which lack the approval in advance of the King. He will be fighting an enemy who rides in the dark of night and strikes without warning, and the sharpest kind of measures will be necessary. More important still is the wording of one phrase, *because I uphold against them your rights and those of the common people*. The reference to the common people was not inserted in the letter to assist in swaying the King to the support of his officer in this crisis. Henry had no concern for the rights of the common people. That this consideration weighed in the mind of Simon de Montfort would incline the King to look on him with suspicion. The reference may be accepted, therefore, as an honest and vehement expression of the thoughts in the seneschal's mind and not as an argument to influence the King. It was so much in Simon's mind that he inserted it even though he knew it would hurt rather than help his cause. It thus becomes clear that in dealing with the men who "ride about at night like thieves in companies" he wanted to protect the common people. The arbitrary methods he adopted in breaking up the baronial combinations can be more easily understood and, in this light, more readily condoned.

Simon went to England and had his talk with the King. The latter was uneasy over the situation, willing enough to have Gascony brought to subjection but fearful of the consequences of the strong measures which alone would avail.

"By God's hand, Sir Count," he said in the tone of bitter faultfinding which had become habitual with him, "I will not deny you have fought bravely for me. But—but in truth there ascends a clamor of grave complaint against you!"

In spite of the royal misgivings, some funds were supplied and the seneschal returned to Gascony with the understanding that the uprising was to be put down with a firm hand. The expected rebellion did not take place, but there was continuous fighting of a desultory nature after Simon's return. He did not find it necessary to go beyond the instructions he had received when in England, but at the beginning of the following year he arrived again in London with only three squires in his train after a mad gallop across France which had worn them all out. He could no longer continue the struggle, he declared, without support from home. He had exhausted all his own funds and had reached the end of his resources. Three thousand marks were doled out to him, and he rode back to Gascony in time to defeat the rebellious nobles at Castillon. It was such a complete victory that the rebels without exception made their peace and promised to sin no more. Simon then returned to England and handed in his resignation. His work was done, he declared, and someone else could now carry on the government in his stead. All he asked was that the King would recompense him for the money he had paid out of his own purse.

Henry proceeded to take a stand which can only be characterized as extraordinary. He not only refused to make any payments to the earl but went further and claimed that the latter must maintain garrisons in all the important castles in the province at his own expense for the balance of his seven years of office. Even the Queen balked at this evidence of the curious way the King's mind worked, but Henry refused to listen to anyone. All the troubles in Gascony were due, he declared openly, to the evil conduct of Simon de Montfort himself. The earl demanded at once that an investigation be held, and with some eagerness the King agreed.

Commissioners were sent to the South to gather evidence and returned with a long train of witnesses, headed by the Archbishop of Bordeaux. The King received them with cordiality, but when Simon de Montfort put in an appearance he was greeted with coldness.

The trial was held in the refectory at Westminster and lasted for five weeks, the commissioners acting as judges. It was conducted with great bitterness on both sides. The bitterest of all the participants was Henry. He injected himself at every stage into the cross fire of question and answer, of charge and countercharge, shouting and losing his temper and making two things abundantly clear: that he wanted Simon to be judged a traitor and to have all his possessions confiscated to the Crown. Even when his brother, Richard of Cornwall, who had governed Gascony many years before and knew the conditions at first hand, testified that Simon de Montfort had taken the only way to put down disorder, the King continued to rail at the seneschal and his witnesses. An account of the trial has been preserved in the form of a letter by Adam Marsh, who attended the proceedings. Adam by this time was an ardent adherent of Simon de Montfort, but he was also a man of honor and a Christian, more devoted to truth than to any cause or friend. It may be assumed that he set down his account with fidelity to truth and that it may be accepted literally.

A dramatic picture emerges. It was a duel between the two men, the King and his subject, Henry attacking the earl with the twisted logic which grew out of his resentment because things had gone wrong, the earl meeting his attacks with the sharpness of a sword thrust. The feeling of the King was no longer the petty malice which had prompted his charge against the honor of his sister; it was hate, a hate of white heat which could be felt in every corner of the long chamber; a hate, moreover, which was returned in full by the smoldering-eyed defendant.

Simon listened to the written charges against him and answered them orally. Some of the statements he denied and gave his own version of what had happened; others he explained on the ground that he had acted on sentences pronounced in courts of justice. He had, in fact, summoned a parliament at Dax to consider the conduct of the "pack of thieves" who were disturbing the peace of Gascony, and it was on the authority of regulations which had been passed there that he had acted in all cases. This statement he elaborated in meeting the charges, showing his conduct to have been governed by parliamentary instruction. That he had sometimes been ruthless in carrying out these instructions, he acknowledged, claiming in extenuation that only by prompt and sharp action could lawlessness be met and checked. Not until the finish did he allow his feelings to get the better of him. Facing his accusers, he cried out in a loud voice, "Your testimony against me is worthless because you are all liars and traitors!"

The trend of the evidence had been running strongly in the earl's favor from the beginning of the hearing, and his concise and powerful summation completed the rout of his opponents. It was now clear, even to Henry, that the Council could return no verdict save one of acquittal. The King continued to interfere, nevertheless, stabbing blindly and bitterly at the man who had accepted this mission in the first place against his will and had suffered so much in attempting to complete it. Simon was stung finally to open retaliation.

"Sir King," he said, "observe the gist of your letter investing me with the government of Gascony for seven years." There it lay on the table before them, the document giving to Simon de Montfort full authority to meet conditions in the South by any means he found necessary. The sensechal added after a moment, allowing his voice to reach a vehement note, "Restore all the money I have spent in your service out of my own resources!"

There was a pause before the King spluttered an angry reply. "No, I will not keep my promises," he declared. "They have no value since you yourself have betrayed me."

The Earl of Leicester was not one of the subservient men who clustered about the King and accepted the edge of his biting tongue in silence. He advanced a step in the direction of the royal dais.

"That word is a lie!" he cried. "Were you not my sovereign, an ill hour would it be for you in which you dared to utter it!"

Henry had passed the lie to many men, but this was the first time that he had to swallow his own medicine. He was too astonished to make an immediate reply.

Having gone this far, Simon allowed himself a further verbal aggression. "Who could believe you a Christian?" he demanded to know. This was followed by a direct challenge: "Do you ever go to confession?"

"I do indeed," answered the King.

"What is the use of confession without repentance?"

Henry now found tongue to answer. "Never," he cried, "have I repented anything so much as that I allowed you to enter England and take over lands and honors here!"

The verdict of the Council was unanimous. Simon de Montfort was cleared of all charges, his conduct in the office of seneschal tacitly approved. That night the candles burned in the chancellery, where the King worked with a coterie of his closest advisers. John Mansel was one of them, without a doubt, for Henry was deferring to his judgment now on all occasions and following his suggestions. In an effort to snatch some shreds of victory from the defeat of the trial, a set of conditions was drawn up and stamped with the royal seal without any responsible member of the Council being consulted. Simon was to return to Gascony, but a truce was to be declared and maintained until he, Henry, could visit the province and settle all questions under dispute. In the meantime certain castles were to be handed back to their owners, certain confiscated properties were to be restored, certain prisoners were to be released. Every point was a concession to the complainants who had been declared by unanimous decision of the Council to have failed in establishing a case.

Realizing that the King had made it impossible for him to carry on his duties with any hope of success, Simon returned to the South of France with the greatest reluctance. Henry bade him farewell with the words, "Go back to Gascony, thou lover and maker of strife, and reap its reward like thy father before thee."

When the seneschal reached Gascony he found that his opponents had already broken the truce. Gaston of Béarn had marched a strong force against Le Réole and was besieging the castle. Collecting such forces as he could, Simon succeeded in defeating the archtroublemaker. He won another battle at Montauban, with more difficulty this time, as the disaffected barons had brought a large army into the field against him. As soon as this battle had been won two royal commissioners appeared and handed him a communication from Henry in which he was sternly commanded to abide by the terms of the truce.

"I cannot observe a truce," declared the seneschal, "which the other party refuses to recognize."

On receiving this reply, the commissioners handed him a second note containing notification that he had been removed from office. This procedure, most clearly, had been carefully planned in advance. The ingenuity of the trap laid for the seneschal's feet suggests that the idea had not originated in the mind of the King. Henry was distinctly lacking in originality. John Mansel seems the most likely concocter of the scheme. He was now deep in Henry's confidence. In the years immediately following, the King's policy would show a cunning and a degree of resourcefulness never displayed before.

Simon de Montfort kicked aside the steel jaws of the trap. He had been confirmed in his office by Royal Council, he declared, and would not retire until his seven-year term had expired. When word of his obduracy reached England a meeting of Parliament was called in an effort to get constitutional sanction for his dismissal. Parliament refused to take action. Henry was thus brought to the need of offering terms. Grudgingly and unhappily he agreed to pay all the debts Simon had contracted in Gascony and to give him seven thousand marks by way of compensation if he would resign his office.

Simon de Montfort accepted these conditions. It was with reluctance that he laid down his baston and departed. The robber barons still "rode about at night like thieves in companies." The common people still suffered the terrors of civil war. Had he been too harsh in his methods and thus responsible for the continuing strife? Or, on the other hand, should he have gone to greater lengths and rooted out the quarreling barons once and for all? The man who crossed the Garonne and rode through Guienne into France was not happy over his first experience as a ruler.

He arrived in Paris at a crucial moment. Worn out with

anxiety for her son at the Crusades and by the exacting nature of her official duties, Blanche of Castile had been taken ill and had died, leaving the state without any head. Fearing that the old dissensions would break out again, the council of peers began hastily to throw a government together. The post of seneschal was offered to Simon de Montfort, special commissioners being sent to him twice to urge his acceptance. The proffer of this important position was evidence that his conduct in Gascony had been watched closely in France and, moreover, with approbation. He refused the offer, stating that he was an English subject and intended to remain one.

4

Henry had the utmost confidence in his capacity to settle matters in Gascony, but he seemed in no hurry to get away, letting almost a year elapse before making any move. Perhaps he was held back by the emptiness of the royal coffers. Empty they were, at any rate, and the King was finding it a difficult matter to replenish them. Knowing that the barons would refuse a subsidy, he fell back on an old order of the Pope's to the English clergy which stipulated a grant to the Crown of ten per cent of all the revenue of the Church to be applied to crusading expenses. The clergy had refused up to this point to obey the papal mandate. The King decided to lay his suggestion that this was the time for the grant to be paid before the Bishop of Ely, that dignitary having been rather more lenient in his attitude than his brother bishops. My lord of Ely, however, displayed no leniency on this occasion. He not only refused to entertain the kingly suggestion but proceeded to lecture Henry for his extravagance. Henry flew into a passion and ordered his officers "to turn out this ill-bred fellow."

By means fair or otherwise he raised funds for the venture finally and was ready to leave by the middle of the following year, 1253. He issued instructions that during his absence Queen Eleanor and Richard of Cornwall were to act as regents jointly. There seems to have been an understanding, however, between the royal couple, at any rate, that Eleanor would exercise the functions of ruler and that the King's brother would act in a consultant capacity. Henry made out a will to confirm this, a brief document which was the only testament he ever drew. The confidence he thus demonstrated in his strong-minded spouse would yield bitter fruit later.

He sailed from Portsmouth on August 6 with a large retinue

of knights and administrative assistants, John Mansel being one of the latter. Prince Edward was brought from Eltham to bid his father farewell. He was now in his fourteenth year and had grown tall, his head being almost on a level with the King's. He was brisk and workmanlike in the use of weapons and was going to make a great soldier, this long-legged heir to the throne; but on this occasion he was no more than a boy who did not like being left behind. Tears streamed down his cheeks as he watched the departure of the royal flotilla.

On reaching Bordeaux, Henry found conditions to be worse than ever. While he had fiddled at home, the fires of Gascon dissension had burned briskly. Gaston of Béarn had supplied yeast to the bread of discontent by making an open alliance with Alfonso the Wise of Castile. The latter was to push his claims to the province with the active aid of the troublesome Gaston and, in the event of success, Gaston was to be made seneschal. Henry was disturbed at the turmoil which existed and found himself at a loss as to what to do. He did what might have been expected of him, therefore; he sent for Simon de Montfort. "We beg you to come," he wrote, "and discuss affairs with us, and show us what you wish to be done."

Simon was still in France and in poor health. Remembering the scenes at Westminster, the hatred Henry had displayed, the accusing forefinger which had been leveled at him, the King's bitter speech of farewell, he must have indulged in a wry smile on reading the communication. His first impulse was to refuse. It was some time, at any rate, before he stirred himself to obey and set out for the southern province with a small following of knights. Henry received him with outward cordiality, and they proceeded to take counsel as to the best method of pacifying the country.

A solution was now in sight. The craftily smiling Alfonso of Castile had always been in the background of Gascon intrigue, and Gaston of Béarn had never been more than a gadfly responding to the fan of Castile. If Alfonso could be persuaded to withdraw his pretensions, the disobedient nobility would be left without any prospect of support and would cease to be defiant. The first step toward such an agreement had been taken before Henry left England, a proposal that the Lord Edward, heir of England, should marry Alfonso's half sister, the infanta Doña Eleanora of Castile. It was decided now to pursue the proposal actively.

Two plenipotentiaries were dispatched from Bordeaux to

open negotiations in Burgos, Peter d'Aigueblanche, Bishop of Hereford, and the inevitable John Mansel. The Castilian ruler was found in a receptive mood. It is doubtful if he had ever entertained serious designs on Gascony. Rather he had been using his claim as a means to an end. The infanta, a lissome girl of ten years with charming manners and the promise of great beauty, pleased the English representatives. The bishop and the resourceful Mansel found one reservation in the mind of the Spanish monarch. English princes in the past had been notoriously fickle in matrimonial matters. The infanta's mother was the Joanna of Ponthieu who had been so unceremoniously tossed aside by Henry himself in his desire to have Eleanor of Provence as his Queen. There must be no playing fast and loose in this case. The Lord Edward must appear in Burgos not later than five weeks before Michaelmas of the following year to claim his young bride. If he failed to arrive within that time, the marriage contract would be canceled.

The major stipulation of the contract was a solemn promise that Alfonso's claims in Gascony would be relinquished. When word of this reached Gaston of Béarn he realized that he had been left to face the consequences of his treason alone. Dissension and civil war ended with dramatic suddenness.

Simon de Montfort was delegated to return to London and report the happy solution of Gascon troubles. He seemed to have regained royal favor, but the rapprochement was all on the surface. The hatred which had flared up at Westminster still smoldered between them. The King was almost certainly laughing up his sleeve at his own cleverness in sending the Earl of Leicester to England to carry the glad tidings that he, Henry of Winchester, had succeeded where Simon de Montfort had failed.

CHAPTER EIGHTEEN

Edward Marries the Infanta— A Trio of Great Kings

HENRY took one precaution when he left the kingdom under the regency of his wife. He deposited the great seal of England in a casket, securely locked, and with instructions that it was to be used only in an emergency. Perhaps the members of the Council had insisted on it; certainly it was intended as a curb. The fair Eleanor, however, had other ideas. She was going to be Queen in fact as well as in name.

She assumed at once some of the dignities and duties of a sovereign, not only presiding at meetings of the Council but seating herself on the bench and hearing pleas. One of her first moves was to make the city of London feel the full weight of her hand now that it held the scepter; and this was a very great mistake indeed. The highhanded way in which she treated the Londoners contributed greatly to the causes of the armed clash of later years.

Eleanor, it is clear, hated the Londoners. Her first aggressive act was to demand back payments on a form of tribute called queen-gold. It had been a prerogative of the Queen to receive a tenth of all fines which came to the Crown. Now one of Henry's favorite forms of exaction was to levy fines on the city on the thinnest and most ridiculous of pretexts. The Londoners, fuming bitterly but not daring to risk open refusal, had met these demands; but with the understanding that in doing so they did not concede the King's right to penalize them in this way. Eleanor claimed that she had not received her percentage (the rule had always been for the King to pay his wife out of the amount received) and that the city must make it up to her. London gasped, first in wonder at such sheer audacity, then in angry denial. The Queen's temper was too sharp to brook any opposition, and she promptly seized the two sheriffs of the city, John de Northampton and Richard Picard, and lodged them in prison. The queen-gold was paid. Later, when the question of raising funds for the war in Gascony came up and the whole nation refused to pay, Eleanor vented her spleen on London. A group of prominent citizens, including the draper Lord Mayor, Richard Hardell, were put in prison.

The violent dissatisfaction she had stirred up in the city spread throughout the country when she summoned Parliament for the purpose of raising war funds. It was reported to the barons and bishops assembled that Alfonso of Castile was planning to invade Gascony with a huge army of Christians and Moors. This was a subterfuge, and a stupid one to boot, because the barons knew that negotiations for peace with Castile were proceeding satisfactorily, based on the proposed match between Prince Edward and the infanta. They had a shrewd notion that an agreement would be reached, and under the circumstances their reply was that they would grant supplies when proof of the invasion was forthcoming, and not before.

That the marriage contract was signed while Parliament debated became known later. Queen Eleanor was arranging to accompany Edward to the South at the very time she was demanding of the House the funds for a full-scale war. It was quite clear to his justly unsympathetic subjects that Henry was now endeavoring to make capital out of a situation which did not exist. It was his hope that Parliament could be hoodwinked into granting a tax for the defense of the Gascon possessions which he could devote instead to his own personal uses.

Parliament knew him too well by this time to be cozened into any such generosity. They laughed in their sleeves and said firmly, no. All that Henry received was five hundred marks which the Queen sent him, the fruit, no doubt, of her misuse of royal power in London.

2

The time has come to deal more fully with Lord Edward, as the heir to the throne was generally called in the records of the day, the prince who was to play such a magnificent role in English history. He is said to have grown into the tallest and strongest man in the kingdom. This is probably an exaggeration, but it is quite true that he never met his match in personal encounter or in any test of strength, and it is equally a fact that he towered over the men of his court. At the age of fifteen, when he married the infanta, he had not attained as yet his full stature, but he was a great gilded youth, very long in the leg and as blondly handsome as Richard Coeur de Lion. His expression, according to one witness, was "full of fire and sweetness." Certainly he was a figure to revive belief in the godlike origin of kings.

None of the sagacity, the earnest desire to be just in all things, which distinguished Edward when he ruled as king, had yet become manifest in the proud and high-spirited youth. He was Edward of England, above curbs and restraints, chivalrous to a degree (chivalry did not count cruelty to the lower orders a fault), and a law unto himself. In his late teens he would be guilty of excesses which could be defended only on the ground of youth and the influence of lawless continental ideas.

He had preceded his mother to Gascony and had been installed as ruler, to the great satisfaction of the people of the province, who were capable of much sentimentality. Queen Eleanor, leaving England in the hands of Richard of Cornwall, arrived at Bordeaux in May, accompanied by a truly royal train. Henry remained behind when Edward and his mother went on to Castile, and Boniface of Canterbury was given charge of the party. Boniface, it seems, could be depended upon to be anywhere save where he should have been, attending at home to his long-neglected duties as archbishop. They reached Burgos, after a tedious journey over the Pyrenees, several weeks ahead of the stern limit set by Alfonso. That subtle monarch exercised his privilege of inspecting the prospective bridegroom before giving his final consent to the nuptials. Fortunately the tall youth, with his fair locks close-clipped below the ears, his strong straight back in stiffened tabard, his handsome legs in long leather riding boots, made the best possible impression, and Alfonso had no hesitation in accepting him for his young half sister. The arrangements for the ceremony were pushed ahead. Tournaments were held while they waited, and at one of them Edward was knighted by Alfonso.

In October the prince and the ten-year-old Eleanora were married at the monastery of Las Huelgas. All royal marriages were made into spectacles of splendor and lavish color, and this was no exception. However, the Castilian monarch had earned for himself the sobriquet of El Sabio, the Wise, and he did not impoverish himself as Henry would have done. Any lack of ostentation, however, was more than compensated for by the picturesque detail of the ceremony, the *jugale*, the vivid coloring of the costumes.

Edward was probably as casual about romance as most boys of his age. As he played his part in the ritual his mind may have been filled with the jousting he had witnessed and the splendid Spanish charger which had been one of his gifts. He must have been conscious in some degree, however, of the brightness of eye of the young girl who took the vows with him, of the soft flush on her youthful rounded cheek. Whatever his emotions may have been, this beautiful ceremony in the high vaulted chapel of Las Huelgas was the beginning of one of the truly great romances of history. Edward and Doña Eleanora of Castile would become ardently devoted to each other and would remain so until death separated them. If Eleanor of Provence was the most unpopular of English consorts, Eleanora of Castile was to be the best liked, and deservedly so.

The nuptials of Edward and Eleanora brought together in one sense the three great kings of the thirteenth century. The first was Edward himself, who would become in time the most illustrious of them all, a framer of just laws, a farseeing constitutional reformer, a doer and not a dreamer. The second was Alfonso, his brother-in-law, who was perhaps the most brilliant of all rulers but who, unfortunately for himself and the people of Spain, lacked the capacity to transmute ideas into actualities. Nevertheless, his subjects coined the name El Sabio for him, and by that term he has come down through the centuries, remembered for his accomplishments in the arts and in the field of science.

Alfonso was a scholar, a poet, an ardent believer in the possibilities of scientific advance. He authorized the collection of translations of all Arabic works on astronomy and supplemented this with the establishment of research organizations in Toledo and Burgos. Nothing made him happier than to assist in the work in the laboratories with his learned doctors. All their manuscripts, for which he wrote the prologues himself, passed through his hands and he spent a great deal of time correcting and rewriting them. He published them at his own expense. There were droves of poets about his court, and between them they composed the famous *Cantigas de Santa María*, a collection of four hundred songs about the Virgin Mary, some of the best of them from the pen of Alfonso himself. He had a history of Spain prepared, the first one with any pretensions to authenticity and value, which is still used under the title of *Primera Crónica General*. He made Castilian the official language, which meant relegating Latin to the schoolroom and the cloister, a change which did not sit well on monkish stomachs, and he established universities at Seville, Murcia, Córdoba, and Salamanca, building great libraries in connection with each of them. Finally he displayed an interest in invention and gave his assistance in the making of instruments, the astrolabe, the water clock, the sun clock, most particularly a remarkable new article called a mercury clock.

Alfonso was too far in advance of his times, and there were many in Spain who suspected a whiff of brimstone about his activities and spread whispers of heresy. He was too trusting, too prone to see only the good in people about him, to be a successful administrator. His great plan for a unified legal code of laws called the *Siete Partidas* had to be laid aside after a brief effort to enforce it. It was not until 1348 that national sanction was won for it. The members of his own family considered him soft and yielding, and they took advantage of him at every turn. The nobility followed the same line and did not hesitate to block his efforts at reform. In the end his own son, Sancho, as a true product of the Middle Ages, a hard and ambitious realist, took the reins into his own hands and kept Alfonso in confinement. The great King spent his last years, therefore, in bitterness, with his books on the stars to fill the long hours, the songs which filled his head his only company. As soon as he died Sancho declared himself King, setting aside Alfonso's will, which left the throne to the son of his deceased heir, Fernando.

It is unlikely that Edward, being so young at the time of his marriage, learned much from his stay at the court of this brilliant monarch. He was not of a studious disposition, and Alfonso's addiction to the arts would meet small response in that active adolescent mind. If their meeting had been after Edward had steadied to a sense of the responsibilities of kingship, each would have benefited from the other. The poet and dreamer might have learned how to apply his finespun schemes. The practical and earnest Edward might have discovered better ways to vent his immense energy than the subjugation of weaker neighbors and so have kept the shield of his accomplishments untarnished.

3

The third of the trio of great kings was St. Louis of France, whose participation in the nuptials came after the return from Spain.

Louis was quite different from the other two, a monarch who achieved luster not by what he accomplished but by greatness of character. This tall (Joinville says he stood a full head over his average subject) and truly saintly man conceived of kingship as a trust from God, and of life as no more than a preparation for eternity. He rose before dawn to hear matins in his chapel, contented himself with frugal meals, refused rich sauces, never allowed himself sweet dishes, and drowned his wine in water. He prayed for two hours each evening after compline and never went to bed until his couch had been sprinkled with holy water. None of the lighter sides of life appealed to him. There were no minstrels or jesters at his court, but if visitors brought their own entertainment he would listen to the singing of *Robin m'aime, Robin m'a* and witness the conjuring tricks with attention but no trace of enjoyment. The money which ordinarily would have been expended in tournaments and festivities went into charity instead. He gave seven thousand pounds each year to the mendicant orders and distributed sixty thousand herrings annually to the poor of Paris. To the members of his court he gave, with a straight face, hair shirts as gifts. He built no castles during the whole of his reign, but splendid hospitals were raised by the royal bounty.

Although Louis was not a reformer in the usual sense of the word and contributed no new laws or economic ideas, the memory of his justice and of his saintly life persisted down the ages.

4

After the wedding Edward was left in Gascony. The rest of the party, including the bride (who was to pass several years in England before becoming a wife in anything but name), traveled over into France on their way home. Henry, happy over a task so well done, went with them. King Louis and Queen Marguerite met them at Chartres with an imposing cavalcade and escorted them to Paris, where they were to be the guests of the French nation. The city was bedecked with flags, the students at the university were released from their books, the citizens suspended all work to help in the welcome.

The Old Temple had been prepared for the use of the visitors. It was a huge cluster of buildings, into a corner of which any of the English royal residences could have been snugly fitted. There were separate houses for the King and the Queen and the young bride. All the King's horses could have been shod at one time in the blacksmithies and all the King's men accommodated in the dormitories with plenty of room left over for, say, a company of palmers and a congregation of bishops. The malthouse was capable of housing all the servants had there not been so much activity around the mash tuns for the purpose of satisfying the thirst of the newcomers. The kitchens and the salthouse, the spicery and the squillery had been packed with supplies, and the stables bulged with hay.

Henry could not allow himself to be outdone. After distributing alms to the poor of Paris with a lavishness which caused his money men considerable alarm, he called his people about him and began to plan for an entertainment such as had never before been seen on land or sea.

He succeeded so completely in his purpose that the meal he served in the great chamber where the Templars had once assembled for their silent collations was called in the annals of the time the Feast of Kings. He insisted that the King of France take the head of the table, to which the magnanimous Louis agreed only after a protest. Henry then took his own place at the French King's right, while the King of Navarre sat on the left. There were twenty-five great peers present, eighteen countesses, and twelve bishops, as well as tableful after tableful of mere knights and ladies of lesser rank, not to mention rows of abbots and priors. After the feasting, which went on for hours, Henry distributed silver cups to all the male guests and silver girdles to the ladies.

It was during this ostentatious and costly affair that Louis turned to Henry and said in an undertone, "If only the peers and barons would consent, what close friends we should be!" The French King, however, was only half right. If his will had not been checked and confined by his council of peers, he would have established a basis for permanent peace between the two countries. Granting this much, the mind recoils from any thought of the condition into which England would have fallen if all restraints had been removed and Henry allowed a free hand.

That monarch's conception of the uses to which kingly power might be put was most pointedly illustrated by what happened in London on the landing of the royal party. Henry was returning in triumph. The Gascon troubles had been ended, a brilliant match had been made for the heir to the throne, the importance of the Crown of England had been demonstrated in no uncertain way in the very heart of the French country. There was due appreciation in London of the mood in which the King was returning, and he was received with great pomp and circumstance. The citizens might have faces purple with cold, but they lined the streets on a wild and blustery January day and cheered loudly for the victorious homecomer. What is more, they had gifts for him, one hundred pounds and a handsome piece of gold plate, beautifully inscribed.

Henry accepted the gifts but with a perceptible lack of cordiality. The reserve of his manner, the smolder in his eye were proof that he had not forgotten the quarrels between the Queen and the city. He was determined to let the Londoners see how much he resented their obduracy, and when it was reported to him that a murderer had been allowed to make his escape from Newgate he seized on this as a pretext. A fine of three thousand marks was imposed on the city.

CHAPTER NINETEEN

The Sicilian Absurdity

IT was December 7, 1254, and an old man lay dying in the ornate brick and colored-marble palace of Peter della Vigna which looked out over the Bay of Naples. In his wasted face above a straggling white beard the old man had none of the gentleness which so often accompanies the passing of the aged. The aggressiveness of purpose which had governed his life had left too strong a mark. His sunken eyes turned restlessly and unhappily as he thought of all the great projects, the plans and intrigues for papal aggrandizement, which he was leaving unfinished.

Close around his couch were relatives, weeping and bewailing the loss which confronted them. There was in the noisiness of their grief more than a hint of appreciation on their part that the era of the golden eggs was drawing to a close. Farther back stood the priests, prominent churchmen for the most part, one of whom at least wore a red hat, the papal physician who is sometimes designated as John of Toledo and sometimes as the English Cistercian, John Tolet. The churchmen were ranged in a circle, a silent group, their minds on the problems which would soon have to be faced.

The dying man made a gesture with one hand, a weak movement which expressed, nevertheless, impatience. "What are you crying for, you wretches?" he asked in a low whisper. "Don't I leave you all rich? What more do you want?"

He had indeed made them all rich, these demanding barnacles. He had plucked benefices for them from all countries of Europe, most particularly from England. He had found glittering sinecures for them in the offices of the papacy. He had even been stuffing the kingdom of Sicily full of his incompetent nephews and needy in-laws, where they reposed like so many wormy raisins. For this old man, dying not in proper peace but in irascibility, was Sinibaldo Fiesco, who had been Pope for eleven years as Innocent IV.

Although the archexponent of nepotism, he had been a strong pope, bringing the struggle of the Vatican against the ambitions of the Holy Roman Emperor, Frederick, to a new pitch of intensity; and had emerged, in the main, the victor. To carry on the war he had been draining the Church of its gold, and such blame as attaches to his name may be traced to the relentless nature of his exactions. He it was who had stared straight through the English envoys at Lyons and had refused to relieve their country of the payments to Rome which were impoverishing the national Church. He it was who had hated Robert Grosseteste so bitterly.

Innocent had ruled the Vatican through tumultuous years, sometimes riding triumphantly on the crest, sometimes driven into exile, a period which would remain long in the memories of men; and yet the one accomplishment which would be linked with his name after everything else had receded into the mists of time was a simple enough matter. He had introduced the red hat as the distinguishing mark of the cardinal. Even here he cannot be given credit for originating the idea. It is recorded that the Countess of Flanders, that mature and active lady of great wealth whose hand in marriage had once been sought by Simon de Montfort, made two social errors in one day in Rome; she mistook a mere bishop for a cardinal, which annoyed only herself, and then addressed a cardinal as a bishop, which was much more serious because it annoyed the cardinal. Accordingly she proposed to the Pope that something be done to make a cardinal stand out unmistakably from his fellows and, it is said, she even proposed that one way to do it would be to give him a red hat to wear.

When Henry of England learned of the death of Innocent he must have experienced mingled feelings of apprehension and relief. The harsh old titan with the face of a weary mastiff had involved the King of England in a desperate gamble. The venture to which Henry was committed had been weighing heavily on him and causing him many uneasy moments, perhaps even a twinge or two of conscience. Would the death of Innocent make his position easier? Or, disturbing thought, would his successor go on with the gamble and prove as sternly demanding as Innocent had been? Would he even adhere to the latter's threat of laying England under an interdict and excommunicating Henry himself if he failed in his obligations?

It was a difficult situation for Henry, because the transaction had been hatched more or less in secrecy. The impulsive King, knowing full well that his Council would not agree, had not consulted his advisers when he decided to take the gamble in partnership with the Vatican. The barons did not know of the letters which had passed back and forth nor of the nature of the negotiations conducted by the King's representative in Rome, Peter d'Aigueblanche. They had no conception of the staggering obligations which their headstrong ruler had assumed.

One thing was certain: the death of Innocent would bring some of the truth out into the open. And this was what Henry, above everything else, did not want.

2

Six years before William the Conqueror won the Battle of Hastings, a youth "of the greatest beauty, strong and brave and furious in battle," who was also a Norman and was known as Count Robert, began the conquest of Sicily. As a result of the efforts of this surpassingly able young man, the island was turned quickly into a Norman possession. The conquering maw drew in gradually all of the southern portions of the Italian boot, Naples, the Abruzzi, Apulia, Calabria. This was the greatest achievement of the roving seamen, more spectacular than the setting up of the duchy in Normandy, weighing much more in the medieval world than the conquest of England. It was a brilliant period, ending after a little more than a century, when Henry I of Germany added Sicily and its mainland possessions to the Holy Roman Empire.

In England the glory of the century of Norman rule in Sicily had been a legend. It was part of the dream of Henry II to unite all Norman possessions into one empire, and it was with this in mind that he married his daughter Joanna to William the Good of Sicily. Henry III, who talked much of great wars and feats of statesmanship but, like all weak men, never progressed from talk to the tremendous personal labor of preparation, had a vague idea that it might be possible to redeem there the loss of the duchy and the Angevin possessions in France. When Frederick of Germany died in 1250 it was reported about that Innocent IV had offered the imperial succession to Richard of Cornwall, although it was more likely the crown of Sicily. There was, of course, a great deal of excitement and interest, but Richard, cool and closemouthed, neither confirmed nor denied the story. If an offer had been made, he showed no signs of accepting. Two years later the papal purpose took a definite form, and one Master Albert, a Vatican notary, arrived in England to negotiate with Richard.

As Conrad, son and successor of the great Frederick, was a friend of Richard's, the answer of the latter was that he would not be a party to a plot for his removal. It is unlikely, however, that this consideration weighed too heavily; Richard was probably actuated instead by a different train of reasoning. His sound judgment would tell him that it was hopeless to conduct a war in distant Sicily against the power of the Holy Roman Empire, and that only disaster and financial ruin would come of it. Then in 1254 Conrad died, leaving as heir Conradin, an infant of two years. Manfred, an illegitimate son of Frederick, assumed the rule of Sicily, acting outwardly as the agent of the infant heir. This was generally believed to be no more than a pretense. Manfred, the son of the beautiful Bianca Lancia, took after his imperial father in many respects. He was a man of great ability and furious ambition. Having no faith in the disinterestedness of Manfred, Innocent decided that, as the kingdom of Sicily was a fief of Rome, the time had come for him to act. Having failed with Richard of Cornwall, he offered Sicily to Charles of Anjou, a brother of Louis of France. Charles would have grasped at the chance but had no means of financing the venture. As a last resort the Pope then approached Henry and proposed that he accept the throne for his second son, Edmund.

Henry was thrilled to the marrow of his bones. The opportunity of which he had dreamed, of redeeming the calamity of Normandy's loss, had come at last. Perhaps he consulted his own inner circle of advisers, perhaps only Mansel. The barons heard there was some talk connecting the young prince with the Pope's deep scheming, but even this had not become general knowledge when the agreement was made. There had been a fast and furious exchange of letters. The upshot was that at Vendôme on March 6, Master Albert, acting for the Pope, formally ceded the kingdom to Edmund. This was confirmed at Assisi two months later by Innocent himself.

The news of what had happened stunned the disgruntled men who were called the magnates of England, even though they did not suspect the truth, which was that Innocent would fight the Germans in Sicily as Henry's agent and that the responsibility for the total cost had been assumed by the English King.

While Henry was thus keeping his magnates in the dark he was almost certainly being misled himself by Peter d'Aigueblanche as to the exact nature of the agreements the latter was entering into as his representative. It had been understood from the first that the grant of a tenth of all national church revenue for five years which Innocent had offered the kings of England and France as the price of their participation in a new crusade would now be allowed Henry for the Sicilian adventure in lieu of taking an army to Palestine. Unfortunately for Henry and the Pope, the bishops in England were resolutely refusing to give the tenth for any purpose whatever, declaring boldly that they had already been bled white. What Henry may not have known was that his agent in Rome was pledging revenue from English bishoprics and monastic houses, without their knowledge or consent, and was using this as security for loans which he was raising from Italian bankers and merchants. The money raised on these false promises were being applied to the costs of the Sicilian campaign.

Not knowing any of this, the barons nevertheless watched and waited with intense anxiety.

Innocent sent an army into the south of Italy under the legate William, and Manfred hastily decamped from his headquarters in Naples. It looked as though the shrewd and resourceful Pope was thus, at the close of his career, on his way to a great triumph. Taking his physician with him, because he was sick enough to realize that he had not much longer to live, Innocent went to Naples. As he crossed a bridge into Sicilian territory, the bearer of the cross which was always carried before him allowed it to slip from his hands. This was a bad omen, and the papal party arrived at Naples in a less confident mood than when they set out. The worst of news awaited them there. Manfred had secured possession of treasure which Frederick had been storing in Apulia at the time of his death and with it had hired more troops. With the army thus improvised he had encountered the legate William at Foggia and had soundly beaten the papal army. He was already marching across country to take possession of Naples.

This unexpected reverse hastened the death of the Pope and perhaps prompted the irritability of the last words he addressed to his greedy relatives. He died with the bitter conviction that his final effort to curb the Hohenstaufen power had been a failure.

Henry waited for news of the election of a successor with great anxiety. When the word came that Cardinal Rinaldo of Segni had been the selection of the conclave and had assumed the name of Alexander IV, he was filled with mixed feelings. Alexander was well liked in the upper reaches of the Church, a stout, ruddy-faced, amiable man. But had he the capacity and the strength of purpose to take up where Innocent had left off and turn what looked like a rout into victory? There was room for much doubt on that score as reports kept coming in of the successes Manfred was scoring. On the other hand, Alexander's more generous character might incline him to be less demanding. It might even be possible to secure from him some lessening of the terms exacted by his predecessor.

One of the new Pontiff's first acts was to repeat Edmund's confirmation as King of Sicily. No progress was made, however, in the matter of ousting Manfred, and each passing month made the situation more desperate. Henry was loaded down with debts, and the whole country was sternly united against any further exactions. He had no money to pay the cost of the futile campaign the papal forces were waging, and the demands from the new Pope became increasingly sharp and insistent.

Finally Alexander sent to England the Archbishop of Messina, accompanied by Rostand Masson, the papal nuncio, to insist on the fulfillment of the agreement into which the King had entered. The men who made up Parliament assembled in the chapter house at Westminster on the Sunday after mid-Lent, 1257, to consider the situation which had brought these distinguished visitors. They were a sober lot. They knew that the King's operations in Gascony had involved him in expenditures in excess of three hundred thousand marks and that much of this staggering total was still waiting to be paid. The barons met on this occasion, therefore, more grimly determined than ever before to put an end to such squandering of public revenue.

Before the papal delegates were heard Henry staged a diversion which he hoped would create a more friendly attitude on the part of his magnates. He brought his son Edmund before the meeting, dressed in Apulian costume, and introduced him to the assemblage as the King of Sicily. Edmund was twelve years old and had developed into a handsome and engaging youth.

"Behold my son Edmund," said the King, beaming with pride, "whom God of His gracious goodness hath called to the excellency of kingly dignity. How comely and well worthy he is of all your favor! How cruel and tyrannical must be they who would deny him effectual and seasonable help, both with money and advice!"

Knowing Henry so well, the assembled magnates were convinced that this was a prelude to more sweeping demands than they had yet encountered. They were not prepared, however, for what followed. The Archbishop of Messina took the floor and laid bare the details of the agreement which had been entered into between the King and Innocent IV. This was the first public acknowledgment of the obligation Henry had assumed to pay all the costs of the Sicilian war, and the magnates sat in a stunned silence while the papal representative presented a balance sheet. England now owed Rome the sum of 135,000 marks. This was not all. Henry, it developed, had promised to lead an army into Sicily to assist in establishing his son on the throne, and the demand was now formally made that he appear with eighty-five hundred men in Naples the following year.

The barons, under these circumstances, proceeded to show how cruel and tyrannical they could be by refusing all financial aid and advice. They had not been consulted and they considered themselves free of all obligation in the matter. Henry protested stormily that in entering into partnership with the Pope he had acted with the consent of the bishops of England. He demanded that the Church give him the tenth which Innocent had pledged and, in addition, the income of all vacant benefices for five years. The bishops declared that they had not been consulted before the agreement was entered into and they asserted their unwillingness to pledge the tenth demanded of them until the lower orders of the Church had been consulted. This was followed by the presentation of a bill of complaint over the administration of national affairs in which fifty specific charges were made.

The outcome of the series of meetings which followed was that the bishops agreed to pay the King fifty-two thousand marks in lieu of the tenth. Henry accepted the offer, although with the greatest reluctance. The barons remained adamant, however, in their refusal to give any form of aid. The King's efforts to make forced loans were not successful, even Richard of Cornwall refusing to accommodate him. The amount finally assembled was so much less than the Pope was demanding that it was decided to send to Rome to represent the nation in this crisis a body of proctors consisting of the Archbishop of Tarentaise, Peter of Savoy, Simon de Montfort, and John Mansel. For some reason, this committee did not reach Rome, and the negotiations with Alexander seem to have been conducted by Rostand, who had taken back with him a full appreciation of the King's difficulties.

Alexander might present an outward suggestion of kindliness, but he acted in this matter with such sharpness and dispatch that Westminster was thrown into a state of dismay. First the Pope discharged Rostand and appointed one Arlotus in his place. Then he made it clear that, although some additional time would be allowed, the money due Rome must be paid. Finally he notified Henry that if he did not appear in Sicily with his army by March 1, 1259, he would be put under the ban of excommunication.

Henry threw up his arms in a rather abject surrender. He made it clear that he would be happy to be rescued from his unenviable position by any means that his devoted subjects might devise. He seems to have wanted nothing so much at the moment as a chance to get out of his bargain and to relinquish for his son the right to the Sicilian throne. The magnates accordingly took matters in hand, making it clear first, however, that their willingness to assume the task was contingent on his agreement to a reform of the whole basis of administration for the future. To this Henry gave his assent.

The negotiations with the Pope resulted in a cancellation of the grant of the kingdom to Edmund, although with the understanding that the King's son could at any time, prior to the crowning of a new king, seek the restoration of his rights by payment of the balance of the debt to Rome. The balance of the debt went unpaid, and thus came to an official end the Sicilian Absurdity.

In later years Henry was wont to say that he would have brought the venture to a successful issue if the barons had not interfered. It became a favorite complaint of his that they had robbed his son of his chance for a crown. He talked continuously of reviving the project but of course never took any definite steps to do so.

3

The immense castle of Wallingford, in the building of which a large part of the town had been demolished, was the favorite residing place of Richard of Cornwall. He was there a great deal, at any rate; and there he was when a party of emissaries from Ottocar of Bohemia arrived to announce that he had been elected King of Germany. It was a cold day in January 1257, and the ambassadors were summoned to a long hall where, in front of a roaring fire, the brother of the English King and his beautiful wife Sanchia were dining in considerable elegance and state.

Richard rose to hear what the men from Bohemia had to say and at the finish he burst into tears. He would accept the crown, he said, but it was not through greed or ambition. His sole object was to assist in restoring prosperity to the German states; his honest desire was to rule justly and well. It was clear to the German delegation, and to the throng of adherents and servants who swarmed into the hall to listen, that he was happy over the fulfillment of his great wish. It must have been quite apparent also that the gentle Sanchia was delighted beyond measure. Now she would be a queen as well as her two older and patronizing sisters.

The news was in no sense a surprise. The death of William of Holland, who had been the leader of the Hohenstaufen interests, had thrown the election open, and Richard's qualifications were such that he had been from the start the leading candidate. He had the support of the Pope, he came from the country which supplied the industrial provinces of Germany with the wool they needed, he was reputed to be the wealthiest man in Europe and could maintain the office with proper splendor. Only one other candidate was actively supported, and this was none other than Alfonso the Wise. The ambition of the Spanish monarch, balked in Gascony, was stirring again, and he would gladly have taken the overlordship of the Empire. Richard had thrown himself into the contest with a right good will, first calling in twenty-five thousand marks which he had out on loan and cutting off much of his wood to raise revenue. He was well aware that it was a costly business to secure the imperial crown.

There were seven electors, and the votes of some of these at least would have to be purchased. Richard's gold won the adherence of the three who governed the industrial West: Conrad of Cologne (his vote cost eight thousand marks), Count Palatine (he was to have one of Henry's daughters as his wife), and the Archbishop of Mainz. On the other hand, the Archbishop of Trier and the electors of Brandenburg and Saxony declared their allegiance to Alfonso. This gave the deciding vote to Ottocar of Bohemia and, when he came into Richard's camp, the victory had been won.

It was part of the tradition that the election be formally declared at the city of Frankfort-am-Main, and accordingly the four assenting electors made their way to that city. The opposing forces, refusing to acknowledge defeat, gained possession of the city and closed the gates to the other party. This made it necessary for the majority electors to stage an unusual ceremony. Riding up in front of the gates, the four raised their arms in the air in token of their agreement that the imperial crown should be tendered to Richard of Cornwall. The honor of notification was given to Ottocar.

The next step was for Richard to appear at Aachen for his coronation, and he proceeded to make the most elaborate of preparations. He was reaping his reward now for all the years of careful financial planning, the vigilance with which he had policed his loans, his expert farming of the English coinage; there was plenty of money available for a truly triumphal entry into the wide-flung dominions over which he was to exercise suzerainty.

Fifty vessels were needed to transport his party to Dordrecht because an imposing train of English nobles went with him. He carried rich gifts for everyone of importance in his domain and had even commissioned the making of a new crown and insignia. Flanders was properly impressed by this magnificence, and the reception accorded at Aachen was all that could be desired. The coronation took place in that city on May 17, Conrad of Cologne placing on the head of the

new monarch the costly crown which he had himself provided.

With commendable energy Richard then proceeded to visit
other parts of his domain, covering all of the Rhineland in less
than a year. Wherever he went he distributed gifts with an
almost spendthrift hand. He won the good will of the important officials by confirming grants in their favor, he greased
the palms of minor officers, he handed purses of gold to the
burghers and jewels to their buxom wives. This prodigality
was necessary because he was a stranger to the people of
Germany and they had not been prepared to accept him with
any degree of enthusiasm. Richard does not seem to have
shown any hesitation about the freehanded scattering of the
wealth he had accumulated so slowly and carefully. Perhaps
he had always kept this end in mind. He seems to have been
happy in his bargain, finding the touch of a gold rim on his
brow an exhilarating sensation. And then there was Sanchia,
happy, radiant; no longer would she need to sit on a stool in
the presence of her two older sisters.

While Richard, pompously subscribing himself *Dei gratia
Rex Romanorum semper augustus,* was enjoying the fruits of
victory, Henry was struggling in the mire of his own feckless
contriving in the Sicilian matter. The usual story had been
repeated again. Henry and Richard had gone into the monarchial market together, the former to buy a crown for his son
Edmund, the latter to buy one for himself. Henry had failed as
usual and had succeeded in getting himself into a sorry mess;
Richard had achieved his aim and now was seated, insecurely,
it is true, on the imperial chair.

CHAPTER TWENTY

The Provisions of Oxford

THAT the elements hostile to Henry would sooner or later turn to Simon de Montfort for leadership was inevitable. They recognized his great ability and his soldierly gifts. At the investigation of his stewardship in Gascony they had seen him stand up boldly to the King, meeting charge with charge, taunt with taunt. They had fallen under the spell of his magnetic personality, his steady dark eyes, his warm smile. They knew him to be deeply and sincerely religious, stanchly loyal to any cause in which he had enlisted, willing always to take heavy risks when necessary. More and more the opposition had been rallying about him.

His actual assumption of leadership, however, can probably be traced to the accident of two assaults on the rights of individuals by the most cordially hated of the Lusignans, William of Valence, who was now proclaiming himself Earl of Pembroke. The King's half brother had developed from the rather effeminate youth who had made such a pretense of chivalric observance into a man of the bitterest pride who believed himself above all law. One morning he sallied out from his castle of Hertford for a day's hunting, and it happened that the fortunes of the chase carried his party into the park which surrounded the palace at Hatfield of the Bishop of Ely. The park was a remarkably fine ten-mile stretch of hunting land and was most zealously guarded by the bishop's people. Centuries later it would become the property of Queen Elizabeth's minister, Cecil, and he would build his magnificent Hatfield House on the site of the bishop's manor. Here, while Spanish counsel ruled England and the smoke of Smithfield fires filled the horizon, Elizabeth would be sitting under an old oak when the messengers brought her intelligence that her sister Mary was dead.

William of Valence and his huntsmen had no right to invade such a closely held domain, but that carried no weight with the King's brother. He led his men into the wood and, after a vigorous day's sport, they came to the bishop's palace to demand refreshment. The bishop was not there, but the servants produced beer for the unbidden guests. This seemed to William of Valence something less than respectful to his person as well as unsatisfactory to his thirst, and he directed his followers to break open the bishop's cellar. "Swearing awfully," as Matthew Paris puts it, the huntsmen smashed the padlocks and broke off the bungs of the casks which held my lord of Ely's finest wine. They were all drunk when they took to saddle, not bothering to stop the flow of the costly wine from the damaged casks.

When informed of what had happened the bishop maintained an air of calm. "What necessity was there," he asked in a mild tone, "to steal and plunder that which would have been freely and willingly given if they had asked for it?" Then his feelings gained mastery of him and a fire began to burn in his eyes. "Accursed," he cried, "be so many kings in one kingdom!"

The Bishop of Ely had put into words the feeling of the whole nation. What he had said passed from mouth to mouth until the phrase, *Accursed be so many kings in one kingdom*, could have served as the rallying cry of revolution. The incident focused again the enmity of the people of England on the Lusignans. All other grievances, even the major discontent with the King's willfully weak rule, seemed secondary to the universal resentment felt for the haughty upstarts.

A similar trespass occurred at the time now reached in the recording of events. The hatred of the people for the many kings had been mounting all the while. It so happened that a steward of William of Valence entered and did some damage to property of Simon de Montfort near Leicester. Simon took the King's brother to task at the next meeting of the Council and was haughtily rebuffed. The pair would have resorted to steel if Henry had not thrown himself between them. Receiving no satisfaction in the matter, Simon brought it up again. He rose in the Hocktide Parliament of 1258, which met in London, and demanded that the injury done him be acknowledged and that compensation be given. William of Valence, his face contorted with anger, strode out to confront his accuser in the open space between the seats of the magnates.

"Traitor!" he cried. Then he further embroidered his accusation by adding, "Old traitor!"

"No, no, William," said Simon de Montfort. "I am neither traitor nor traitor's son. My father was not like yours!"

Steel was out this time when the King, fearing for the safety of his brother, thrust himself between them again, thereby bringing the royal legs into considerable jeopardy. The kingly person might have suffered some hurt if others had not intervened also.

Although nothing further seems to have been done at the time, the incident did not end there. By openly attacking the most hated of the Lusignans, Simon had made himself the one man around whom the opposition could group themselves. They were ready from that moment to stand behind Simon de Montfort and to fight against these continuous assaults on their rights and feelings. The Hocktide Parliament had begun its deliberations on April 9, and the quarrel took place immediately. On April 12 Simon was one of seven nobles who made a compact among themselves to stand together, to help one another to their rights "without wronging any man."

The party of resistance was taking organized form at last.

2

The Earl of Leicester was now a dominant figure among the malcontents, but two other noblemen loomed up strongly.

The first of these was Richard de Clare, Earl of Gloucester, who for one reason or another had been a spectacular character all his life. A grandson of William the Marshal, he had been made a ward of Hubert de Burgh at the age of eight, when his father died. His secret marriage when fourteen with Hubert's pretty and ill-fated daughter Meggotta had plunged his guardian still deeper into the bad graces of the King. As poor Meggotta died almost immediately thereafter, the youthful earl was married off promptly to Maud de Lacey, a daughter of the Earl of Lincoln. On growing up he was considered the most prominent of the old nobility, and he had played his part in all the important events of the reign. In 1253 his ten-year-old son Gilbert, called the Red because of the color of his hair, was married to Alice of Angoulême, daughter of Guy de Lusignan and therefore a stepniece of the King. The Earl of Gloucester took this alliance with royalty seriously, but as he was intensely proud and most tenacious of his rights as a leading peer, Henry had never been able to count on his support. At the Hocktide Parliament he had, somewhat reluctantly and with a great deal of grumbling, placed himself in opposition.

If there had been any doubt as to the Earl of Gloucester's final position, the loose tongue of Henry's evil genius, William of Valence, settled the issue. In the course of an angry discussion the latter charged that the earl was in league with the Welsh because the lands of Gloucester had been spared in the last raids. It was an idle and senseless assertion, exactly the kind of thing the King was in the habit of saying at the wrong time. The insult certainly could not have been timed worse. Richard de Clare ranged himself at once on the side of the King's enemies.

The spokesman of the barons was a more attractive figure than the unpredictable Earl of Gloucester. Roger Bigod, Earl of Norfolk, had been initiated as marshal of England when the last of the five Marshal sons died, his mother being the oldest daughter of the Good Knight. Further luster had been added to his name by marriage with Princess Isabella of Scotland. He was outspoken and courageous, with a stronger hand on the lance in a tilting than a head for serious counsel, a temper which was famous for its brevity and flaming quality.

Because he was marshal of England it was natural for him to act as spokesman, but it was manifest to all that he could never be considered a leader. Roger Bigod was a remarkably good lieutenant and admirable in the role of sword arm. He was, moreover, without guile; and the leader of a popular cause must have cool inner reserves, a capacity for shrewd planning and contriving, a willingness even to sacrifice men and some part of principle to the main issue.

Henry came to the Hocktide Parliament in dire straits. He asked for a tallage of one third of all belongings in the kingdom, a stiff demand. The magnates were equally stiff in their attitude. Roger Bigod, as their spokesman, declared that the day of vague discussion had passed and that the barons must have more than sworn promises which would be broken as fast as the King could get his absolution from Rome. They were no longer willing to have the nation involved in madly extravagant adventures and, to prevent their recurrence, there must be reform in administration from top to bottom. The main offices under the monarch—justiciar, treasurer, and chancellor—must be filled by men of substance and no longer by glorified clerks of the King's own choosing. There must be a commission, finally, to direct the measures of reform.

Henry had never been faced so openly before with the determination of his subjects to be free of his weak personal rule. The challenge of the barons was as straight and fierce as a sword thrust. He backed away, incensed beyond measure, his pride in a splutter of protest. The coterie to whom he listened—the Queen, the Lusignans, John Mansel—were all against compliance. With the exception of Mansel, they advised taking a high hand. Mansel favored the opposite course: dissemble, he whispered to the King, maneuver, make promises, outwit them, play for time.

This was all very well, but certain ugly facts had to be faced. The King was now completely without funds and weighed down by his debts. Pressure on the monasteries and the Jews was yielding almost nothing. Only by direct taxation could Henry's difficulties be solved. In addition to this ugly fact he was faced by men who seemed to him equally ugly in their determination.

On the last day of April the barons attended the session in full armor. They had left their swords at the door, but this did not serve to allay the King's alarm.

"What is it, my lords?" he cried, looking at the stern faces above the coats of mail. "Am—am I your prisoner?"

The answer, delivered by Roger Bigod, was intended to be reassuring. Violent intent was disclaimed. It had been a gesture, nevertheless, which could not be misunderstood.

Reluctantly and bitterly the King yielded. On May 2 it was announced that he had agreed in principle to the demands of his barons and that Parliament would adjourn until June 11 at Oxford to work out the details.

His yielding, it was believed, meant the end of personal rule. A feeling of optimism took hold of the country, a conviction that at last the weathercock King would be securely anchored.

3

Oxford in the thirteenth century was not what it became later, a much-restricted and law-bound lodginghouse for the university. It was a city of the first importance, the western tip of the sickle of forts securing the line of the Thames, the point where roads fanned out to the Marcher country, the field headquarters of the mendicant friars. It was a national sounding board, echoing the birth of ideas, the spread of opinion, the mutter of sedition.

When Henry arrived for the adjourned meeting of Parliament he found that the barons had taken advantage of an impending campaign in Wales to bring their followers with them. The place was like an armed camp. The brown-habited Franciscan and the yellow-garbed Jew had been shoved into the background by knights in chain mail and squires in coats of *cuir-bouilli*. More longbows were in evidence than grammars at St. Martin's, which served as the center of town, at St. Frideswide on the edge of the Jewry, in Beaumont Palace and Oxford Castle. Men were camped on Banbury Road, Hogacre, Greenditch, Portmeadow, even at the approaches to Folly Bridge, where in a strange tower lived the strangest man, the greatest man, that this magnificent century produced: Roger Bacon, scientist and iconoclast, his back bent in the brown habits of the Minorites, his hands stained with the acids of experiment, his mind racing on the cold outer edges of time and space.

The King who had stammered and gasped when he saw his barons sitting in Parliament in their armor had double reason to pause at the spectacle of Oxford in arms, and he met their demands in a mood which could only be described as submissive. This session, which later was given erroneously the title of the Mad Parliament, could not have been held at Beaumont palace, which lacked the space for such numbers. More likely the magnates assembled in Oxford Castle, where the keep and the square lower tower afforded plenty of room. One chronicle places the meeting in the monastery of the Dominicans.

The principles which had been approved at London were expeditiously applied to a reorganization of the machinery of state. A committee of twenty-four, half chosen by the King, half by the magnates, was appointed to handle the details of the operation. Henry's nominees included his three half brothers, John Mansel, and the leading peers who were standing by him. The baronial half included Gloucester, Simon de Montfort, Roger Bigod, and Walter Cantilupe, the Bishop of Worcester. This body set to work at once.

Out of their deliberations came the creation of two new administrative bodies. The first was a permanent council of fifteen men who would sit continuously with the King and advise him on all points of policy and who would have, moreover, the power to restrain him; a gentle method of applying the right of veto. The second was a body of twenty-four to deal specifically with the difficulties of the King and find ways of meeting them. It was ordained that three sessions of Parliament were to be held each year at specified times for the discussion of state problems. The filling of the responsible offices under the King was to be a function of the council of fifteen.

It will be seen that these regulations, which came to be called the Provisions of Oxford, were more than a curb of the King's power. Cloak their intent in the most careful and polite of phrase and they still constitute a transfer of final authority to the council of fifteen. That Henry agreed to terms as humiliating as this can be accepted as evidence of the panic into which he had been thrown by his recent mistakes and failures. Early in August he published his consent, after taking a solemn oath to abide by the Provisions, a step which was demanded also of Lord Edward.

One of the first acts of the Council was to have the Crown resume control of all royal castles, a move directed at the royal favorites among whom the bulk of the strongholds had been distributed. A list of peers, nineteen in all, was drawn up to undertake the responsibility in their stead. Simon de Montfort placed Kenilworth and Odiham in the hands of the Council at once, but the Lusignan half brothers, who had already refused to swear obedience to the Provisions, declared their intention of retaining control of all the castles in their hands. William of Valence clashed again with the Earl of Leicester on this issue, and the latter said to him grimly, "This hold for sure, either you give up your castles or you lose your head!"

The hated King's Men had not been under personal attack during the proceedings at Oxford. They had served on the committee of twenty-four and they would not have been disturbed had they not elected to stand out against the Council. Even though Prince Edward came forward boldly in their favor, the four Lusignans were convinced by the bitterness of the storm raised throughout the country that flight was the only course left them. They attempted to get away but, realizing the impossibility of making their escape, took refuge in Aymer's castle at Winchester. Here they were joined by Edward, but this did not stop the baronial party from laying siege promptly to the place. Lacking the supplies for defense, the brothers were compelled to surrender.

They were treated with more consideration than might have been expected under the circumstances. They were told they must leave the country, and a choice was presented to them: the first, exile for all of them; the second, a proposal that Guy and Geoffrey abjure the realm while William and Aymer were to be retained in custody in England. The brothers chose the first course. Dover was then fixed as their port of departure, and it was agreed that they might take the sum of six thousand marks with them. All their properties in England would be confiscated, but a subsistence arrangement would be made for them after their departure.

There was a recognized method of dealing with men who had agreed to abjure the realm. A point of departure was fixed and a certain number of days allowed for the land journey. The abjurer had to wear the garb of a condemned criminal, a tunic of the cheapest cloth. He walked barefoot and carried a wooden cross in his hand. He was not permitted to stray from the most direct road nor to stay more than one night in any one place. If no vessel was available on his arrival, he was compelled to wade out into the sea up to his neck each day as evidence of his intention to depart at the first opportunity.

There was no thought of invoking any of these regulations in connection with the departure of the much-execrated Lusignans, although the public would have howled its delight at the spectacle of the belligerent Aymer tramping barefoot to his appointed fate or the exquisite Wiliam wading out into the waves. There was, however, considerable delay in getting them off. The wind blew finally from the right quarter and they put out to sea, landing at Boulogne, where they were received with suspicion and hostility.

Their departure was hailed with almost universal delight. There would be fewer kings in England now. The greed of the King's Men would no longer stir enmity, their influence would no longer be felt in matters of state.

4

On an occasion during the late summer, after the Provisions had been ratified and put into effect, the King elected to go from Westminster to London by water. A thunderstorm blew up while he was on the way. As the King had a great fear of thunder and lightning, it was decided to put ashore. The bargemen, selecting the first water stair which offered, landed him at Durham House, which Simon de Montfort was occupying as his city home.

The latter appeared at a gate in the high masonry wall to receive them. As the King and his party were well drenched, he met them without donning hat or cloak. "Do not be alarmed," he said. "The storm is spent."

Henry was desirous of gaining shelter as quickly as possible, but he turned at this and regarded his brother-in-law with a hostile eye. "By the hand of God," he declared, "I fear thee more than all the thunder in the world!"

The earl accepted this declaration of his liege lord's enmity without any change of countenance. "You should not fear me, my lord," he answered. "I am your true friend and my sole desire is to preserve England from ruin and you from the destruction which your false counselors are preparing for you."

There is good reason to believe that this was an honest reflection of Simon de Montfort's feeling at this time. His hatred of the King might have played some part in driving him into the ranks of the opposition in the first place, but there can be no doubt that a sincere belief in the need for change now actuated him. He was never known to blow hot and cold; once committed to a course in which he believed, he was wholehearted in his adherence, even fanatical.

The charge has been lodged against him that it was ambition which spurred him on to organize the baronial party into a fighting unit. This may have some basis of truth. The Earl of Leicester was an ambitious man, without a doubt, knowing himself to possess the qualities of leadership. In times of crisis destiny has the habit of beckoning to one man. Simon de Montfort knew himself the favorite of destiny in the situation created by the reckless government of the self-willed King. No one else was capable of stepping into the shoes of Stephen Langton, certainly not the undependable Gloucester or the brave Bigod. There was no reluctance on Simon's part to step forward in response to the beckoning of the unerring finger. There was in him a furious gladness that now at last, after years of wrangling and shilly-shallying, the issue would be joined.

But if personal ambition had been the predominating impulse, he would have followed a different course after the baronial victory at Oxford. The reins of power were within his reach had he cared to gather them in. Henry was in a thoroughly penitent mood and, for the time being at least, incapable of facing the aroused magnates. His quavering, "Am I your prisoner?" spoken at London in April, was an indication of the craven mood into which he had lapsed at the first shaking of the baronial fist. The King must have realized, moreover, that he was alone in this crisis. His favorites had been seized and bundled unceremoniously out of the country. Richard of Cornwall was in Germany, attending to his complicated affairs and seeing his slowly accumulated wealth vanish like the snows of April. Edward was too young to count. The men who had been running the country under the King, even the clever Mansel, were lacking in stature. It was cold and lonely for the weathercock King, high up on his monarchial ridgepole, with such strange and bitter winds causing him to gyrate madly on his gilded pedestal. He must have been in a mood to welcome able assistance, even that of his detested brother-in-law; particularly if he could, by detaching him from the baronial party, deal a blow to the solidarity of his enemies.

In arriving at any understanding of the inner motives of this militant champion, Simon de Montfort, it must be borne in mind that the men of this day, steeped in feudal traditions, had no conception of government save that of the monarchial state. The barons were striving for nothing more drastic than a sounder basis for the exercise of the King's powers. It was not in any of their minds that Henry should be removed as head of the state. Simon de Montfort had no such thought, as became clear after the battle of Lewes. The Provisions of Oxford contained the germs of constitutional government, but there was a clear understanding that they were temporary in character and designed to provide a workable system against the day when a permanent solution could be found.

Had Simon de Montfort been actuated by ambition he would have seen a much better role for himself than that of leader of the opposition. A strong man acting under Henry in accord with the Provisions would have been the solution most acceptable to the mind of the age instead of a continuation of the struggle to its inevitable end—the extinction of royal power or the final defeat of the barons. It would not have been a difficult matter for Simon to slip into the spot once occupied by Hubert de Burgh. His wife would have favored a reconciliation and might have served as the go-between. Henry was in a sufficiently desperate frame of mind to respond, provided he himself retained all the semblance of kingship and could be assured of relief from the mortifying difficulties in which he wallowed. He had done so once before. When he had arrived in Gascony and found himself facing conditions he did not understand, he had sent for the man he had vilified with such blasts of hatred in the hearing at Westminster.

Such a partnership would not have lasted long, of course. A spirited war horse could not travel for any length of time in double harness with one which had never learned discipline. This, nevertheless, was the solution a purely ambitious man would have sought, power and wealth under the King. Leadership of opposition is a cold and thankless task at best.

It was leadership of opposition which Simon de Montfort selected. Perhaps he knew that to accept power under the King would be a temporary matter, an arrangement doomed to an explosive termination. Perhaps he was wise enough, and unselfish enough, to realize that the success of the government under the Provisions would depend on vigilant opposition and that he himself was the best qualified for the role of watchdog.

It is certain that he had become by this time almost fanatical in his devotion to the cause of better government. This he demonstrated in his first serious altercation with the Earl of Gloucester. During the meeting of Parliament in February of the following year the two earls clashed over the terms of ordinance. Gloucester wanted the advantages gained at Oxford to apply only to the nobility. Leicester stood out for an engagement whereby the peers would extend to their dependents the same rights they were exacting from the Crown for themselves. Gloucester was so insistently opposed that Simon flared into anger.

"I care not to live and act with men so fickle and so false!" he cried.

He not only withdrew from the deliberations but from

England as well, crossing the Channel into France, where he moodily concerned himself with personal matters.

This outburst was not the chagrin of a leader balked by the opposition of his supporters. Simon was the heart and soul of the cause, but Gloucester's name had appeared first in the Provisions; they still shared the command. It was an impulsive and irrational act and it endangered the success of the cause. Why did Simon behave in this way? It was not in keeping with his usual statesmanlike attitude. Perhaps he saw in the quarrel an opportunity to bring things to an issue and to oust Gloucester from the equality they were sharing. Perhaps—and this is the more reasonable assumption—it was caused by the passionate resentment of an overworked and overwrought man who saw something very close to his heart being weakened and debased.

The most telling evidence as to the sentiments which actuated this able and darkly passionate man is supplied by none other than the King's son, Lord Edward, who would from this moment forward play an important part on the great stage. In late summer of 1259, while the King was in France in connection with the French treaty, word reached London that the prince was paying the city a visit in advance of the October meeting of Parliament. This caused speculation of a decidedly apprehensive character. Edward had not been behaving himself well. He had been keeping about him a company of young knights, mostly recruited from abroad, who caroused wildly and pillaged wherever they went. Having no concern over matters of detail, he was leaving the management of his castles and lands to stewards who were enriching themselves at the expense of the tenants. It was even reported that he had killed a youth of common parentage without any provocation. His very young wife being still in France, the prince had been displaying an interest elsewhere, in the dark-eyed Alice of Angoulême who had married the Earl of Gloucester's son. Alice had inherited some of the beauty of her grandmother, the late Queen Isabella, and as she was very flirtatious and provocative, she had caught the eye of her step-cousin Edward. The people of England who had been ready to love and follow the tall prince were beginning to dread the day when he would rule in Henry's stead. They feared to find in him another John.

The Edward who rode into London on this occasion was a grown man. Managing his horse with sure hand, his surcoat embroidered with the three leopards and laced to his metal skullcap, the chausses of steel which covered his thighs the longest in the kingdom, he was an impressive figure. He made his entrance with fitting sobriety; no curvetting of horses in youthful display, no wild caracoling, no exuberance of any kind. The prince, in fact, showed a grave face to the Londoners who watched his arrival. There was an almost somber air about him, as though he realized the extremity which affairs had reached and was deeply concerned over the part he was to play.

Simon de Montfort was in London at the time, having returned at the insistence of the magnates, who needed his sure hand on the rudder. He was again at Durham House, which lay out beyond Cheringe Village, now Charing Cross. The champion of the people was prone to deep spells of unhappiness, and in his moods of melancholy he would stand in the stone turret at the water's edge and watch the wool barges going by; and wonder, perhaps, what was in store for this realm of England, what the future held for these brisk and cheerful people. What part in the life of centuries to come would the wool merchant have, and the bargemen and the shevel-gabbit custodian of the river stairs shouting hoarse-voiced greetings to acquaintances on the river? The earl had no longer any concern with normal things. He brooded constantly over the situation in England. His eyes had turned to the future.

Edward rode straight to the Tower of London and took up his quarters there. All of walled London lay between the Tower and Durham House, but the two tall men, the fair-headed prince and the dark peer, were constantly in each other's company nevertheless. They rode and walked and talked together with every evidence of accord. In the streets and the inns of London, in all the mean hovels as well as the palaces, speculation was rife. What did this mean? Edward had sworn to obey the Provisions with open reluctance. Why did he now consort on amicable terms with the man chiefly responsible for forcing the assent of the King to these ironclad regulations? It was to be expected under the circumstances that wild rumors would spread in London, the wildest of all being a story that the heir to the throne and his godfather were plotting to anticipate nature and put Edward in the King's place.

It is purely a matter of speculation as to how far the relationship between the two men developed. There was no thought between them of supplanting Henry. Edward's love for his father would have made him recoil from such a course. It is equally clear, however, that he had been won over temporarily to a belief in the popular cause, and this was remarkable because he had been the most militant of his father's supporters.

It is easier to conceive of the nature of their talks. The sage earl and the eager neophyte discussed the best ways of governing a country like England and, no doubt, the responsibilities of subject to King, and King to subject. More than anything else, they talked of the science of warfare, in which Edward took the most intense interest. He could not have found a better teacher than Simon de Montfort. The battles the latter had fought in Gascony had never been large enough to be called important, but he had always commanded his inadequate forces with the greatest skill. He had never lost a brush with the enemy and had never besieged a castle in vain. So brilliant had been his performance there, in fact, that he was now generally conceded to be the best soldier in Europe. Edward, willing to learn, listened to this master tactician with respect and admiration.

What had brought about the change in Edward's attitude? A belief clearly in Simon de Montfort, a recognition of the deep sense of idealism which governed the baronial leader. The turn that affairs had taken in England had changed Lord Edward from the roistering leader of bachelor knights into a man with a serious concern for the inheritance into which he would come someday. He would never have given his friendship and trust, even for so short a time, to a man actuated solely by hostility to the King or personal ambition.

CHAPTER TWENTY-ONE

War Becomes Inevitable

THERE was simplicity and informality in everything that Louis of France did. He was prone to call in his ministers and peers to his chamber and have them sit on the side of his bed while they discussed affairs of state. Sometimes even the humblest of petitioners were summoned to the royal bedroom for a talk over their claims, for Louis delighted in honoring the old tradition that even a beggar from the city gates could approach the King. Often he would sit on a bench with his advisers about him or on the ground, "in his plain camel's-hair coat with sleeveless surcoat of tiretaine," with them grouped about him tailor-fashion.

It was in some such manner that he discussed with the members of the council of twelve the peace he had made with Henry of England. It had taken a long time to negotiate this treaty which was hopefully believed to have made everlasting peace possible between the two countries. The main reason for the protracted nature of the discussions had been an obstructive attitude on the part of Simon de Montfort and his wife. Eleanor, now a mature but still beautiful woman, was not content to have her claims to land in France brushed aside and lost for all time. Henry had never gone to the trouble of reclaiming her dowry in full from the Marshals after the death of her first husband, and this had been a bitter bone of

contention between them. If Henry wanted to have the treaty
signed and sealed, then let him remedy the neglect of so many
years: thus, Eleanor, and it is impossible to blame her for it.
In this stand she had the firm and emphatic backing of her
husband. Louis, for his part, refused to ratify a treaty which
left any unsettled claims to rise up and vex him in the future.
With glowering reluctance Henry had agreed finally to allow
his sister the sum of fifteen thousand marks out of the funds
that Louis would pay him, a small enough settlement. The
treaty had then been drawn up and signed with great pomp
and circumstance.

Henry renounced for all time his claims to Normandy,
Poitou, and the Plantagenet possessions of Anjou and Maine.
He was to retain Gascony and to receive by way of compensa-
tion lower Saintonge, the province of Angenais, the lands of
Quercy, and the dioceses of Cahors, Périgueux, and Limoges,
for all of which he would do homage to Louis. In addition
Louis was to pay Henry the cost of maintaining five hundred
knights in the crusading field for a period of two years.

The French council objected bitterly to the cession of these
lands in the South to the English King, particularly the rich
provinces lying between Gascony and La Marche. They
agreed it was wise to secure the renunciation of all English
rights in Normandy and the great provinces in the North and
West. But why give up the rich dioceses of Périgueux and
Limoges to a king no more formidable than a boy with a tin
sword? For that matter, they argued further, it would not be
difficult to wrest Gascony from him if France had any desire
for such an enterprise.

These were the arguments they advanced against the unpopular treaty, seated perhaps in somber and frowning rows on
the ground about the King or on benches facing him. There
was nothing they could do about it if the King persisted in
what seemed to them a weak and sentimental course. France
had set up no manner of safeguards against the power of her
kings, and Louis might do as he pleased. They were outspoken
enough, however, to make it clear that in pampering his
brother-in-law of England he was seriously affronting his own
nobility and disregarding vested rights in the ceded territory.

Louis, holding his hat of swan's-down in his hands as unpre-
tentiously as the humblest of them, his splendid face grave and
intent, was convinced in his own mind, without a doubt, that
from the standpoint of realistic statesmanship they were right.

He was not going to allow himself to be swerved, however, from a stand to which he had given long and prayerful thought.

His brief answer, delivered in a quiet voice, might well be remembered as a truly great utterance, "I give these lands to the King of England in order that there may be love between our children and his."

2

Henry did not return to England immediately after the signing of the treaty. He lingered on in France on one pretext and another. The main reason given for the delays which continued month after month and extended finally into the middle of the following year was the need to tie up some loose ends of the treaty. This is not entirely convincing. The final disposition of details could have been attended to without the bodily presence of the King of England. Such a splendid messenger service had been developed that letters could be exchanged between Westminster and St. Omer, where Henry was making his headquarters, in six days. The royal carriers did not wait for favorable winds to cross the Channel, and relays of horses were maintained so that mail could be carried at top speed. There was, clearly, another reason for staying in France.

John Mansel was with the King and had served as his chief adviser throughout the long and tedious negotiations. This gifted commoner is one of the most baffling characters in English history. Little actually is known about him, but the few available facts whet the appetite for more. He must have been a man of infinite resource, a Richelieu or Wolsey, operating on a much more limited scale; their equal in point of clever planning and adroit execution but lacking, first, the personal ambition shown by the two great cardinals and their vision, and, second, a master of the right caliber and temperament to give him a chance to show his mettle. Before the rise of Mansel, Henry's course had been weak and maladroit. He had drifted aimlessly, shifting from one party to another as events dictated. Then he began suddenly to show a greater steadiness of purpose and at times such flashes of ingenuity, such evidence of machiavellian planning, that one cannot fail to wonder about the reason. This was not Henry's own work; natures do not change in the middle years so suddenly and remarkably. Inevitably it is necessary to accept the fact that

Mansel, working unobtrusively behind the scenes, was pulling the strings. The skill he displayed in all the missions with which he was entrusted marks him as of sufficient capacity. It could not have been anyone else. The Queen had always been at the King's side, and her advice had always been bad. Henry had ceased listening to the Queen's Men, and his own brothers were a blundering, blustering lot. Richard of Cornwall had his hands full in Germany. Mansel, therefore, it must have been.

It was Mansel, clearly, who kept the King so long in France. He knew that Henry had already recovered from the panic which had caused him to accept the Provisions of Oxford. Henry's pride had been so trampled on that he had now one purpose in life, to be his own man again and resume the easy methods of personal rule without any dictation. Two courses were open to him. He could return to England and repudiate the Provisions openly. This he preferred, naturally, but he did not need a John Mansel to point out that doing so would lead to civil war. The other course was to whittle at the Provisions, to break them down one clause at a time, and to resume personal rule by such easy stages that the barons would find it hard to take a stand. This was the course Mansel would favor, and it is easy to believe that Henry remained in France in accordance with a careful long-range plan. The whittling process could be started better there.

Only on such grounds could Henry have been restrained from returning. He knew that Simon de Montfort had gone back to England, taking war horses with him and a small squad of mercenary soldiers. What was the man up to? Was he planning to make war? To add to the King's uneasiness, stories began to seep back of the continued friendship between Simon and Prince Edward. Were they plotting to get rid of him? Henry was so alarmed that he began to write frantic letters to prominent people in England, even to leading citizens of much-despised London, beseeching them to be on their guard and to work in his interests. He ran to Louis of France and Queen Marguerite and told them of conspiracies being hatched against him. But still he did not return.

A persistent hand was needed on the tail of the royal supertunic to keep the apprehensive King from hurrying back home to protect his interests. That, and a conviction that his interests would best be served by waiting.

The Provisions called for three meetings of Parliament each year at stated times. This was one of the most revolutionary clauses. Parliament had always met when the King summoned it and not before, and had always been properly humble about the whole matter. It was one of the most mortifying of all the restrictions to Henry's pride. The first step, then, in the whittling process was to establish the fact that, in spite of the positive intent of the Provisions, Parliament could not meet when the King was not there. The time drew near for the first session of the three, which was set for February 2 and would be called the Candlemas Parliament, and still Henry lingered in France. Finally he wrote to the chief justiciar that he could not get back and so the meeting would have to be postponed.

This caused a flurry of angry talk in England. The magnates did not relish the necessity of breaking so soon the rule established in the Provisions. But, after all, could Parliament function without the King? With one exception the magnates finally accepted the necessity of a postponement. The exception was Simon de Montfort.

Simon had been unhappy over the way things were going. The solidarity of the baronial party had been shaken by the inevitable quarrels in the rank and file but even more so by the uncertain course of the Earl of Gloucester. Simon had been watching the merrytotter tactics of his fellow leader with a somber eye. He himself had not veered by as much as an inch from the stand he had taken at the start. He would not remain in the country if compromise measures became necessary. Nothing would suit Simon but strict adherence to the terms of the Great Charter and the methods of administration established in the Provisions. There must be no more squandering of national wealth on foreign favorites, no more bestowing of lands and heiresses on royal relatives from abroad, no further levying of illegal taxes.

Simon became morose in temper and thin in body. There were deep lines of care on his dark face. His temper was short. It was at this stage that Adam Marsh found it necessary to admonish the earl and his princess wife not to allow their tempers to strain the marriage bond. Eleanor seems to have shared her husband's dark view of the future, and her temper suffered accordingly. But the gentle Franciscan need not have been alarmed. Nothing could seriously shake their deep devotion.

That Simon was prepared to see Parliament meet while the King was absent was most significant of his state of mind. The feudal conceptions which ruled the thinking of the times were losing their hold on him. He had reached the stage of believing that, in some matters at least, the King should be the servant and not the master of the state. This meant inevitably a weakening of the power of his own class, for King and peer fitted into the same pattern. The leader of the baronial party had come a long way in his thinking; but, as events were quickly to prove, he had come alone.

The plans of the King—or perhaps it would be more accurate to say the plans of John Mansel—were forced into hasty application by word that Simon and Prince Edward were planning to call a Parliament in London in spite of everything. Instructions were sent across the Channel on March 27 to the justiciar to summon a selected list of one hundred or more barons on April 23 to join the King and to be in readiness for armed action. The list included the Earl of Gloucester but not the Earl of Leicester. Richard of Cornwall, free for the time being of his not heavy responsibilities as King of the Romans, turned up in London. An inner council was set up in the King's interests, consisting of Richard, Gloucester, the justiciar, and a few top royal officers. They closed the gates of London tight and issued orders that no adherent of Leicester or Prince Edward were to be allowed within. Armed guards stood on all the gates and along the walls to see that these orders were carried out.

Henry himself arrived in London on April 30 with three hundred knights at his back. Most of the barons who had been summoned were already there. The situation was well in hand.

Henry, preferring to remain for personal safety behind the walls of London, made St. Paul's his headquarters. Edward appeared in a contrite mood and was admitted to the city, but not at first to his father's presence, the King not being able to bring himself immediately to forgiveness. The prince had been carried away by the ideals of his godfather, but when it came to a definite issue such as this he could not ally himself against his father. The ideals, however, had taken root and later they would sprout and grow and, finally, bear magnificent fruit.

It was several days before Henry would see his son, but he gave in at last and the reconciliation between them was affectionate and complete. Edward, a little ashamed over his sowing of ideological wild oats, organized a party of his bachelor knights and set out on a tour of France to break lances with the champions of Gaul. There was no bad blood at this stage between the prince and Simon de Montfort. Edward knighted one of the earl's young sons before leaving, and the parting between the two men was on terms of personal amity.

The King now moved vigorously against his brother-in-law. He drew up a list of charges, a lengthy document which revived memories of his all-embracing indictments of Hubert de Burgh. It recited the full history of their financial disagreements. It listed in repetitious and monotonous detail the complaints which had been brought against Simon as seneschal of Gascony and which had been unanimously dismissed by the Council but which Henry now revived as though they had been proven. The other clauses were of the irrelevant kind to which he was much addicted, including a complaint that Simon had not said farewell to him when he left Paris.

It was decided, on the insistence of Louis of France, who seems to have admired Simon as one of the great figures of the day, to have the charges heard before a panel of peers. Simon defended himself with his usual skill, his main point being that he had acted as a sworn counselor of the King and in accordance with the oaths of office he had taken. No conclusions were announced and the King's charges were shelved.

In the meantime troubles were brewing in Wales. Llewelyn ab Gruffydd, taking advantage of the division in England, led a force into the valley of the Wye and captured the important castle of Builth. It was decided to meet the invaders with a two-pronged drive, and armies were ordered to concentrate at Chester and Shrewsbury. Simon de Montfort's military abilities were badly needed in this emergency and, in spite of the charges still hanging over him, he was appointed by Henry to command the army at Chester! Intimidated by these preparations, Llewelyn decided to withdraw from the Wye, and a truce for two years was signed before Simon had an opportunity to do any fighting on the King's behalf.

Henry's position was well consolidated by this time. He was making his personal headquarters in the Tower of London and he held the line to Dover strongly. The barons of the Cinque Ports had been forced reluctantly into line, and this assured the possibility of bringing in, if needed, reinforcements from France. This careful planning was in great contrast to the haphazard and farcical campaigns Henry had conducted in France and may be accepted as proof that the King's affairs were now in good hands.

Mansel had not remained, however, to see the working out

of the arrangements which undoubtedly he had initiated. He had hurried off to Rome on a delicate mission, to get from Pope Alexander an absolution of the oath Henry had taken to observe the Provisions of Oxford. It took time, apparently, to convince His Holiness, for it was not until April 14, 1261, that the bull of absolution was issued.

Things moved rapidly then, and according to plan. A body of mercenary troops from France under the command of the Count of St. Pol arrived in the country. Henry went to Winchester, accompanied by some of the foreign soldiers. On June 12 he announced the bull of absolution.

"I have resumed royal power," he declared proudly.

3

The country was stunned and incensed by the publication of the bull and the implication that Henry did not intend to act any longer in accordance with the Provisions. That he was taking back into his hands the reins of personal rule was clear when he began to supplant officials who had been appointed by the committee of fifteen in the administrative departments by men of his own and to select new sheriffs without tolerating a word of advice. Simon de Montfort, who still held to his policy of no appeasement, was infuriated by the weakness his fellow barons showed at this juncture. They were ready to compromise, to negotiate, to make concessions. Convinced that they could never be held together as an active force, he left the country and settled in France, a disappointed and saddened man.

Henry followed him to the Continent, and the French King made an effort to reconcile the embattled brothers-in-law. Henry made peace impossible, however, by raking up all the old charges against Simon. They seem to have become an obsession with him. At every opportunity he reached a hand into the packet of the past and brought out the now familiar indictments, reciting each old charge with unction and enjoyment. King Louis, who had heard it all before, abandoned the effort to restore the two men to a friendly basis.

Henry and his party were caught in Paris by an epidemic. The King became so ill that it was a long time before he could attempt the journey home, and he was so weak when he landed that he could ride no farther than Canterbury. Here the royal party spent Christmas. An outbreak of hostilities occurred in Wales in the midst of the festivities, and in a despondent frame of mind the King wrote to Edward, who was still breaking lances in France. "This is no time for laziness or boyish wantonness," he said. "It is a disgrace to you that Llewelyn spurns the truce which he promised to maintain with us." At the same time he wrote to the justiciar that, in view of the disturbed conditions, no sessions of Parliament would be held.

Edward answered his father's appeal by returning and taking charge of operations along the Welsh frontier. He found things in a badly disorganized state. The old Marcher barons had been dying off. Richard of Gloucester, who had been the commanding figure in the West because of his immense landholdings in Gloucester and Glamorganshire, had died in July of the previous year. His son, Gilbert the Red, was in his twentieth year and had become an ardent supporter of Simon de Montfort. Other young men who had succeeded to positions of power distrusted the King with, it must be said, the best of reasons. They saw no reason yet to place any faith in Edward.

The result was that the prince found it impossible to accomplish much in spite of the fact that he demonstrated energy and a fine military instinct. The young Marchers held back from him, unwilling to help consolidate the royal power.

Simon de Montfort returned to England around the end of April of the following year, 1263. This time he came in a new role. There could no longer be any doubt of his status and his purpose in coming back. He was the acknowledged leader of the barons, the unchanging champion of the Provisions of Oxford. His purpose was to organize and command the forces of dissent in the armed struggle which had become inevitable.

CHAPTER TWENTY-TWO

The First Moves of the Civil War

SIMON de Montfort had come back to make war, and all men knew it. All men knew that no peaceful agreement into which Henry might enter would be carried out. At the first opportunity he would run to the pope for absolution of his vows, and thus the familiar performance of repudiation would be repeated. It was impossible to get the better of the King in this kind of contest because his very weaknesses made him a formidable opponent. It was like buffeting a straw man suspended at the end of a loose rope.

Late in May, Simon was at Oxford for a council of war with his chief supporters. He had selected the university city because it was strategically situated, having the Marcher country back of it. Perhaps he had it in mind also that the meeting place of the Mad Parliament would be a logical starting point for the armed struggle.

Many of the men who assembled at the Earl of Leicester's call were, strangely enough, new to the cause. Some of the original members were present, but many of them had died and many had been won over to the royalist side by one inducement or another. There was a predominance of youth in the baronial ranks at Oxford, and the explanation of this can be found in the personality of Simon de Montfort. Young men found him irresistible. He was a magnetic figure, this

Anglo-Norman peer who had won for himself the reputation of being the best soldier in Europe. He appealed to their sense of idealism because they knew him to be fervent in his faith and unswerving in his devotion to the cause. When the choice lay between this knight in shining armor and the weak King, the crabbed, complaining old incumbent of the throne who had been an almost comic figure for so long, they did not find it a hard decision to make. If Edward had been older and had behaved himself better during the years of his adolescence, he would have split their allegiance. As it was, they flocked to Oxford and clanked in full armor about St. Martin's, clamoring for armed action.

The most sensational addition to the baronial ranks was Henry of Almaine, the oldest son of Richard of Cornwall. Henry was a thoroughly likable youth, brave, amiable, personable; but, as it developed, inclined to be fickle and certainly without any great force of character. He had accompanied his father to the crowning at Aachen and had shortly after been sent back because the Dutch and German subjects of the new King had objected to so many Englishmen in the imperial train. Young Henry was just old enough now to come into some properties of his own and to take an interest in politics. At first he was an ardent advocate of the cause of his uncle, the King, and refused positively to take the oath of obedience to the Provisions of Oxford. He even took sides with the Lusignans although he did not go to the length of following them to Winchester in their final gesture of defiance. Shortly afterward he became the close friend of Gilbert the Red and, perhaps because of this, he was drawn into the youthful circle which saw in Simon de Montfort the hope of England. He arrived in Oxford with shining-eyed enthusiasm, the most eager neophyte there. And no doubt a spark passed through the ranks when they saw him come riding in with the baronial cross on his shoulder.

The next recruit in point of rank was John de Warenne, Earl of Surrey, who had married Alice de Lusignan and was therefore the King's brother-in-law. He was in his early thirties and had been a member of the inner royal circle, even being chosen for the great honor of knighthood at the hands of Alfonso at Las Huelgas. An ardent royalist in the early stages of the struggle, he also had come under the influence of the baronial leader, and now he was at Oxford with a long train of knights and men-at-arms.

Gilbert the Red had come back into the ranks. It was clear, perhaps, to the leader that this twenty-year-old peer was already showing some of the defects of character which had made his father such a difficult partner. He had a tendency to sudden enthusiasms and to equally sudden processes of cooling off. If Simon had studied him with prophetic eye he would have been slow to welcome this youth with his blazing pride and his tinderlike temper, seeing faintly in the future a field of battle where the sudden appearance on the other side of the three chevrons of the house of Clare would turn the tide. At the moment, however, the mercurial though brave young earl was a fiery adherent of the baronial leader and ready for any risk beside him.

One of the recruits was Roger de Leyburn, a Kent man of the second rank. This passionate knight was always in trouble but possessed such a capacity for making friends that the consequences of his folly passed him by. Ten years before he had killed one Arnold de Montigny in a tilting, and it had been discovered later that he had neglected to cover the point of his lance with the customary socket, a fact which sat ill on men's stomachs when it was recalled that he had suffered a broken leg in an earlier jousting with the unfortunate Arnold. To cover up this unsavory episode he took the cross but did not go to the East, being given the appointment of steward to Prince Edward. There must have been unusual qualities in him which made other men like him, a devil-may-care gaiety, perhaps a hint of diablerie in his bold eye. He became at once a great favorite of Edward's, the leader of his train of bachelor knights. Nothing he did, not even the summary hanging of some servants of the house of Gloucester over a dispute, seriously disturbed his place in the prince's regard. He had, however, a predilection for the baronial side of the long struggle, and it was said that he had been instrumental in bringing his royal master and Simon de Montfort together. The King seems to have liked him in spite of this, but Queen Eleanor took a different view, regarding Leyburn with the cold eye of suspicion. She feared his influence over her son and may in addition have disliked the rakish side of the man. It was due to the Queen's insistence that in 1260 a demand was made for an accounting of his stewardship, as a result of which he was stated to be short in his accounts to the extent of one thousand pounds.

Leyburn violently denied the justice of the verdict and

removed all his goods from his various manors to prevent seizure. His properties were declared confiscated and, with characteristic boldness, he announced himself a rebel. When the return of Simon de Montfort brought the national issue to a head Leyburn was still at outs with the law and the leader of a group of youthful malcontents in the Marcher country. It was natural enough for him to throw his allegiance to Simon and to bring his companions with him. They were in force in Oxford and the most strident of all in support of the policy of armed action. Simon was to have little good of them, however. Their adherence hurt the cause in the eyes of many sober men who regarded them as outlaws. The Leyburn enthusiasm, moreover, which was real enough at the beginning, was not equal to the pressure which would be exerted later to make him change his coat.

The most loyal of the younger men was John de Vescy from Alnwick Castle in Northumberland, a grandson of Eustace de Vescy, who had played such a prominent part at Runnymede. It was not surprising to find him a zealous believer in the baronial cause and devoted fanatically to Simon de Montfort. John de Vescy remained true to his vows and fought through to the end of the struggle.

The decision of the council of war was to send a final demand to Henry. The Provisions were to be observed both in letter and spirit, and all who refused to abide by them were to be considered enemies of the realm and treated as such, the only exceptions being the King and the members of his immediate family.

Henry was not convinced that the barons meant to fight or that they could win if they did. He rejected the proposals.

2

The baronial forces were not large, but their commander had gained his reputation for generalship as much by the speed as the fury of his strokes. The suddenness with which he now went into action caught the royalists off guard.

Simon moved his forces out of Oxford and struck westward, his purpose being to secure command of the Severn River and his communications with the Marches. He met with no opposition, sentiment in the West being at this time against the King. Gloucester and Bristol opened their gates to him. While thus engaged he permitted his followers to exact tribute from the landowners who were known to be royalist in sentiment.

The estates of Peter d'Aigueblanche, Bishop of Hereford, were plundered, and Peter himself was captured and imprisoned at Eardisely. The ill repute in which the bishop stood as a result of his part in the Sicilian transactions accounted, perhaps, for the severity with which he was treated. Others had their fields burned and their livestock seized to support the army on its eastern drive. This may have been a necessary war measure, but it was to prove a serious mistake in policy. The plundered landowners never forgave Simon de Montfort and remained his implacable enemies to the end.

Simon now proceeded to demonstrate the vigor of his generalship. He did not sit himself down to the siege of castles while waiting for more of the dissenting barons to rally around the banner of revolt as any other leader of the day would have done. He knew that in order to win he must win quickly. London must be made his permanent base; the Cinque Ports must be secured because they meant command of the sea. Satisfied with his lines of communication, he turned and marched for London with a speed which threw dismay into the advisers of the King. The approach of the baronial army convinced them that it would be wise to seek a peaceful settlement. The task of opening negotiations was delegated to the King of the Romans, who had returned to England. Richard took to horse and rode furiously to Wallingford, hoping to intercept Simon as he led his steel-clad knights past Oxford. He was too late. The barons had not paused at Oxford but were already streaming down the Thames Valley. Richard turned and rode to Reading, but again he was too late. The roads between Reading and London were already thick with the dust raised by the marching feet of the barons.

By another surprise move Simon did not continue on to London but swung south between Windsor and that city and drove straight for the heart of Kent. This seemed the height of rashness. Kent was strongly held by the enemy. But when the weary and dusty army reached Romney on July 9 it became clear that the Earl of Leicester had been right in his calculations. The men of Kent came out to welcome him, and the barons of the Cinque Ports rallied to his side. Simon's main purpose had been accomplished. He had control of the Channel and the approaches to the kingdom in his pocket.

The royalist party realized their peril. Henry hastened in a panic to the shelter of the strong walls of the Tower of London and lent an assenting ear to the pacific counsels of the

King of the Romans, who had arrived after the tumult of the passing of the barons died down. Those of the King's party who had favored a bolder course now scented danger for themselves and hastened to get away. Boniface of Canterbury, who had faced the fury of London mobs once before and desired no more of that medicine, took ship on the Thames and got away to the Continent. John Mansel, not relishing the role of scapegoat which he knew would be his, followed the example of the archbishop and fled to France. London rose up in defiance of the King.

Henry was thankful for the strength of the Tower walls when he saw the narrow streets below him filled with angry mobs. As always, the rioters vented their first fury on the foreign residents of the city and the Jews, who were believed to have financed the long-continued obduracy of the King. Stephen Buckrell, the marshal of the city, was the leader of the demonstration, although its first violence was the work of a firebrand named John Fitzjohn. In one long night of horror many hundreds of the unfortunate Jews, including Kokben Abraham, the wealthiest of his race in the country, were slaughtered and their homes looted. Flames still rose from the Jewry when the sun came up over the estuary. The mobs, drunk on blood and the looted wines of the Gascon vintners, were not yet satisfied. They thronged the streets below the Tower and roared defiance of the anxious watchers on the ramparts.

Queen Eleanor chose this moment to think of escape. All night long, by the side of her spouse, she had watched the violence below and she feared that the rioters would now storm the Tower. Orders were given that the royal barge be prepared and manned for a race down the river to Windsor.

In another century the surface of the Thames would be crowded with large balingers and crayers with rounded bow and stern, but it is practically certain that the royal barge in this day would be of the galley type, which was, of course, much slower. It would have a large square mainsail of colored cloth or even silk, loose-footed and boomless, with a small cabin above the level of the rowers. Ordinarily the royal standard crackled sharply in the breeze at the prow, but discretion may have resulted in its removal for this precarious venture. Every pair of eyes in London, however, had rested many times on the royal conveyance as it plied up and down the river, the King's minstrels strumming and tootling in the stern and the deck gay with rich costumes. It was recognized as soon as it put out from the Tower wharf.

Old London Bridge was three hundred yards long and, even though the center was lined with houses and shops, it provided plenty of room for spectators. The bridge was black with people when the barge headed out into the river and steered for one of the narrow arches through which the water roiled and churned. A loud chorus of vituperation arose as soon as it became certain that this was the Queen and her ladies seeking to escape. Hands reached for rotten eggs and vegetables, for dried mud and stones and loose pieces of paving with which to pelt the hated Queen-consort.

Eleanor was now in her forty-first year. As she had been in ill-health for some time, it may be assumed that the freshness of her early beauty had deserted her. She was still of fine presence, however, and in spite of the plainness of the attire she had donned, it was not hard for her jeering subjects to pick her out from the group surrounding her. Alderman and thief, merchant and beggar joined in a furious shout.

"Down with the witch! Drown the witch!"

Eleanor, the only queen in English history to be subjected to such a demonstration of hatred and contempt, had never learned to school her emotions or to hide resentment. Her face was livid with anger as she listened to the execrations of the people she disliked more than any on earth, "these clowns," as her royal husband called them. But the hatred which caused her to register mental vows of retaliation was merged with fear. It was clear enough to everyone on the barge that to run the turgid water under the bridge would result in calamity. The order was given to turn about and put back to the Tower.

Later, escorted by royal troops, she ventured into the streets and ensconced herself in the sanctuary of St. Paul's. If she encountered any opposition on the way it is not recorded.

Henry had no stomach for adversity. He had always yielded quickly under pressure, and the treatment accorded his Queen had made him thoroughly apprehensive. His supporters were scattering, and there was no longer any hope of succor from his brother-in-law of France. Under these circumstances he gave in. It was announced on July 16 that he had accepted the terms proposed by the popular party.

All through the years of his long reign Henry had been making his peace thus, after being caught in flagrant error and wrongheadedness. It had always been possible to wriggle out of things in due course, breaking his oaths and finding pretexts for non-observance of promises. The stern and sardonic man who rode in from Kent to take control of things was not likely, however, to condone any breaking of pledges. Had Henry finally committed himself to promises he would have to keep?

Under the shrewd and incisive direction of Simon de Montfort it took three days only to set up a provisional government. Hugh le Despenser became chief justiciar. Nicholas of Ely took the custody of the great seal from Walter de Merton, the King's own appointee and familiar. New castellans were selected for the royal castle, even Prince Edmund, the stickit King of Sicily, being ordered to vacate Dover. The baronial army in the meantime marched into London, hard on the heels of the hastily retreating King and Queen.

3

The King had given in, but Prince Edward was in a far different mood. The first warlike move of the barons at Oxford had roused in the heir to the throne a mighty fighting spirit.

Having under his command a body of troops he had been using in the Welsh campaign, and lacking funds to hold them together, Edward went to the New Temple, where his mother's jewels were being held as security for loans she had received. He presented himself with a bodyguard and declared that he wanted to be assured as to the safety of the Queen's property. A request of this kind being not at all unusual, the custodian took the prince back into the center of the great cluster of buildings which constituted the New Temple until they came to the vaults. Edward and the men with him then took possession of the keys and proceeded to help themselves. It is recorded that the prince not only went away with the jewelry but ten thousand pounds in money as well, most of which had been placed there on deposit by London merchants. With the funds thus secured the prince was organizing a force at Windsor when the unexpectedness of Simon de Montfort's march into Kent brought royal resistance to an end. This, however, did not weaken the prince's resolution to go on with the struggle.

The period of his youth had come to an abrupt ending; he was now a man and with a man's work to do. He lacked at this time all sense of restraint, as witness his looting of the Temple. He never lost entirely, in fact, the conviction, so strong in him as a youth, that the end justifies the means. While the man he now recognized as the archenemy of his house proceeded to reweave the fabric of government, Edward set himself to the task of rebuilding the royal strength.

As shrewd in his untamed early manhood as Simon at the peak of his powers, Edward knew the weak spots in the baronial armor. He made the young men around Simon his special target. Roger de Leyburn was won back. That violent opportunist needed no more than a promise that the sins of the past would be forgiven to bring him into the royal camp. His influence being as strong as ever with the other members of the group, it was not long before Henry of Almaine and John de Warenne followed his example. The young Earl of Gloucester, being of stouter fiber and owing his opinions to no other man, withdrew temporarily from the heat of things, leaving himself in a position to jump in either direction. Lesser members followed the trend, however, and appeared at Windsor to make their peace.

Henry of Almaine was a youth of good principles, and he could not regard the changing of his coat as easily as some of the others. After deciding that his duty lay in the other camp he went to Simon and announced the fact.

"I can no longer fight against my father, against my uncle, against all my relatives," he said. There was in his attitude a kind of desperation over the difficulties of his position. "That is why I must leave you, Sir Earl, but I shall never bear arms against you."

The interview, a brief one, brings out a weakness in the leader of the popular cause. Simon was a little deficient in sense of humor. Instead of recognizing the mixed loyalties which had thrown Henry of Almaine into such a confused state of mind, he glowered at the embarrassed young man.

"I fear your lack of loyalty, Messer Henry," he answered, "more than I fear your arms."

The phrasing of this speech makes it clear that Simon was fully aware of the danger of his position. His following had been small enough when he had raised the standard of revolt, and now the defection of the younger wing was leaving him without sufficient strength to consolidate and hold what he had gained by his march into Kent. The desertion of one as inconsequential even as Henry of Almaine was not a matter to be treated with any lightness. It was a loss to a cause which in his eyes had become nothing short of sacred.

4

It was the Earl of Leicester's realization of his waning strength which induced him to agree to Louis of France as arbitrator between Henry and his subjects.

Prince Edward had been stirred to a pitch of fighting fury possible only to unbridled youth. He was using every weapon on which he could lay his hands to defend the crown which one day would be his. The savagery of his methods became clear at the meeting of Parliament called on October 13 in the hope of arriving at a compromise. The obstructionist tactics of the prince and his young lieutenants made any discussion impossible, and the meeting broke up in confusion.

That night four citizens of London, all of the wealthier class, brought word to Edward that Simon was staying at Southwark with a small following and that they could guarantee the closing of the city gates if an effort were made to capture him. The prince moved with haste to get his hands on the man he now hated, but, fortunately for the baronial cause, the efforts of the four wealthy citizens to seal the gates of the city aroused suspicion. Simon was the hero of the common people of London, and word was carried out to him that it would be safer to find lodgings inside the walls. When the mounted followers of the prince surrounded the house in Southwark, they found that the bird had flown.

It may be assumed that Simon agreed to arbitration because the situation was out of hand and he was not anxious to seek the solution in an immediate appeal to arms. There can be no doubt, however, that he believed the arbitration would be limited to a definition of method and not of principle. Before the brief meeting of Parliament had been broken up by Edward's supporters the King had again asserted his intention of abiding by the Provisions. His affirmation seemed to remove the possibility that the French King's inquiry would have any bearing on the validity of what had been done at Oxford. Whatever was in Simon's mind, however, the fact remains that he signed his name to the invitation, agreeing to abide by the decision. Among those who signed with him were the bishops of Worcester and London, the chief justiciar, and Humphrey de Bohun.

Even had Louis shared the understanding of the barons as to the limited scope of his arbitration, his appointment would still have been a mistake from the standpoint of the popular cause. Louis had a deep sense of justice, but he was, after all, a king. It was unthinkable to him that subjects could tell a king how he was to rule and what servants he might employ in carrying out his will. So closed was his mind on these points that it took him a very short time to arrive at his conclusions. He had not been expected to render his verdict before Pentecost. Henry arrived early in January at Amiens, where the hearings were to be held, but Simon de Montfort did not put in an appearance. It had been the intention of the latter to present the baronial case, but on his way he was thrown from his horse and his leg was broken. The hole in the road near Catesby which caused this accident may have changed the course of history. Simon was a powerful advocate, and it is possible he could have given Louis a clearer view of the rancorous conditions which had existed so long in England. He might, at any rate, have established in the mind of the French monarch an acceptance of the limited scope of the inquiry. If the nature of the Mise of Amiens had been different, it is probable that further fighting could have been avoided.

Louis did not allow the absence of the baronial leader to delay his decision. On January 23 he gave out his findings, which were in Henry's favor on every point. The Provisions of Oxford, which Henry had sworn to observe on so many occasions, were declared null and void. The King of England might rule as his judgment dictated and he might appoint his own ministers and officers, employing aliens as he saw fit. Two provisions were added which put some degree of restraint on the King's hands: the award did not apply to the liberties of the realm as established "by royal charter, privilege, franchise, statute or praiseworthy custom," which was meant to apply to the Great Charter only, and there must be no punishment of individuals.

England was stunned by the nature of the Mise of Amiens, as the decision of the French King was called. Simon de Montfort proclaimed at once that Louis had disregarded the established limitations and that, moreover, a decision recognizing the Great Charter could not at the same time rule out the Provisions of Oxford. He had no intention of accepting the rulings. "Though all should forsake me," cried Simon, "I will stand firm with my sons in the just cause to which my faith is pledged! Nor will I fear to risk the fortune of war."

He had no reason to fear that he would stand alone on this ground. The diplomatic defeat of the barons proved to be the means of uniting them again. Sentiment throughout the country stiffened. The city of London would have none of the award. The barons of the Cinque Ports were up in arms about it; the rank and file of the baronial party fiercely proclaimed their unwillingness to abide by one-sided findings to which they had not committed themselves.

The attitude of the Vatican proved a further stimulant to opposition. A new pope had succeeded Alexander two years before under the name of Urban IV. He was a Frenchman, Jacques Pantaléon, the son of a shoemaker. Urban was Gallic in his thinking and he agreed with the findings of the French King. The Mise of Amiens was given papal confirmation on March 16. Urban then made a tactical error, however, in appointing another Frenchman as papal legate to England, Cardinal Guy Fulcodi of Sabrina, with full power to declare a crusade against all who opposed the restoration of Henry to his former powers. Guy Fulcodi was an able man, a jurist who had worked closely with Louis in national matters before taking holy orders. He was a forward thinker in some respects, but he had an unshakable belief in the absolute power of kings. This made him incapable of understanding the attitude of Englishmen who had taken up arms against their monarch, even though he must have had some inkling of the almost imbecilic weakness of Henry's rule. The papal intervention acted as a bellows in blowing the coals of national discontent into flames.

Henry came back to England in a complacent frame of mind, announcing somewhat smugly that he would "receive into his peace" all who were ready to swear their acceptance of the award. To his huge dismay he found the country echoing with preparations for war.

CHAPTER TWENTY-THREE

The Battle of Lewes

THE castle at Northampton was one of the strongest in the kingdom, and the walls of the town were high and thick. To Simon de Montfort, still nursing his broken leg in London but losing no time in organizing a force of townsmen, it seemed that this midland stronghold, commanded by his cousin, Peter de Montfort of Beaudesert, and his son Simon, was an unconquerable outpost. He had not yet seen any evidence of the skill Prince Edward was acquiring in the art of war, but this he was due to discover at once.

Edward had learned one lesson from Simon himself, that battles were won by speed of movement and use of the element of surprise. On April 3 the royal army moved out of Oxford, where it had been mobilized, and struck north. The grades of the Chilterns lay east and south, and so the road to Northampton was straight and level enough. Edward led his men over the thirty-five miles in little more than one day, startling the baronial garrison by arriving suddenly under the walls the following afternoon.

The youthful impetuosity of the prince, which was responsible for this miracle, almost resulted now in throwing away the fruits of his energy. Having no sense of fatigue himself, he ordered his dusty followers to attack the city at once. They were repulsed, as might have been expected.

That night, while Edward sat gloomily under the stars, his armor beside him on the ground, there came to him the prior of the Cluniac monastery of St. Andrew which stood in a corner of the wall near the north gate. The prior was ardently royalist in sentiment and was prepared to give the same help to the prince that the woman who lived on the wall at Jericho rendered the besieging army of Israel. His monks were making an excavation under the walls through which the forces of Edward could file into the town. Dawn found the prince and his men pouring into the streets. Young Simon fought bravely to hold them back, but he was overborne and captured. The following day the castle surrendered.

William of Valence had returned to England after publication of the Mise of Amiens, on direct invitation from the jubilant Henry. He had marched under Edward's banner and was now given the task of pillaging the country around Northampton, extending as far as the Montfort estates at Leicester. This was a task which suited perfectly the haughty and vengeful Lusignan. He went about the razing of manor houses, the burning of villages, and the slaughtering of innocent people with thoroughness and relish. In the meantime the prince was demonstrating how well he had learned his lesson by following up his victory without delay. Consuming no more than five days in the operation, he marched south with his weary but triumphant followers and captured the town of Winchelsea. Tonbridge Castle, which belonged to Gilbert of Gloucester, fell soon after.

One of the prisoners taken at Tonbridge was Gilbert's wife, Alice of Angoulême, who was Edward's half cousin and a special favorite with both the prince and the King. Gossip had it, in fact, that the dark-eyed and vivacious Alice was a very special favorite; that as the young wife of the prince was still in France and would be kept there until things settled down in England, Edward had been solacing himself with the company of this fair Poitevin relative. There was probably some truth in the story because Edward had not seen his child wife for some time. The countess was released with great courtesy and, perhaps, inner regret.

The strategy followed by the prince thereafter was sound, being based on the truth that whoever was master of Kent and Sussex was master of England. If the royalists could control the country south of London, they could keep communications open with France and so prepare the way for the arrival of the forces which Queen Eleanor and John Mansel were mobilizing in the ports of Normandy. The Cinque Ports being baronial in sympathy, the royalists were under the necessity of occupying the country back of them with the intention of taking them over gradually.

There were two main roads leading from the Channel ports to London, the one most frequently used running from Dover to Canterbury and then by way of Rochester to the capital. The other ran from Hastings and Battle to Lewes and Croydon, which meant that some part of it went through the Weald. The first was the preferable one for the royal army to take in any movement directed against London, but Simon de Montfort was attacking Rochester with great vigor. Still unable to sit a horse with any comfort, he had been directing his men from a curious vehicle in which he had traveled from London and which resembled a chariot with four wheels. This had not handicapped him seriously because he had already captured the town and was pressing his attack against the castle when the royal forces began to march up the more westerly road from Hastings with the object, clearly, of attacking London. Simon, who lacked strength to guard both roads at once, had to give up the siege of Rochester and take his relatively small army to Fletching, which lay nine miles north of Lewes. Here, his men concealed for the most part in the eastern approaches to the Weald, he watched and waited.

2

When the royal army reached Lewes, King Henry took up his quarters in the Cluniac priory of St. Pancras, which lay on the southeast, between the town and the river Ouse, while Prince Edward was lodged in a castle belonging to William de Warenne on the west. Time was on their side, and they could afford to wait until the Burgundian and Brabanter mercenaries of Queen Eleanor arrived. They knew, however, that they had a decided superiority in numbers over the army of the barons and they were eager to engage them.

Perhaps because of this discrepancy in strength the barons made a final effort to reach a peaceful settlement. The bishops of London and Worcester carried a peace offer to Henry on May 13. The barons would grant the King fifty thousand marks if he would again affirm the Provisions and swear to observe them strictly. Such a proposal, coming from a meager army skulking in the shelter of the Weald, seemed to Henry and his advisers a confession of weakness and despair and was rejected with scorn. Prince Edward is reported to have said, "Peace is forbidden to them, unless they all find themselves with halters on their necks, and bind themselves over to us for hanging or for drawing." There was nothing for Simon to do now but fight.

That night the baronial leader moved his army from its well-concealed base at Fletching and marched through the darkness to a position beneath the ridge of the Downs immediately north of Lewes. There had been talk of attacking during the night, but this suggestion Simon had rejected as treacherous. The hours until dawn were spent instead in prayer and the hearing of confessions. After a sleepless night Earl Simon donned a plain surcoat over the chain mail which enveloped him from head to foot and buckled on his long two-edged sword. He said a silent prayer as he gazed up at Black Cap over which the sky had turned faintly gray. The day of the great test was at hand.

Each man wore the white cross of the Crusades on back and shoulder as a sign of the barons' belief in the justice of their cause. There was a practical purpose in this as well, because they would be able to distinguish friend from foe in the heat of conflict.

Earl Simon, it should be explained at this point, was not as badly crippled as the royalists thought. He had recovered sufficiently to take to the saddle, and during the day he would demonstrate his fitness by remaining in the thick of the fighting. He had used the chariot in getting to Fletching, however, thereby convincing the enemy, who had spies everywhere, that he was incapable of active leadership. The chariot now contained the four merchants who had tried to betray Simon to the prince. The earl did not forgive treachery easily and had some drastic punishment in mind for the unhappy quartet.

North of Lewes the Downs rise to a height of about four hundred feet and then shelve off abruptly to the level of the Ouse. The escarpment above looked black and formidable when the army of the people began their ascent. Black Cap stood up against the ebony of the sky, and off to the east rose the somewhat lower hilltop called Mount Harry. There were two roads which could be used in getting to the crest: a steep incline leading up between the two peaks, and a longer but less severely graded route which wound slowly around Mount

Harry on the east. The heavily armored troops and the knights on horseback took the latter way while the foot soldiers and archers in their light leather jerkins went scrambling up the sharp cut between Black Cap and the line of the hills.

Simon de Montfort rode in the van with the armed horsemen, a prey to the most intense anxiety. Would he find the passes above well guarded? If any part of the royal army had been posted behind the jagged crest of the Downs it would be impossible to gain a foothold and the upward thrust of the baronial forces would end in disaster. It was a bold gamble they were taking, but no other course had been open which held out any chance of victory. It has already been pointed out that time was on the side of the King. To win the test by battle the barons must win before the royalist strength was augmented by mercenary levies from abroad. If they could gain a foothold on the Downs, moreover, the royal forces would be placed at a severe disadvantage, compelled to fight uphill and with no facilities for retreat in case of defeat.

Simon de Montfort knew the risks he was taking and as he rode up the incline he strained his ears for any of the sounds which might betray the presence of the enemy: the neigh of a horse, a voice raised indiscreetly, the muffled tramp of feet. All was silence. Did this mean they would be allowed to seize the heights?

The knights in the van emerged cautiously from the road circling Mount Harry and found themselves on the downward grade to Lewes. Over their left shoulders they could see the sky turning to the light gray of dawn, shot with shafts of red. Under them were the lights of Lewes, where, it was said later, the royal troops in the priory had been drinking in expectation of an easy victory. The slopes immediately ahead of the debouching troops were clear, but a sound of galloping came back out of the darkness to warn them that scouts were carrying word to the town of their advance.

Simon de Montfort made his dispositions for battle. His army was small, numbering perhaps a little in excess of four thousand men. The center was given to the command of Gilbert of Gloucester with two veteran campaigners to assist him, William of Montchesni and John Fitzjohn. The right wing was entrusted to Simon's two sons, Henry and Guy, assisted by John de Burgh and Humphrey de Bohun. The left wing was made up of a small body of knights under Nicholas de Segrave and the citizen bands from London, who were lightly armed and lacking in military experience. Little was expected of the left. They were to advance down a ridge on the east with the Ouse immediately beneath them, and so constitute a threat to the royalist right without coming into close contact. A considerable reserve was assembled on the high ground near Black Cap, and here Earl Simon set up his standard, placing it above the four-wheeled chariot so that the impression might be maintained that he himself was stationed there like Moses directing the battle of Rephidim with uplifted arms from afar.

It had been overconfidence which had led the royal leaders to post a single sentry near Black Cap (he was sound asleep in the bushes) instead of occupying the roads up to the Downs. They were sure Simon de Montfort was still suffering from his injuries, a leader so downcast by the sweep of the King's army and so conscious of his meager strength that he had gone on the defensive by taking shelter in the Weald. They expected him to play the part of a Willikin on a much larger scale, using the Weald as a base from which to harry the royal army. It had never entered their heads, clearly, that he would have the magnificent audacity to lead his men up the steep escarpment and offer battle in the open.

Henry had never been a real soldier, and even in his civilian capacity he was indolent. Pulling himself together with commendable speed, however, the King brought his forces along Antioch Street and out into the open north of the town, where Edward was marshaling the army with furious energy. The prince seems to have performed prodigies in the small time allowed him. At any rate, the royal forces were drawn up in battle array before the army of the barons came within striking distance.

It would have been better for the royal cause if the King had stepped back and allowed his son to take full command, for Edward was filled with an explosive energy and a savage will to fight which the mild King lacked. If the prince had commanded in the center, the responsibility of holding the battle lines together would have been his and he would not have given rein to his youthful impulsiveness in following up an initial advantage.

The King refused to relinquish command. Henry never seems to have accepted the fact of his limitations in spite of a lifetime of failures. He had a blind faith in himself which caused him to stumble into impossible situations, blithely convinced that he would discover in his meager resources of mind and spirit the capacity to face and beat back the whirlwind. The command of the army must be his. Was he not the King?

Stationing himself in the center where, from the nature of the terrain and the dispositions of the enemy, the heaviest pressure would be encountered, Henry flung his gaudy dragon banner to the breeze. This banner was, perhaps, Henry's greatest military achievement, the handsomest flag in all Christendom. He had planned it himself more than twenty years before, when the dream was still in his mind that he would lead victorious armies in the redemption of the lost Angevin empire. It was made of scarlet samite and with the head of the dragon so placed that each flutter of wind caused the tongue to ripple and spit scarlet flames and the eyes of the beast, made of rubies, to roll in a fine martial frenzy. Was anything but victory thinkable under such an inspiring banner?

The right wing, made up of cavalry, he entrusted to Edward and the left to Richard of Cornwall. As things turned out, a more ill-advised disposition could not have been made.

To understand what followed, the spirit of the two armies must be taken into account. The barons had been inspired by their belief in Simon de Montfort to sharing his sense of the sacred nature of their cause. As they marched in close formation down the ridged slope they were filled with the same confidence which had led him into taking this gamble, the assurance that God would smile on them. The sun emerged as they marched, lighting up the little town and picking out the tower of the priory in the rear. Simon called a halt at this and raised a hand in the air.

"Behold, comrades and followers!" he cried. "We are about to fight this day for the better government of the kingdom, for the honor of God and the blessed Virgin and all the saints. Let us pray to the King of all that, if our undertaking pleases Him, He will grant us strength and aid to overpower the malice of our enemies. To Him we commend body and soul."

It might have been the eloquent tongue of the great Grosseteste which thus exhorted the baronial host to do battle in the right spirit; for it was this faith and humility which the militant bishop had taught Simon as a youth and which Adam Marsh had been preaching in all his letters. The men dropped full length on the ground and spread out their arms to form the semblance of a cross.

"Grant us, O Lord, our desires," they intoned in unison, "and give us a mighty victory to the honor of Thy name."

There was in this prayer a fervor, a fanaticism even, which these hardbitten men had caught from their leader.

Henry was religious also, but he was more a lover of the outward forms. He took a sensuous delight in the beauty of fine churches, in rich vestments, in the peal of great organs and the chanting of monkish choirs. Ritual fascinated him, and he was always ready to spend long hours on his knees. It is doubtful if he shared to the same degree the deep-seated faith of the baronial leader. There was little trace, therefore, in the royal ranks of the fervor which animated the advancing ranks. The King's men were very sure of themselves and contemptuous of the enemy. They did not seem to realize the difficulties under which they must fight.

Edward, filled with martial ardor and impatient to repeat his success at Northampton, started the clash by charging the London levies streaming down the eastern ridge with a shallow picket of mounted knights in the lead. These presumptuous traffickers in wool and fish and wine, these men of low degree, would feel the weight of his steel! William of Valence, that most chivalrous of knights, was with him and would share avidly in the sport. They opened the battle with "a terrible clang of trumpets," charging up the ridge with a thud of horses' hoofs and a mad rattling of accouterments.

The poor Londoners had courage but little else with which to face this onslaught. They were on foot and lightly armed, and unused, moreover, to the bloody business of battle. The royal horsemen broke through the thin cover of knights and swept the citizen bands aside like chaff. The bewildered Londoners sought safety by scrambling down into the hollow between the ridges, from which they were routed out later by the foot soldiers who followed in the wake of the charging cavalry, or they threw themselves over the steep sides into the river, where they drowned in vain efforts to get to the other side.

It was said afterward that his bitter recollection of the way his mother had been treated in London caused Edward at this stage to throw military discretion to the winds. These were the men who had pelted the Queen with stones and offal from London Bridge when she was trying to escape from the city on the royal barge. He could hear above the roar of battle the loud jeers of the London mob, "Down with the witch! Drown the witch!" This whetted his appetite for revenge to such an extent that he led his troops in pursuit beyond the crest of the escarpment and for a long distance beyond, some say as far as four miles. The pursuit was so vindictively maintained, at any rate, that a large part of the London bands had been wiped out before the order was given to desist from the drive.

It was not an easy matter then for the prince to gather his scattered horsemen together into battle array and lead them back to the field, and it was early in the afternoon when they rode in some weariness up the slope which Simon de Montfort's army had climbed in the light of early dawn. On the flat space in front of Mount Harry they found the banner of the baronial army still flying over the chariot and no guards save a few camp followers and servants. After killing all of the latter who could be laid by the heels, the tired horsemen surrounded the chariot, expecting to find the leader of the people's army there.

"Come forth, thou devil Simon!" they shouted. "Come out, vile traitor!"

When they discovered to their great chagrin that the Earl of Leicester was not in the chariot, they did not pause to identify the unfortunate occupants. The four men whose efforts in the royal cause had placed them in this situation were killed forthwith. The victorious cavalry then turned to ride down the slope with the intention of attacking the baronial forces in the rear.

But they had come back too late. The battle was over.

The rout of the Londoners had been so sudden and devastating that nothing could be done to stem the tide on that flank. To have committed the reserves to the task of bolstering the left wing would have been a useless sacrifice. All Simon de Montfort could hope for was that the flaming exuberance of the prince and his men would lead to a protracted pursuit, and he seized the golden moment when they went thundering out of sight around Mount Harry. Ordering up all the reserves, he led the way down the slope and attacked the royalist center and right with every bit of strength he had.

Few details are available of this phase of the struggle. It was man against man, a clashing of battle-ax and mace and sword, a bloody give-and-take with the dead falling under the feet of the combatants and the wounded lying unheeded in agony while the battle swayed back and forth over them. It is said that King Henry fought well, that he had a favorite charger killed under him and called for another in order to go on with the struggle. On the left the King of the Romans did not do as well. He was a good enough soldier and had fought bravely on occasions, but when his lines sagged under the hammer blows of the baronial drive he could not rally his men to renewed efforts. They broke first and took to flight, each man racing for the one bridge over the Ouse which offered the only means of escape. The center broke soon after, but the King managed to reach the priory in safety and with enough of his men to hold its walls against attack.

Earl Simon, who had been in the thick of things, took prompt steps to assure the victory. He placed some troops on the plain north of the town to take care of Edward when the latter returned from his pursuit of the Londoners and then seized the end of the bridge, finding this a difficult operation because of the press of fugitives on the road leading to it. He isolated the priory to make sure of the King's ultimate capture.

In the meantime the King of the Romans, who was as willing as any knight or soldier in the ranks to survive the disaster, had taken refuge in a windmill called later the Mill of the Hide. It was surrounded immediately by a company of jeering soldiers demanding that he come out. He had never been popular with the people in spite of his many good qualities. Perhaps he had been a little too successful in his money-lending and more than a little too acquisitive in all his dealings to capture the fancy of the man in a London alley or the villein on a midland mark.

"Come down, come down!" shouted the soldiers. "Come down, thou worst of millers! Come down, thou who would be called by no meaner name than Augustus!"

The King's brother finally emerged, a crestfallen figure covered with the dust of the mill, his face black with cobwebs. His captors were delighted to catch him in such an unkingly plight and marched him into the town with the grime of the mill still on him. A song was made of this incident which was sung later with much sly delight.

> *Richard, tho thou be ever trichard,*[1]
> *Tricken shalt thou never more.*

[1] Trickster.

It was at this stage that the horsemen under Edward arrived back on the scene. It required little more than a glance to convince them that the battle had been lost in their absence. The royal standard had been torn down from the walls of the town and only a limp pennant of the Earl of Surrey, floating above the castle, held out any evidence of continued resistance. Edward wanted to fight on, even though faced by the whole strength of Simon de Montfort's army, but his closest advisers had seen as much of battle as they could stomach for one day. One by one they flitted away, seeking safety in the marshy lands west of the town and all of them getting through to Pevensey to the south. The prince succeeded in cutting his way through the frenzy of the streets and reaching the priory finally, where he found his father sitting glumly in the ashes of defeat.

3

A legend died at Lewes. Fulk FitzWarine was killed in the battle, fighting on the side of the King.

The name of Fulk FitzWarine had attained as much celebrity in the country as Robin Hood did later. There were four of that name in direct descent, barons of Shropshire and great fighting men, and it seems likely that the exploits of all were combined in the story of one. The second Fulk, who contributed the most to the legend, was raised at the court of Henry II. In the course of a game of chess Prince John broke the board over young Fulk's head and the latter retaliated by kicking the future King in the stomach. The incident still rankled in John's mind when he ascended the throne, and Fulk had the discretion to take to the woods. He remained an outlaw all through the reign of the wicked King (the records contradict this, but so runs the legend), robbing the rich, helping the poor, keeping John in a state of apoplectic rage. A master hand at disguising himself, he appeared in all manner of unexpected places in the guise of a monk, a juggler, a minstrel, a merchant, as the fancy seized him. Finally he went to the Crusades and added international luster to his fame as a champion.

It is said that in one battle on the Continent the commander of the opposing forces cried:

"Now, my lords, all at Fulk!"

The English exile answered, "And Fulk at all!"

As a figure of chivalry he takes rank just below Roland and

Amadis de Gaul and on a level with Garin de Loherain. The death of the fourth Fulk at Lewes was like a personal loss to Englishmen who had been raised on the ballads. Unfortunately the last of the line did nothing in the battle to add to the legend. He was drowned in the retreat. His horse became hopelessly mired in the swamps and he was suffocated in his heavy body armor.

4

Peace does not return as soon as the outcome of a battle is assured. The town of Lewes was a madhouse during the early hours of the night. The streets were piled with dead bodies and the untended wounded, and a search was being made through the houses for fugitives. The discovery of hidden survivors would lead, if they did not give in at once, to a renewal of tumult, a mad outburst of shouting and cursing and the sound of blows in the dark.

The barons made one effort to scale the walls of the castle but, failing to get inside, desisted in sheer physical weariness. The garrison retaliated by shooting Greek fire into the town and setting some houses ablaze. There was fear for a time that the conflagration would spread.

Earl Simon had drawn his lines closer around the priory, but it seemed wise to him to arrange a surrender without more bloodshed. He accordingly offered a truce to discuss terms of capitulation. Henry and Edward agreed. Simon and his chief followers made their headquarters somewhere in the town, and negotiations were carried on for several hours with the trapped royalists in the priory. The intermediaries were priests, and there was a constant coming and going of men in monkish robes as the differences were slowly resolved.

The group in the priory were a dispirited lot. The King, who had been wounded slightly in the fighting, was eager enough to get matters settled if he could save a few shreds of dignity and authority. Even in his most craven moments, however, he had a tendency to chaffer and splutter and protest his rights, and this dragged the negotiations out to an interminable length.

This night was for Edward the most humiliating moment of his life. He was still young, just under twenty-five, and had been confident he could measure his strength against the godfather from whom he had learned so much and for whom he now held a bitter hatred. The day had started so well, with confidence and high spirits and great élan; and now, as he sat in the glum group about his father, he knew himself the chief agent of defeat. Not only had he failed to match in strategic conception the experienced and cool military brain of the baronial leader, but he had thrown away all possibility of victory in the excitement of the fighting.

But make no mistake about this tall young man in blood-stained armor with a frown of concentration on his handsome face. Edward was not taking refuge in any of the excuses or illusions which weak men seek in adversity. He knew he had made grievous errors that day and was letting the lesson sink in deep.

His active and brilliant mind was concerned with the future, with the repair of the great mistakes he had made. This was apparent when he insisted on one clause in the terms of capitulation which would later serve the royal cause well, that the young men from the border country should not be held captive. They were needed, he contended, to hold the unruly Welsh in check, these devious young men, Roger de Mortimer, Roger Clifford, above all, that stormy character, Roger de Leyburn. He was so concerned in getting them their freedom that he agreed to remain as a hostage, he and his cousin, Henry of Almaine. This was shrewd, very shrewd indeed. Edward knew that his own liberty was something which could be achieved in time, that there would be continual pressure to have him freed; and in the meantime the men thus released could foster the royal cause and set on foot a nationwide intrigue against the victorious barons.

An agreement was reached during the night to which both Henry and Edward attached their seals and which became known as the Mise of Lewes. As no copy of this document is in existence, it is impossible to say how much of the final terms of capitulation it contained or whether it defined the basis on which the country was to be run while recovering from the effects of civil war.

CHAPTER TWENTY-FOUR

Simon de Montfort, the Statesman

IT was apparent at once that a firm hand had grasped the tiller of state. Peace was proclaimed throughout the kingdom, and men on both sides were bidden sternly to return home and resume their lawful occupations. Arrangements were made for the exchange of prisoners. Steps were initiated to compensate those who had sustained losses in the struggle.

The King accompanied Simon de Montfort to London and took up his lodgings at St. Paul's, where an eye could be kept on him much easier than at Westminster or Windsor. The castellans who had been most active on the royal side were replaced by baronial leaders. Some of the old sheriffs and wardens were retained, but those who were unacceptable to the new order were replaced.

Across the Channel there was much activity. Henry's defeat at Lewes had been a staggering blow to the Queen and her party, which included the archbishop, Peter of Savoy, and John Mansel, but they rallied and began to recruit mercenaries and hire ships with feverish speed. The young noblemen who had escaped from the battlefield had crossed the water by this time. They threw themselves into the work with great energy in an effort, perhaps, to compensate for the panic in which they had abandoned Edward at Lewes. Although the French King had expressed, with some reluctance, his willingness to assist in an arbitration, there was no surety that he would not come to the aid of his distressed brother-in-law and throw the weight of France behind an invasion. Such a move would have the blessing and support of the Vatican.

Never a believer in half measures, Simon prepared to meet the threat by recruiting the man power of England on a wider basis than had ever before been attempted. A national levy of men and money was proclaimed and "Down with the alien!" became the slogan. Watchers were maintained along the coast from the far North to Cornwall. The inland counties were called upon to provide men in accordance with their population, and a large army was gathered at Barham Downs. The King, acting partly under pressure, partly because of a genuine fear for his hostage son, wrote letters to Queen Eleanor, urging her to cease all hostile preparations.

Cardinal Guy Fulcodi, the legate who had never set foot on English soil, sent messengers to notify the new government that he now proposed to visit the country and exercise his powers in bringing about a proper peace. Knowing full well the kind of peace the legate would consider proper, Simon saw to it that the messengers were intercepted as soon as they landed at Dover. Their papers were taken away from them and they were sent back on the next boat, carrying notification to the cardinal that he must insist on the disbanding of the army of invasion and that, moreover, he must see to it that none of the money Louis of France was paying to Henry for the maintenance of knights on crusade be diverted to the war chest of Queen Eleanor. The cardinal responded with a furiously hostile letter in which he declared that "the earth marvels and the heavens are stupefied by the ingratitude of England." He declared the powers of the Pope to be unlimited and made it very clear that he would be content with nothing short of the full restoration of Henry's powers and the banning of the Provisions of Oxford.

In the meantime a session of Parliament was held at which a council of nine was appointed to guide the King in all his official acts, of whom there would always be three at his side. The intention seems to have been that any three of the nine would serve as the close advisers of the ruler, but in practice the select trio became Simon de Montfort, Gilbert of Gloucester, and Stephen Birkstead, the Bishop of Chichester. Of the three men who thus assumed the actual control of the kingdom, the Earl of Gloucester was too young and unstable to have much hand in things and the bishop was content to serve in an advisory capacity. Simon de Montfort became, therefore, the real ruler. It is likely that he maintained the fiction of divided responsibility, but he it was who made the decisions. He acted promptly when quick moves were necessary and notified his colleagues later of what he had done. He had no title. Some men called him the Protector; in a few instances he was cited as *count justiciar*. He came very close to being a dictator.

He made mistakes, but in the main he used his dictatorial powers with vision, courage, and dispatch. The soldier became the statesman; the general who had led his men up the face of the escarpment at Lewes did not hesitate to act with equal boldness in the government of the country and in his dealings with the hostile outside world. After making what seemed a reasonable effort to find a basis of arbitration in which the King of France and the papal legate would have a part, he refused to yield beyond that point, having no intention of allowing another Mise of Amiens declared. The diplomatic ball was held in play for some considerable time, long enough to put such a strain on the purse of Queen Eleanor that the unpaid mercenaries drifted away and the waiting ships had to be dispersed. The clouds cleared over the Channel; the threat of another invasion dissolved into the mists.

When Cardinal Guy, who was sometimes called the Fat, came out unequivocally against the victorious barons, he was met by a decision of action which he most certainly had not anticipated. The bishops of London, Worcester, and Winchester had carried Simon's final terms for arbitration to Boulogne. Guy sent them back with orders to promulgate the papal sentences against Simon and his chief associates. The bishops were met at Dover, their luggage was searched (without any objection on the part of the churchmen), and the bulls were torn to pieces and scattered at sea. The legate retaliated by excommunicating Simon de Montfort, with bell, book, and candle, at Hesdin on October 21.

There was a corresponding vigor and decision in every move the Protector made during these first months. He realized the gravity of the situation and the strength of the forces working against him, and he did not hesitate to inject the audacity of the soldier into the decisions of the chancery. He maintained a semblance of order and official sanction. All communications were issued in the name of King Henry and with the royal signature. The King seems to have accepted the role and to have fallen into line with this pretense of solidarity.

2

There was still a sharp division among the nobility. In the West the young men released on Edward's insistence after the rout of Lewes confirmed his shrewdness by coming out openly against the provisional government. Most of the great barons of the North stood aloof, refusing to acknowledge the summons to join in restoring peace.

There were divisions also in the Church, but the royal faction, in spite of the papal position, was small and inactive. The heads of the Church were on the baronial side almost to a man. Simon's strongest supporters had been the bishops of Worcester, Chichester, London, Lincoln, Salisbury, Winchester, and Coventry. They had not only stood by him through thick and thin, but they now protested jointly to Rome against any measures of deprivation and the anathemas pronounced by the angry cardinal across the Channel. In the second Parliament called by Simon one hundred and twenty churchmen took part as against twenty-three representatives of the nobility. The parish priests, who lived close to the people and shared in some degree at least their beliefs and aspirations, were as strongly for the baronial cause as the Franciscans, who, remembering the robust guidance of Grosseteste, preached the new order up and down the land. The students of Oxford raised the strident voice of youth on the same side.

There can be no doubt that the common man was for Earl Simon. There had been too many kings in the land, and the news of the victory of Lewes had been wildly acclaimed. The heavy losses sustained by the London levies were a blood pledge to the cause. This was a day of political songs, and the towns rang with loud refrains of victory. "Now England breathes again," proclaimed *The Song of Lewes,* a long paean of triumph penned in Latin by a Franciscan whose identity has not been established. The English people, went on this political epic, had been despised like dogs, but now they could lift up their heads. The *Song* contained a lengthy defense of the popular cause, leading to the conclusion that "law rules the royal dignity, for law is right and rules the world . . . It is one thing to rule, which is the duty of a king, another to destroy by resisting the law. . . . Read this, ye English," proclaimed the triumphant author, "concerning Lewes' fight under the protection whereof ye live defended. Because if victory had yielded to those who are now vanquished, the remembrance of the English would have been vanquished and become worthless."

But the acclaim of the people, while gratifying, was not as important as it might seem. The vociferous townsman who emptied a mug of ale in a London tavern to "Sir Simon the Righteous" might have no more than a penny or two by way of property and would not count in the financial levy which was being made. The student who left his seat in the straw at the feet of his master in Oxford to shout himself hoarse in the streets was probably too young to bear a pike. What counted was the support of the men who owned the land, the proud barons. Most of them had been against the bad government and wastefulness of the King, but now they found it went against the grain to see one of their own number in a position to dictate to them.

Simon realized that a final and public understanding must be reached with Henry and the heir to the throne. Accordingly a meeting was held at Canterbury on August 12 which the King and Prince Edward attended. A document was drawn up confirming the terms agreed to on the night of the battle of Lewes and making them mandatory as long as Henry lived and for a short period after Edward's accession. To this was added a summary of the steps which had been taken since the battle, including an ordinance forbidding the employment of aliens by the Crown. Finally it was provided that no man was to be punished or molested for the part he had played in the civil war. This agreement, called the Peace of Canterbury, was signed by Henry and Edward.

The Peace of Canterbury was enacted while the country was still strongly held by the victorious party. The terms, although sharp and conclusive, were not, therefore, excessive. Simon had done no more than secure confirmation of the basic concessions for which the barons had taken up arms.

He had hoped, no doubt, that it would be possible after Canterbury to settle down to a more orderly administration and that peace would return to the country. In this he was disappointed. The great landowners of the North refused to have any part in these moves toward pacification. The young Marchers in the West continued to flaunt their defiance. The air was filled with rumors and alarms. It was widely believed that the Queen had managed to enter the country in disguise, bringing assurances of support from Louis of France; that Prince Edward had escaped from captivity and had joined the insurgents in the West; that the Pope would lay England under an interdict again; that the Seven Knights, a term used to designate the western barons because they had planted seven flags on the walls of Bristol, were creating a large army and were now ready to sweep down the line of the Thames with fire and sword. Peace was not possible in a land which listened daily to stories such as these.

There was some basis of truth in the last-mentioned rumor. When Edward was removed from Dover to Wallingford for safer keeping, the Seven Knights made a bold attempt to set him free. A considerable force under Sir Warren de Basingbourne, who had been Edward's favorite companion in the field, made a surprise attack on that strong citadel. They carried the outer wall and were pressing forward with such spirit that the defenders sent out word that, if they persisted, the prince would be delivered to them but "bound hand and foot and shot from a mangonel." To make certain that his friends appreciated the danger in which he stood, Edward appeared on the inner wall and shouted to them that he was sure his captors meant what they said. Sir Warren desisted from the attack at this, and the knights returned reluctantly to their base in the West. To prevent any further attempts at rescue, the prince was taken from Wallingford to Kenilworth, where his uncle Richard had been detained since his capture at Lewes. The midlands about Kenilworth were solidly baronial in sentiment.

3

At Kenilworth the Countess Eleanor was presiding over a household which resembled a royal court in size and importance. Her signature appears on many state documents as witness, and so it is apparent that much of the business of the realm was being transacted there. This meant a constant influx of visitors, officials from Westminster with bags packed with papers, bishops and barons and envoys from other countries with long trains of horsemen. Simon arrived at intervals and never with less than one hundred and fifty lances behind him. This would present his princess wife with serious problems. One hundred and fifty men to feed and find accommodation for without advance notice! Somehow it would be done. The loaves and the salt fishes, the haunches of beef and the gallons of flattish beer would be found, and at night straw and rushes would be spread around all hearths in which there had been fire, and the unexpected guests would use their cloaks as pillows, snoring the night away in as much comfort as they might have expected.

The earl was in the habit of discussing the situation with his wife. This is certain because she acted with decision and a sure knowledge of the situation when the final crisis arose. They would get their heads together and he would pour out his troubles. Anxiously they would discuss the continued recalcitrance of the Marchers. Should they be ignored in the hope of a gradual subsidence, or should the peace be disturbed by an armed excursion against them? What designs were hatching in the brain of that proud and selfish young man, Gilbert the Red? How long could the young lion, Edward, be kept caged?

There was so much correspondence handled at Kenilworth that three carriers were used to insure a quick exchange of mail. The household Roll, to which earlier reference has been made, gives the names of the trio, all good Saxon names, Dignon, Gobithesty, and Truebody. Good Saxon names, in fact, predominated at this great castle of the earl's, Haude and Jacke in the bathhouse, Hicke the tailor, Dobbe the shepherd.

It has not been unusual for royal ladies, even the most realistic and shrewd, to believe that time would have to stand still for them. Although Eleanor had been a very great beauty indeed, she seems to have been under no such illusion. She was now in her forty-eighth year, and although still a handsome woman, without a doubt, she was no longer the madcap charmer who had wedded Simon of Leicester under such romantic circumstances. It is not known if she used dyes or other beauty aids, but the testimony of the Roll makes it clear that Adam Marsh would no longer have found it necessary to chide her for extravagance in dress had he been alive. She spent little on her own wardrobe during this, the most important year of her life. The items for dress materials concern the one daughter of the house, a charming girl of twelve, named Eleanor after her mother, but known to everyone as the Demoiselle.

4

It would be a pleasant task to provide clothes in the thirteenth century for a child of budding beauty. The flowing draperies of feminine attire were graceful in the extreme, and in the matter of materials it was a period of great extravagance. This was the day of the first importation of silks and satins and velours from the East; silks interwoven with gold thread and brocaded in flower designs; the six-threaded samite; a magnificent thing from the land of the Syrians called baudekin, which was a combination of silk and gold thread and which glowed as though the rays of the copper sun had been caught and imprisoned in it; transparent silks called sarcenet and fine cloth known as brunette. Rich materials such as sendal were used for linings. Furs were employed to trim the robes of the great, miniver and ermine and vair.

The girdles which bound the flowing robes of the nobility at the waist were set with precious stones. Often they consisted of solid gold links.

The chief chance that ladies had for originality in dress was in the coverings they devised for their necks. They began to go to somewhat foolish extremes with wimples and peplums. The wimple became large enough to muffle the neck up to the chin, being worn with fillets over the forehead. Mantles of Honor, made of gaily colored cloth, were worn over the shoulders. Sometimes these mantles were very gay indeed, with blue groundwork and scarlet borders and with a profusion of white scallops.

As was to be expected, the train had become an important part of feminine attire. They were so long at court that boy pages had to be in attendance to carry them. Priests saw vanity and worldliness in the use of elaborate trains and preached bitterly against them. The ladies, however, went right on having them cut long in spite of pulpit wrath. A belief grew up that invisible demons rode on the trailing skirts of great ladies and, in tacit acceptance of this, the wearers fell into the habit of stopping at intervals and giving their skirts a vigorous shake to dislodge any grinning imps which might be clinging to them. They did not take the story too seriously because, imps or no imps, they went right on wearing trains.

The tailor, in fact, was a very important person in the household of a prominent nobleman. The ladies condescended to take his opinion on all matters pertaining to their appearance, and even the men, who liked to strut in garments of white damask and handsome tabards, consulted the man with the needle. A popular ballad of the day was called the *Song of the Tailors* and began, "Gods ye certainly are."

It was a pleasure decidedly for Eleanor de Montfort to dress her slender daughter in the finest garments which the gods of the basting threads could devise, particularly when affairs of state brought Llewelyn of Wales to Kenilworth and his eyes followed the Demoiselle to the exclusion of everyone else.

5

With the exception of Richard, who was still in his teens, the Montfort sons were now out in the world and deeply involved in the political situation: Henry, Simon, Guy, Amauri, a handsome lot, tall and dark and strong. Their mother was intensely proud of them, and it is not strange that her chief concern had ceased to be her own adornment and had become political so she could share the interests of her husband and sons.

Eleanor endeavored to make life as agreeable as possible for the gloomy and depressed nephew who came to Kenilworth after the failure of the daring enterprise of the Seven Knights. Edward had always been fond of her, and he seems to have responded in some degree to her efforts in his behalf. It must at times, nevertheless, have been a silent trio who sat at the head table in the Great Hall; a hall so great, in fact, that it had two immense fireplaces and five tall windows. The King of the Romans, now callled Richard the Trichard by impudent men in London, sat in the center because of his imperial rank, a much-worried monarch who realized that his imprisonment was adding every day to the insecurity of his position in Germany. On his right sat the heir to the throne, his head filled with schemes for escape and plans for the day when he would strive to reverse the decision of Lewes. On his left was the countess, who alone of the Montfort family could sit with them, being the daughter of a king. She sought to play the part of hostess, but on occasion it must have been apparent that her eyes also contained a speculative gleam. It was generally believed that she expected someday to sit beside Simon at Westminster. At times thunderclouds hovered over the far from festive board and a sense of the strain penetrated even to the trestle tables at the far end of the long hall where humble men sat beneath the salt.

6

It has already been said that Earl Simon made mistakes during the year that he controlled the affairs of the country. They had nothing to do with state matters but were entirely personal. There was his desire to let his sons share his authority. Henry was made governor of Dover and was given the custody of Prince Edward after the latter's brief sojourn at Kenilworth, an arrangement which irked the prince exceedingly. Simon, the second son, was put in command of the forces of Surrey and Sussex. Earl Simon took into his own hands all the western possessions of the prince, Bristol, Chester, and in the North, Newcastle, to hold until permanent peace had been achieved. His closest adherents were given charge of other royal castles, Corfe, Bamburgh, Nottingham. This may have seemed advisable to the man on whose shoulders rested the responsibility of maintaining peace, but to the proud nobles who had played their part in the struggle and who felt themselves being excluded it seemed more a determination to advance his own family and consolidate his personal power.

The one who felt most bitterly about this was the Earl of Gloucester. This brave and mercurial young man had in him a belief in the rightness of the cause but also, by way of inheritance from his less admirable father, a pride which took fire easily and a strain of hauteur which made a secondary role intolerable to him. He had played no more than a supporting part at Lewes, and since then he had felt himself being relegated more and more to the background. This preyed on his proud spirit. It was becoming a matter of time only until he would change sides as his father had done.

It is likely that Simon de Montfort would have held his temperamental lieutenant in line if he had taken pains to placate him, to bolster his pride. That he did not do so is not entirely to his discredit. He had his hands full with matters much more pressing and important than the coddling of a demanding young man of limited capacity. He was guiding the ship of state through one of the most tumultuous periods of English history. There was not only the threat of invasion to meet and the sharp hostility of the Pope, but the need to restore order in a land torn by hate and fear. The injured feelings of a sulky young nobleman seemed, perhaps, to the harried leader a minor problem. But minor it was not. The failure to keep the Earl of Gloucester at his right hand was the most disastrous of major mistakes.

Simon took decisive action in the West, following the attack of the Seven Knights on Wallingford. He moved against them in sufficient force to capture their key castles of Hereford, Ludlow, and Hay. Roger Mortimer, who was looked upon as the leader of the western insurgents, was forced to meet Simon at Montgomery and make peace on behalf of the others. They were to surrender all the royal castles they held and leave the country for a year and a day, going to Ireland if they so desired. In addition they were to give up at once the prisoners they had taken in the royalist victory at Northampton and leave hostages for their own good behavior.

This was strong medicine, calculated to bind their hands for the whole of the crucial period. If the country could be rid of them for a year and a day, the new government would have time in which to establish a basis of peace. The young men swore to obey the terms laid down, and Edward's consent was also obtained.

CHAPTER TWENTY-FIVE

The Great Parliament

THE monks who wrote the chronicles of the day had a habit
of connnecting noteworthy events with curious phenomena of
nature. A great wind swept over England when John died and
it continued to blow with unexampled fury for several days,
as though sent to purge the land of all traces of his presence.
There are continual references to iron frosts, to black storms,
to drought and plague and other manifestations of divine displeasure. During the year following Lewes there was for a
long time a comet in the sky, blood-red and shaped like a
sword.

Surely on March 8, 1265, there was in the sky a great
blazing sun, a sun strong enough to burn away at least one set
of shackles from the wrists of men. On that day of days there
assembled in London a parliament such as had never been
seen before, a parliament in which common men sat and
voted with lords and bishops. This truly unheard-of event was
the work of Simon de Montfort. On the thirteenth of the
preceding December, after holding the tiller of state with a
firm hand through seven violent months, he had summoned
some of the peers of the land, most of the bishops, two knights
from each shire, and from two to four "good and loyal men"
from each city and borough to meet and discuss the business

of the realm. This was the first time in history that plain men—the socman, the franklin, the merchant, the alderman—had been judged worthy of a voice in framing the laws under which they lived.

Nothing much is known of this momentous gathering. Not a name, not a scrap of description, not the faint echo over the centuries of one spoken word: nothing but the bare outline of the one decision reached. This is unfortunate, for living history was made in Westminster Hall.

It is not even known how they were seated, the baron, the bishop, the plain knight, and "the bran-dealers, the soap-boilers and clowns," as someone has phrased it. That they were arranged sectionally is hardly likely. More probably the barons and bishops had the front rows and "the good and loyal men" were far in the rear. The citizens, it may safely be assumed, took pains to present as good a front as their means allowed. Their cloaks and tunics would be of good cloth and warm colors, and no doubt some of them would have a show of miniver or vair at neck and wrist; but at best they would seem sober and as common as twist against the ruffling splendor of the barons and the costly vestments of the high churchmen. What a pity it is that no poet Gray has turned his imagination and his pen to picturing them, the rude forefathers of the modern House of Commons, the mute, inglorious Pyms and Hampdens who had answered the summons to sit with their betters!

There were no rules of procedure in these early days, no set parliamentary ritual. They met, they listened to the King or the minister delegated to expound his views, they debated, and they voted. Some sessions were noisy and voices were raised high in anger and wounded pride. This particular Parliament, however, provided no dramatic moments. A program was presented. The voice was the voice of Henry, but the will back of it was the will of Simon. It had all been decided upon in advance, and it was carried with a good will, without delay or senseless babble.

The provisional government set up in the Peace of Canterbury was to continue. Edward was to have his liberty, but he must continue under restrictions for three years. During that period he must not leave the kingdom and he must not bring in aliens or seek the return of adherents abroad: this on pain of disinheritance. Both Henry and Edward must swear again to abide by the Great Charter and the Provisions of Oxford and must bind themselves not to seek absolution of their oaths.

Three days later there was a solemn ceremony in the chapter house at Westminster to announce publicly that Prince Edward had been released and delivered into the keeping of his father. Henry, wearing crown and royal robes, was present when the declarations to which he and the prince had sworn were read to the gathering. At the finish nine bishops stepped forward in full pontifical robes and, with the customary dashing out of candles at their feet, declared the excommunication of anyone who broke or transgressed the agreements which had been reached.

This ceremony marked the peak of Simon de Montfort's power. His will had prevailed. The King and the heir to the throne had made their peace and sworn to all the terms, stern though they were, which he had deemed necessary for continued peace and the future good government of the realm. He played no part in the ceremony, but as he stood in his place with the rest and watched he must have found it hard to keep a light of triumph from showing in his eyes. This was the culmination of his years of steadfast adherence to an idea, long years through part of which he had stood alone. For this he had risked life and fortune; for this he had gambled on war and had dared the climb at Lewes.

Perhaps other and more exalted thoughts had their place in his mind as well; that he looked at the good and loyal men from the towns and boroughs and saw a vision of the gradual shifting of power which in time would vest in the hands of their successors all legislative control.

2

It is called the Great Parliament, not because of what it accomplished but on account of the momentous precedent it set.

Did Simon de Montfort include the commoners because he realized he must depend on the cities and towns for his main support in the struggles ahead? Was it a purely selfish expedient to bolster his power and insure a more generous response to the calls he must make for financial aid? This viewpoint, which is widely held, must be given full consideration because it is not an unreasonable assumption. The leader of a great cause must have something of the opportunist in him. He must be alive, at any rate, to obstacles and ready to make use of the best weapons which are available. Simon, without a doubt, was aware of the advantages he might derive from his epoch-making invitation to the men who soiled their hands, not in the killing of other men, but in useful occupations.

But he could not have taken the step without being aware of other considerations. He was fully conscious of the tension in the ranks of the barons. He knew how suspicious they had become of him, how easy it might be to offend them still further. How would they react to this daring innovation which made the vote of a vintner or a fishmonger as good as that of a belted earl? Would they see in this another excuse for deserting the ranks? He must have remembered a line from *The Song of Lewes;* "See! Now is a knight subjected to the sayings of clerks. Knighthood put under clerks has become of little esteem."

Summoning the commons was a questionable expedient from the standpoint of political advantage alone, one which might harm the cause more than it helped. There is reasonable ground to doubt if as farseeing and able a leader as Simon would have risked this step if he had thought of it as a temporary expedient and nothing else.

There is at least as good reason to believe that he was thinking of the future as much as the present; that he was ready to throw feudal conceptions to the winds and admit that the common man must have a part in shaping his own destiny for all time thereafter. Simon de Montfort was more than the leader of a political faction. For years he had been the symbol of a cause, the stern exponent of new principles. There had been indications of the way his mind was tending. There was the reference in the one letter which remains in his handwriting, *because I uphold against them your rights and those of the common people*. He alone had been in favor at first of calling a meeting of Parliament without the King. This revolutionary stand, a retreat from all feudal beliefs, might be expected to lead to still more radical acceptances on his part.

There is no way of determining what was in the mind of this daring and passionate leader when he took his long step in the direction of democratic government. This much, however, may not be gainsaid: it was in his mind that the conception first grew of a house of governmental control in which all classes of men would have a voice and vote, and he it was who had the sublime courage to make the experiment. Edward in later years, when he had succeeded his father on the throne, would give the principle permanent acceptance by summoning commoners to all meetings of Parliament. Could this have been one of the things they talked about during the brief interlude when Edward, in youthful enthusiasm, ranged himself by the side of the popular leader?

They share the credit and the glory of it between them, Simon de Montfort and the young Edward. There is plenty for both.

CHAPTER TWENTY-SIX

Tales of Fair Ladies

A NUMBER of women, all of them fair by repute, were to play parts in the drama which now unfolded. First there was Queen Eleanor, who was still in France and moving heaven and earth to find support for the royal cause and to get her husband out of captivity. She had pawned all her jewels and personal possessions and had contracted debts of such size that their redemption later swallowed up all of the fine of twenty thousand marks paid by the city of London. Nothing could discourage the firm-minded Queen, not even the letters of warning which Henry (under pressure, without a doubt) addressed to her.

Then there was Eleanor de Montfort. The sister of the King was to demonstrate in these violent and eventful months that although she took her looks from her beautiful mother she was all Plantagenet in character. She had the decision and resolution which Henry so conspicuously lacked, and these qualities she was now to have an opportunity of displaying. The princess wife of the popular leader appears to rare advantage in the climactic stages.

Alice of Angoulême was also to have a part, a not particularly creditable one, it must be confessed. In the few glimpses of her which the records supply she appears in the role of troublemaker, flirting with Prince Edward while he waited for his

303

young wife in France to grow up, even casting an eye on the aging Henry, who responded in kind for perhaps the first time in his long married life. In support of the latter assertion there is only one bit of evidence, a letter from Queen Marguerite of France warning her sister that Henry was too fond of the company of his capricious niece. Marguerite seems to have developed into a prim and proper woman, the result, perhaps, of being married so long to a perfect man. The part Alice played in the drama indicates that she placed royal allegiance ahead of wifely obligations. She does not appear, however, until after the main issue had been decided.

Of less exalted rank was the fourth fair lady to take a prominent part in events. She was the wife of Roger de Mortimer, the quarrelsome, avaricious, and generally disagreeable lord of Wigmore who had been the most active enemy of Simon de Montfort in the West. Born Maud de Braose, she had been a great catch, for the Braose holdings to which she succeeded comprised a large part of Breconshire and a share as well in the immense Marshal inheritance. Her father was the gallant but unfortunate William de Braose who had been detected in an illicit relationship with Joanna, the wife of Llewelyn (and illegitimate daughter of John of England) and had been publicly hanged by the Welsh leader. This would make her a granddaughter of the unhappy Maud de Braose who was starved to death by John in a cell at Corfe Castle.

She was beautiful and nimble-witted, and the one glimpse that history gives of her is an advantageous one.

Finally there was Margot the Spy. She could not have been of noble birth or the fact would have been recorded, but she was as courageous as the others and, from the nature of the part she played, as pleasing to the eye, undoubtedly, as any of them.

2

With the calling of the Great Parliament the sun had seemed to reach its zenith for Simon de Montfort, but immediately after the ceremony with which the meetings concluded things began to go wrong.

First there was the death of Urban IV. Eighteen of the twenty-one cardinals being available, they were shut up in conclave at Perugia to elect a successor. For months they disputed and balloted, in perfect good humor, it was reported, but without result. To break the deadlock it was decided to make a compromise selection, and the choice fell on one of the three absentees, Guy Fulcodi, the legate to England. Unaware of the great honor which had been done him, Guy did not reach Perugia until two more months had passed. He accepted the election doubtfully and took the name of Clement IV.

Although Clement was to prove himself an able pontiff, the choice was not a fortunate one for England. He had not changed his mind with reference to the struggle between the King and his subjects. One of his first acts, in fact, was to appoint Ottobuoni Fiesco as legate in his place and in the course of his instructions to write bitterly of "that pestilent man and all his offspring." Simon realized, of course, that now he could expect nothing but the most aggressive hostility from the Vatican.

The barons, moreover, were in a disgruntled mood. They were angry because the pledge made at Lewes for the restoration of prisoners on both sides was being carried out. They were hungry for ransom money from the band of wealthy nobles who had fallen into the baronial net in that battle. The situation came to a head when John Giffard of Brimpsfield claimed two prisoners who had been taken in the priory and was angrily insistent on making them pay through the nose for their liberty. When Simon refused to give in, Giffard retired to his estates in a towering rage.

Disturbing information came to Simon's ears almost immediately thereafter. The Earl of Gloucester was in the Forest of Dean and had collected about him a considerable force of armed men. John Giffard had joined him there. It was rumored, moreover, that the pair had opened communications with Mortimer and Leyburn, the ringleaders of the Seven Knights. Determined to bring matters to a head, Simon went to Gloucester, taking the King with him.

The Earl of Gloucester attended the meeting but in his own manner. He came with a band of armed horsemen and camped on a wooded hillside just outside the walls of the town. The first night his campfires lighted up the sky, convincing evidence of the strength in which he had arrived. Counting the fires from his window in the royal castle, Simon realized that Gilbert the Red had come in war and not in peace.

A temporary arrangement was made between them, nevertheless, through negotiations conducted by the Bishop of Worcester. It was not very satisfactory to either side. Gilbert was still incensed over the preponderance of power which Simon held and what he believed was an unfair division of the spoils of victory, despite the fact that his own share had been quite enormous.

At this juncture word reached the court at Gloucester that William of Valence and the Earl of Surrey, who had been among the refugees from Lewes to reach France in safety, had landed at Pembroke with a handful of men. This could mean one thing only, that the royalist supporters were preparing to renew the struggle. Simon knew full well that William of Valence would not thrust his effeminately handsome head into the lion's mouth in this way unless certain of adequate support. Before moving against the new arrivals Simon had a final talk with Earl Gilbert, finding him evasive and unfriendly and willing enough to let it be seen that he could no longer be depended upon in the impending clash.

3

Maud de Mortimer is given credit for finding a way to get Prince Edward free. She is said, in fact, to have planned each step of the ingenious stratagem employed.

Edward was technically in the custody of his father, but a close watch was being kept over him. He had sworn not to leave the realm for three years, and it had been ruled that this barred him from entering the Marcher country, which was not at peace; an interpretation to which, apparently, he did not subscribe. Edward was a different man from the impetuous youth who had failed so signally in his first great test. Since the bitter lesson of Lewes he had been living in constant mortification, compelled to agree to conditions which chafed his spirit and to give public assent to them. He was now filled with such a consuming fire to take up arms again that he was prepared to adopt any means of getting free. Staying at Hereford Castle, the heir to the throne knew that a few miles away his friends were gathering in force and were waiting for him to place himself at their head. The details of Lady Maud's plan were conveyed to him and he assented eagerly.

On May 28, in accordance with the plan, the day was spent in the open. Edward and his usual companions, which included Henry de Montfort, who went along to keep an eye on things, rode out some distance from Hereford and proceeded to race their horses. Edward was in a gay mood, taking a share in the sport and riding several horses at different stages.

Finally he mounted one which was capable of outdistancing all the others and which, through clever manipulation, had not yet been used in any of the racing. Cantering casually and easily on his fresh mount, the prince managed to get himself free from all his companions on one flank without rousing any suspicion as yet in the mind of his guileless cousin and guardian.

At this point a horseman appeared some distance away and raised an arm in the air. This was the signal the prince had been expecting. Touching the flank of his horse with his silver prick spur, he made off at top speed. The rest of the party, on their partly winded mounts, had no chance whatever of overtaking him. They fell back hopelessly and saw their charge join a party of horsemen who emerged from the woods ahead to act as his escort. The fugitives set off in the direction of Wigmore Castle, which was twenty miles away.

The fair Maud, anxiously scanning the road from the southeast, which wound up the rocky ledge on which the castle stood, was dismayed at first when she saw a solitary rider approaching. Had her plans gone wrong? Alarm changed to satisfaction, however, when she realized from the length of leg doubled up above the stirrups that it was the prince. In his impatience he had outridden his party. Galloping into the courtyard, he leaped to the ground; dusty and a little weary but in a jubilant mood and as eager for action as a lion loosed from its cage.

He remained at Wigmore just long enough for refreshments. The chatelaine, who of course had attired herself to the best advantage, kept busy in the background to be sure that everything was being done properly for the royal guest, that the wine had been sufficiently cooled and the mutton properly browned over the fire. While doing so she must have cast many appraising glances at the heir to the throne, about whom she had heard such conflicting reports: his wildness, his occasional cruelties, his much-discussed interest in the foreign lady, his cousin, and on the other hand his determination to continue the fight which his father seemed willing to consider ended. She must have been impressed by the appearance of the fugitive as he bent over his hurried meal, the gravity of his manners, the look of preoccupation in his eyes. It must have seemed to her that at last there was a real leader for the royal cause.

He would not be too preoccupied to wave his hand in

parting to the fair chatelaine of the castle, but at this point the pages of history close over Maud de Mortimer.

From Wigmore, Edward rode to the rather squat Norman castle of Ludlow on the banks of the Jug, a distance slightly under ten miles. Here he found waiting for him the man he wanted to see above all others, Earl Gilbert of Gloucester. Roger de Mortimer was there also, and the three men sat down together and discussed the future. Edward appreciated the importance of detaching Gilbert the Red from Simon de Montfort's side and he agreed readily enough when the stipulation was made that the country must be governed in accordance with the Provisions of Oxford. On receiving this promise the young earl agreed to transfer his allegiance to the King's side.

When the word spread that the prince had escaped and that Gloucester had joined him, the whole West blazed up into martial activity.

4

The Countess Eleanor received the disturbing news while at Odiham Castle, to which she had removed from Kenilworth. She knew that it meant war again and she proceeded to demonstrate how much she had been in her husband's confidence by acting with great decision. Waiting until night had fallen, she had a horse saddled and rode from Odiham to Porchester Castle to join her son Simon, taking one companion only. She had selected old Dobbe, the shepherd, to accompany her because he knew the roads over the hills and could guide her in the dark. They arrived at Porchester in the morning and, without waiting to rest, the countess began preparations for the test which lay ahead of the Montfort family.

It was clear to her that the Cinque Ports must be kept in line so that no aid for the King could be brought over from France. As her husband would have his hands full for some time in the West, she decided to make it her concern to keep the door to France closed. She started immediately for Dover, traveling by way of Bramber Castle, Chichester, Wilmington, Winchelsea, and Sandwich. To her intense relief, she found the South solidly for Simon. Her following grew every day until she had eighty horses in her train and many vehicles, including a chariot drawn by five horses which the Countess of Arundel sent for her personal convenience.

Eleanor knew how easily loyalties may be shifted in civil war, however, and she went to the greatest efforts to win adherents in all the towns through which she rode. At Winchelsea she gave a dinner for the people of the town and had two oxen and fourteen sheep roasted for their entertainment. Three days later she dined the people of Sandwich on a similarly lavish scale. Reaching Dover, she found that her oldest son Henry, who was castellan of the great stone entry gate of the kingdom, was in the West with his father. The garrison, however, was loyal to the baronial cause.

The gallant and energetic lady breathed easily for the first time since the news had reached her that the prince was loose. The barons had control of the Channel. The sails of the men of the Cinque Ports swept the straits and no help could reach her brother, the King, from his wife and sympathizing brother-in-law in France. London, solidly against the King, was filled with martial ardor.

The situation in the East, in fact, was well in hand.

5

Before proceeding with the story of the last phase of the struggle it will be advisable to pause and take a look at Simon de Montfort, the man about whom the storm was raging. There can be no doubt that the suddenness with which the tide had turned against him had been a shock. It becomes clear that he had expected peace would follow the assembling of the Great Parliament. In believing this he had been far from realistic; he had allowed faith in his own capacity and his popularity to dictate his thinking. The defection of Gilbert of Gloucester had been a blow, but Simon had been half persuaded it would happen. What had shaken him was not the fact that the undependable young earl had turned his coat finally but the fury with which royalist sentiment had swept the West. This he had not expected, being convinced that to the people of England the royalist cause was a bankrupt one.

He was old and he was tired; fifty-seven years old, a great age for that day and particularly for a man of his temperament. There was neither philosophy nor calmness in him. He believed deeply, he loved and hated passionately, he worked hard. And the length of the struggle had been taking its toll.

His face was thin and his eyes were deep pools of conflicting emotion. He longed for peace.

He acted, however, with his usual sagacity. His oldest son Henry was with him, a loyal son but one not likely to be of any great help, cast down already by his blindness in letting Edward escape. It was to Simon, the second son, that the earl, therefore, sent his instructions. Simon was to collect what strength he could in the South and East and march at once to join the forces under the earl himself. Speed in following out these orders was most emphatically enjoined. The army of the baronial state must be ready not later than the forces Edward was gathering in the West.

Before learning of Edward's escape Earl Simon had crossed the Severn River with a double purpose, to strike at the base of the Marchers' strength in Glamorganshire and the valley of the Usk and to establish contact with his ally, Llewelyn. Edward, at liberty and entering the fight with the fury which had been growing in him each day of his captivity, took advantage of his opponent's position by sweeping up the interior side of the Severn as far as Gloucester, which he succeeded in capturing. Only one part of Simon's mission could, therefore, be accomplished. He made a treaty with Llewelyn which bore on its surface the desperation of his mood. Concessions were made to the Welsh leader which would never have been considered if the need for help had not been so great. The independence of the portions of Wales over which Llewelyn ruled was recognized as well as his right to retain all the conquests he had made in the Marches. In return he was to pay thirty thousand marks in ten annual payments and to supply military aid. None of the money, which Simon needed badly, was paid over at once, and the military assistance consisted of a paltry force of several hundred Welsh archers.

Realizing that time pressed badly, Earl Simon now made a move which did not turn out well. Instead of marching north for Hereford at once and turning the flank of the royal forces, a movement which could easily have been carried out and which would have made it possible to join forces with the troops from the East under young Simon, he marched down the Usk with the purpose of crossing the Severn at a point where he could strike a blow at the prince and the Seven Knights. For this he has been severely blamed. It has been easy for armchair strategists, writing centuries after the event, to contend that Simon de Montfort should have taken the easy, the safe, way. It has been assumed that his age was dictating his plans, that he fumbled and lost time, and did not resort to the proper plan until juncture with his son was impossible.

The exact opposite seems to have been the truth. In planning to cross where the Usk and the Wye flow down into the Severn, with Bristol straight ahead, Simon was endeavoring to repeat his success at Lewes, where he had led his men up the heights to face an enemy superior in numbers and strength. He hoped, no doubt, to reap again the reward of audacity, to get across the river at the point where it seemed most unlikely that he would strike. The enemy had the whole river to watch. He might catch some portion of them unprepared on the other side; or, at worst, he might succeed in driving through them with a clear path to the East ahead of him. If his son had acted promptly on his instructions he might already be moving up behind the royalists, who would then be caught between the baronial pincers.

Unfortunately for him his son at this point was a very great distance away and moving with a sad indecisiveness. More important still, the leader on the opposite bank of the Severn was not the overconfident prince who had been content to place one sentry on the heights of Lewes. The Edward who faced him now had learned much from misfortune. He was wary and cool and, above all else, he was watchful. Simon found that the forces facing him were strong. The boats he had counted upon for the crossing, moreover, had been captured already or destroyed.

Realizing now the impossibility of getting across, Simon followed the course which, it is contended, he should have adopted in the first place. He turned and marched up the west bank of the river toward Hereford in the north. As he led his army, briskly enough for a man weighed down with anxiety and already gripped in the cooling process of the years, his mind was filled with one speculation. Where was his son Simon with the reinforcements from the East? He realized that no good would come of this campaign unless a juncture could be effected, and that in the shortest possible time.

6

Margot the Spy, disguised as a man, brought news of the greatest importance to Edward, who was making his headquarters at Worcester. Nothing is known about this woman; who she was, how she came to be playing a role in the struggle, what became of her later. She may have been a camp follower who had been hired to keep her eyes open. More likely she was the wife, daughter, or mistress (very probably the latter) of someone in a position to know what Simon the younger was about, and that she was acting as a go-between.

The news she brought was of the most welcome kind. The dilatory Simon, a full month after receiving his instructions, had arrived with his forces at Kenilworth, more than thirty miles to the north. With Simon the elder still at Hereford on the wrong side of the Severn, there was no danger of an immediate union of the baronial forces. Edward at Worcester lay squarely between them, enjoying in that way the greatest possible military advantage, the opportunity to fight on interior lines. His army was at least equal to the whole of the baronial strength: employed against either of his opponents, it would have enough weight of steel to make victory comfortably certain and, because of his position, he could strike first at one and then at the other.

It was an easy decision to attack the younger Simon first. Simon the elder's men were weary from much marching and weak from lack of food, but they were under the command of an inspired soldier, a daring and unpredictable general whose whole career had been one of victory. Margot the Spy had brought news, moreover, which was enough in itself to settle the issue. Simon the younger, feeling himself at home and certain that the enemy was a long way off, had not thought it necessary to shelter his men behind the impregnable walls of Kenilworth. He had left them in the open, some billeted in the town, some in tents around and about the castle. An immediate attack would catch him even less prepared than the royalists had been at Lewes.

Edward acted with all the decision and vigor his great opponent would have employed under the circumstances. He took his whole army out of Worcester, even calling in the mounted patrols along the river, and struck north for Kenilworth. A march of thirty-four miles lay ahead of him. He covered this distance in a matter of twelve or thirteen hours, arriving at Kenilworth just before dawn on the following day, July 31. Such a march seems commonplace by the military standards of succeeding ages when the need for rapidity of action had been realized. In the age of chivalry, the most stupid stage of warfare, men refused to learn and went on fighting as they always had done, encumbered with armor, armies moving and creaking along like a circus on wheels. In this lumbering, lute-twanging, looby age of warfare, Edward's march was nothing short of astonishing.

To digress for a moment: the knights of Europe, after more than a century of warfare against light-armed and fast-moving opponents, had learned exactly nothing from their general lack of success in the Crusades. They still put their faith in heavy body armor, they still conceived of battles as clashes between cavalry. The importance of the foot soldier and the archer was so little understood that the puffed-up lords of privilege in their mail shirts preferred in reality not to have them about. The role of men on foot was to handle the baggage train and the horse lines and to be cut to pieces unmercifully if the horsemen on the other side got the better of the chivalrous encounter on the field of battle. Edward, however, proceeded in the most thorough way to break with tradition. He took with him every man he could find —knight on horseback, humble foot soldier with bill on shoulder, archer with longbow, greasy knave from the wagons—and shoved them along at an unprecedented pace on the road to Kenilworth.

He broke another precedent when he arrived in the darkness just before dawn. Simon de Montfort had refused to attack his opponents at Lewes during the night, holding such a course to be unfair and unchivalrous. Edward had made many discoveries during the year of his humiliation, and the most important conclusion he had reached in his thinking about war was that it was the business of a leader to kill more of his opponents than they could kill, without regard to outmoded conventions or the hampering rules which minstrels liked to glorify in song. Finding the army of Simon the Slow sleeping warmly in town beds or under canvas, as had been reported, he gave the signal for an immediate attack.

It was a foray in the dark rather than a battle, a one-sided butchery which resulted in the scattering of the baronial forces. Some very much surprised and chagrined baronial leaders, including the Earl of Oxford, were made prisoners. All the baronial horses were secured and, for good measure, thirteen banners. Some of the bewildered soldiers swam across the moat and took refuge behind the walls of the castle. Among these was Simon the Slow himself. Others, in the thousands, scattered over the countryside.

Edward did not pursue the fugitives. He had learned the folly of headlong pursuit at Lewes. Believing his victory complete enough to put this branch of the baronial army out of the reckoning, he gathered his troops together. Without a pause for rest they started back to deal with the elder Simon. The captured horses relieved some of the strain on tired legs. The captured banners, elevated proudly above the marching files, raised the spirits of the soldiers equally high with their reminder that half of the victory had been won.

CHAPTER TWENTY-SEVEN

The Battle of Evesham

A TIRED man led a hungry army across the Severn on August 3.
Simon de Montfort had arrived at the river the night before,
accompanied by King Henry and a badly equipped force of
not more than four thousand men, including the few hundred
Welsh archers whose services had been contributed by Llewelyn. It had been necessary to keep custody of the King's
person for two reasons: to have the royal signature on communications and manifestoes, and to make sure that Henry
did not slip away to join the prince. The pretense of royal
authority must be kept up. Henry, most unhappy about it,
must still play his part in the masquerade.

It took the whole day to accomplish the long-desired passage of the river, there being few boats available. The crossing
was made at Kempsey, which was four miles south of Edward's base at Worcester, so it is certain that Simon de Montfort knew of the withdrawal of the royal army. He was apprehensive as well as tired, realizing that the disappearance of the
prince with his army of ten thousand men meant he had
marched eastward to deal with the reinforcements under
young Simon. It is certain he did not know of the terrible
mistake his son had made and of the disaster which had
overtaken him in consequence. Otherwise he would have
taken care not to march into the jaws of a victorious enemy

but would have slipped away on the road to London, where alone he would have a chance to augment his meager forces. He was hoping, it is clear, to get to his son's assistance before the prince could deliver his attack. Not daring to take the direct route to Kenilworth, which would bring him dangerously close to the royal lines, he marched instead for Evesham, which lay in a loop of the Avon, a distance of fifteen miles away.

The tired man had acted with more expedition than Edward had anticipated. When the prince arrived in the vicinity of his Worcester base late in the day on August 3, confident that Simon the younger would play no further part in the campaign and prepared to deal next with Simon the elder, he discovered to his surprise and dismay that the old earl had already crossed the river and disappeared with his ragtag army. Where was he heading, for Kenilworth or London? Then the prince's busy spies brought him a welcome piece of information. Earl Simon was now crossing the Avon at Pershore, which meant he was headed for Evesham. From there he still had a choice of routes; but Edward, knowing the valiant heart of his veteran opponent, had no doubt that the earl's intention was to get to his son's aid.

There was still time to prevent a junction of the two wings of the baronial army. Trumpets sounded in the royal camp where weary men were settling down to enjoy a rest after three days of marching and fighting. They fell into line again, grumbling furiously, and began in the falling dusk to move eastward over the rough roads and wooded country between Droitwich and the Vale of Evesham.

Military experts disagree as to the roads they took and at what stage the army was divided into three parts; two flying wings being constituted and confided to the command of Gilbert of Gloucester and Roger de Mortimer. The fact remains that at some hour of the night, while his equally weary foes were slowly filing into the Vale of Evesham, that lovely and fertile strip of country, Edward found himself astride the road to Alcester and so between the two baronial armies. A little later the prince extended his line as far east as Offenham, after fording the eastern side of the loop at what came to be called later Dead Man's Ait.

A council of war was held at some time during the night with the two young leaders of the supporting wings in attendance. It was held at a spot still known as Council Green, and in some accounts Roger de Mortimer is given credit for the plan of battle then adopted. This is not an acceptable version in view of the subsequent records of Edward and his lieutenant from the Marches. Edward's conduct of the campaign thus far had been marked by flawless strategy and great speed of execution. It is not reasonable that at the final moment he would find it necessary to lean on the advice of a man of inferior capacity. Mortimer was opinionated and talkative, and it is probable that his tongue clacked a great deal during the discussion, leading to the suggestion that he was guiding the tactical decisions for the next day. It is certain that Gilbert of Gloucester had little to say. He was not a soldier of experience, and it is possible he was listening to another sound while the voices about him were raised in debate, a faint but disturbing noise which might have seemed to him like the jingle of thirty pieces of silver.

The plan decided upon was simple, sound, and effective. Gloucester was to take his wing down the west arm of the Avon to prevent a retreat toward the Severn. Mortimer was detailed to cross the east arm of the loop and not only block the one bridge across the river but get himself astride the London road, a minor role. Edward, with the bulk of the army, would drive straight against the baronial forces in the town.

The trap had closed.

2

Before daylight the mounted scouts of Simon de Montfort detected the approach of armed forces north of the town where Green Hill dominates the sky line. Edward, who was neglecting no possible advantage, had resorted to the stratagem of sending the banners captured at Kenilworth ahead of him. The scouts, in consequence, got the impression at first that this was young Simon and his men marching to join them. If this report was carried back to the leader (there is every reason to doubt it), the truth soon became apparent. It was growing light now, and a barber of the town, who had stationed himself in the bell tower of Evesham Abbey, detected the imposture and cried out in great alarm that the enemy was on them.

It may be taken for granted that Simon would not have remained in such a vulnerable position if his men had not been worn out by the hardships through which they had been passing and if he had been free of the importuning of the King. Henry wearied easily in the saddle and he had slept all night, arising in the morning to demand time for prayers and the celebration of mass. It would have been wiser if the harried earl had decided in this desperate juncture to jettison his dangerous captive. The presence of Henry, and his acquiescence in measures, had been necessary as long as the ruling of the realm alone was in question. As soon as civil war broke out again, he had become no more than a prisoner. Perhaps Simon indulged instead in a line of reasoning which would not have seemed strange to any man of that violent day. All this hatred and dissension in England, this fighting and bloodshed and destruction, had been caused by the obstinate determination of one incompetent man to rule the land as he saw fit. With a bloody battle impending, should the author of it all be removed safely to the rear where he would have no share in the tumult and fury? Should he be made comfortable while thousands paid the price in death of his never-ending obduracy?

Whatever the reasoning which governed the decision, the King was hastily accoutered for battle. Chain mail was buckled over his pourpoint jack, steel cuisses were fitted on his broad thighs. Allowed no distinguishing crest and no banner to identify him, he was put into the saddle, knowing the odds and realizing the probability that he would die under the blows of those who were fighting to free him. If this situation had been deliberately contrived, it was a strange revenge which Simon was visiting on the King.

So they rode out together, King and subject, crowned autocrat and leader of the popular cause, with the memories of nearly twenty years of trouble and fighting and hatred between them. The curtain had risen on the last scene of the long duel.

Simon had no illusions about his own fate. His position was a desperate one. Ahead of him, covering the fifteen-hundred-yard gap which divided the arms of the Avon, lay the army of Edward, twice the size of his own. His scouts had already reported the presence of Mortimer on the southeastern side of the river, which blocked any possibility of retreat. It was an evidence of Simon's greatness that his first impression was one of admiration for the troop dispositions of the prince.

"By the arm of St. James," he cried, "they come on well!"

With a sense of soldierly pride he added, "It was from me he learned it."

Then the hopelessness of their position caused him to say to those about him, including his sons Henry and Guy, "May God have mercy on our souls, for our bodies are theirs!" It did not enter his head to hoist a white flag or to throw himself on the mercy of the King. Henry might have welcomed this way out of the dangerous dilemma in which he was placed. Edward would have refused any offer from the barons to lay down their arms, however, unless they came to him with halters around their necks. It is certain that Simon de Montfort preferred death to humiliation.

The old leader had reason to believe that his son Simon had reached Alcester, which was about ten miles away at the junction of the Alne and the Arrow rivers, and this dictated the course he elected to follow. He decided to form his men into a wedge and drive up the hill into the center of the encircling forces of the prince. If Edward had thinned his line in spreading out to cover the whole gap, the desperate gamble of a frontal attack might conceivably be successful. The armed knights were directed to lead the drive, with the English foot soldiers following and the Welsh archers bringing up the rear. The order for the charge was given.

At this moment the convulsion of nature which medieval writers demand for historic occasions came about in actual truth. A black cloud appeared in the sky above the elevation where the royal army stood, a grim and evil cloud which seemed at once to form a part of the menace facing the trapped barons. It did not move with the slow stateliness of casual clouds but as though in a mad hurry to blot out the light of the sun. The advance rack raced like cavalry scouts, tossing in the wind. The cloud brought anger and thunder but little rain, which added to its effect because it seemed unreal and contrary to nature. Men could see little of the faces of their neighbors, and back in Evesham Abbey the monks who, through sheer force of routine, paraded two by two into choir loft and stall to chant their perfunctory plain song while history was being hammered out in a din of steel a few hundred yards from the calm walls, could not read the words spread before them. It was believed later that the Lord had sent this black pall over the earth to hide the grim tragedy being enacted on the slopes of Green Hill.

The first shock of the baronial wedge carried them well into the royal line. But the line did not break; it bent, and, as often happens when column meets line, the wings closed in on each side. The earl and his followers found themselves hemmed in, the impetus of their attack expended and wasted. It was well for Simon de Montfort that the most furious action centered where he spearheaded the baronial effort. He had no time to think of anything but keeping the protection of his shield with its silver fork-tailed lion between him and the blows of hostile battle-axes while he flailed about him with his heavy sword. He no longer had time to think that he himself must die, although the probability of that had come to him with his first glimpse of tossing plumes above Green Hill. He could not pause—and this was mercy indeed—to realize that here was the end of everything, that the cause of liberty was dying with him, that Henry's maddening persistency had won after all; there was time only for parry and thrust, for the deadly give-and-take, the air about him filled with hostile spear and mace.

It is certain that he did not know Henry was spared all share in the carnage. Someone on the royal side heard and identified the King's high-pitched and beseeching cry of "I am Harry of Winchester, your King; do not kill me!" A gauntleted hand—some say that of Edward himself, but this is too contrived for belief—seized the bridle of his horse and he was hurriedly guided out of danger. For the rest of the time that the battle raged he was well beyond the possibility of hurt, his helmet removed to give him freedom to breathe, his eyes avid as he watched the decision of Lewes being wiped out in a river of blood.

"Such was the murder of Evesham, for battle it was not," wrote Robert of Gloucester in his story of the event. Of the hundred and sixty knights who accompanied Simon on the field, only twelve survived. Hugh Despenser and Ralph Basset fell by his side. His son Guy was badly wounded and captured. Then Henry, his first-born, was cut down before his eyes.

"It is time for me to die!" said the earl in great anguish of spirit.

He made a final and desperate effort to cut his way through the circle of his foes. It failed and he was beaten down and slain, with a cry of "God's grace!" on his lips.

The war had engendered so much hatred that the death of the great leader of the barons did not satisfy the thirst for revenge which his foes felt. The body of the dead earl was hacked to pieces as it lay on the ground. Roger de Mortimer, who had crossed the river to join in the fighting, is supposed to have been the leader in this vandalism. The head was cut off, then the legs and arms were removed with savage blows. Even the trunk was mutilated.

Simon the younger, who might in full truth be called Simon the Tardy, arrived within sight of the field as the final stages of the battle were enacted. He had spent the night at Alcester, had dined there the previous evening, and had breakfasted before setting out. If he had not stopped at Alcester at all, he could have reached his father's side before the gap was closed by the fiercely energetic Edward. The full enormity of his mistake was borne home to him when he reached a point back of the hills where he could see, under the inky pall of the clouds, the ground strewn with corpses and could hear the delirious shouts of triumph rising from the followers of the prince. His horrified senses recoiled from one trophy of the victory, the bloody head of his father carried high above the press on the point of a royalist lance.

"Feebly have I gone!" he cried out in his remorse and grief.

There was nothing he could do now, so he gave orders to his men to turn about and begin the long march back to Kenilworth.

Silence fell slowly over the field of Evesham. The black cover rolled away and the sun came out. But there was no real sunshine in any part of England that day. The cause of liberty had been defeated with the great earl. Harry of Winchester rode back into Evesham with a loud blast of trumpets, the undisputed master of the realm, his mind filled with plans for the use of the power which had been restored to the fribblery of his hands.

3

It might be said that Edward the great King was born at the battle of Evesham. He had achieved the victory by a display of remarkable military skill and the exercise of a truly magnificent will to win. His reactions after the battle were the proof of an awakening greatness in him. As soon as the battle fever subsided in his veins he began to feel compassion for the foes he had destroyed with such thoroughness. He stood beside the body of Henry de Montfort, who had been his first playfellow, and wept with grief. He then gave orders that what was left of the mutilated body of the baronial leader should be collected and buried at Evesham Abbey. As hostile as ever to his dead foe, he was too generous to condone the barbarities of his vengeful followers. He even went to the abbey and watched gravely as the shattered bones of Simon were laid away.

From that moment on he was the leader of the party which stood for moderation and leniency. William the Marshal, the Good Knight, had seen the need for quick national recovery after the defeat of the French forces of invasion in the first year of Henry's reign and had not been exacting in the terms he imposed. Edward now saw things in the same light and opposed those who hurried to fill the only too willing ears of the King with counsels of vengeance. In all that happened after the final collapse of the baronial cause the prince was to show himself of statesmanlike stature and perception.

He had not succeeded in recovering all of the body of the dead leader. The head of Simon de Montfort was carried to Wigmore Castle, where it was raised that night in the Great Hall, still on the point of the lance. Here it seemed to watch, with the stern disapproval the earl would have shown if he were alive, the revelry going on below. Perhaps the men, drunk with victory and strong wine, felt this. They began to gibe at the grim trophy, bowing and scraping before it and calling Simon "king." The head disappeared soon after, tossed out into the courtyard, it was believed, to be trampled under horses' feet and pecked to pieces by preying birds.

One other fragment of the body was missed also, a foot. This was in the possession of John de Vescy, one of the most loyal of Simon's men, who had been wounded in the battle and made a prisoner. He took it with him when he was given his release later and kept it at his castle of Alnwick, encased in a silver shoe. When the castle was confiscated as part of De Vescy's punishment for bearing arms against the King, this relic of the great man was removed to Alnwick Abbey, where it was kept a long time in great secrecy and veneration.

When miracles were reported at the spot where Simon de Montfort had fallen they were reported doubtless to Rome, but at the Vatican "that pestilent man" was held still in violent disesteem. No efforts were made to attest the truth of the rumors. Throughout England their truth was generally accepted and the name of the dead leader was coupled with that of Thomas à Becket. People came in great numbers to bow their heads at the pool where he had died, watching its waters turn blood-red, confident that their physical disabilities would be cured.

The memory of the stern leader, the brave upholder of the rights of man, was kept green for many generations.

CHAPTER TWENTY-EIGHT

The Disinherited

WITH great Simon dead, it might be expected that the record of the years immediately following Evesham would have some of the dreariness of anticlimax. Instead they resound with excitement; what is of much more interest, they produced important results. Something worth while was salvaged from defeat. Of these sorry days there is much, therefore, to be told.

Henry has been praised because he sent none of the prisoners to execution. This is hardly worth comment. There was no need for block or gallows tree after the murder of Evesham. So much blood had been spilled there that the most sanguinary natures recoiled from wasting more. The demands for vengeance, short of death, however, were so insistent that the wise counsels of Edward, the giver of victory, were swept aside. His brother Edmund, who had played no part in the fighting, clamored for the utmost severity, being rewarded himself with the earldom of Leicester and the state offices of the dead leader. Nothing in the way of punishment and confiscation was sweeping enough for the rapacious Mortimer, the demanding Giffard of Bath, the King's Men and the Queen's Men, who returned with outstretched palms for a share of the spoils. Henry himself was in favor of wholesale confiscation, which would relieve him of debt. His hands itched for the feel, if not of the throat of London, at least of its pockets.

A meeting of Parliament was held at Winchester on September 8 to settle the question. The moderate party of Edward, to which Gilbert of Gloucester allied himself at first in an outburst of generosity, suffered a defeat. Resolutions were adopted which gave the conquered over to the violence of the conquerors. All the adherents of Simon de Montfort, which meant a full half of the substantial owners of property in the country, were disinherited and their lands given to the King for disposal. The charter of London was annulled. The De Montforts were stripped of everything and banished from the kingdom. The heads of religious houses and the militant bishops were summoned to buy their forgiveness.

The King, sufficiently normal in spirits to order the cleansing of a painting in an altar where he had prayed and to issue explicit instructions for the reception of Edward's wife, who was now expected to join the prince, left Winchester for Windsor and from there gave instructions for mobilizing such forces as might be needed to subdue London. The citizens did not wait for any action of this kind. They gave in and were told to send forty of their number to Windsor under safe-conduct to make their submission. The Lord Mayor elected to go himself, accompanied by the richest and most influential of his fellows. In spite of the safe-conduct, they were seized and lodged in cells in the tower of the castle. Henry refused to see them. He left for London, leaving orders that they were to be held in solitary custody at his pleasure, save the Lord Mayor and four others, who were judged the special prisoners of Prince Edward, to be disposed of in any way he saw fit.

In London the King proceeded to administer the punishment he had been storing up for the men who provided so much of the wealth of the kingdom, the hated bran dealers and soap boilers. The houses of many of them were handed over to friends of the King. Merchandise was seized and disposed of, and much of the land held outside the walls by residents was escheated to the Crown. The city was fined twenty thousand marks, half of which was to be paid at once. A charter of remission was granted the city, reading in part, "Know ye, that in consideration of twenty thousand marks—that we have, and do, by these our presents, remit, forgive, acquit . . ." None of the other fines and seizures were remitted, however, and it was not until all this had been done that the forty prisoners at Windsor were released.

It soon became apparent that the policy of Winchester had been a mistake. Had the followers of Simon been subjected to heavy fines, they would have paid gladly enough and the royal coffers would have overflowed, for the first time in the whole course of this long and troubled reign. Finding themselves faced instead with confiscation and with nothing to lose save their lives (life without honor and possessions meant little to men of their stamp), they elected to fight on. Resistance centered in Kenilworth and in the Isles of Elȳ and Axholme. The ships of the Cinque Ports were loaded with the families and possessions of the owners and set out to sea, where they resorted to piracy as the only means of subsistence. Every county had its sanctuary in the woods where some of the Disinherited stood out against the King's vengeance. In the South there arose a remarkable champion, one Adam Gurdon, a knight as tall and powerful as Edward himself. Once a bailiff at Alton in Hampshire, Adam had fought under Simon and he now proceeded to make himself as troublesome to the King's men as Willikin of the Weald had been to the French in the first year of the reign.

After several years of struggle to bring the country to subjection, during which Henry had to keep armies in the field at a ruinous cost, his rosy dreams of affluence changed to despair. He was close to the brink of bankruptcy when he gave in finally and allowed the terms which the moderates had advised in the beginning.

2

On October 29, 1265, Queen Eleanor returned to England, landing at Dover and accompanied by Doña Eleanora, the young wife of Prince Edward. The King and his heir met them at Dover with becoming state and ceremony.

Doña Eleanora, who must henceforth be called by the Anglicized form of Eleanor by which she is known in history, was now twenty years old. She had been in England at intervals before the start of the war and had borne her husband two children, a boy named John and a daughter. The great romance of the thirteenth century which links their names may be said to have started, however, on this bright October day when Edward saw that the bright-eyed princess who had been wedded to him at Las Huelgas had developed into a lovely woman, as sweet and gracious and intelligent, moreover, as she was beautiful. Her quite unusual attractiveness may have been due to the mixture of blood in her veins. Her grandmother had been the Alice of France who was affianced to Richard of the Lion Heart and whose charms had won the affections of Richard's father, Henry II. Her mother was the Joan of Ponthieu who would have been Henry III's wife if he had not become so enamored of the reputation of Eleanor La Belle of Provence (not to mention the lush romance she had penned) and who subsequently married Ferdinand III of Castile. Eleanor had lived through the years of turmoil with her widowed mother at Ponthieu.

If Alice of Angoulême had ever held any real place in Edward's affections, which is doubtful, she was never given a serious thought from that moment on. Certainly Edward gave Gilbert of Gloucester no further reason for jealousy on the score of his flirtatious Alice. Eleanor suited him so completely that he was happy only in her company. She is given credit for the mellowing of his character, which began to manifest itself at this stage.

Although he had been against the measures which now embroiled his father in the hornets' nest of continued civil war, Edward was saddled with the responsibility for all military operations. He had won over the garrison at Dover the day before his wife and mother arrived and had arranged the departure for France of Eleanor de Montfort and her two youngest sons, Amauri and Richard. His treatment of the widow of the slain leader had been most considerate, and he had promised to see that the members of her household were restored to their homes, a promise he did not fail to carry out, sending written instructions in the matter and referring to the unfortunate lady as "my dear aunt."

In the late fall of that year the Disinherited roused themselves to serious resistance and the prince led a force into the northern counties. He captured Alnwick Castle, where John de Vescy held out bravely but briefly, and then proceeded against the Isle of Axholme, where the young Simon de Montfort was in command. The latter was prevailed upon to cease resistance and to have a personal interview with the old King. Richard of Cornwall took Simon in to see Henry, and the talk seems to have passed off well enough. Young Simon agreed to surrender Kenilworth Castle in return for certain concessions. Once again, however, the extremists gained the King's ear and the concessions were referred to arbitration, with the certainty that they would be rejected. Under these circumstances the garrison at Kenilworth refused to give in, asserting that they held the castle for the countess and could surrender only on her command. Hearing that he was to be imprisoned for life, Simon managed to make his escape from the country and join the rest of the family in France.

In the meantime Edward was taking energetic measures to restore order in the country. He sent Henry of Almaine to subdue what disaffection was left in the North and gave command in the Marches to Mortimer. He himself took the southern shires in hand. At Whitsuntide he defeated Adam Gurdon's little army in Alton Wood and in doing so provided the annals of English chivalry with one of the most pleasant and colorful of stories. In the course of the battle he encountered the leader of the band, and the two tall men decided to fight it out singlehanded. As in the case of Fitz-James and Roderick Dhu in Scott's *Lady of the Lake*, the mighty champions clashed with broadsword in one hand, shield on arm, the woods ringing with the sound of clashing steel. They seem to have been evenly matched, but in the end the youth of Edward told and the result was the same as in the other contest; the commoner went down to defeat.

Edward treated Adam Gurdon with great generosity. He saw to it that his opponent's wounds were bound up and then rode by his side from the shade of the Berkshire woods into the higher country of the chalk Downs. Here, standing high above the market town of the same name, was the castle of Guildford which had been given to Princess Eleanor as her official residence. It was Guildford Castle which Henry had ordered to be prepared for the beautiful Spanish bride, specifying that her chamber was to have "glazed windows, a raised hearth, a chimney, a wardrobe, and an adjoining oratory." When the prince and his company came within sight of the place it was apparent that something was afoot. Flags in profusion flew above the battlements, and the sound of trumpets greeted them as they rode in under the portcullis. Inside it was found that the stables were filled with horses and that smoke was pouring from all the kitchen chimneys as evidence that much food was being prepared. Edward realized from the buff-and-blue costumes of the armed men in the outer bailey that his mother had honored him with a visit, for these were the colors of Queen Eleanor's Brabanters.

The young chatelaine was frightened when she found that her blond giant of a husband had returned in a badly battered condition. Edward reassured her and led the way to the Great Hall, giving orders for Adam Gurdon to follow. There he told the story of the Homeric conflict, blow by blow, and at the finish the two Eleanors agreed that so gallant an opponent should be given his pardon.

Adam Gurdon was not only pardoned but was taken into the service of the prince, being given a post at Windsor. He is mentioned as fighting under Edward in the Welsh wars in succeeding years. The two tall men remained the best of friends thereafter.

Eleanor brought another son into the world, as handsome as the first one, and he was named Henry after his royal grandfather. Edward was fond of his little brood but had small chance to see them. He still had the reduction of Kenilworth on his hands and he was dreaming of going on what he had hoped would prove the final Crusade. Until the Disinherited had given in fully he could not be spared. It was not until the spring of 1270 that he was free to fulfill his great ambition. Eleanor was determined to go with him.

"Nothing ought to part those whom God hath joined," she declared. "The way to heaven is as near, if not nearer, from Syria as from England or my native Spain."

3

When the two Eleanors had arrived at Dover they were accompanied by the new papal legate, Ottobuoni Fiesco, the cardinal deacon of St. Adrian, who had been sent by Pope Clement to assist in restoring peace. Since the death of the "pestilent man," Clement had been in a forgiving mood and his instructions to Ottobuoni had been to lend the weight of the papacy to a more moderate view than was prevailing at that moment. "Clemency is the strength of a realm," wrote the Pontiff to King Henry.

Ottobuoni, an old and somewhat feeble man, was not an entirely unfamiliar figure to the English. He was distantly related to Queen Eleanor, and quite a few of his relatives had been holders of English benefices. He was an able administrator. His name meant, literally, Eight Good Men, and his admirers asserted that he was the equal of a thousand. In spite of this, there was some uneasiness over his selection as mediator. His first moves increased the tension because they had to do with the question of the punishment of the prominent churchmen who had been closely leagued with Simon de Montfort. Walter de Cantilupe, Bishop of Worcester, was in dying condition, and the consequences of the excommunication which had been pronounced on him allowed him no peace of mind. To have the ban raised, the old man went through a form of recantation, asserting that he had been wrong in supporting Simon. The three remaining bishops who had been militantly engaged against the King, London, Winchester, and Chichester, were packed off to Rome to face an inquiry before the Pope himself. The Bishop of Winchester died while there. London and Chichester remained firm and outspoken in their faith, asserting that the baronial cause had been a just one and that it had been necessary to take up arms against the King in the interests of the people. They were held for seven years in a severity of exile which amounted almost to imprisonment. Finally they were allowed to return, old and saddened men but still firm in the faith.

Ottobuoni's share in the negotiations with the outlaws was more to his credit. He strove earnestly to convince the King that he must be more moderate in his demands and to bring the Disinherited to the acceptance of terms; and in the end he succeeded in both.

The siege of Kenilworth began in June 1266. Henry of Hastings had assumed command of the garrison in the absence of all the sons of the dead leader, and he waged a grimly determined defense. The castle was at the time the strongest in England. It was surrounded by a lake artificially deepened, which covered more than one hundred acres and thus formed an impassable moat, with a series of earthenworks known as the Brays around the outer edge as an additional precaution. The Norman keep, called Caesar's Tower, stood eighty feet high on a solid rock base. There were other towers almost equally formidable, notably the Strong Tower at the northwest angle of the walls (Sir Walter Scott named this later Mervyn's Bower), the Swan and Lunn's. The latter had been erected by John, a cylindrical building more than forty feet high. Ironically enough, some of the strength of this great midland fortress was due to Henry's interest in building. He had felt impelled to tinker with it and had constructed the Water Tower at his own expense.

The garrison was so confident that they kept all the gates wide open during the daytime as a gesture of defiance. Parties rode out across the moat on sudden forays, still wearing the white cross as a sign that the defeat at Evesham had not affected the validity of their cause. They harried the attacking forces and even raided the meadows where the royalists kept their horses and cattle. They kept the King's army at bay so easily that Cardinal Ottobuoni found it advisable finally to come down and apply ecclesiastical pressure. Stationing himself within eyesight of Caesar's Tower, he excommunicated all of the garrison with the customary ritual.

The ban of the Church was beginning to lose some of its potency as a result of the indiscriminate use to which it had been put for the past century or two. Men had become accustomed to seeing the lifting up and the dashing down of candles, to hearing the solemn pronouncement of the sonorous words, as bishop cursed King and abbot cursed knight and wholesale decrees were proclaimed for the most trivial reasons. The garrison at Kenilworth was so little perturbed over the doom pronounced in the thin voice of the stooped old man in his red cope that they followed with a mock ceremony of their own. One of their number, a clerk named Philip Porpeis, appeared on the walls in burlesque canonicals and went through the motions of banning every man, woman, and child on the royalist side, from the King himself to the blowziest female camp follower and the scrawniest army mule.

The castle had seemed amply stocked when the siege began, but a garrison in excess of one thousand men can consume huge quantities of food. Gradually the stores diminished and the Disinherited had to go on short rations until they became weak and thin. Time, the unbeatable weapon, was making itself felt. When the legate finally persuaded the King to save the face of the besieged by holding Parliament in the neighborhood of Kenilworth for the sole purpose of arriving at a peaceful solution, the garrison professed themselves willing to co-operate.

The Parliament selected a panel of twelve members to discuss the situation. These commissioners finally arrived at a basis on which peace could be made, not only at Kenilworth but throughout the country as well. This measure became known as the Dictum, or Ban, of Kenilworth, and because of its definition of the relationship between the King and his subjects it is worth studying. It provided first that all confiscated lands could be redeemed in whole or in part on payment of fines running as high as five years' rental in accordance with the degree of culpability established in each individual case. It then went on to "beseech the King, and respectfully press on his piety, that he appoint such men to administer justice as, seeking not their own but what is of God and justice, may duly settle his subjects' business according to the laws and customs of the realm." The most important clause read as follows, "Let the King establish on a lasting foundation those concessions which he has hitherto made of his own free will and not under compulsion, and those needful ordinances which have been devised by his subjects and by his own good pleasure."

This reinstatement of what the barons had been fighting for was accepted by the King. The temper of the people's demands had, of course, changed. The King was beseeched to act according to the Great Charter and the Provisions and to select good ministers, whereas it had been Simon de Montfort's contention that he *must* govern according to rules duly established and laid down. The dead leader had been far ahead of the times in his conception of constitutional safeguards, too far for any chance of permanent acceptance at that early stage. The Dictum of Kenilworth is chiefly important, therefore, because it established the fact that the will of the people had not changed, that the King was expected, in spite of the triumph of the royal arms, to adhere to the new basis of good government. The vanquished had not fought in vain. Simon de Montfort was dead, but out of defeat had come this recognition of the essential justice of the people's demands.

The garrison accepted the terms and marched out in December, a much-depleted and emaciated band. Meager rations for two days only were left when this peaceful termination of the spectacular siege was reached.

4

Even after the Dictum there was no peace. Properties were withheld from men who had surrendered and paid their fines. On the other hand, many of the Disinherited refused to consider themselves bound by what had happened at Kenilworth. The Marcher barons, for their part, were furious at the prospect of having to disgorge what had been given them in the first flush of victory and returned to their distant strongholds in high dudgeon.

Toward the end of March 1267, Alice of Angoulême sent word secretly to the King that her husband, the Earl of Gloucester, was planning to seize London. No serious attention was paid to this warning at first because it was known that Ottobuoni had invited the earl to come to London. His visit there, it was believed, could have no more serious purpose than a discussion with the papal legate.

The unfaithful wife had been correct, nevertheless. Earl Gilbert had been an unhappy man since the battle of Evesham, conscious of the hatred in which he was held by the old comrades he had abandoned, aware also that the King was seeking ways of escaping from the pledges to which he was committed. The young earl, it may be taken for granted, had a sincere belief in the principles which had led him into the baronial camp in the first place. Now, seemingly, he was prepared to lift the mantle which had fallen from nobler shoulders and wear it himself. When he reached London it was with a sizable army in fighting order.

Gilbert the Red camped at Southwark but was unable to hold his men in hand. Terror gripped London, a state which was added to by the unexpected appearance of John d'Eyvill, Nicholas Segrave, and William Marmion, who had been holding out on the Isle of Ely. Was another civil war in the making?

The legate now found himself in a very awkward position. His invitation to the earl had been the cause of all this trouble. Not knowing just what to do under the circumstances, the legate took what was probably the wisest course. He locked himself up in the Tower of London.

It is doubtful if the young earl intended to lead a second rebellion. His occupation of London was intended more likely as a warning to the King that the will to oppose him was not dead. He carried his gesture to a dangerous extreme, however, digging a ditch around the city walls and permitting his men to raid Westminster. The raid resulted in much looting and the killing of some royal servants.

After two months of occupation Gloucester found himself facing an army under the command of the King. Ottobuoni had been at work, however, and had convinced Henry of the wisdom of a pacific attitude. As a result a settlement of all outstanding points of dispute was reached. The terms of the Dictum would be carried out promptly and to the letter. The rights of London would be restored. On June 18 the King rode into London with the earl in his train.

The violent gesture of Gilbert the Red seems to have had the desired effect. The air cleared. The turmoil throughout the country died down. The civil war had come to a final end.

One effect of Gloucester's drastic move was a widening of the rift with his wife, leading shortly thereafter to a divorce.

5

Ottobuoni should not be dismissed without telling how he came to be elected Pope on his return to Italy. It had taken more than two years to choose Gregory X and, to prevent anything as harmful as this from happening again, very severe regulations had been drawn up. Gregory promulgated a new constitution by which ten days only were allowed after the death of a pope for absent members of the Sacred College to arrive. The electing members were then to be locked up in one of the papal palaces. They were to be allowed no communication with the outside world, and food was to be supplied through a closely guarded window. After three days the food would be reduced to one meal a day; after five only bread and water and a little wine would be allowed.

Charles of Anjou, the overbearing French prince who had married Beatrice, the youngest and loveliest of the four Provençal princesses, and was now King of Sicily, had very decided views as to the choice of popes. He wanted a friendly pope so much that he decided to go even farther than the regulations prescribed in Gregory's *Ubi Periculum*. He had the Lateran Palace, where the nineteen cardinals had assembled, walled up so securely that only air, and not much of that, could find its way in. He was watchful to see that, after the fifth day had passed, nothing reached the embattled cardinals but the prescribed bread and water; although it was said at the time that some way had been found to supply plenty of warm and sustaining food to the French cardinals who were striving for the election of someone favorable to Charles—one of themselves, no doubt. It is difficult to see how this could have been done, as a common existence had been decreed. The cardinals had their meals together, such as they were, and they were not allowed separate cells for sleeping.

Days passed and still no smoke arose from the chimney to announce that a decision had been reached and the ballots burned. Finally a rather meek message was sent out for Charles of Anjou. Would he consider Ottobuoni Fiesco a suitable choice?

Ottobuoni had not been the candidate Charles favored, but the latter gave the matter consideration. His answer was, Yes, Ottobuoni would do.

The cardinals, weak from long fasting and the bitterness of the contest, emerged like wraiths. The most reduced of them all was the new Pope, who had taken the name of Adrian V. When his relatives came forward in a body to congratulate him, he answered in a rather dismal tone:

"Why are you glad? A live cardinal could do more for you than a dead pope."

It was realized later that there had been a note of prophecy in this cheerless speech. A few weeks later the new Pope was dead at Viterbo, where he had gone to escape the summer heat. There had not been time even for him to be inducted into holy orders.

Dante charges this brief holder of the holy office with love of gain and tells of encountering him in the fifth cornice of hell where "the effect of avarice is here made plain in purging of converted souls." This seems a harsh judgment on a man who, in the most serious labor of his life, the mission to England, strove most earnestly and successfully to achieve peace without any thought of personal advantage. The mission had the distinction of elevating three members of its personnel to the papacy. One member, Teobaldo Visconti, had already served as Gregory X. A third, belonging to the family of Gaetani, took office later as Boniface VII.

6

When Simon the younger rode back to Kenilworth on the day of Evesham and told the story of his father's death, the castle was filled with rage and despair. The dead leader had gained such a hold on the affections of his men that they wanted to avenge his death. Richard of Cornwall was still being held a prisoner in the castle, and it required all the authority that young Simon could exert to prevent them from taking the King of the Romans and treating him in like manner. They wanted to hack him in pieces, to cut off his head and elevate it on the point of a lance, to sever his limbs from his body and roughly dandle what was left of him on the paved courtyard. Richard knew the peril in which he stood and always thereafter gave Simon credit for saving his life.

In the meantime the newly made widow had been allowed by Edward to depart for France, accompanied by three of her children, the two youngest sons, Amauri and Richard, and her daughter, the Demoiselle. The sons took the sum of eleven thousand marks with them. It was alleged later that some of the money belonged to York Minster, where Amauri, who had entered the Church, had served as canon and treasurer. This charge was never proven.

Eleanor hired French ships to carry her furniture and personal belongings across the Channel, fearing that she would never see England again. The vessels were attacked by pirates and everything of value was taken, so that the once proud princess arrived in France in a destitute condition. She went finally to the Dominican convent of Montargis. It was not, however, to a quiet and contemplative life that she resigned herself. Her spirit refused to be subdued by disaster. From her retreat she sent a continuous stream of demands to her brother and later to Edward. In a tone which bordered on the shrill she beseeched the championship of Louis of France and of the Pope for her claims. Henry had banished her from England forever and from this decision he would not depart, but he finally agreed to allow her a pension from her dower lands, amounting to five hundred pounds a year.

The family of De Montfort was one of the most powerful in Europe, still centering at Montfort l'Amauri in Normandy, where the archives were kept. It was not as homeless exiles, therefore, that the sons of dead Simon lived but as scions of a famous family with influence of the most potent kind behind them. Guy, the third son, seems to have inherited much of his father's military genius. He joined the forces of Charles of Anjou in Italy and he did so well, particularly at the decisive battle of Alba, that Charles made him vicar-general of Tuscany. He married Margherita Aldobrandescia, the daughter and heiress of the count palatine of Pitigliano.

Amauri went to the University of Padua and later was appointed a papal chaplain. He continued to call himself treasurer of York and, having in full measure the contentious spirit of his mother, he spent the rest of his life in litigation, petitioning for this and suing for that, getting a great deal of support in high places but achieving no substantial satisfaction.

Richard, the youngest of the sons, disappeared from the scene early. There is no record of his death, and some writers have assumed that he passed the rest of his days in obscurity. It seems highly improbable, however, that any member of this spectacular family could remain for long unnoticed and unidentified. It is more probable that the unkind fate hanging over the progeny of the dead earl marked young Richard for an early death before he could be brought to notice in the tempestuous twilight of the family.

Eleanor, her perturbed spirit never at rest, spent the balance of her life at Montargis. The Demoiselle had fulfilled the promise of her girlhood and had ripened into a beauty of beauties. She lived with her mother, dreaming of the day when it would be possible for her to join her lover in Wales. Llewelyn ab Gruffydd, Prince of Wales, had visited Kenilworth during the year of great power when Simon de Montfort had been head of the state, and he had been attracted instantly to the daughter of the house. It had been settled then that they would marry when the Demoiselle became old enough. The shadow of Evesham had fallen between the lovers, and it must have seemed to the pining beauty at Montargis that she would never see Llewelyn again.

The unhappy countess died in the spring of 1275, and only Amauri and the Demoiselle were with her. It was a sad ending for the once gay and always ambitious sister of the English King. It had been her hope to establish a dynasty, to see her handsome and virile sons in high places and her beautiful daughter on a throne of her own; and it had come to this, only two of her brilliant progeny beside the narrow cot on which her last hours were spent, the austere walls of her cell close about them. Her will divided the sum of six hundred pounds between the surviving children, all that was left of her great fortune.

After Eleanor's death the Welsh prince took matters into his own hands, with the result that he and the Demoiselle were married by proxy. Somewhere around the close of 1275 the bride set out to join him, accompanied by her churchman brother, Amauri, and a party of French and Welsh knights; the name of De Montfort still having enough magic to make the marriage a matter of international importance. The vessel on which they sailed was captured off the Scilly Islands by four English ships which had been lying in wait. The bride was held in captivity at Windsor for three years, a great asset for Edward in the struggle he was waging with the head of the Welsh state. At the end of the three years, despairing of union by any other means with the wife he had not seen, Llewelyn made his submission to Edward. The couple were formally married at Worcester on October 13, 1278. Edward, having achieved his purpose, was in attendance in a benign mood.

It seems to have been a happy marriage, but the same unkind fate which hovered over the sons of Simon de Montfort overtook the Demoiselle (the childhood name clung to her throughout her life) in the end. She died in childbirth in 1282, and the daughter who thus cost the princess her life was taken to England when Llewelyn died in battle shortly after. The little Princess Gwenllian now presented the same problem as the unfortunate Pearl of Brittany had in the first half of the century. The high authorities did not want the line of Simon de Montfort perpetuated nor that of the Welsh royal family. And so the infant, while still in her cradle, was taken to Sempringham and spent her life there as a nun.

7

It was at Viterbo that the most tragic scene in the story of the De Montforts was enacted. The lava-paved town, lying high above Rome on the main road to Florence, had been making history for centuries. Here it was that England's only Pope, Adrian IV, met the all-powerful Emperor of Germany, Frederick I, and compelled that haughty monarch to dismount and hold the papal stirrup. Here popes came to spend the midsummer months in the shady gardens of the beautiful old town. Here many pontifical elections were held; here many of the popes died and were buried. Here the wars of the Guelphs and the Ghibellines surged back and forth about the high stone walls. But never had it seen anything to equal what happened on a warm morning in March 1271.

In the center of Viterbo there was a paved square surrounded by the stone houses of the gentry and one parish church, that of San Silvestro. From the square a narrow street led to the cathedral where for more than two years eighteen cardinals had been struggling to elect a pope in succession to Clement IV. They were almost hopelessly divided between two factions, the Italian and the French. At this stage Charles of Anjou, whose interests were in the hands of the French faction, arrived in the hope of breaking the stalemate. He was accompanied by his nephew, the new King of France, Philip III, and Henry of Almaine. The latter was returning from the Crusades, where he had won praise from Edward and had been entrusted with a mission to settle some new difficulties in Gascony. He had traveled through Italy in the royal train of Charles.

At the same time also there arrived in Viterbo Guy de Montfort, riding at the head of a party of knights and accompanied by his brother Simon and his father-in-law. He came, in all probability, to consult Charles, his liege lord, on points connected with his stewardship in Tuscany. He was twenty-eight years old and at the peak of his physical powers; handsome, full of high spirits, and certain in his own mind (a conviction generally shared) that a great career lay ahead of him. Simon was three years older, less flamboyant in appearance and talent, very much sobered, moreover, by his experiences in the civil war.

Thus by an evil coincidence the three main actors in the tragedy were brought together.

The stone houses on the square were so tall that they cast long shadows across the paved enclosure and aided the palm trees in keeping the air cool. Spring came early in Viterbo, and on March 13, 1271, the vines on the walls were a luxuriant green and there were flowers in profusion everywhere. Henry of Almaine had been assigned one of the houses as his residence while in the town, and this morning he sauntered across the square to hear mass in the little church with no more than an attendant or two to keep him company. He could not have failed on this warm, scented day to feel at peace with the world and happy in the pleasant prospects ahead of him. He was a handsome man, the blending of the Plantagenet and Marshal strains apparent in his height, his fairness of hair and skin, his well-modeled features; more Marshal than Plantagenet in disposition, for he was amiable, easy-speaking, kindly rather than proud.

Guy de Montfort was of a passionate, brooding nature. The death of his father had affected him so deeply that even during this period of his fast-mounting success he thought constantly of the revenge he would exact someday. He hated everyone who had been on the other side of the struggle. Perhaps he had special dislike for Henry of Almaine, who had been among the first of the young men to desert Simon de Montfort. It is not believed, however, that there was premeditation in what followed. Guy did not seek out the son of the King of the Romans deliberately; it was, rather, part of the evil coincidence that he and his brother Simon and his father-in-law, with the usual train of knights and servants at their heels, elected also to hear mass that morning in the little church on the square. They entered in a body, and Guy recognized at once the man kneeling in prayer before the high altar.

If there had been any room for wise considerations in his mind at the moment, he would have turned instantly and left the church. He had greatness ahead of him, he had wealth and a lovely wife, he had the respect and admiration of men. But a wild upsurge of hatred banished such considerations from his mind, and he loosened the dagger at his belt.

"Traitor!" he cried in a loud voice, striding up the aisle. "Thou shalt not escape!"

One account has it that Henry gave way to panic when he saw what was in the minds of these violent men. Instead of defending himself, he clung with desperate hands to the altar, begging for mercy under the sword strokes of his assailants. He died quickly, though not mercifully, his mutilated hands losing their hold and allowing his body to fall on the stone steps of the altar.

"I have had my revenge," said Guy, turning to leave the church. It was now almost empty, the frightened Lenten worshipers having made their way out with loud cries of alarm.

One of Guy's knights, who had shared in the killing, was not yet satisfied. He stared down darkly at the body of their victim.

"How so?" he demanded. "They cut up the body of your father and dragged it about."

Guy turned back. He seized the long locks of the dead prince. With the aid of his followers, who took rough hold of the arms and legs, he dragged the body down the aisle of the church and out to the cobbled square. Here they hacked the inoffensive clay, dragging it about and echoing the grim shouts of triumph which had accompanied the mutilation of Simon de Montfort on that black morning in the Vale of Evesham.

CHAPTER TWENTY-NINE

The Magnificent Century

WHILE England was taking remarkable strides in the direction of freedom and establishing principles of democratic rule which the world would accept later, Englishmen had been sharing also in other activities of this great and beneficent period.

The twelfth had been the century of the Crusades, a memorable, gallant, resounding century. Men marched away singing and died in battle or were captured and sold into slavery; and comparatively few came back. The heroic but badly managed efforts to wrest the Holy City from the infidels kept Christendom in a continuous flurry of exultation, of preparation, of loss and despair. But something grew out of it. Those who came back brought the first hints of a new life.

They brought books and medicines and maps and Eastern magic as well as new foods, new diseases, new heresies. Spices from the East awakened the dull palates of Christian people. Knowledge from the lands of the hot desert enlivened their sluggish minds. Europe would have roused slowly from the lethargy of the Dark Ages, in any event, but the breaking of barriers between East and West stimulated the process. It would have been a quicker burgeoning if the nations of Europe had not started warring among themselves. During the last decades of the twelfth century there were civil wars in

Germany and Italy, religious troubles in France, dynastic in England. As a result the cloud lifted a little, but a little only, and the light which came through was fitful. Men continued to suffer unceasingly. Those of high station lived in dank stone castles and those of low degree in mean hovels without chimney or window. They clothed their bodies in dun shoddiness and counted a man a meacock who wore an embroidered band on his tunic. They had faith in God but believed just as surely in the devil. Men died early, in the wars, on the rack, or with a searing hot pain in their insides about which they knew nothing and for which nothing could be done. Women began to bear children in their teens and died in their thirties after losing all their bloom and most of their teeth. All this was as it had been.

Then the thirteenth century dawned—and a great change came over things. Wars went on just the same and ignorance lost only a little of its grip. Lepers went on dying in woeful neglect and in the stench of lazarcotes. The first dark cruelties of the Inquisition were felt. It was a vastly imperfect century, with everything wrong from the Dark Ages carried over into it in some degree. That must be accepted at the outset.

But it was magnificent because it saw the beginnings of so much. Men began to think new thoughts, to dream again, to rediscover beauty which, like dyes for the making of gay cloth, had almost been lost. Science, which had started with Plato and Aristotle, Euclid, Archimedes, and Pythagoras, may be said to have been born a second time in the thirteenth because it was then that the principles of scientific research were discovered. These years from 1200 to 1300 were to see progress in all directions. Invention, after lying fallow for centuries, was to bloom again with the suddenness which can turn a desert into a riot of lupine overnight.

It was a century of great men. They stand out from the darkness like pillars of light, their achievements undimmed by distance, their personalities vivid in spite of the scantiness of the records. Consider them for a moment, forgiving the inevitable use of superlatives which cannot be avoided in dealing with a superlative period in the march of time.

Thomas Aquinas and Duns Scotus represent the fields of philosophy and theology, and they were, it will be admitted, authentic giants. The teachings of the former are as much regarded today as when he labored by the light of a tallow dip over his *Summa Theologiae*.

Giotto, the shepherd's boy who humanized painting, paved the way for the Renaissance in art, while Nicola Pisano was doing the same for sculpture. Greater than either stands a figure of supreme luster, an Italian named Dante, who would not produce his great work in the thirteenth but would acquire his training and draw his inspiration from that century.

Innocent III, one of the most justly acclaimed of popes, might be classified under many resounding titles, but one may be selected because of its humanitarianism, the father of the modern hospital. Genghis Khan, the Tartar who overran Asia and whose lieutenants shattered the armies of Western chivalry, was on every count the most devastating conqueror of history. There was a king in France, Louis IX, who was so enlightened of spirit and so filled with desire to make kingship what he conceived God had intended it to be that men called him St. Louis. A monk in a Dominican monastery, one Vincent of Beauvais, conceived the idea of an encyclopedia which would be revived five hundred years later to set the modern standard; and, moreover, he wrote the first one all by himself, a monumental effort.

A courageous English churchman named Robert Grosseteste may be called the greatest teacher of the age because he imparted to his pupils the first glimmer of scientific truth.

Roger Bacon, that man of mighty intellect and fascinating mystery, raised the torch higher and taught the principles of research and experiment on which scientific advance has been based, applying them himself in many inventions. Believers in the Baconian cult will say that a century which did no more than produce this inspired Franciscan monk might rest content with its share in the annals of progress.

2

A few examples of thirteenth-century activities will suffice to convey an idea of the spirit of the times. Toward the end of the twelfth century the spires of churches began to rise higher. In the thirteenth they soared into the heavens in a glory of carved stone and with a daring which told of the release of men's minds. With height went a conception of new beauty in all detail. G. K. Chesterton speaks of Late Gothic, the gift to the world of the thirteenth, as fighting architecture, its spires like spears at rest, its arches clashing like swords. It was that, of course, but much more. It was a manifestation of faith so great that man wanted to carry this symbol of it right up to the stars. Of all the signs that the curtain of ignorance and inertia was beginning to fall, the new type of church was the clearest and most marked. It flaunted, moreover, a return of interest in beauty and a general desire to create it.

This amazing span of years produced in France the cathedrals of Chartres, Reims, Amiens, Bourges, and Le Mans. In England, following the more subdued lines of English Gothic, came Salisbury, Ely, Lincoln, the great Yorkshire abbeys which rank above everything else for sheer purity of design.

It was possible quite early in the century to walk into buildings in almost all large cities of Europe which were so different from other structures that they instantly aroused wonder as to the purpose they served. They were generally of a single story. They had a few rooms only, and these were large and the ceilings high, the windows spacious enough to admit plenty of light and air. Almost invariably they were located near running water so there would be plenty for all uses and waste matter could be carried away quickly, this latter a curious consideration indeed in the dirt of medievalism. They were hospitals, and this will be hard to believe because of the conception man has of the hospitals of any period before the middle of the nineteenth century; a picture, and a true one, of unclean hotbeds of disease and suffering, dark and fetid, with crowded beds and mortuaries filled with untended bodies.

The hospitals of the Holy Ghost came about in this way. Innocent III, in some inspired moment when he laid aside his plans for bringing the whole Christian world into one great federation under the active control of the papacy, conceived the idea of having in Rome a model hospital which would serve to enlighten the nations in the proper treatment of the sick. Knowledge of medicine had been limited through the dark centuries to accepted ideas and practices, a great deal of superstition, a jumble of absurd cures from leech-books, a little practical understanding of the use of herbs, and very considerable skill in surface surgery. Connected with the school of medicine at Montpellier, France, there was, however, a physician who had created an institution for the sick which was a model of organization and new thought. This man, Guy of Montpellier, was summoned to Rome and given a free hand by the Pope. He built the hospital of Santo Spiritu, which fulfilled every desire of the forward-looking Innocent. Thereafter it was pointed out to every churchman who came to Rome and the suggestion made that he should carry back with him a determination to create hospitals of a like nature. Many were built along these lines, mostly in Germany, France, and England.

The premature death of Innocent resulted in a loss of impetus, and it may be taken for granted that the finer type of hospital was found only in the larger cities. The Tonnerre in Paris was one of the best examples, having wards 270 feet long and 55 feet wide, the roof high and vaulted to admit plenty of air and light. In Germany at least one Holy Ghost institution still stands, exhibiting the admirable features which made them so remarkable in this early age. In London five royal hospitals were built or reorganized during the thirteenth century and had, no doubt, some of the new ideas: St. Thomas's, St. Bartholomew's, Bethlehem (which later became known as Bedlem), Bridewell, and Christ's Hospital.

It must be conceded that the picture of medicine remained, in spite of this, a dark one. The number of houses for the segregation of lepers rose before the year 1300 to the staggering figure of nineteen thousand in all Europe, and the physician of the day seems at this distance a combination of quack and native medicine man. Still, an Italian named Salvenus de Armat invented spectacles in 1280, a somewhat crude aid to eyesight but a definite step in the forward direction.

Something in the nature of a miracle (or so it seemed to those who saw it) would be performed on rare occasions, and this is worth telling about. When a great nobleman had been thrown from his horse in the course of a tilting and a splinter of steel had become lodged in his head, or a bishop had fallen and suffered a fracture in a great fat thigh, the physician summoned to the case might resolve to ease the pain of what had to be done. His assistant always carried a bag wherever they went, containing a book in which the tides of the ocean and the phases of the moon were recorded (it being considered important not to do anything at the wrong time), and such varied items as saffron seed, soda, dried frogs' legs, yarrow, belony, asses' hoofs, and powders of crushed precious stones. From this assortment the assistant would produce a not overly clean sleeping sponge. A sleeping sponge was a very rare thing, and its use was something to be whispered about in awed tones. The doctors knew little about the strange power it contained and were loath to make use of it. It was a plain sponge, nevertheless, which had been dipped at some previous time in a mixture of the juices of opium, hyoscyamus, mandragora, and conium and then dried in the sun.

The assistant, an overworked and usually not very clean individual who drew the teeth and administered clysters and such routine work, would dip the sponge in warm water. The doctor would then take it and place it over the mouth and nostrils of the sufferer. Sometimes, of course, nothing happened, but sometimes the patient would begin to breathe stertorously, indicating that he had fallen asleep and would continue unconscious while the doctor went to work with knife and searing iron and splints.

This secret was lost some time thereafter. The mists closed in again. Even as late as the nineteenth century people would suffer excruciating pain during operations, with no more aid to endurance than a glass of brandy or rum. But write it down to the credit of the thirteenth century that the mercy of anesthesia was known then, although not fully understood and most sparingly used.

3

A creative urge was felt in all the arts. Men composed, painted, wrote, with an almost feverish new interest. The beauty of the magnificent churches was reflected in the poems, the romances, the pictures, the Latin hymns, which this inspired century produced. It was then that *Dies Irae* and the *Stabat Mater* were first sung; that the songs of the Crusades, polyphonic and sonorous, grew out of the marching feet turned eastward. It was a poor parish church indeed which did not have a biblical painting, usually depicting the Second Coming, on its walls. An inn lacking gay decorations was counted no better than a spittlehouse. The meanest home had something to distinguish it, a boldness of line, a carved sign, a vigorous splash of paint.

The mind of man, awakening from its long torpor, had turned with vigorous energy to progress. He was no longer content with what he had known before, the narrow limits and interests of the life he had been forced to live. He was questing in all directions, thinking, asking, demanding, inventing. New weapons were being produced, new types of ships built. Clocks were put up in church towers, at Westminster, Canterbury, St. Albans, to the great wonderment of Englishmen, and one Robertus Anglicus was experimenting with a mechanical clock which would be operated with weights.

Most remarkable of all, the inspired English friar, Roger Bacon, was beginning to speak of curious things, of glasses which would make it possible to see clearly across the Channel from Dover to France, of vehicles which would soar unsupported through the air, of a powder of the most secret kind, made up largely of saltpeter, which would explode with a flash of fire like lightning in the sky and a roar to equal the terror of winds at the end of the world.

CHAPTER THIRTY

Merrie England

THE weak efforts Henry had made to regain the lost provinces across the Channel had disturbed the even tenor of life
in England scarcely at all. The long struggle with the barons
took its toll in lives, in financial loss, in trade disturbances, but
again the effects on the common people were relatively light.
The country was prosperous in the main through the years of
this long reign. The soil seemed to have grown in fertility. The
painstaking Cistercians raised the standards of husbandry, and
the value of English wool soared. The country became prosperous in a new sense, the cities grew larger, the villages
around the castles teemed with active life.

In spite of poor government and the strife it produced,
England was merrie.

2

There was a law that any yeoman with less than one
hundred pence a year in land was obligated to have a bow and
to practice regularly. This was no hardship, for one of the
great pleasures of the common man was shooting at the butts.
During the hours of leisure, sounds of loud laughter and
approving cries of "Shotten!" would be heard from the arch-
ery grounds. The thud of arrows striking the clout squarely

old the story of the skill English hands were developing with
the mighty longbow. They came to the targets eagerly, these
heavy-set men of the land, with their bows as tall as they were
themselves, their arrows a yard long. They were not content
to shoot at the marks which men of other countries used.
They took willow wands instead, and rose garlands, and a very
special target called a popinjay, an artificial parrot or pheas-
ant. Every village produced its champions, and it was no
wonder that in later days it was easy to recruit the expert
bowmen who won the great victories of the Hundred Years'
War.

Boys, always eager to ape their elders, had bows of their
own and would cover up their lack of skill by capering and
singing:

> *"All in a row, a bendy bow:*
> *Shoot at a pigeon and kill a crow,*
> *Shoot at another and kill his brother."*

Younger children amused themselves on teeter-totters,
although the name used then was merrytotter. They often
played a game called Nine Men's Morris, which required a
whole field.

The English, in fact, were great lovers of sport. In winter
they fastened the bones of animals to their feet and skated on
frozen ponds and streams. Those who could afford such
luxuries had a kind of skate with a metal edge, but they did
not call them skates; they were termed scrick-shoes. A very
popular game was known as bandy-ball, in which a crooked
stick was used to clout a ball about a field. This form of
amusement sired two quite different types of game, *goff* and
shinny. Men bowled on the green and also played kayles or
closh, a form of ninepins. They differed from most people in
preferring games in which they could participate. Whole
villages would turn to kick a ball or frisk around a Maypole.

At the same time they were avid followers of less healthy
forms of sport in which they played the part of spectators—bear-baiting, bull-running, badger-baiting, and cock-
fighting.

The recreations of the nobility were somewhat more
dignified. The tournament was the great amusement of the age
and it drew all classes of people. Between joustings the brave
knights kept the eye in for the next splintering of lances by

practicing at the quintain, a special type of target. Sometimes live quintains were used, men who covered themselves with a shield and defied the champions to bowl them over.

Hunting and hawking engaged most of the waking time of the nobility. Ladies of gentle blood took an active interest in both. Their participation sometimes took the form of sitting in an enclosure and shooting arrows at game driven past them. This, needless to state, did not suffice for the bolder ones who preferred to go into the field with their own harehounds. Ladies became expert hawkers and were seldom seen in the saddle without a hooded marlyon on wrist. The love of hawking, in fact, was universal. The poor man with his tercel and the yeoman with his goshawk (a certain type of hawk was designated for each class) were seen as often as the earl with his falcon and the knight with his sacret.

The indoor amusements of the nobility included chess and an early form of backgammon. After supper in the great hall the minstrels would fill the hours with their ballades while the well-stuffed guests drank their wine. Minstrels were often well paid for their efforts, it being a not uncommon thing for the host to reward a particularly good performance with a gift of the cloak he was wearing or a drinking cup from the table.

3

When people are happy they turn to music, and so it is not surprising that during the years of this remarkable century there was a great revival of minstrelsy. The bardy-coats (so called because of the shortened garments they wore) went up and down the land, singing the songs of Assanduan and Hastings, the ballades of Richard the Lion-Heart and Henry and the Fair Rosamonde. They were a race apart, these itinerant musicians, capable of playing on harp or vielle (which the common people called a fydel, or fiddle), with the use of an arched bow which produced a long-drawn-out accompaniment called a "drone bass." Sometimes the vielle was operated by the turning of a handle, which made it the distant ancestor of the modern hurdy-gurdy. Sometimes the bardy-coats would lay their instruments aside and tell losel tales instead; and then the villagers would roar with laughter and slap their muscular thighs over anecdotes of scolds and cuckolds and fustian adventure. Sometimes a party of entertainers would roam up and down the land, consisting of jugglers and tumblers as well as minstrels, and even girls who danced on the shoulders of the gleemen.

The better class of minstrel found employment in the household of a nobleman. He then wore a distinctive dress, a red jacket over a parti-colored tunic and a yellow hood, the costume later used by court jesters. Even these musicians of a relatively lordly stature were under the ban of the Church, however, being forbidden the sacraments; which placed them in the company of excommunicates, sorcerers, prostitutes, and epileptics.

Music up to this time had been largely liturgical, the one-voiced Gregorian plain song which had the sanction of the Church. Now folk music, which went back some centuries and was polyphonic, began to come into its own at last. In England folk singing in the form of the *motet* can be traced back centuries before the Conquest. The first records of actual music for more than one voice are found, therefore, in the island kingdom. The *motet* sounds very confusing to the modern ear. It has three parts, each with a different number of syllables to the measure and each with different words. There can be no doubt that dramatic intensity was achieved by this method, and by the end of the thirteenth century it had come into steady use, even in the secular church. The center had shifted from England to France, where in the cathedral later known as Notre Dame there was a quite fabulous musical school under the direction of the great Magister Perotinus Magnus.

The Church did not accept these innovations with any gladness. In fact, there was much opposition and much thundering of threats against those who composed these disorganizing songs and those who sang them. The refusal to admit minstrels to the sacraments was part of the effort to maintain plain song as the one form of musical expression. This had no effect: let churchmen inveigh as much as they liked, the love for polyphonic music grew. Wherever men and women gathered and the opportunity arose for song, on communal green, on the roads where groups plodded along together, the new music would be heard, voices blending in *motet* and *hocket*.

The Church was particularly opposed to a class of singers who became known as *goliards*. These wandering minstrels were sometimes renegades from clerical life, sometimes students who had failed to achieve anything at the university and had taken to a vagrant life, wining, wenching, dicing, singing. They seldom attempted to do more than entertain peasants at village inns, knowing how darkly the eye of authority turned on them. They lived and died, therefore, in obscurity, and this is unfortunate because many of them were brilliant fellows, capable of composing music of a delightfully melodious turn and of writing words to match. Collections have been made of such of their songs as have survived, and these make it clear that they produced love lyrics and nature songs of rare artistry. For the most part, of course, they specialized on different fare, knowing the tastes of the people on whom they depended for a living. Their drinking and gambling songs were bawdy in the extreme. They even indulged in obscene and sacrilegious parodies of the church litanies.

England produced her full share of *goliards*. They went from tavern to tavern, cutting their capers, singing their rowdy songs with much drollery, getting an occasional penny and free meal, couching a hogshead (sleeping in a barrel) when in town, curling up under a hedge when in the country. It was a short life and a merry one for the *goliard*. He died in a brawl or at the end of an official rope for thievery, his François Villon type of life seldom bringing him a moment of peace in life or an orderly departing therefrom. He helped considerably in making life more bearable for the common man, so peace to his memory.

The people of the century had many instruments on which to express their love of music. There were organs in the churches, of course, and a portable variety which had as many as seven or eight notes. The keyboard had not yet been invented, and so the music was produced by striking the strings with clenched fist or elbow. Then there was the guitar, which was called a gittern in England; the fydel, already mentioned; small portable harps with a limited number of strings, which were much favored for the singing of ballades; the psaltery, a wooden box with strings stretched across it; flutes, double-whistles, bagpipes; the shawm, a kind of oboe with a double reed which the watchmen in London began to use on their rounds at some stage of the long reign of Henry III; finally, the trumpets, cornets, and bugles used in battle and for the announcements of the heralds.

4

The people of the thirteenth century danced long and feasted heartily at weddings. They went regularly to fairs and spent their few farthings on ribbons for their wives and sweethearts, and often enough were hauled up before the Pie Powder Courts for infractions of the peace. They danced around the Maypole with an abandon which told of a complete lack of concern for the morrow. They worked hard but they laughed loud.

They seem to have had an instinctive good taste and a well-developed sense of order. The tillers of the soil kept their hedges well trimmed and their furrows as straight as the flight of an arrow. The artisans in the towns produced the finest of cloth, neat-fitting garments, and the cockiest of hats.

Norman castles still frowned down on them from hillsides and strategic fords, and the distinction between the two races in the land had not yet been obliterated. The nobleman still spoke Norman French; the workman kept alive the more virile tongue called English. The tillers of the soil still whispered of the days of Edward the Confessor and great King Alfred, but the memory was growing dim. A national solidarity was forming which would be completed in the following reign.

In the meantime England was merrie enough, much more carefree in mood than France, where the iron bonds of feudalism still weighed heavily on the common people. Men remembered the Great Charter, and there was a feeling in slum and toft that the calling of commoners to Parliament would lead to real emancipation. On the whole, the artisan and the yeoman had reason to be merrie.

CHAPTER THIRTY-ONE

Roger Bacon

At Folly Bridge near Oxford there stood a small stone tower with a ponderous gateway, and over the gateway there was a long, dark room. It was a mysterious room, with a furnace at one end and tables covered with the retorts, alembics, and crucibles of science, with books and manuscripts in great quantity; a dusty, gloomy room, filled with the odors of acids and old leather and dead fires. But give scholars a choice: to have for study today all the royal castles of England in the thirteenth century, and the chancery offices at Westminster, including the cubicle where Henry fretted and sulked, and the chapter house at Canterbury where the frustrated monks would meet in secret midnight sessions in an effort to impose their puny wills on the Crown in the matter of new archbishops—in fact, almost all of England of that period—or that one long room, complete to the last scrap of manuscript and sooty fingerprints on cucurbit and bellows. The choice would certainly be for Folly Bridge and its tower; for there Roger Bacon lived during his years of study and experiment at Oxford, great Roger Bacon, the man of mystery of the Middle Ages, the Doctor Mirabilis, the scholar so far in advance of his time, that tragic and compelling figure.

Although this Franciscan friar has become a figure of the first historical importance, very little is known about the

354

man. It is generally conceded, on the strength of occasional hints about himself in his writings, that he was born in 1214 or thereabouts, either at Ilchester in Somerset or Bisley in Gloucestershire. It is certain he went to Oxford and became a student under the incomparable Grosseteste and the kindly Adam Marsh, absorbing gratefully the enlightened scientific theories of the one and the gentle philosophy of the other. About the year 1240 he left Oxford for Paris and remained in the French capital for ten years, teaching, studying, experimenting, his mind filled with visions of a different world and burning to correct the methods and beliefs of a complacent, wrongheaded age. It was almost certainly during his first Paris period that he joined the Franciscans, feeling, no doubt, that the work he planned required the background and secure retirement of the Minorite order.

After his ten years in Paris he was back again at Oxford, and it was during this second term, lasting from 1250 to 1257, that he occupied the tower at Folly Bridge. While the struggle between the King and his barons mounted in intensity and Oxford was a storm center of politics and war, Roger Bacon's ideas took final form and he gained his clear conception of an orderly universe with fixed laws, the nature of which could be proven by scientific approach. It was during the turbulent fifties that this intense man in the brown habit of his order, this angry, critical man who lashed out at the stupidities of medieval thinking and did not hesitate to attack the leaders of the day, even the saintly Thomas Aquinas and the learned Alexander of Hales, began to say to the world that its absorption in the subtleties of theological dispute was wrong and that the time had come for a realistic study of life and the universe. He was the one man with feet planted solidly on the earth, the voice of reason and common sense in an age of hairsplitting. The teachers of the day were saying, "Believe that ye may understand." Roger Bacon countered with, "Understand that ye may believe."

He was not, however, a mere theorist in the realm of scientific thought. He knew how to apply the principles in which he believed. If he had conceived it his part to complete some of his visions of the shape of things to come, and if he had not been working with the fewest and poorest of tools, he might have brought some of his discoveries to applied use. In that case the world would have had a telescope and a microscope three hundred years before they were evolved. He knew how to make gunpowder, and undoubtedly did make it, but had no conception of it as a great new force in warfare. In a prophetic attack on the future he saw the airplane and talked of vehicles which would fly through the air, but in this case he does not seem to have had more than the vision. It was an impossibility for him to glean any hint of how a flying machine might be built or of the force which would serve to drive it through the air; too many discoveries would have to be made first as to the nature of materials.

All this, however, is beside the point. It is unimportant whether Roger Bacon actually discovered gunpowder in the age of the crossbow and arrows or conceived the principles of the telescope while the windows of the world were filled with waxed linen instead of glass. The great and all-important thing is that he contributed new light to the world, that he saw the simple and direct method by which knowledge could be won. He preached the demonstration of fact by experiment, by experiment repeated over and over again until the following of effect after cause could not be doubted. He preached that only from one truth thus established could man go on to more experiments, to more truths. In other words, this farseeing friar, hampered by the shackles of medieval thought from which he could not entirely free himself, had grasped the principle, nevertheless, which was applied in later centuries to all scientific research and has proven the keystone of knowledge.

Inevitably it became common belief that this lonely man, poring over his manuscripts and making secret experiments in his dark tower room, was a practitioner of the black arts. His indiscreet talk, his hints of things to come strengthened the fancy. The verbal buffetings he administered to the self-satisfied gods of the medieval classroom made enemies for him who were only too ready to foster belief in his heresies. Stories were told that the devil, forked tail and slavering tongue complete, had been seen going in and out at Folly Bridge. It was believed that Roger Bacon had sold his soul for the secrets the Prince of Darkness could give in exchange, that he could make himself invisible, that he could transport his body through space with the speed and ease of angels, that he could see into the future. Out of these beliefs grew the legends which persisted down the ages and led in time to the not very amusing or original anecdotes about Friar Bacon and Friar

Bungay, out of which not very amusing or original plays and stories were concocted.

In this respect the great Franciscan was faring no worse than others who had striven to upraise the torch of reason. The heresy hunt which kept nipping at his bare heels had already involved, to quote one case only, a wise man from Scotland who preceded Bacon in his pryings into scientific truth by relatively few years. A digression seems necessary at this point to speak of Michael Scot and the curious vagaries of popular belief which turned him into a sorcerer of the blackest hue.

2

The manner of the death of great men and the time and the place are always known; their beginnings are almost as certainly shrouded in mystery. The arrival of children was a matter of small importance in the Middle Ages.

Michael Scot, supposedly, was born at Balwearie in Scotland, but the evidence is far from conclusive. It has been calculated that he arrived in this world about 1180 and that as a youth he went to the university at Oxford, but again there are no definite facts. The trail becomes definite only when he appeared in Germany, a slight, dark man with a luminous eye and an air which set him apart, and gained recognition at the court of Frederick II. That most courageous supporter of learning saw great possibilities in the young Scot, who had already won for himself some reputation in the mastery of the sciences. Scot remained at the court of the Emperor for a number of years and then went to Spain, where it is supposed he became immersed in the study of black magic. What is certain, however, is that he went to Spain to further his researches in mathematics and astronomy. He occupied himself while there in making a translation of the Latin Averroës, which, when completed, won him a high place in the regard of scholars.

He returned to the court of Frederick after ten years in Spain, worn out from long and arduous labors and the strain of incessant poring over manuscripts. The Emperor was glad to welcome him back and sought to find papal appointments for him in England and Ireland. A benefice was offered him in Cashel, but as it would have meant exile from all the sources of knowledge and as Scot himself was honest enough to rebel against plural appointments, he refused it. He remained at court, therefore, practicing medicine, poor, rather unhappy, as jealous as ever in his pursuit of knowledge, particularly in the three branches of science which interested him most, mathematics, astronomy, and medicine.

After his death he became a legend. It was believed he had known the secrets of the East and had been a great sorcerer. The legend grew out of a popular belief that he had a gift for prophecy, that he had not only predicted the time and manner of the death of the Emperor but of his own as well. He was said to have declared that Frederick would die at gates of iron in a town named after Flora of the Romans, and it was assumed that this meant Florence. It happened, however, that the head of the Holy Roman Empire fell ill in the town of Firenzuola in Apulia. He was put to bed in a tower with his head against a masonry wall which had been built to fill in an ancient gateway. When the eyes of the sick Emperor saw that the iron staples of the gate still protruded from the wall, he knew that his time had come.

"This is the place," he said to those about him. "The will of God be done, for here I shall die."

He passed away soon thereafter, and the reputation of Michael Scot waxed rapidly because of this.

As to the manner of his own death, Scot had declared that a bolt from the sky would strike him on the head and kill him, and he was so convinced of his danger that he invented and made a special plate of steel to wear under his hat when he ventured out. One day he neglected to wear the steel bonnet and as he passed the bell tower of a church a stone was dislodged from the wall by the motion of the bell rope. It fell and killed Michael Scot.

Because of this, the belief in his magic powers grew rapidly. The name of Michael Scot became one to cause shudders, and soon it was classed by a credulous world with the great magicians and sorcerers of the past, even with Simon Magus and Merlin. The stories and myths about him multiplied with the years. He was supposed to have written down all the dark secrets he had known and the unholy spells and incantations he had used, and men of ill will sought for this book with as much zest as honorable men searched for the Holy Grail. It is possible that he had made experiments in the realm of the occult, for all scholars of his day seem to have entertained some measure of belief in magic. In his scientific work, however, he remained realistic and free from the taint of charlatanism. As a delver into the secrets of the heavens and as a mathematician he won words of praise from the usually critical Roger Bacon, and that may be accepted as proof of his great ability as well as of the soundness of his ideas. As a doctor of medicine he seems to have been regarded as an enlightened practitioner. This, of course, was before the black mantle of the legend had been wrapped about him like the trailing sheets of a ghost.

The record of his substantial achievements in the world of science was soon lost in the wild stories which the world invented and believed of him.

3

During the years when his most important work was done, between 1240 and 1257, Roger Bacon spent two thousand pounds of his own money in study and in acquiring the books and equipment he needed. After that date, his resources exhausted, belonging to an order which set a watch on him and seemed ready to detect in him the signs of heresy, he proceeded with great wariness. He had a small circle of friends in whom trust could be placed and he used two young assistants who were intensely loyal. One of the assistants, a youth named John, had been a beggar in Paris and had been befriended by the great Franciscan. Bacon had trained John carefully and used him on errands of the greatest importance.

It is certain that during the years of his second visit to Paris Bacon began to set down notes on the discoveries he had made. He worked in great secrecy, being fearful of interference and, perhaps, of punishment. It is now widely believed that he went to the extent of inventing and using a Latin cipher. He had given up all hope of making any impression on the world of his own day. The mind of authority was closed against him and all he represented. Determined that his discoveries should not be lost, he had begun to look to the future, hoping that in succeeding generations there would be more tolerance.

In 1265 there was a turn of events in his favor. Guy Fulcodi had become Pope, taking the title of Clement IV. When a cardinal and the papal legate to England, Fulcodi had heard of the mysterious friar and the work he was doing and had become interested. Now his word had become law and he wrote to Bacon, asking him to send to Rome at once any material he might have written, warning him to proceed in the matter with the greatest discretion but without permitting any hostility among the heads of his own order to interfere. Bacon had not committed anything to paper in a form suitable for pontifical consideration and so he began at once, in a spirit of aroused hope and enthusiasm, to prepare a statement of his beliefs, his theories, and something of his experiments. Working secretly because the nature of the papal instructions made it dangerous to consult any of his superiors, he succeeded in the course of eighteen months in preparing the three great works on which his reputation is based, the *Opus Majus,* the *Opus Minus,* and the *Opus Tertium.* In these huge documents he covered the whole field of scientific and philosophical knowledge and pleaded with Clement as God's representative on earth to give sanction to teachings along his lines. He wrote with frankness and an enthusiasm which stemmed from the hopes which the papal invitation had aroused in him. The course he was proposing was not one, however, which Clement could adopt. If the Pope had committed the Church to these startlingly new principles there would have been a storm such as Christendom had never experienced before. The Church was not ready for the revolutionary methods of Bacon, nor was the world it ruled. The support of the Pope would not have sufficed to bring about the changes the Franciscan was so boldly advocating.

The three books, together with a spherical crystal lens which Bacon had made as a gift for the Pontiff, were given into the care of the trusty John, who set off with them for Rome. They were delivered, if not actually into the hands of the Pope himself, at least to officials who were close to him. Buoyed up with hope that the world might be brought after all to accept the truth of his teachings, Roger Bacon waited for word from Rome with as much patience as he could summon.

Time passed and the silence at Rome remained unbroken. The interval stretched out into a year, the ailing Clement died, and still no word of the manuscripts had been received. The unhappy friar came to the realization finally that his work had been in vain.

It is doubtful if Clement ever laid eyes on the *Opus Majus,* the most important of the three volumes, in which the truth of Bacon's great discovery was convincingly set forth. He had been a sick man when raised to the pontificate, too sick in body and weary in mind to undertake the study of this formidable manuscript. It is recorded that he sought diligently to repair his health, consulting in particular a French physician in whom Louis of France placed the greatest reliance. The physician studied the swollen feet and legs of the Pontiff and prescribed a treatment of such rigor that the suffering Clement complained he found the cure harder to bear than the disease. A year after Roger Bacon's messenger reached Rome the sick old man yielded to his ailments. The manuscripts, in the meantime, had been allowed to rest in some dusty niche in the archives.

They had not been entirely neglected, however. Eyes, unfriendly eyes, had spied out the nature of these revolutionary documents. Perhaps Clement had instructed members of the Vatican staff to read and digest what Bacon had written, a normal form of procedure. If this were the case, he may have received reports of such a sweepingly critical nature that he decided hastily to proceed no further in the matter. However it came about, the Baconian theories had been read and emphatically censored before they were filed away.

It was fortunate for the author of them that the new incumbent of the papacy was a man of similar mind to the deceased Clement. Nothing was done to punish the daring English friar while the three great tomes, containing the secret of future world progress, were allowed to repose in complete disregard on some forgotten shelf.

This immunity could not last forever. In 1277 Jerome of Ascoli became head of the Franciscan order and, with the support of the Pope of that period, he condemned the Baconian doctrines as dangerous. The inspired Englishman was sentenced to imprisonment in a dark cell. No communication with the outside world was allowed him; no opportunity was afforded for study or work in any form. For fourteen years that great mind languished in solitary confinement.

He was close to death when a new minister-general of the Franciscan order, Raimondo Gaufredi, ordered that he be released. He emerged from his cell a bent and sick man of nearly eighty years. Long imprisonment had not, however, blunted his mighty spirit. Being allowed to return to England, he had two years of life and freedom and used them to prepare a final book, the *Compendium Studii Theologiae*. He died at Oxford, convinced that he had failed, that the light of the great truth he had preached would be extinguished forever. He was buried on June 11, 1292, in the Gray Friars in the university city where his greatest work had been done.

4

The original manuscript of the *Opus Majus* was found in the Vatican library in recent years by one Monsignor Pelzer. This discovery, important though it was, cannot be compared in interest with a later find. In 1912 Mr. Wilfrid Voynich, a bibliophile of New York and London, visited a castle in Italy and found there a collection of illuminated manuscripts in an ancient chest. Among them was an unadorned manuscript of very great age. He studied it carefully and decided that it dated from the latter half of the thirteenth century. The drawings illustrating the text seemed to indicate that the reading matter was given over to a discussion of methods of making various objects such as the telescope and microscope. The text was written in what obviously was a Latin cipher.

The history of the manuscript has been traced since with great ingenuity, and it has been established with what seems reasonable accuracy that it passed from the possession of a sixteenth-century Englishman, a collector of Baconian manuscripts, to the Emperor Rudolph. From the Emperor it was transferred through various hands into the care of someone in Parma; and there it had remained for a very long time in the battered old chest, dusty and almost undecipherable, regarded as of small interest by those who examined the rest of the contents.

A continuous effort has been made since to find the key to the cipher. Some progress has been made, enough perhaps to establish it as a relic of the great Franciscan's work, but the final secret still eludes the scholars who labor over it. If the key can be found, it is considered more than probable that the story of Bacon's experiments in applied science will be revealed and that in this personal account of his work, penned perhaps in his own hand, will be the proof that he had made not only a telescope but a microscope as well.

What other secrets are buried in this ancient manuscript? How much light may it shed on the life of this remarkable recluse? Will it bear out the belief which many hold that Roger Bacon, lost in the darkness of the Middle Ages, hampered by his lack of facilities, was one of the great intellects of all time?

CHAPTER THIRTY-TWO

The Death of Henry

THE surest method by which a king may enhance his place in the esteem of his subjects and on the pages of history is to reign a long time. If he sits on his throne for a relatively short period, his achievements and mistakes, his personal idiosyncrasies are limned sharply against the record of the years, and he goes down to posterity as The Great, The Good, The Unready, The Simple, The Cruel, or perchance no more than an almost forgotten name linking two years. But let his reign go on and on, let the years accumulate and his head become rimed with frost, let him totter toothlessly on the brink, and no matter how good or bad a ruler he may have been, people will begin to think of him with affection and call him the Old King; let him go on still longer with the business of living, and inevitably he will become the Good Old King. Age, if it acquires some tinge of pathos, is a great restorer of reputation. Those with the most reason for thinking badly of an ancient monarch have died or have been caught themselves in the mellowing process. Public memory is short and public taste sups avidly on sentiment. No manner of evidence from the past weighs against the spectacle of a stooped old pantaloon going about the affairs of state and subsisting on gruel. If he has been a good king, his merits are exalted; if a bad one, there is always a chuckle in his misdeeds and a certain pride because he has been a gay dog in his day.

Henry III reigned for fifty-six years. Before the end people were calling him the Old King, even perhaps the Good Old King. There is no evidence that he had changed much, except in appearance. He had become stouter, he shambled as he walked, his face had changed to the semblance of a campaign map, the defect of the drooping eyelid had become more marked. Son of the worst of kings and father of the best, this fatuous ruler continued to the end to exhibit the qualities which made his reign an interlude of folly and comedy leading inevitably to tragedy.

The closing years of the long reign, nevertheless, were peaceful. Men were too weary to continue the struggle. They had salvaged something out of the defeat of a cause and perhaps they sensed that things would be better when Edward stepped into his father's shoes. They were ready to sit back and wait, and even to watch the proceedings of the busy old King with detachment.

Henry came, therefore, at one and the same time to the end of his days and the completion of his single great work. There had always been on the part of the Norman and Plantagenet kings a deep sense of reverence for Edward the Confessor. Good Queen Mold, Henry I's wife, had set the example. Of Saxon blood herself, she made it a custom to go barefoot and in sackcloth to his tomb to pray. She placed there the hair of Mary Magdalene and in many ways fostered the traditions which clustered about the pious King's memory. Her grandson, Henry II, secured the canonization of the Confessor, having the tomb opened for the ceremony and revealing the fact that the body had been most completely preserved, which was considered a miracle in itself, the delicate long features remaining as they had been in life, the frail white hands and the patriarchal beard unchanged in death. This respect for a memory had been deeply embedded in the mind of Henry III. He always celebrated the day of St. Edward in a fitting manner. With his nobles he would attend the vigil in white garments, remaining all night in the abbey church to watch and pray. It became an obsession with him that the edifice where the body of the Confessor lay must be converted into something of surpassing beauty.

When the work was started in 1243 the plan had been enlarged to provide for making the abbey into a place of royal sepulture. The rebuilding was from that time forward the major interest in the King's life and, it must be added, the chief contributing factor to his financial delinquencies. Even while involved in his long struggle with the barons he was giving close attention to the work of the masons, the stone carvers, the carpenters. Orders were being sent off in all directions: to the Lord Mayor for one hundred barges to move gray stone to Westminster; to Edward the treasurer, that one phase of the work must be finished by a certain time if it meant employing a thousand workmen on it; to Odo, the goldsmith, for vessels of wondrous design for the chrism. The work never stopped entirely, not even when dusty riders galloped into London with the news that Simon de Montfort had defeated the King and made him a prisoner at Lewes.

The general plan, which was carried out with discrimination and a real creative instinct, was to extend the church beyond the high altar and create an apsidal chancel, in the center of which the new tomb of the Confessor would be placed. This was elaborated on as the work progressed, a vast and well-lighted triforium being erected over the apsidal chapels. Estimates of the total cost vary from thirty thousand to five hundred thousand pounds. The Crown assumed this immense burden, except that wealthy individuals were expected to make donations, and some money was raised on the revenue from town fairs. It is on record that the widow of a London Jew gave more than two thousand pounds, and so it seems certain that considerable funds were obtained from private donors.

Henry was always at his happiest in supervising the work on this huge undertaking. He had a notable corps of chief aides, the first among them being an anonymous genius who is known only as Master Henry. When Master Henry dropped from sight in 1253 his place was taken by Master John of Gloucester, who seems to have been also a man of rare ability, being rewarded by his royal master with gifts of houses as well as incidental baskets of fine wine. The King did not confine himself to personal contact with his supervising heads. He was continually strolling about under the high piers and the dusty scaffolding with words of praise or criticism, often the latter, for the royal tongue remained sharp to the end; not wearing his crown, as shown in some ancient prints, but dressed certainly in foppish splendor. There would be pearls on the broad band of his hat, his tabard would be well padded and extravagantly tufted, his belt would be of solid gold links, his shoes of green leather (he had a passion for green) would have gilt leopards in the frets, his gloves would be jeweled. Looking like an oriental bird which had wandered by mistake into the haunt of a flock of sparrows, he called his greetings to Master Peter the Roman, who was responsible for the Italian note in the decorations, Master Robert of Beverley, Master Odo. Never was there anything but praise for Walter of Colchester, the magnificent artist who was responsible, among other things, for the lectern in the new chapter house. His tone in discussing affairs of state was invariably querulous and his temper was short, but on his daily strolls under the echoing arches and in the dusty workshops he could be jovial and carefree. "Ha, Master Odo, I like that, I like it much," or "Come up, Master Robert, you must do better for me than this!"

The royal enthusiast was consulted about everything, from the use of Italian mosaics to the size of the flying buttresses and the relation of the vault to the clerestory windows. He would leave the chancery at any time to attend a discussion on the iron tie bars. It is a simple deduction that he would have been more successful as a builder than he proved to be as a king.

That the structure became a thing of magnificence, of glowing beauty, may be ascribed chiefly, therefore, to the good taste and discerning eye of the architect King, and equally to his willingness to divert every penny of royal income if necessary to the good of this overriding ambition. It is the one abiding contribution of the King to the splendid record of progress of the Magnificent Century.

The work reached a stage of completion which made it possible to hold the ceremony of translation on October 13, 1269. It was a great day for the stout and asthmatic King. For a quarter of a century he had labored and persevered. Much of his life had been spent in the shadow of debt that this work might go on. Wars had been fought and battles lost, but he had never faltered. And he had lived to see the completion of the great church which was to serve as his final resting place. He must have realized as he walked with some difficulty in the procession from St. Paul's that the time was drawing near when his servants would gird his bones in and he would be laid in this elaborate grave he had provided for himself in the environs of the city against which he had always contended.

The members of the royal family, with the assistance, no doubt, of some strong baronial arms, carried the coffin of the Confessor back into the abbey and deposited it in the new tomb.

2

The King had three years to live after the ceremony of translation. The days were filled with lawsuits arising out of the restoration of confiscated lands and the bitter grumbling of royalist followers who were being forced to disgorge. They were acrimonious days for the contestants, quiet days for everyone else, and so no purpose would be served in going over the various stages of legislation made necessary by the tangled problems of restitution.

As Prince Edward had started off for the Crusades, taking his brother Edmund with him as well as the wife from whom separation was now unthinkable, his pockets comfortably lined by the huge sums granted him by the Church, the burden of government fell on the bent back of the King. Henry allowed himself as always to become immersed in detail. He passed a statute forbidding Jews to acquire the lands of their debtors. He decided to pay homage to the new King of France for his possessions in that country and borrowed a large sum from merchants of London to cover the expense of traveling; then changed his mind and did not go, using the money for other purposes. He protested bitterly against any lifting of the ban on the murderers of Henry of Almaine, even though Guy de Montfort, the chief offender, followed the Pope on foot, naked save for an undershirt and with a halter around his neck, begging to be forgiven. He wrote to Edward in Palestine on February 6, 1271, telling him that the royal physicians gave him no hope of recovery from the ailments which beset him and entreating his son and heir to finish with the Saracens and hurry home.

When a dispute between the people of Norwich and the church authorities reached a stage of bloodshed, the King felt called upon to travel there in an effort to settle matters. Having imposed heavy penalties on the townspeople, he began the return journey and was stricken suddenly at Bury St. Edmunds. It became apparent to everyone in the royal train that his end was drawing near. He moved with the greatest difficulty, his face was gray, his hands shook. Nevertheless, he was determined to reach London as soon as possible. He came to the Tower in dying condition.

It was perhaps to be expected that the people of London would be rioting over grievances at this very moment. The streets were filled with the contentious townsmen. Henry had never been able to get along with London, a lifelong rift for which he was himself responsible. There was to be no amelioration of this condition at the last: he was fated to die at Westminster with the rebellious tumult of the city sounding faintly in his ears.

He breathed his last on Wednesday, November 16, 1272, the weathercock King, the unsteady, unready, unreliable King, the generally unpopular and sometimes hated King, now at the finish the Old King, the Good Old King.

He had outlived almost everyone who had played parts in the saga of these eventful years. The actors had been a colorful lot, numbering among them some outright villains, many supposedly chivalrous knights with false hearts under their chain mail, a few amusing clowns, many curious and devious individuals. But the period had been noteworthy for the many great men it produced, for the eagles in the sky who beat their wings, sometimes with little effect, against the adverse winds. Two of the authentic eagles were alive: Edward, now the King, and Roger Bacon. The rest were gone: Stephen Langton, the sage leader of the reform movement, who had died in the surety that the Great Charter was forever safe from interfering hands; Simon de Montfort, the passionate crusader for the rights of common men, who had been less fortunate in his final moments but whose work would be carried on; the somewhat less notable eagles of this notable era, the Good Knight, Robert Grosseteste, Edmund Rich, even, with somewhat tarnished wings, Hubert de Burgh; gone to find loftier eyries, beyond a doubt, than the skies of England afforded.

Index

Index